Changing the Subject

CP

1

Changing the Subject

The impact of national policy
on school geography
1980 – 2000

Eleanor M. Rawling

Geographical
Association

Acknowledgements

Many acknowledgements are due. First and foremost, this work would not have been possible without The Leverhulme Trust, which awarded me a Leverhulme Research Fellowship for 1999-2000. I am indebted to Leverhulme for this award. I am also grateful to the Qualifications and Curriculum Authority which gave me a secondment from my post as Principal Officer (Geography) so that I could not only undertake the work but also return to my post afterwards. Thanks to John Westaway and Barbara Jones for covering the work in my absence. The Oxford University Department of Educational Studies made the year so much more enjoyable and productive by extending my Honorary Research Associate status and providing me with office space, library facilities and, more importantly, intellectual stimulation, advice and support. I would like to thank Professor Richard Pring and all the academic staff, particularly Professor Kathy Sylva, Dr Geoffrey Walford, Dr Harry Judge, Professor Sally Tomlinson, Dr Brian Woolnough and Dr Graham Corney.

During the research period, I undertook five interviews with key people who had been involved in the process of policy making or had new insights to offer – Professor Norman Graves, Dr Nick Tate, Dr Ian Colwill, Pat Wilson and Dr Rob Phillips. I thank them for giving their time and views so freely. Less formally, but equally productively, I sought views and advice from Jo Armitage, Professor William Balchin, Trevor Bennetts, Dr Graham Butt, Simon Catling, Martin Curry, Professor Richard Daugherty, Professor Mick Healey, Professor Bill Marsden, Mick Naish, Paula Richardson, Dr Frances Slater, Peter Smith, Rex Walford, John Westaway and Professor Michael Wise. I was also given substantial help by the library staff at OUDES and at QCA, the staff of the RGS-IBG and the GA and, in the final stages, Judi Holloway, who assisted with the word-processing of charts and tables. My thanks to all these people.

The author

Eleanor Rawling is Principal Subject Officer (Geography) with the Qualifications and Curriculum Authority (QCA) London, and Honorary Research Associate at the University of Oxford, Department of Educational Studies (OUDES). During 1999-2000, she undertook a secondment from QCA to be a Leverhulme Research Fellow at OUDES, examining the politics and practicalities of recent curriculum change in geography. The book, *Changing the Subject: The impact of national policies on school geography 1980-2000*, was one outcome of this work.

Eleanor is a member of both the Geographical Association and the Royal Geographical Society with Institute of British Geographers. She was President of the GA in 1991-92, Chair of the Council of British Geography in 1993-95, and was awarded MBE for services to geographical education in 1995. Eleanor has produced many articles and books, including co-authoring and co-editing *Geography into the Twenty First Century* in 1996.

Hardback: ISBN 1 903448 34 4; Paperback: ISBN 1 903448 87 5
First published 2001
Impression number 10 9 8 7 6 5 4 3 2 1
Year 2004 2003 2002

Published by the Geographical Association, 160 Solly Street, Sheffield S1 4BF. Tel: 0114 296 0088; Fax: 0114 296 7176; E-mail: ga@geography.org.uk; websites: www.geography.org.uk and www.geographyshop.org.uk
The Geographical Association is a registered charity: no 313129.

The Publications Officer of the GA would be happy to hear from other potential authors who have ideas for geography books. You may contact the Officer via the GA at the address above.

Copy edited by Rose Pipes Publishing Services
Index by Liz Cook
Cartography by Paul Coles
Design by Arkima Ltd, Leeds, UK
Printed and bound by Titus & Wilson, UK

Contents

Preface

Many books about educational policy and its impact on schools and teachers have been published over the past 20 years – indeed 'policy studies' has flourished as an area of educational research. Particularly influential has been the policy sociology approach, developed by Stephen Ball and drawn on substantially in this book. There are also some notable recent studies of the impact of policy on individual school subjects, particularly Rob Phillips' impressive book about the making of the National History Curriculum (Phillips, 1998) and the work of John Evans and Dawn Penney on National Curriculum Physical Education (Evans and Penney, 1999). However, as far as I am aware, there is no study which provides an overview of the changing fortunes of one school subject, and places this within the wider context of educational change throughout the full 1980-2000 period. This book undertakes this task and, in so doing, fulfils two purposes. It is a curriculum history of school geography, a narrative which will have particular resonance and meaning for the geography subject community. It is also a case study of the impact of national policies on school subjects, using geography to illustrate general points about subject knowledge, subject identity and the politics of curriculum change. I have called this a 'curriculum policy case study', and I hope it will be of interest to policy researchers in general and to those who wish to compare the experience of other school subjects.

I should make clear that, in order to take this approach, it has been necessary to focus at the macro level. This is a story of national specifications, of committees and working groups, of subject associations and national interest groups, of ministers and political advisers and of national debates. It is not a book about classrooms, teachers and pupils, though their crucial importance in interpreting, amending and re-creating national specifications is recognised, particularly in Chapters 6 and 10. By focusing on the national level and on the complex interaction between the policy-making process and the factors influencing the subject curriculum, I hope to highlight the implications for the status and identity of school subjects. However creative we are in our research and in our classrooms, national policies and procedures increasingly set the boundaries within which a school subject is identified, its contribution assessed and its practitioners allowed to operate. As Ball explains 'we do not speak the discourse, it speaks us' (1994, p. 44). All subject communities need to recognise this situation and to plan their strategies to encompass both the macro and the micro levels. I hope this book will be an aid to the geography community in undertaking this task.

One further point about the focus of this book is that national, in this context, refers to England. Northern Ireland and, particularly, Scotland, have different curricular structures and processes. Also, while it was normal in the 1980s to refer to England and Wales when talking about the curriculum, this is no longer the case. As a result of the increasing distinctiveness of curriculum and assessment arrangements in England and Wales in the 1990s, a feature accelerated by devolution, Wales is no longer subject to the same policy-making processes as England. Despite the initially similar Geography Order (1991), the geography requirements for England and Wales now show differences and are subject to some distinctive influences.

As with most books, this one has its origins in my own experience. Over the past 25 years, I have been involved in curriculum change and policy implementation or policy-making at various levels, from school classroom to national subject association to government working group. I cannot claim to be an unbiased reporter of events. Indeed the details of my involvement, and the advantages and disadvantages I see arising, are all explained in Chapter 1. Nevertheless, in Chapters 2-9 I have tried to maintain an objective distance from my analysis, drawing substantially on other sources of evidence and viewpoints to clarify the picture. For Chapters 1 and 10, I have allowed myself more personal comment and reflection on the situation. For me, involvement has added motivation and intellectual stimulation to the task – I hope and believe that it will have added some zest and new perspectives to the story.

To read the full story it is necessary to follow the chapters through from 1 to 10. However, the chapters can be read in their own right, as well as providing a stage in the narrative. Each chapter follows a similar format: an introductory section summarises the main purpose and emphases of the chapter; the middle sections provide the analysis and the sources of evidence; and the conclusion draws together key findings. Throughout the text there are figures as appropriate, and at the end of some chapters are boxed studies. These present further information or case studies, providing added interest or a diversion, but they are not essential to the story.

Full acknowledgments are given on page 4, but I want to express special thanks to Richard Daugherty, Bill Marsden, Richard Pring and Peter Smith who encouraged and supported me throughout, and provided the constructive comments and questions which forced me to tackle the difficult issues. Finally, of course, I am grateful to my family (John, Helen and Richard) who saw (and tolerated with good humour!) the best and worst sides of the creative processes involved in writing a book!

Responsibility for the views expressed, the materials used and any inaccuracies that may have occurred, is my own.
Eleanor M. Rawling
May 2001

Footnote: The 2001 General Election (7 June) resulted in the return of a Labour government for a second term. I have taken the opportunity to ensure that the text is as up-to-date as possible in its references to new government departments and initiatives. Thanks to the Geographical Association for making this possible, despite the publishing schedule.
Eleanor M. Rawling
July 2001

Curriculum Change, Policy Studies and Geography

'It is obvious that you must have some history and some geography; you are not a complete person unless you have that knowledge' (Margaret Thatcher, Sunday Times, 15 April 1990).

Introduction

It may have seemed obvious to Margaret Thatcher that history and geography were well-established school subjects, and that the areas of knowledge they provided were important for everyone but, in practice, curriculum construction has never been as easy as this! As Head and Merttens pointed out in the preface to Ross's book, *Curriculum Construction and Critique* (2000), questions surrounding the content and structure of the curriculum touch on the most fundamental issues for education, for example issues about the purpose of education, the structure of knowledge and the nature of society. In fact, in the 1990s, the implementation of the Thatcher government's education policies, specifically the creation of a national curriculum, seems to have contributed significantly to a decline in status of those very subjects mentioned in the quote. What is more, the 1990s were characterised by continuing and often heated debates over the details of subject content for both history and geography. Ministers and their political advisors have sometimes seemed to stand in direct opposition to the views of professional educators in both disciplines, and the national press has revelled in publicising these differences.

The aims of this book are two-fold: first, to investigate the impact of changing curriculum policies on the character and status of school geography in England 1980-2000; and second, to use this case study to highlight key points about curriculum change, school subjects and the impact of policy making in general. This chapter will introduce the issues to be explored, explaining my approach to the task and the methodology I have used, particularly my own involvement in the last three decades of geography's curriculum history. Finally, I will briefly explain 'where we are now' for school geography – the strengths and the weaknesses of the situation in 2000 and, hence, my reasons for writing this book.

Approaching the task

The story of the geography curriculum 1980-2000 reveals that, despite Margaret Thatcher's apparent support for the subject as an element in the new ten-subject national curriculum (NC), it has not experienced curriculum stability. Since the Education Reform Act of 1988, geography has been subjected to a substantial amount of controversial curriculum change and threats to its status. My initial aim in carrying out the research for this book was to write a 'curriculum history' for geography, in order to describe and explain just what has been happening. I had read Ivor Goodson's work in which he used geography as a case study of curriculum change (1983, 1987, 1988a), his interest developing as a result of his work on the contested nature of the 'curriculum newcomer' environmental studies and its conflicts with geography (Goodson, 1988b). He referred to Layton's three-stage model (1972) and traced the way in which, starting from a low status utilitarian and informational school subject in the early twentieth century, geography was gradually promoted by the subject community and developed with a university base and academic respectability. By 1970 geography was a popular and well-respected subject in secondary schools. According to Goodson 'the battle for high status had been won and geography had finished its long march to acceptance as an academic discipline, from now on its future would be determined not in the school classroom but on the intellectual battlefields of the universities' (1988a, p. 177). However, Goodson's analysis of school geography finished in the mid-1970s and, as we now know, his forecast has not been proved correct. Although there have been momentous changes in academic geography, they have hardly been reflected in the school curriculum. A whole range of other events and agencies have made their impact felt since 1970: the curriculum development movement and new ideas in pedagogy of the 1970s and 1980s (Rawling, 1991a); the growing importance of the somewhat different model of development followed by primary geography (Catling, 1991); wider societal concerns about the environment and world development gathering pace in the 1990s; and the politicisation of the curriculum and the era of centralised control after 1988. What is more, a well-documented 'gap' seems to have opened up between the geography taught in schools and the geography taught in higher education (Goudie, 1993; Bradford, 1996; Brown and Smith, 2001) – a gap which the subject community made considerable efforts to close during the 1990s (Rawling and Daugherty, 1996). My idea was to follow up Goodson's work and to continue the story where he left off. The book would then have focused on the theme of 'curriculum change' and my particular task would have been to analyse the historical processes through which geography had developed and changed in the 1980s and 1990s. Goodson had explained the importance of shifting the emphasis from questions of the intrinsic and philosophical nature of subjects to the human motives and activities inherent in their construction and maintenance. For me, this clearly signalled the need to consider the motives and actions implicit in the national curriculum exercise and so to assess its significance against the more traditional change agents – academic geography, classroom teachers, resources and texts.

As the preliminary work progressed and the story unfolded, I realised the significance of 1988 and the Education Reform Act   it was in a very real sense a curriculum watershed. Before 1988, influences on the school curriculum were many and varied and school subjects were the result of a long process of debate, decision making and sometimes conflict, but always involving a trade-off between the practitioners and advocates of the subject, and society at large. At different times, different interest groups dominated this process (for example academic geographers in the late 1960s and early 1970s, curriculum developers in the late 1970s and early 1980s). After 1988, all curriculum development seemed to be centralised in the government and the involvement of subject practitioners was carefully controlled centrally. The pattern thus seemed to change from one of competing influences to one of a single powerful influence – that of the state. In retrospect, as this book will reveal, the situation has been far more complex than that, but there *were* significant changes after 1988. Since that date, it is no longer possible to trace a story of the changing curriculum, for any school subject, without understanding the new relationships. There is a complex interplay between ministers (empowered by the 1988 Act to intervene in curriculum decision making); the government department responsible for education in England (currently the Department for Education and Skills (DfES)); the central advisory agencies such as the Qualifications and Curriculum Authority (QCA) and Teacher Training Agency (TTA); the school inspection agency, Ofsted; and the schools and teachers who are on the receiving end of central policy decisions. There are civil servants and bureaucrats concerned with curriculum matters whose jobs did not exist pre-1988. There is a whole new language of statutory orders, attainment targets, national tests and targets which has evolved since 1988, and there is avid and relentless media interest forever generating new issues, as well as picking over the existing issues (Wallace, 1993). Not surprisingly, a whole new area of educational research, focused on educational policy making, has developed in the late 1980s and 1990s. Researchers such as Dale (1989), Ball (1990, 1994), Hatcher and Troyna (1994), and Carr and Hartnett (1996) have analysed aspects of the 1988 Education Reform Act, particularly the national curriculum, and studied the consequent impact on schools and teachers.

One special area of interest has been the importance of ideologies and, in particular, the influence of the New Right political thinkers. Curriculum studies and curriculum development have declined as research areas, the general assumption seeming to be that all curriculum change stopped with the national curriculum. Kelly encapsulates this view arguing that, apart from central change, 'all forms of change and development have been arrested since deviation from the prescribed form is not permitted' (1999, p. 101). Yet, central power has been balanced by implementation. Many of the latest developments in policy studies have moved into micro-level analysis (schools, classrooms, teachers) in order to trace policy implementation and practice (e.g. Ball, 1993; Helsby and McCulloch, 1997a). The policy sociology approach pioneered by Ball gives a wide definition of this work, covering not only the development and creation of policies but also their impact and outcomes at all levels in the education system. In particular, I was attracted by the approach outlined in Bowe and Ball with Gold (1992). They warn of the dangers of following a linear approach to policy studies, explaining that this leads to a separation of policy generation from policy implementation, as if 'policy is what gets done to people'. They propose instead recognition of a 'policy cycle' (Figure 1a) comprising three policy contexts – the 'context of influence' in which the interested parties struggle to dominate the prevailing discourse; the 'context of text production' in which the official policy texts (e.g. NC Order, non-statutory guidance) are produced; and the 'context of practice' in which the official policy is received and subject to interpretation and possibly re-creation by the teaching profession. At a broad level, the policy cycle idea seemed to provide a framework with which I could bring together the experience and insights from curriculum change with the new perspectives gained from policy studies and policy sociology.

Figure 1: The Geography National Curriculum:
(a) the policy cycle and (b) its application to the GNC. (Note: Dates are notional).

Source: (a) Bowe and Ball with Gold, 1992, Figure 20.

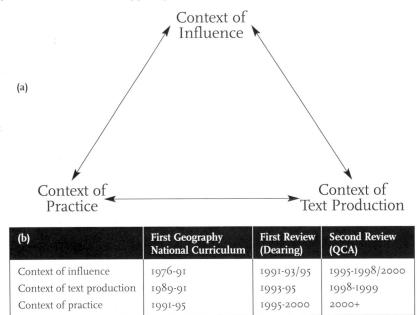

(b)	First Geography National Curriculum	First Review (Dearing)	Second Review (QCA)
Context of influence	1976-91	1991-93/95	1995-1998/2000
Context of text production	1989-91	1993-95	1998-1999
Context of practice	1991-95	1995-2000	2000+

My intention therefore is to undertake what I have called a curriculum policy case study, using the experience of one subject, geography, to trace the impact of curriculum policy on the definition, character and status of a school subject. This will be an example of what Ozga (1999) refers to as 'research *on* policy' as opposed to 'research *for* policy'. Ozga regrets the increasing dominance of research *for* policy and promotes instead the use of critical theory by researchers to 'assist the profession by insisting on complexity, resisting homogeneity and recovering lost histories' (1999, p. 131). This study will attempt to take this approach by questioning the social and political relations which have affected the geography curriculum over the past decade. There has been research on individual aspects of the geography curriculum and its impact on teaching, learning and assessment (e.g. Daugherty and Lambert, 1994; Roberts, 1995), and Walford (2001) has written a history of school geography 1850-2000. As far as the author is aware, there has not been any overview of the 'big picture' for school geography, set in the wider context of educational policies 1980-2000. It is hoped that this book will fill the gap.

The characteristics and advantages of such a curriculum policy case study are outlined below.

Some methodological issues

The advantages of using a curriculum policy case study approach are:

■ *One subject as an example*
It will provide case study exemplification of ideas and theories developed from more general overviews of policy making and implementation. The analysis will draw on recent research in educational policy making and policy sociology (e.g. Ball 1990, 1994; Bowe and Ball with Gold, 1992; Hatcher and Troyna, 1994; Carr and Hartnett, 1996). It will also make use of current thinking and research about the curriculum (e.g. Young, 1998; Kelly, 1999; Ross, 2000). School geography provides a good case study because it has experienced significant changes to its character and status since 1980. Chapters 3, 4, 5, 6, 7 and 8 will analyse the detailed influences on the subject over this period. The resulting analysis will explain how things are and how they came to be that way for school geography, thus extending the curriculum history study of Goodson.

■ *Identifying new perspectives on policy making*
It should be possible to identify some new perspectives on policy changes 1988-2000 and to highlight key points about the changing nature of educational policy making since the election of a New Labour government. The experience of one subject might suggest lessons from the past and signposts for the future. The conclusion to each chapter will make general as well as subject-specific points, where appropriate, and Chapters 9 and 10 will also address these broader issues.

■ *Time-scale to cover several policy cycles*
It will analyse the policy cycle over a longer period than just one cycle. There have been other studies of the impact of policy on individual subjects (e.g. Evans and Penney for PE, 1995 and 1999; Phillips for history, 1998). However, they have tended to focus on the initial national curriculum text production process, whereas I wish to trace the experience of geography through the whole 1988-2000 period, covering not just the creation of the original national curriculum, but also the two subsequent reviews and the newer structures and processes of policy making developed under New Labour. This will allow comparison of policy-making processes and impacts, and it will highlight key issues about the current situation (Chapters 3, 4, 5, 6, 7 and 8).

■ *Positive re-consideration of curriculum theory and thinking*
Because of the opportunity provided by Chapter 6 to consider national curriculum implementation and practice for one subject, the approach will allow curriculum change, curriculum planning and curriculum development to be re-considered in a positive way, in terms of what their role is, or might be, in a centralised curriculum. Chapter 6 will explore this particularly in relation to the role of the teacher, while Chapters 9 and 10 will pick up discussion of the role of the subject associations and wider community. This approach should avoid the more negative focus which has dominated some comment ('curriculum development is dead') and also limit the tendency to itemise only what has been lost with a national curriculum.

■ *Raising big questions about subject knowledge and the subject community*
Through the experience of one subject, this approach will raise, and to some extent try to answer, big questions about curriculum policy making and subject knowledge – e.g. What guarantees a particular subject a place in the school curriculum? Who decides what subjects/areas of understanding should be included in the curriculum? How do subjects change and develop as a result of changing political discourse? What role does or should the subject community play in this process? (Chapters 9 and 10.)

I believe that all this will be of interest to educationalists generally, to those involved in policy studies particularly and to other subject communities who may wish to emulate the approach. For geography educators and the geography subject community, there will be a special interest not only in understanding what has happened to the subject, but in considering how to react and respond in the future.

Ball (1994) expanded his policy cycle framework to include two more contexts, both of which have potential value for geography educators and to which I shall refer in this book. The 'context of outcomes' is a wider analysis of the effects of policy, not just focusing on immediate implementation and practice but identifying wider outcomes, for example in relation to justice, equality and individual freedom. In many ways this gives a useful structure for considering how pupils and society may be affected by geography's lowly curriculum status and utilitarian image. How does geography's marginal image and status at KS4 (14-16), for example, square with society's apparent concern and priority given to sustainable development education and global understanding? Chapter 8 will pick up these points in dealing with the current politics of the curriculum, and Chapter 10 more generally.

The 'context of political strategy' is concerned with the identification of a set of political and social activities which might more effectively tackle issues in the future. This, as Ball recognises, is where the relatively objective process of analysis moves into a more critical and targeted social research, aiming to be of use to those who wish to change the current situation. In Chapter 10, based on the preceding analysis, I allow myself a more personal perspective and the opportunity to suggest strategies for the future of geographical education.

In order to undertake such a detailed study of the geography curriculum 1980-2000, it has been necessary to focus my analysis mainly on the national curriculum (originally planned for the 5-16 age group, but by the mid-1990s covering only 5-14 year olds). However, Chapter 2 will provide a background to the 1970s and 1980s curriculum development activities, prior to the national curriculum, and Chapter 7 will deal in a more summary way with the important issues surrounding geography's place and character in the 14-19 curriculum. It should be noted that the book focuses predominantly upon the macro-level, attempting to draw together the many sources of data about geography and curriculum change at the national level. Chapter 6 does consider implementation and teachers' responses to the curriculum at a more micro-level, the evidence being mainly derived from Ofsted, SCAA/QCA and published research.

As for any historical enquiry, the study draws on secondary source material, in particular:

■ policy documents and other official papers (e.g. statutory National Curriculum Orders, DES papers, Ofsted reports, minutes and papers of meetings);

■ material produced by the subject associations, LEAs and schools themselves (e.g. promotional literature, schemes of work, curriculum guidance);

- research papers, journal articles, methodological texts and other publications providing different interpretations and views, both from within the geography community and from educational researchers generally.

In addition, I have made comprehensive use of my own personal notes, diaries, papers and publications produced during the period. Following Marsden I will attempt to use 'a methodology which respects evidence, which enjoys sorting through the detail of events, which justly and comprehensively selects and balances the data, acting as a counterpoise to the tendency to over-generalise and resort to deterministic explanation' (1980, p. 2). One methodological issue which this raises concerns my own role as writer of this curriculum history. I am not an unbiased observer of the events unfolding, but have been closely involved throughout the 1970-2000 period at all levels of change from school through subject association to national policy making. The 30-year period coincides with my professional life in geography education. My career profile, after finishing my degree in 1970, has to some extent followed the 'ups and downs' of school geography's curriculum fortunes. During this period I have been a school geography teacher, Associate Director and National Co-ordinator of two curriculum projects (1976-91), a senior officer and President (1991-92) of the Geographical Association during campaigning for the subject and supporting national curriculum implementation; member of the government appointed Geography Working Group (GWG) 1989-90; and Principal Officer for geography at the curriculum and assessment authorities (1994-present) during two reviews of the national curriculum.

In this respect, this is very much a personal journey I am describing. As Barber explains in his book about the national curriculum:

> 'I do not write as a detached observer, still less as a disinterested historian of these events, but as a participant who might be expected, like other participants, to attempt to justify or explain the positions I took up as the events unfolded. A degree of bias is inevitable' (1996, p. 41).

However, I have tried to lessen the bias and reduce the subjectivity by, for example: careful attention to detail and to original documents; by reliance on published accounts and documentation rather than only on my own notes and diaries; by an assiduous process of cross-checking or triangulation, so that any statement or event is corroborated by at least two other sources as well as myself.

As the work has progressed, however, I have become convinced that there are numerous advantages to being a participant observer in the events described. At the most basic level, I have access to papers, such as GWG minutes and meeting notes. Exploring these sources might have otherwise been impossible or taken an inordinate amount of time to arrange, or access to them would have been uneven. Also, the official documents and texts tell only one part of the story: as Goodson points out, 'only what is prepared on the drawing board goes into the school and therefore has a chance to be interpreted and to survive' (1998a, p. 6). Equally important to a curriculum case study is an understanding of the editing process – i.e. what was left out and why. I have a wider understanding of this editing process for many occasions. In a more general sense, my experience of involvement in different camps – as a policy maker, on behalf of a subject interest group, and as a teacher – all give me a range of perspectives from which to view the changes occurring. At times, such as during my participation on the GWG, such multi-perspectives caused an undoubted conflict of interest and considerable personal stress. At other times, such as on numerous occasions acting as subject officer at QCA and the School Curriculum and Assessment Authority (SCAA), this ability to empathise with both policy makers and subject enthusiasts has allowed me to act more effectively. Whatever the personal gains and losses of my career track (and this is perhaps the focus for a different book!) I conclude, like Susan Semel that 'writing history as a participant and former participant is a valid form of research' (1994, p. 204). Indeed, a final point which Semel emphasises from her history of

Dalton School, New York, is that the participant has a special motivation and enthusiasm to undertake this task. In my case, geography has filled my professional life and provided a vast range of professional 'highs' and 'lows'. Exploring its curriculum history has probably been a necessary and therapeutic activity but also, I believe, one which will be of value to the geography and wider education communities. As Glesne and Peshkin pointed out:

> 'my subjectivity is the basis for the story I tell. It is the strength on which I build. It makes me who I am as a person and as a researcher, equipping me with the perspectives and insights that shape all I do as a researcher, from the selection of a topic, clear through to the emphasis I make in my writing. Seen as virtuous, subjectivity is something to capitalize on rather than exorcise' (1992, p. 104).

School geography 2000: the strengths

Considered from an international perspective, geography now occupies a relatively strong position in English schools. It is part of the statutory ten-subject national curriculum for pupils aged 5-14 years and it is still a popular optional subject with high entries for public examinations at 16+ (GCSE) and 18+ (A-level), ranking sixth or seventh in the subjects offered for GCSE through the late 1990s, and sixth or seventh in the A-level tables. There are now central guidelines for the subject at all these levels (National Curriculum Orders, GCSE and A/AS-level Criteria), containing considerable detail about the subject content to be taught in physical, human and environmental aspects and about the standards expected (Figure 2). Since 1999, geography is also a recognisable component in the Early Learning Goals for 3-5 year olds (QCA, 2000a), appearing as 'knowledge and understanding of the world'. In higher education, geography occupies a relatively strong position. At the beginning of 2001 there were 93 departments of geography in the UK (source RGS-IBG), each offering undergraduate degrees, post-graduate opportunities and supporting research in the subject. According to Walford (1999) geography graduates were highly employable in 1999, ranking alongside modern languages and mathematics. Given the need to train teachers of geography, there is also a strong tradition of teacher education for geography. Since the late 1960s this has become predominantly a university-based activity with graduate entry. In 2000, there were 46 institutions offering the secondary Post-Graduate Certificate of Education (PGCE) in geography and a significant number of institutions offering three-year BEd courses and/or four-year BEd or primary PGCE. There is, then, a framework as a basis for development into the twenty-first century. This is undoubtedly a strong position compared with that of geography in the education systems of most other countries of the world. Biddle (1999) undertook a comparison of school geography in New South Wales (Australia), England, Finland, USA, Japan and Hong Kong. He noted that the strength of the situation in England lay in the relatively continuous nature of geography provision available from primary years through to university, and in the high levels of geographical knowledge and expertise held by most teachers.

A range of national subject associations exist to maintain and promote the subject. The largest is the Royal Geographical Society with Institute of British Geographers (RGS-IBG). The RGS originated in 1830 as a direct response to exploration and imperial interests. In 1933, the academic geographers broke away from the main body to form the IBG, but rejoined with it again in 1995 to face external pressures as one organisation. The RGS-IBG, with 13,488 members in 2001 thus represents a wide spectrum of interests from exploration and fieldwork through public and professional involvement with environments and places to research and teaching in higher education. As a result of its long and prestigious history and many connections with the great and powerful, the RGS-IBG has been able to play a valuable role in lobbying for the subject in schools and in universities. Indeed the Geographical Association (GA) was established in 1893, as an initiative promoted by individuals in the society and supported by the RGS as a whole. Its focus has always been the advancement of geography in schools, although it has also attempted to maintain a close relationship with academic geography.

Figure 2: A summary of school geography 5-19 in England, 2000.

Note: A foundation stage of the curriculum (3-5 years) is also recognised and there are Early Learning Goals for this stage. They do not comprise a curriculum but establish expectations for most children to meet. These goals include 'knowledge and understanding of the world', in which a geographical contribution may be recognised.

	5-7 years (KS1)	7-11 years (KS2)	11-14 years (KS3)	14-16 years (KS4)	16-19 years
Status in the curriculum	Compulsory (but schools were not required to follow the programmes of study in geography for a temporary two-year period 1998-2000)	Compulsory (but schools were not required to follow the programmes of study in geography for a temporary two-year period 1998-2000)	Compulsory and with statutory teacher assessment at 14 years	Optional but popular subject for public examinations at 16 (GCSE) (some aspects of geography in national vocational qualifications, e.g. Leisure & Tourism GNVQs and after 2002 vocational GCSEs).	Optional but popular subject for public examinations at 18 (A/AS) (some aspects of geography in national vocational qualifications, e.g. Leisure/Travel/Tourism GNVQs and vocational A-levels (AVCE)).
Central guidelines	National Curriculum Geography Order (programme of study)	National Curriculum Geography Order (programme of study)	National Curriculum Geography Order (programme of study)	GCSE Criteria for Geography (details of specifications left to awarding bodies)	A/AS Subject Criteria for Geography (details of specifications left to awarding bodies)
Main emphasis	Four aspects of geography (geographical enquiry/skills; places; patterns and processes; environmental change/sustainable development) are developed throughout. ■ locality of the school and a contrasting locality ■ basic locational knowledge ■ mainly local scale but awareness of wider world	Four aspects of geography (see KS1) are developed throughout. ■ contrasting localities and wider range of themes, e.g. water, settlement, environmental issue ■ locational knowledge ■ mainly local, regional and national scale	Four aspects of geography (see KS1) are developed throughout. ■ two countries in different stages of development and a wide range of physical human and environmental themes ■ locational knowledge ■ full range of scales, local to global	■ full range of geographical enquiry and skills ■ balance of physical/human/environmental geography ■ range of places and scales ■ issues about places/environments ■ contribution to sustainable development, key skills, etc.	■ full range of geographical enquiry and skills, ability to undertake investigations ■ people/environment interactions ■ human and physical processes (selected for AS-level) in relation to chosen environments) ■ range of places and scales (full for A-level) ■ contribution to key skills
Issues	Increasing marginalisation due to National Literacy and Numeracy strategies and emphasis on English, mathematics, science.	Increasing marginalisation due to National Literacy and Numeracy strategies and emphasis on English, mathematics, science.	Relatively sound, but school inspections reveal weaknesses in quality relative to other subjects. Also unknown effect of government's KS3 strategy (e.g. literacy, numeracy, ICT).	Declining numbers and competition from other academic subjects with protected status, from vocational courses and from new initiatives (e.g. citizenship).	Declining numbers, since 1998 and unknown effect of lower GCSE numbers, introduction of modular A-level syllabuses and new AS courses from 2000.

In 2001, the GA is one of the largest subject teaching associations in England (it also covers Wales, but not Scotland, where geographers are represented by the Scottish Association of Geography Teachers), having a membership of 10,003 that covers teachers in primary, secondary and further education, teacher educators and advisors and a decreasing number in higher education. Whereas the RGS-IBG now represents the subject in acadaemia, public life and on behalf of the general public, the GA is the main source of expertise in all matters concerned with school education, teacher education, curriculum, assessment and pedagogy. To a large extent the organisations are complementary, although there is growing overlap (so far on a co-operative basis) in secondary education matters. Between them, the RGS-IBG and GA offer representation and support for all the many sub-groups concerned with school geography. The RGS-IBG has an Education Committee and many sub-groups concerned with research in the specialist areas of geography. In the GA there are committees and working groups concerned, for example, with primary geography, fieldwork, teacher education, environmental education and sustainable development, use of ICT in geography, and research in geography education. In addition, there are some separate or semi-autonomous national groupings which add to the picture, for example the group covering University Department of Education Tutors for Geography, the Geography Advisers and Inspectors Network (GAIN), the primary geography research register and the British Geomorphological Research Group (BGRG), loosely affiliated to the RGS-IBG.

It is important to mention the Council of British Geography (COBRIG), an umbrella body which represents all those organisations concerned with geography or geographical education in England, Wales and Scotland. COBRIG was formed in 1988 when it seemed that pressures for centralised curricula and assessment arrangements being felt in all parts of the UK demanded an organisation which could speak for the whole geography community. With limited funding and varying degrees of support from the constituent bodies, COBRIG has, nevertheless, managed to play a significant role in lobbying for and promoting the subject during the 1990s. Its submissions to the two national curriculum reviews carried some weight and its organisation of the biennial COBRIG seminars has been instrumental in bringing the higher education and school sectors back into dialogue. However, inter-association rivalries and the increasingly different policy-making contexts in England, Wales and Scotland have probably inhibited the achievement of greater influence.

At international level, the UK is an active member of the International Geographical Union (IGU) in which, since 1952, there has existed a separate Commission for Geographical Education (CGE). This has predominantly been concerned with school and teacher education (see Wise, 1992), although during the late 1990s, growing interest has been shown by geographers in higher education interested in teaching and learning issues. Also of note is the newly formed International Network for Learning and Teaching Geography in higher education (INLT), which was established in 1999 with particular interests in higher education, but recognising from the outset the need to involve pre-university level educators in its activities. The papers resulting from the preliminary conference in Hawaii in 1999 are published in the *Journal of Geography in Higher Education*, 24, 2, and include one about the links between schools and higher education (Bednarz *et al.*, 2000).

School geography 2000: the weaknesses

It is important to recognise these strengths; equally we need to be aware that geography's status is declining at all levels in the curriculum. In primary schools, geography's position has progressively been marginalised as the national inspection regime, national tests and the introduction of the National Literacy and National Numeracy strategies have reinforced a curriculum hierarchy which places English and mathematics at the summit and leaves geography languishing at the bottom along with history, music, art and physical education. Two reviews of the national curriculum, although ostensibly slimming the curriculum, have significantly reduced content only for the 'non-core' subjects. Not surprisingly, Ofsted inspections (1999a; 2001) and monitoring by the national curriculum agency (SCAA, 1997e; QCA, 1998b) have found that, despite some good practice and excellent support from the subject associations, overall geography is not accorded high priority in primary schools.

For geography in secondary schools, the most severe blow to status came when the Dearing National Curriculum Review (Dearing, 1993) proposed and the government confirmed (1994) its optional status in the key stage 4 curriculum. Subsequently, it has had to compete for curriculum time with other national curriculum subjects (e.g. history), non-national curriculum subjects (e.g. business studies) and the newly created general national vocational qualifications (e.g. GNVQ Leisure and Tourism). The latest National Curriculum Review for 2000 failed to make the situation more flexible and instead added to the already full statutory requirements by introducing a new Citizenship Subject Order and a framework for personal, social and health education (PSHE). Although geography is still a popular subject (normally ranking sixth or seventh in GCSE candidates), a decline in numbers of pupils opting for GCSE geography is taking place (Westaway and Rawling, 2001). The reduction in candidates registered in 1998, 1999 and 2000 was 8.5%, 3.1% and 2.21% respectively, and there are fears for the likely negative impact on take-up of 16-19 courses. A decline in A-level numbers took place in 1999 (6.02%) and this was followed by a 12.05% reduction in candidates in 2000.

This situation leaves school geography in England secure only at KS3 (11-14 year olds) but Ofsted inspections note some signs of poor quality teaching and learning at this key stage compared with other similar subjects such as history (Ofsted, 1998a). There are fears that this problem may be exacerbated by reduced staffing and resourcing consequent on its lower 14-19 status in schools.

There are signs of pressure elsewhere in the system. The numbers of students accepted for geography degree courses showed a small decline in 1997-98, but has since risen slightly (RGS-IBG information). Of more concern is the fact that a small number of institutions have ceased to offer geography at all, partly because of competition from newer subjects (e.g. media studies). Also of concern is the declining entry for geography teacher education courses. Recruitment to geography secondary PGCE courses has been between 15 and 20% below target in most years since 1996 and geography was declared a shortage subject by the TTA in 1999. This classification allows students to access extra financial assistance, and the £6000 training salary, announced in 1999, is also helping. However, in 1999-2000, although the situation seems to be slowly improving, recruitment was still only 85% of the DfEE target (source: TTA). A conference was held in 1999, sponsored by the TTA and the RGS-IBG. The resulting report (Rawling, 2000) revealed that although the geography situation was only mirroring a more general decline in the popularity of teaching as a career, there were some features special to geography and some adverse implications for the whole geography education system. The 'hard-hitting' article by Gardner and Craig (2001) in the *Journal of Geography in Higher Education,* is both a sign of the seriousness of the situation and an attempt to encourage academic geographers into action. A TTA sponsored programme, managed by the RGS-IBG, is under way to try and address the issue of teacher supply in geography, particularly by working with higher education geography departments to promote teaching as a career. It will be some time before the results are apparent.

The frustrations in this situation are many. Politicians exhort schools to 'inspire children to become global citizens' (Estelle Morris MP addressing a conference, October 1999), to tackle education for sustainable development, to 'heighten awareness of Europe and the wider world' (Tony Blair, 1998) and to develop in our students creative and enquiring minds. Geography educators respond by saying 'yes, these are the things our subject is about, these are its strengths'. Thus the GA's *Position*

Statement talks of the wide range of knowledge, skills and understanding developed through geography and refers to the subject as 'an essential component in preparing young people for life in the twenty-first century' (GA, 1999a, p. 164). The 'Education for Life' leaflet prepared jointly by the RGS (with IBG) and the GA (1998) refers to geography's key role in developing cultural understanding, sensitivity and tolerance; environmental education and responsibility; understanding of the interconnected world; and a unique combination of skills. Despite this promotional literature, the national press and politicians seem to hold a different view of geography as a traditional utilitarian subject concerned mainly with low-level learning about countries and regions, natural landscapes and maps. In the real world, where policies are made and funding is allocated, the focus in 2001 is on literacy and numeracy, on English and mathematics, on national tests, on reconsidering the science curriculum, on supporting citizenship, on key skills and on vocational GCSEs and work-related learning. At times it seems that geography is, at best, given a kindly nod (yes, do add the words 'sustainable development' to the Geography Order) or ignored. At worst, it is thrust even further to the far horizons of the curriculum landscape (please move geography down the list of options at KS4 to make room for citizenship).

The frustration is made more acute because of the discontinuity or 'gap' which has been recognised as existing between the academic subject and the school subject (Goudie, 1993; Brown and Smith, 2001). Geographers in higher education believe that theirs is a dynamic, vibrant discipline, bursting with new ideas and perspectives on people, places and environments and crucial as a tool to help solve local, national and global problems. As Massey *et al.* (1998) explained, geography increasingly does matter, since in today's global and environmentally demanding times, the spatial perspectives which the subject brings are being recognised as crucial to understanding all types of social, economic and political relationships. Internationally, human geographers are highly regarded in academic circles. Soja went so far as to claim that:

> 'the humanities and social sciences have been experiencing an unprecedented spatial turn. In what may, in retrospect, be seen as one of the most important intellectual developments in the late twentieth century, scholars have begun to interpret space and the spatiality of human life with the same critical insight and interpretative power as have traditionally been given to time and history (the historicality of human life) on the one hand and social relations and society (the sociality of human life) on the other' (1998, p. 261).

In physical and environmental matters, geographers are also at the forefront of research in areas such as climate change, environmental monitoring and resource appraisal. Yet despite all this activity and their growing academic reputations, academic geographers have hardly made an impact on or been involved in decisions about the school curriculum or teacher education. Neither the Geography National Curriculum nor the GCSE and AS/A-level syllabuses show much evidence of current influences from geography as it is developing in the universities. This is particularly worrying for A-level which lies at the interface between schools and higher education. It also raises crucial questions about the image of school geography 5-14 and its ability to respond to a curriculum increasingly concerned with citizenship, global interrelationships and sustainable development education.

Conclusion

These, then, provide powerful reasons to write this book. It is important to explore and explain the disjunction between 'the vision' – what geographers think the subject has to offer the education of young people – and 'the reality' – what contribution it is allowed to make and what status it really has in the school curriculum for the new millennium. A curriculum policy case study of school geography 1980-2000 will attempt to investigate these issues and, at the same time, to draw out some general conclusions about school subjects and curriculum change.

2

School Geography and Curriculum Change 1970 to mid-1980s

Introduction

Prior to the mid-1960s, the term 'curriculum' normally referred only to the full range of subjects offered in a school (i.e. the school curriculum), while the list of content to be taught in one particular subject was referred to, certainly in secondary schools, as a subject syllabus. Although changes to the whole-school curriculum might be activated by the occasional 'expert' report commissioned by the government (e.g. the Norwood Report, 1943; the Crowther Report – DES, 1959) the changes suggested were often organisational more than curricular. Both the range of subjects accepted as the school curriculum and the content of the secondary geography syllabus or topics in primary school were relatively stable at this time.

Graves, referring to the situation in secondary schools, explained:

> 'When I began teaching in 1950, I do not believe that the staff of the school in which I taught ever discussed the curriculum operating in the school, except marginally, such as, what to do with the sixth and upper fifth forms after the examinations were over... It was almost assumed that the curriculum was in a stable state unlikely to change and not worth discussing' (1975, p. 100).

Similarly, Blackie commented in 1967 'geography ... is not dramatically different from what it was in primary schools thirty years ago' (1967, p. 100). This chapter will show how, in the late 1960s and 1970s, the situation changed dramatically. The so-called 'new geography', introducing quantitative methods and the concepts and theories of spatial analysis, was disseminated from university geography departments, and three major secondary geography projects were established and worked with schools in England and Wales. In primary schools the most significant changes in this period were not in content but in pedagogy as geography teaching was included in the move towards a child-centred philosophy, given official recognition by the Plowden Report (DES, 1967). Such changes made an impact on the nature of geography as a school subject and on its readiness to face the more politicised curriculum change processes after 1988.

The following two sections set the scene by examining the nature of school subjects, the rationale for geography as a school subject and the nature of its relationship with academic geography.
This chapter will then provide background about school geography before 1970, and about the curriculum development activities which took place after this date.

Geography as a school subject

The national curriculum in England is a subject-based curriculum and, despite two reviews and the amendments made, it still bears the strong imprint of the original (1988) ten-subject structure. The subject curriculum has, in fact, been the dominant curriculum structure for English education over the past century. Marsden commented that so enduring was this structure that 'the standard combination of subjects in the secondary school timetable seems part of the established order of things' (1976, p. 47). Geography, though not a first order subject, has been a respected part of this traditional subject curriculum, having been accepted in the late nineteenth century as providing knowledge about the world and attitudes of citizenship essential to an imperial power. Marsden (1989) argued that, particularly in the inter-war years, geography was one of the 'Empire group' of subjects (with history and literature). The 1904 Secondary Regulations, strangely anticipating the national curriculum line-up 84 years later, had recognised geography as one of the necessary subjects and throughout the twentieth century it developed as one of the most popular subjects for public examination.

However, curriculum history shows that subjects are not totally fixed features. New ones are occasionally accepted into the list (for instance biology in the early twentieth century) and other subjects wax and wane in importance (e.g. the growth of business studies and the decline of economics in the 1990s) or change in character (e.g. home economics). One view (the social constructionist) is that the structure of knowledge is relative and is determined socially, according to the views and influence of those controlling curriculum decisions at the time (Young, 1971). In this view the traditional subject-based curriculum of 1904 derived from the 'high culture' (or classical humanist) view of knowledge held by decision makers. Its reappearance in the 1988 Education Reform Act was a result of the desire of the New Right political group to 'culturally restore' the traditional curriculum (hence the term 'cultural restorationist'). Social constructionists believe that there is nothing sacrosanct about this list of subjects. It can and probably should change as the needs of society, and of individuals within it, change. Countering this view are those who argue that there is an underlying structure of knowledge, derived from a long and complex process of understanding experience, and that the curriculum does, and always should in some way, represent this structure. Hirst (1965) is the best known proponent of this view. Hirst regarded the major long-established disciplines (such as mathematics) as *forms of knowledge,* each one having distinctive concepts, logical structures, critical tests for truth and specific techniques and skills for exploring experience. Slightly different were the *fields of knowledge* (such as geography) lacking such tight structures but held together by subject matter and to some extent crossing the forms of knowledge for their concepts and techniques. Although in his early work (1965) Hirst seemed to link the major school and university disciplines (mathematics, history, literature) with the forms of knowledge, later (1974) he seemed to suggest that few disciplines related directly to the underlying forms of knowledge. Most were multi-form, being developed for a specific educational purpose. More recently, writers such as Pring (1972, 2000a) seem to confirm this looser relationship. While the curriculum does and always should in some way represent the underlying structure of knowledge, 'the way we come to organise, select, value and transmit our knowledge is, to some extent, explicable by reference to those who do the organising, selecting, valuing and transmitting' (Pring, 1972, p. 28). In any case, geography has never been recognised as a pure form of knowledge, but always seen as one of a number of disciplines whose character is more diffuse and whose distinctiveness results from an assemblage of criteria. Marsden (1976) noted that these include the way in which concepts (particularly spatial ones) are used, the scale of study, the interest in people-environment relationships and the use of maps. Balchin and Coleman (1973) claimed that the range of spatial and map skills summarised under the heading of graphicacy, formed a fundamental fourth basic skill for schools to rank alongside reading (articulacy), writing (literacy) and arithmetic (numeracy). Haggett, speaking at a Council of British Geography (COBRIG) seminar in 1994, referred to 'some central and cherished aspects of geographical education; a love of landscape and field exploration, a fascination with place, a wish to solve spatial conundrums posed by spatial configurations' (1996, p. 17). In other words, geography can provide strong links to the underlying forms of knowledge and can lay claim to a distinctiveness which justifies its place in the curriculum, even though its specific form and character have changed over time. This is the view taken in this book. Geography's failure to fit into neat classifications of knowledge and its crossing of the physical and human sciences boundary have caused problems as curriculum planners are unsure how it fits their systems. The Norwood Report commented on 'the expansiveness of geography', pointing out that this quality made it likely that geography enthusiasts would 'widen their boundaries so vaguely that definition of purpose is lost' (1943, pp. 101-2). However, Marsden (1976) and Graves (1979) suggested that these characteristics have often been a positive quality in curriculum debates, allowing geography to justify itself as a bridging subject. Such an argument was used in the GA's campaign to have geography included in the national curriculum. In a letter to the Secretary of State, Kenneth Baker, in August 1986, the GA pointed out that 'geography has powerful integrating qualities in itself with strong links to both the sciences and the arts'. The National Curriculum Geography Working Group made a similar claim in its final report 'because of its breadth of content and methodology, school geography has many links with other subjects in the curriculum and contributes to cross-curricular themes, skills and dimensions' (DES and WO, 1990, p. 7, para 4.8).

The relationship between the school subject and the academic subject

The way in which the discipline is perceived (from a social constructionist or a more philosophical position) will influence the way in which the relationship between different levels of the education system is understood. If a social constructionist view is taken, then it may be argued that since there are separate social and economic factors influencing schools and universities and different objectives in place, then there is every reason for the subject to take on different forms at each level. On the other hand, if the underlying structure of the discipline is considered to be set and relatively unchanging – either as a result of the concepts and content or because of essential methodology – then it would be the task of lower levels of education to introduce these ideas and methods at an appropriate level as a foundation for later work. The difference between the subject at school and in higher education would be one of conceptual difficulty and range and breadth of study. One characteristic of this position is that it implies a relatively static and unchanging view of the discipline, with case studies and examples changing but the structure and focus of disciplinary work remaining constant. A middle position would suggest that although there is an underlying core of big ideas and questions, there are also many social, economic and political forces impacting on the subject as it appears in universities and schools. These three positions are consistent with the analysis provided by Stengel (1997) in which she suggested three possibilities for the relationship between the academic discipline and the school subject.

1. that academic disciplines and school subjects are essentially continuous, the school subject being a lower level or simpler version of the academic subject;
2. that academic disciplines and school subjects are basically discontinuous, the factors influencing their formation being so different as to result in different forms;
3. that academic disciplines and school subjects are related by common aims and broad principles, but develop in different ways as a result of different pressures. Stengel notes that they may be related in one of three ways *either* the academic discipline precedes the school subject *or* the school subject precedes the academic discipline *or* there is a dialectic relationship between the two.

Goodson seems to see geography as an example of the third model and of the situation in which the school subject precedes the academic discipline:

'the story is not one of the translation of an academic discipline devised by ("dominant") groups of scholars in universities into a pedagogic version to be used as school subject. Rather the story unfolds in reverse order and can be seen as a drive from low status groups at school level to progressively colonise the university sector' (1987, p. 78).

While agreeing with the broad trends of the story presented by Goodson, many geographers do not interpret it quite so starkly as a 'bottom-up' relationship, preferring to accept the idea of a dialectical relationship. Marsden (1997a) explained how the early pioneers of geographical education such as Sir Archibald Geikie, Sir Halford Mackinder and James Fairgrieve all saw themselves as academics and educators. They were as concerned to expand the subject in schools as well as in academia. Mackinder's famous paper 'On the scope and methods of geography' (1887), outlining geography's role in linking physical and human aspects, was regarded by him as equally applicable to all levels of education. Indeed in that year he was appointed reader in geography at the University of Oxford. Unwin (1992) explained how university geography in England 'got off the ground' in Oxford and Cambridge and was influenced by wider views from the scientific community (particularly the natural sciences) as well as by its growing popularity in schools. Throughout the twentieth century, the GA, itself an initiative which originated from the academic geography community in 1893 (Balchin, 1993), laid great emphasis on the dialogue between academics and school teachers. This point was continually reiterated by Presidents of the Association, such as Alice Garnett (1969) and Michael Wise who called for 'a co-operative effort from us all in universitities, colleges of education and schools' (1977, p. 257).

School geography before 1970

Before 1960, both in the school sector and in the universities, geography, though popular and in many cases well taught, had become a rather static component of the curriculum providing mainly systematic physical and human geography, or regional studies (Walford, 2001). There was an emphasis on description and on discursive explanations, often with a deterministic slant. In *Education Pamphlet 59*, (DES, 1972) HMI described how 99% of secondary schools in England and Wales offered geography as a distinct component of the curriculum and in virtually all cases pupils would be receiving a similar diet. The overwhelming emphasis was on the relatively unchanging features of physical geography, on a mainly static, deterministic view of human societies and on racing through a regionally based coverage of world geography. HMI pointed out that this led to 'generalisation and superficiality that left pupils with a skeleton of knowledge rather than an understanding of a living pulsating world' (DES, 1972, p. 30). One main stimulus for change was coming from young academic geographers (particularly Richard Chorley and Peter Haggett from the University of Cambridge). They were keen to introduce a more conceptual approach and to make greater use of quantitative techniques and models, aiming to provide geography with greater rigour and a stronger claim to be part of the scientific community (Chorley and Haggett, 1967). Goodson saw this as a natural strategy for a subject which, despite its successes, still held a relatively low status. The close relationship with school geography meant that there were considerable efforts to disseminate the new ideas to secondary schools. Hall (1991) described the excitement and stimulation provided by the Madingley Conferences of the mid-1960s at which some of these ideas were introduced to school teachers. Articles, textbooks (e.g. Everson and Fitzgerald, 1969), further conferences (e.g. DES Short Courses, Charney Manor) and eventually inputs into examination syllabuses followed and many secondary classrooms experimented with the new approaches. However, because of the different contexts of school and university, even as early as 1970 there was some concern about their wholesale adoption in schools, swelling to quite a reaction by 1980 (e.g. Newby, 1980). Some feared that the fascination implicit in studying real places would be lost altogether if there was too great an emphasis on hypothetical models; perhaps more significantly, others were concerned that the positivist philosophy within which the new approaches were framed would dominate school geography to the exclusion of the humanistic and radical approaches appearing in the 1970s.

In primary schools, the influence of academic geography was even weaker, though still apparent. In the late 1960s, as John Blackie's book *Inside the Primary School* (1967) revealed, primary education had not changed much in purpose or content during the previous 30 years. A distinct component of geographical work was normally recognisable and usually included some study of the neighbourhood, some coverage of the British Isles and some reference to distant places. Maps, atlases and pictures were in evidence in most schools, and some teachers made use of the film projector or the television set. The most significant developments of the 1950s and 1960s were probably in the gradual take-up of less structured and more activity based teaching methods. The Plowden Report (DES, 1967) certainly gave impetus to these developments but it noted that according to an HMI survey of 1964, about one third of primary schools had already been substantially affected and one-third a little affected by these methods and that this applied right across the range of subjects and topics taught. It is probably true to say that from 1970, primary schools were relatively open to new ideas about teaching and learning but relatively resistant to developments which seemed to emphasise the content and structure of geography itself, seeing these as inimical to good child-centred practice. Despite this, 'new geography' did make some progress, for example through the Cole and Beynon textbook series (1968). Interestingly, the HMI *Education Pamphlet 59* recognised the different pressures on schools, noting that it was important to keep a balance since 'the geography teacher (primary and secondary) is both a geographer and an educationist' (DES, 1972, p. v).

By the 1970s, then, geography in universities and secondary schools (less so in primary schools) bore a close relationship, founded on important ideas and methods in the discipline. The relationship between the school subject and the academic discipline may be seen as a good example of Stengel's third model (schools and universities holding a dialectical relationship and united by aims and broad principles). However, developments in academic geography were not the only influence on the school curriculum after 1970.

Gordon *et al.* (1991) referred to the 1944-64 period as marking the 'ending of curriculum consensus', as the local education authorities, nominally in partnership with central government, were busy coping with the curriculum consequences of the tripartite system of grammar, technical and modern schools. Also, a number of new initiatives – for example, comprehensive reorganisation of schooling gaining momentum after 1965 (Circular 10/65), the introduction of the Certificate of Secondary Education (1965) and the Plowden Report on primary education (1967) – all accentuated the feeling that it was time to stand back from a purely academic view of the curriculum and to reconsider the wider purposes of schooling. An increasing central interest in the curriculum was reflected first in the formation of the short-lived Curriculum Study Group in 1962, paving the way for the establishment of the Schools Council in 1964. For the first time, there was a specific body, independent of government, charged with promoting and funding curriculum reform and development in schools. A more specifically subject-based influence was provided by the American High School Geography Project (AHSGP), a large educational programme funded by the American government in the 1960s which produced six packages of innovative enquiry-based materials. Although dissemination of these outside the USA was limited, journal articles and chapters (e.g. Graves, 1968; Fitzgerald, 1969; Helburn, 1983) were written about the project and helped to swell the interest in curriculum change. Having initially funded curriculum development projects in science and English (and the Nuffield Foundation funded an influential mathematics project), the Schools Council turned its attention to the humanities after 1970. Norman Graves, then Professor of Education at the Institute of Education, London, suggested that in the 1970s we were faced with a quite novel situation in English education: 'a series of curriculum development projects in which teams of teachers are actively experimenting with new curricula to find out whether they are capable of being usefully introduced into the majority of schools' (1975, p. 102). In one sense then, the formation of geography curriculum projects only reflected the fact that it was geography's turn to participate in this general trend.

Curriculum development: 20 years of change for school geography

The curriculum development projects

The major period of pioneering curriculum development activity was the 1970s when the three secondary geography projects (Geography for the Young School Leaver (GYSL); Geography 14-18; and Geography 16-19) worked through their initial funding and several primary projects (including History, Geography and Social Science 8-13) made a more limited impact on primary geography (see Study 1, pages 28-29). Throughout the 1970s, these projects worked with enthusiastic project schools and teachers, developed new courses and new approaches and produced the first sets of project materials, later published for wider dissemination. The emphasis was on moving school geography away from regional and descriptive work and focusing more on active learning styles and more relevant thematic content. Some aspects of the 'new geography' were incorporated (e.g. use of models and theories, key ideas) but there was also a strong move into more humanistic, qualitative and issues-based approaches. Because there was secure funding and relatively stable project teams, each project took the opportunity to rethink the kind of geography appropriate to a specific age group rather than merely to add to existing offerings. Curriculum development was seen as a large-scale activity, requiring involvement in and amendment to all parts of the national curriculum system – textbooks, in-service activities and resources – as well as to school-based curriculum development. All the projects undertook wider dissemination and, in this respect, GYSL with its three-tier local, regional and national structure, was the most successful, reaching at one point 98% of all secondary schools in at least a superficial way (Macdonald and Walker, 1976). The three secondary projects also became involved with examination boards and project examinations (first O-level and CSE, then moving easily into GCSE) as a means of legitimising the innovative approaches to the subject. By the late 1980s, there is no doubt that a substantial number of secondary teachers were involved in or affected by the geography curriculum projects. Many pupils were entered for project GCSE and A-level examinations; the Geography 16-19 Project, in particular, had the largest of all A-level entries by 1994, 27.6% of the total entry. The influence of the primary projects is less easy to gauge, given their cross-curricular emphases and the small numbers of specialist geography teachers in primary schools. Marsden (1995) suggested that the History, Geography and Social Science 8-13 Project, though making a relatively small impact directly on schools, was significant because it showed how the contributing disciplines could be used in curriculum planning, whether or not the subject labels appeared on the timetable.

Times were harder for curriculum development generally in the 1980s. Funding was more difficult to obtain, teacher release became more problematic and support systems were reduced. The Schools Council was first reviewed – the Trenaman Report (DES, 1981a) – and then, despite a reasonably favourable report, disbanded (1982-84). A body which had given birth to so many radical innovations in education, initially at a time of plentiful funding, found itself increasingly out of sympathy with the new educational discourse (see Plaskow, 1985; Kelly, 1999). Without the Schools Council, there was less money and less enthusiasm for curriculum development. Responsibilities for curriculum and assessment were split apart and the influence of the teacher unions and LEAs was marginalised. The curriculum successors to the Schools Council – the School Curriculum Development Committee (SCDC) (1984-88) and later the National Curriculum Council (NCC) (1988-93) – ostensibly took on some of the curriculum support and monitoring roles. In fact, both bodies were essentially created to allow the government to exercise firmer central control over the curriculum and assessment. The SCDC handled the final period of funding for the Geography 16-19 Project and support for Geography 14-18 national co-ordination.

There were fewer curriculum initiatives in the 1980s. In 1986, GYSL obtained funding from the Manpower Services Commission (MSC) in order to develop the potential of GYSL-style geography to the courses developed by the Technical and Vocational Education Initiative (TVEI). The acronym

GYSL-TRIST was used for this work. At about the same time, Geography 16-19 schools were exploring modules offered by the Business and Technical Education Council (BTEC) and the contribution of geography to the Certificate of Pre-Vocational Education (CPVE). The Humanities and Information Technology (HIT) Project was set up by the National Council for Educational Technology in 1988 to explore and support the effective use of IT in the teaching of secondary geography and history. The Geography, Schools and Industry Project (GSIP) was established by the GA in 1984 with the specific remit to examine and develop the contribution of geography to economic understanding and to school-industry work. Funding was obtained from a variety of business and industrial organisations as well as, originally, from the MSC and the Department of Trade and Industry (DTI). These examples reveal that the curriculum development movement's response to the more constrained situation of the 1980s was to become more focused, particularly on geography's contribution to aspects of national concern (IT, industry) and more creative about finding sources of funding, often linking the bid to an existing initiative. However, this did not lead the curriculum developers to narrow their approach or retreat from some of the gains made in the 1970s. In each case, the GYSL-TRIST, HIT and GSIP teams built on the good practice established by the earlier projects in relation to the processes of curriculum planning and the adoption of active enquiry learning styles. In the case of GSIP (Corney, 1992) a start was made in extending these more effectively to primary schools.

It is important not to overestimate the immediate impact of the projects, particularly in primary schools where geography was not normally taught as a separate subject. Despite their high profile and major dissemination programmes, in the short term it was really only the relatively small numbers of pilot schools that received a full immersion and involvement in curriculum thinking and many schools continued with traditional examination syllabuses wedded to a regional approach. The projects undoubtedly laid the foundations for a changed discourse about school geography, but it needed the additional stimulus of many smaller scale and less threatening initiatives to persuade the ordinary teacher to try curriculum change.

Developments beyond the projects

During the 1970s, there was what Walford referred to as a 'powerful "underground" publishing movement' (2001, p. 162), characterised by the production of relatively short-lived and informal publications which helped to challenge traditional textbooks and introduce new ideas about quantitative approaches and models. *Classroom Geographer* (founded in 1972 and edited by Neil Sealey from his own home) was one example, Richard Aylmer's *Setwork* pamphlets were another. The *Bulletin of Environmental Education* published by the Town and Country Planning Association from 1971, encouraged geography teachers, among others, to pay more attention to the urban and built environment. In 1967, the GA established a series of *Teaching Geography Occasional Papers*, it being one of the few outlets available at that time for the publication of teaching ideas derived from 'the rapidly evolving geography of the research frontier'. These *Occasional Papers* sold well initially and provided secondary geography teachers with a well-respected source of both practical classroom ideas and more serious debate, ranging across the full geography/educational spectrum. However, its role was eclipsed from the mid-1970s by the launching of the new journal *Teaching Geography* in 1975, and the last *Occasional Paper* was published in 1982.

Also of significance were the activities of the university department of education tutors for geography in drawing together and translating new ideas for a predominantly secondary school teacher audience. A whole range of methodological texts (Walford, 1969; Bale *et al.*, 1973; Graves, 1971, 1972, 1975, 1979; Bailey, 1972; Boden, 1976; Hall, 1976; Marsden, 1976; Slater, 1982; Huckle, 1983) surveyed and summarised the dynamic scene. Most of the books gave as much weight to curriculum thinking and the significance of general educational theories as they did to new ideas in geography.

Secondary teachers were also well provided with textbooks in this period. Textbooks influenced by the 'new geography' included, for example: *Settlement Patterns* and *Inside the City* by Everson and Fitzgerald (1969, 1972); *New Ways in Geography* by Cole and Beynon (1968); *Pattern and Process in Human Geography* by Tidswell (1973) and *Beginning the New Geography* by Briggs (1979). Walford (2001) provides a fuller discussion of these activities. A wave of new project-influenced textbooks and resource materials appeared, mainly in the 1980s. Many of these started from project ideas – for instance enquiry-based learning or an issues-based approach – but then developed these on the basis of practical experience. Thus, for instance, *Worldwide Issues* (1985) was authored by a team of teachers led by Clive Hart of the Geography 16-19 Project team, and the *Enquiry Geography* series (early 1990s) had Graham Ranger, an ex 14-18 and GSIP teacher, as its main author. In 1979, Simon Catling, then Headteacher of Sheringham Primary School, London, noted that, although secondary colleagues were well served, there were not enough curriculum planning models and examples of teaching/learning strategies for primary teachers (Catling, 1979). A year later, the GA's *Geographical Work in Primary and Middle Schools* (Mills, 1981) provided an immediate source of practical help, but it was the late 1980s before the appearance of a more considered look at curriculum matters (Bale, 1987) and two years after that before the GA's journal *Primary Geographer* was launched. It is difficult to find hard evidence – other than anecdotal – for the influence of these books, journals and articles. However, they were read by thousands of PGCE and MA/MEd students and by numerous practising teachers and undoubtedly changed the context of influence for school geography.

At local level, the local education authority geography or humanities adviser became an increasingly influential figure for curriculum development in the 1970s and 1980s. Bailey (1992) estimated that about one-third of English and Welsh LEAs had qualified geographers on their advisory staff by the mid-1980s. In the reorganised local government context after 1972, such individuals were in charge of budgets targeted specifically at subject development and were given considerable freedom to promote the subject in schools and establish informal teacher networks. The result in many LEAs was a package of in-service support, providing county geography advisory groups, in-service courses and frequently newsletters or guidance material (Maund and Wyatt, 1980). The Geography Advisers and Inspectors Network (GAIN) was established in 1981 to support advisers in their work. Much of this activity was geared to secondary geography initially, since most LEAs managed support for primary colleagues through primary generalist advisers.

Overlapping with LEA activities and reinforcing them at regional rather than local level were the activities of the GA Branches. It is difficult to be concise about the number and strength of GA Branches, but Balchin (1993) estimates that a maximum of 75 Branches were operating at any one time, and the 1970s and 1980s were certainly periods of activity. Run by committees of local teachers and/or university department of education tutors, usually with strong support from the LEA, many Branches were breaking away from the traditional offering of twice-termly sixth form lectures by academic geographers. Judged by a brief survey of some GA Branch programmes, the 1970s was the period in which Branches began to offer teacher workshops on curriculum matters, new quantitative techniques or the work of the Schools Council projects. Branch activities predominantly supported secondary teachers in the 1970s. It was not until the 1980s that events aimed at primary teachers made an appearance on Branch programmes.

Of particular significance for secondary geography at national level were the DES Short Courses in geography, organised and run by the HMI Geography Committee between 1969 and 1992 when Ofsted came into existence. Providing for teachers the rare opportunity for a week-long focus on new trends and developments in the subject, and offering high-profile speakers and tutors, the impact of these courses on those admittedly small numbers of teachers attending should not be under-estimated. Further dissemination was ensured because many of the delegates went on to positions of influence in the GA, to write textbooks or to take up posts in advisory or HMI work. HMI planned the programmes on the basis of perceived need as arising from inspection evidence. The first four courses, held at Maria Grey College, Twickenham (with two northern courses held in Doncaster College of Education), dealt with the models and quantitative techniques filtering down from academic geography, and so were primarily concerned to translate the new geography into a school context. It is clear from the programmes for successive years (when the course moved to new locations) that by the late 1970s and 1980s, there was more of a curriculum focus and more emphasis on participant involvement in planning activities (source: Trevor Bennetts, HMI Staff Inspector 1979-92). Many university departments of education were active in offering teacher in-service events in the 1970s (e.g. Institute of Education, London; Charlotte Mason College, Ambleside) so were some university departments of geography, still seeing it as part of their role to update teachers (e.g. University of Leicester). Mention should be made of the 'Burwalls' Geography Conferences established in 1972, originally as an initiative from Peter Haggett, but taken on by the extra-mural studies department of the University of Bristol. After 1973, the main aim was to disseminate the work of the secondary geography projects. These courses, though small in delegate numbers, were popular and significant events, contributing to debate about the subject. They ceased in the mid-1990s (though the RGS-IBG has used the venue for teacher residential courses again since 1998).

Conclusion

The 1970s may, with some justification, be described as the decade of curriculum development for geography. Overall, there was a remarkable growth of interest and activity in new ideas in geography, new classroom approaches and new resources and guidelines for the subject, particularly in the secondary sector. In primary schools, Marsden (1995) suggests that there was less enthusiasm for subject-centred initiatives. He regrets the subject-centred/child-centred dichotomy which existed, hinting that such attitudes were partly to blame for the slower take-up of geography-based curriculum developments in primary schools during this period. In the longer term, such developments undoubtedly changed the nature of the discourse about school geography. They moved it inexorably towards a more progressive and (despite the primary teachers' perception) child-centred ideology and moved it further away from a close relationship with the academic discipline. *Geography into the 1980s* – the publication arising from a conference held to consider the contribution of the three Schools Council (Geography) Projects to geography in secondary education (Rawling, 1980) seemed to set an optimistic tone for the next decade. This conference brought together the teams of all the secondary geography projects with a range of LEA advisers, teachers and teacher educators. There was a feeling of excitement, some satisfaction at the progress made in the 1970s, and an expectation that, if the projects could clarify the gains and losses of the previous decades, then teachers would be well-prepared to weather the new developments, despite the increasingly politicised situation for curriculum decision making. In retrospect, geography educators were under-estimating the increasingly politicised nature of curriculum decision making and the growing influence of the New Right.

Changing the Subject. The impact of national policy on school geography 1980 – 2000

27

Study 1

Geography: The curriculum development projects

The Schools Council was responsible for launching and funding a number of curriculum development projects which had a significant influence on the geography curriculum in the 1970s and 1980s. There were three major secondary projects. Geography for the Young School Leaver (established 1970) aimed 'to examine the contribution that geography can make to the education of average and below average pupils between the ages of 14 and 16' and 'to produce schemes of work and supporting resources which can be used either in a subject or an interdisciplinary context'. The Project team, led by Rex Beddis at the Avery Hill College of Education, took on what Graves (1982) has called an *interventionist* model of curriculum development, emphasising the production of high quality resource materials, initially in the form of three theme-based multi-media kits for teachers (*Man, Land and Leisure*, 1974; *Cities and People*, 1974; *People, Place and Work*, 1975). An extension project published further booklets about geography and development in the mid-1980s. The Geography 14-18 (Bristol) Project, set up in the same year as GYSL, and led by Gladys Hickman at the University of Bristol, identified what it called 'a vicious circle of curriculum underdevelopment' (Tolley and Reynolds, 1977, p. 2) for 14-16 year olds. Traditional examination syllabuses and a narrow focus on essay-style assessment were resulting in courses which were predominantly factual and descriptive, demanding little intellectual challenge and a limited range of skills. The Project set out to break this cycle by establishing a '14-18' O-level syllabus (University of Cambridge) – characterised by innovative forms of assessment, including coursework and individual study – and by involving teachers in developing their own courses based on the Project's syllabus framework of key concepts and principles. Graves suggests that this was an example of the *independence model* – a style of curriculum development which assumes that the teachers in the field are the best people to undertake curriculum change. The Geography 16-19 Project, working from 1976 at the Institute of Education London, was not directly concerned with the school geography curriculum 5-16. However, since its second aim was to help teachers 'appreciate their roles as curriculum developers' and since many teachers were the same people who taught lower down the school, its influence on curriculum development was inevitably wider and more significant then its title might suggest. After setting out broad aims for 16-19 year old students, it established a curriculum framework incorporating a distinctive people-environment approach to geography and an enquiry-based approach to learning. A wide range of courses and syllabuses, including the 16-19 A-level syllabus (University of London), and exemplar materials, were derived from this framework (Naish *et al.*, 1987). Geography 16-19 is seen by Graves as an example of the *co-operative* model of curriculum development, involving teachers at the same time as providing firm central control. The primary project with the greatest influence on geography was probably the History, Geography and Social Science 8-13 Project, established at the University of Liverpool in 1971 (Blyth, 1973). This Project followed a collaborative style of development similar to Geography 14-18, seeking to help teachers identify and develop significant intellectual skills and key concepts common to all contributing disciplines. It later became known as Place, Time and Society 8-13 (Blyth *et al.*, 1976), Environmental Studies 5-13 and Science 5-13 were two further projects which developed materials relevant to primary geography, as examples of new content (particularly environmental content) and different teaching strategies.

Further reading
Ash, S. and Mobbs, D. (1987) 'The GYSL-TRIST Project', *Teaching Geography*, 12, 5, pp. 222-3.

continued

Blyth, A. (1973) 'History, Geography and Social Science 8-13: a second generation project, in Taylor, P.H. and Walton, J. (eds) *The Curriculum: Research, innovation and change*. London: Ward Lock Educational, pp. 40-51.

Blyth, A., Copper, K., Derricot, R., Elliott, G., Sumner, H. and Waplington, H. (1976) *Place, Time and Society 8-13: Curriculum planning in history, geography and social science*. Bristol: Collins-ESL.

Boardman, D. (1985) 'Geography for the Young School Leaver' in Boardman, D. (ed) *New Directions in Geographical Education*. London: Falmer Press, pp. 65-83.

Dalton, T.H. (1988) *The Challenge of Curriculum Innovation: A study of ideology and practice*. London: Falmer Press.

Graves, N.J. (1982) 'Geographical education', *Progress in Human Geography*, 6, 4, pp. 563-75.

Hickman, G., Reynolds, J. and Tolley, H. (1973) *A New Professionalism for a Changing Geography*. London: Schools Council.

Naish, M. and Rawling, E. (1990) 'Geography 16-19: some implications for higher education', *Journal of Geography in Higher Education*, 14, 1, pp. 55-75.

Naish, M., Rawling, E. and Hart, C. (1987) *Geography 16-19: The contribution of a curriculum development project to 16-19 education*. Harlow: Longman for SCDC.

Orrell, K. (1985) 'Geography 14-18' in Boardman, D. (ed) *New Directions in Geographical Education*. London: Falmer Press, pp. 85-98.

3

Contrasting Ideologies and Unresolved Issues 1980-89

Introduction

Michael Naish suggested that the curriculum development movement had provided 'a sound, exciting and provocative basis for further development of the role of geography in education through the 1980s' (1980, p. 64). Many geographical educators assumed that curriculum planning principles would be used to guide any future centrally directed curriculum initiatives as signalled by Callaghan's 1976 'Ruskin College' speech. In the event, this was not the case. The 1980s saw the end of funding for the major curriculum projects (see Chapter 2). The curriculum development movement in geography did not play a major part either in winning geography's placing or in shaping the eventual Geography National Curriculum Order. The new educational discourse, framed by the 'New Right' and forming the basis for the Conservative's education policies, started from the 'deficit view' of school geography. In this analysis, school geography had failed its pupils who were consequently lacking in basic map skills and world knowledge. The 'progressive' developments of the 1970s, and particularly the Schools Council curriculum development projects, were seen as the problem and a main cause of the perceived decline in standards.

Initially, it was not even a foregone conclusion that geography would be a part of the 'core curriculum' for all schools, as Richard Daugherty, then Joint Honorary Secretary of the GA warned colleagues at the Charney Manor Conference of 1980 (Daugherty, 1981). The energies of the geography education community were channelled at national level away from pedagogical issues and into the political campaign to ensure geography a place in the new national curriculum. This chapter will seek to explain how, although geography won its place and established its national curriculum status, geographical educators found themselves increasingly out of step with the prevailing curriculum discourse of the late 1980s. When the official National Curriculum Geography Working Group (GWG) began work in 1989, there were so many unresolved issues that some degree of confusion was almost guaranteed.

This chapter will first trace the growth of the New Right and its influence on the educational discourse in the 1980s, then it will examine some of the main curriculum gains from the curriculum development movement and show that there were many unresolved issues which left the geography education community dangerously exposed in the curriculum-making processes of the late 1980s. The final section of this chapter deals with the role of the GA during the 1980s, noting how the Association sharpened its political campaigning skills and 'played the utilitarian card' in order to ensure geography's place in the national curriculum.

The growth of influence of the New Right

School subjects are not merely random selections of content from their static academic counterparts. The social constructionist viewpoint (Young, 1971; Ball, 1990) states that all school subjects are socially constructed – that is they reflect the values and interests (the ideologies) of those individuals and groups influential in constructing them at different times. While I accept that ideologies have a strong influence on school subjects at different times, I also believe that geography's claim to curriculum status has a deeper philosophical basis (see Chapter 2, page 20). An ideology may be defined as a strongly held set of beliefs or principles. It can be a positive force, expressing clear principles in a benevolent way and promoting constructive discussion, or it can be a more negative force when it seems to distort reality and result in polarised debates. Figure 1 presents a simplified view of the significant educational ideologies which have affected school geography in England over the past 100 years. It must be remembered that at any one time the curriculum is likely to reflect a mixture of ideologies; Figure 1 merely highlights the dominant influences at different times.

Prior to the mid-1970s, the curriculum was not the concern of central government. Schools and LEAs wielded considerable autonomy which, for most subjects, meant that the subject community was the controlling influence on change in content and approach. A pre-1975 'curriculum history' (Figure 1) could be elucidated by exploring the processes of negotiation, dialogue and compromise taking place between different parts of the academic and school-based subject communities. In the case of geography, negotiations over identity and definition have been a recurring activity throughout its history (Johnston, 1991a; Livingstone, 1992; Walford, 2001). In the late nineteenth century, geography had become a significant part of the elementary curriculum but was considered mainly as an informational subject with a low status, although Marsden (1989) reminds us that the promotion of citizenship and international understanding through the subject also played a strong role. Geography hardly appeared in the secondary grammar school curriculum. During the twentieth century, it gradually achieved acceptance as a secondary school and university discipline and, consequently, higher status in schools. Goodson (1988a) and Walford (2001) show that this move to bring geography respectability, and a place in the more rigorous liberal humanist tradition, was planned and promoted as a deliberate strategy by influential individuals such as Douglas Freshfield, A.J. Herbertson, Alice Garnett and by the GA. By 1975, not only had this policy 'paid off' by expanding the popularity and prestige of school geography, but the 'new geography' with its rigorous and quantitative methodology seemed all set to disseminate from universities into schools and to reinforce even further the academic credentials of the subject. In fact, new geography and academic influences did not dominate in the 1970s, as curriculum development activity promoted the more progressive, child-centred educational ideology. The curriculum projects revealed that the subject could also be a vehicle for developing general skills and abilities and the exploration of values. Some geographers also worked with more radical and reconstructionist approaches, particularly in the 1980s (see Huckle, 1983).

What is important about this brief curriculum history is that before 1970, although different ideological traditions were apparent, the subject community (in its different forms – university academics, school teachers, teacher educators) was controlling and manipulating the subject and the way it appeared in schools. Even conflicts and disagreements for example about the place of 'new' geography in schools – were 'in-house'. Prime Minister Jim Callaghan's 'Great debate' speech of 1976 is frequently taken as marking the starting point of a period in which the situation changed significantly, and Ministers began to involve themselves directly in policy making about the form and content of the curriculum. This increasing centralisation eventually resulted in the 1988 Education Reform Act and the establishment of the national curriculum, with geography as one of the ten foundation subjects. Although the curriculum debates at national level were not narrowly ideological in the early 1980s (see, for instance, the aims set out in *The School Curriculum* (DES, 1981b)), Stephen Ball's work (1990) illustrates how these activities vastly increased the likelihood of ideological conflict. Ball traced the growing influence of right wing thinkers, the so-called New Right, on educational policy in the 1970s and 1980s. His analysis reveals the importance of using this

Ideological tradition	Characteristics	Impact on school geography in England
Utilitarian/informational	■ education primarily aimed at 'getting a job' and 'earning a living' ■ a focus on useful information and basic skills	■ nineteenth century emphasis on locational knowledge ('capes and bays') and on useful knowledge about the countries of the world ■ the 1991 GNC reinstated an emphasis on maps, locational knowledge and world geography
Cultural restorationism (as promoted by the New Right in English policy making in the 1980s and 1990s)	■ restoring traditional areas of knowledge and skills (cultural heritage) ■ providing pupils with a set package of knowledge and skills which will enable them to fit well-defined places in society and the workplace	■ economic and regional geography related to Britain's early twentieth century empire and trading links ■ the 1991 GNC seemed to stress factual information and to focus on the geography of Britain in a relatively unchanging world
Liberal humanist (also called classical humanist)	■ worthwhile knowledge as a preparation for life; the passing on of a cultural heritage from one generation to the next ■ emphasis on rigour, big ideas and theories, and intellectual challenge	■ the development of geography as an academic discipline in the 1950s and 1960s and the resulting higher status accorded to the subject in schools ■ stress on scientific methods, theories and quantitative techniques in the 'new geography' of the 1960s and 1970s
Progressive educational (also called child-centred)	■ focusing on self development or bringing to maturity the individual child/pupil ■ using academic subjects as the medium for developing skills, attitudes, values and learning styles which will help them become autonomous individuals	■ the geography curriculum development projects of the 1970s and 1980s (Geography for Young School Leaver, Bristol Project, Geography 16-19) ■ emphasis on enquiry, active learning and development of skills, attitudes and values through geography ■ child-centred primary education 1960s-1970s ■ 'thinking skills' (late 1990s)
Reconstructionist (also called radical)	■ education as an agent for changing society, so an emphasis on encouraging pupils to challenge existing knowledge and approaches ■ less interest in academic disciplines, more focus on issues and socially critical pedagogy	■ geography's involvement with, e.g. environmental education, peace education, global education, in the 1970s-1980s ■ the current interest by the New Labour government in sustainable development education and citizenship seems to offer opportunities for reconstructionism, but may only be a relatively utilitarian reaction to changing societal concerns
Vocationalist or industrial trainer (Note: in some ways this cuts across all the other traditions)	■ provide pupils with knowledge and skills required for work ■ or use workplace and work-related issues as a stimulus for learning skills/abilities ■ or use work-related issues for questioning status quo	■ the Geography, Schools, Industry Project (GA sponsored, 1983-91) used work-related contexts in a progressive way for curriculum change and active learning. More recently, government-promoted careers education, work-related initiatives and key skills have been more utilitarian in character (skills for work).

Figure 1: **Ideological traditions and geography:** a simplified analysis.

approach not only to view the whole curriculum but as a means of understanding individual subjects. In his 1990 book, he looked in detail at the subjects of mathematics and English. He made it clear that, in the making of national curriculum subjects after 1988, the values of the subject communities were no longer taken as authoritative; instead the predominantly New Right views of politicians, political advisers and Ministers assumed prominence as the basis for policy making.

The New Right was not a homogenous group but included, for instance, both neo-liberals who emphasised market forces, individual choice and competition, and the neo-conservatives who focused their attention on social order, stressing a return to traditional values through re-valuing the family, discipline, traditional learning and the nation's history and culture. Both views influenced policies in the 1970s and 1980s and sometimes the conflicts and contradictions between them resulted in confused policy making, so that Ball (1990) warns against making a simple translation directly between philosophical discourse and political action. On the whole, however, neo-liberal influence is best seen in structural and economic measures such as opting out, open enrolment, local management of schools and the establishment of City Technology Colleges, while neo-conservatism may be seen to have had most influence on the curriculum. Kenneth Baker's insistence on establishing a full ten-subject traditional national curriculum, rather than the more minimal framework for the core subjects favoured by Margaret Thatcher, is commonly seen as a victory for neo-conservatism (and, as it turned out, advantageous initially for geography).

Much of the New Right's thinking had its origins in the hostile critique of modern progressive education provided in the Black Papers of the 1960s and 1970s (Cox and Dyson, 1969a,b, 1970; Cox and Boyson, 1977). Briefly the main arguments were that standards of pupil performance and of discipline were declining and that the curriculum and teaching methods reflected left wing political ideology. Although little hard evidence was provided for these assertions, and geography as such was hardly mentioned, the Black Papers were crucial in persuading the public that there was an educational crisis. Neo-conservative thinkers were ready with the answer. Ball suggests that the neo-conservatives were promoting a hard-line version of the old humanist philosophy recognised by Raymond Williams (1962). Ball refers to this as 'cultural restorationism' – since it promoted a re-invention of tradition, a cultural restoration. For geography, it overlaps to some extent with the nineteenth century view of a utilitarian and informational geography of Britain and Empire but with a stronger focus on traditional knowledge and understanding (Figure 1). Ball also recognises a reforming humanist ideology, represented by many civil servants and HMI, and which tended to bring a more modern industrial or technological slant to traditional subjects. This might be represented in new geography and in the schools-industry movements which influenced geography in the 1980s (e.g. GSIP). All through the 1970s and 1980s the cultural restorationists grew in strength and their opposition to progressive education crystallised into the establishment of right wing pressure groups and think tanks – such as the Conservative Philosophy Group (1975), the Salisbury Group (1977), the Hillgate Group (mid-1970s) and the Campaign for Real Education (1987). These groups produced pamphlets and other publications and their proponents (e.g. Roger Scruton, Rhodes Boyson, John Marks) also spoke to popular audiences through newspaper articles and radio/television programmes. Carr and Hartnett point out that such tactics were highly effective: 'The New Right, through its techniques of persuasion and by hard work and the imaginative use of language and the media, created a new populist form of discourse based on pamphlets and the funding of think tanks' (1996, p. 159). The New Right gradually took over key posts in policy making and government (Callaghan, 1995), particularly after 1979, when the 'Believers', as Callaghan calls them, found a natural home in Thatcherism. This was what Ball calls the growing 'context of influence' which led up to the 1988 Education Reform Act.

Some of the New Right literature does refer to school subjects, but mainly to English, mathematics and history, and there are few specific references to geography. Certainly there is no evidence for a cultural restorationist 'blueprint' for geography. However, what is important is to appreciate how significantly the New Right changed the terms of the educational debate and how strongly this contrasted with the more progressive ideologies being explored by the school geography community.

Contrasting ideologies and unresolved issues

Figure 2 identifies some of the significant impacts of curriculum development in geography (column 1) and highlights some of the unresolved issues existing in 1989 (column 2). The third column presents a typical New Right response and is derived from the publications of the New Right proponents and from Ball's analysis of the situation (1990, Chapters 2 and 3). It is not suggested that all the characteristics in column 1 had been taken on by a majority of schools. For most of these, appearance in the list merely suggests that curriculum innovation over the years had revealed potential benefits.

Main impacts of curriculum development	Unresolved issues for geography (1970s and 1980s)	Suggested typical New Right response
Process of **school-based curriculum planning** introduced with focus on strong role for subject teacher in developing and implementing the curriculum	How can school-based planning be accommodated in an era of central control and a national curriculum?	A national curriculum will set required 'knowledge, skill and culture on which our society has been founded' (Hillgate, 1987, p. 3). There is no need for schools to develop the curriculum, only to deliver it.
Key ideas and concepts identified as framework for teaching and learning	Is it possible to ensure that the resultant approach does not neglect locational knowledge and study of places?	Specific prescribed content should be the basis of the curriculum and for geography the emphasis should be on locational knowledge, place knowledge and map skills.
Geography recognised **as an educational medium**	Will this move school geography away from the academic subject? Will it lead to an over-emphasis on social and cultural aspects (human)? or on skills?	The role of traditional subjects is to master a body of knowledge not promote vague attitudes or skills that are common to many subjects.
Geographical enquiry approach promoted as integral to learning the required knowledge and skills	What does enquiry mean? Does it reject or include traditional whole-class methods? Does it only refer to individual pieces of enquiry work?	Traditional subject-specific skills should be emphasised. Approaches to learning should be formal and disciplined.
A curriculum-led view of assessment promoted – i.e. assessment as part of the learning process	Is it possible to resolve the tension between assessment for learning and assessment for accountability?	Most important are formal national tests and examinations because these provide 'objective evidence' about school performance.
Role of **teacher as professional** highlighted with inputs to curriculum development and pedagogy	What professional role is there for teachers with a highly prescriptive NC to 'deliver'? Is it possible to preserve some teacher input and a range of teaching strategies?	Teachers should be trained to 'deliver' national requirements, using their enthusiasm and expertise, but remaining formally in control of the passing on of 'cultural heritage'.

Figure 2: Curriculum development: impact and unresolved issues for geography.

Curriculum planning

Curriculum development experience had revealed the importance of curriculum planning – that is of formulating clear aims and objectives and of using these as the basis for selecting content and teaching/learning experiences and making decisions about assessment. All the Schools Council projects provided structures or frameworks which helped teachers to do this: History, Geography and Social Science 8-13, Geography for the Young School Leaver and the Geography 14-18 projects used an objectives model of curriculum planning based on the ideas of Tyler (1949), but not in the narrow behavioural sense. Their approaches reflect what Marsden calls a 'middle of the road' (1995, p. 63) view, where objectives are more akin to principles. Geography 16-19, with its curriculum framework, is an example of applying a process model of curriculum planning. In this, as Kelly explained, the knowledge content of the curriculum is selected 'in relation to its likely contribution to the development of the pupil' and the aims and purposes of the approach are seen 'not as goals to be achieved at some later stage in the process, but as procedural principles which should guide our practice throughout' (1999, p. 76). By clarifying the curriculum system and providing central frameworks, the projects helped teachers to appreciate their own creative roles in reviewing their existing courses, interpreting project frameworks to develop new courses and designing and implementing new approaches to teaching, learning and assessment. Shared responsibility for curriculum change between national and local levels, co-operative professional development work with other teachers and the celebration of local innovation – these were all features of this school-based curriculum development.

Even the many schools not involved in the Schools Council projects were exposed at least to the broad principles of curriculum planning by other means. There were the methodological texts of the 1970s and 1980s (e.g. Graves (1979), which provided a curriculum process model for geography), the teachers' guides of textbook series (e.g. *Reformed Geography*, Dinkele *et al.*, 1976) and even continuing reminders from HMI (Bennetts, 1985). The pages of *Teaching Geography* show that teachers were actively experimenting with curriculum planning (e.g. Boardman, Developing a GYSL unit, 1976; Walker, Curriculum innovation, 1976; Waters, Creative approach to geography, 1986). Primary teachers of geography were somewhat slower than their secondary colleagues to warm to the idea of subject based developments and the HMI *Aspects of Primary Education* document (DES, 1989a) revealed that there was generally a lack of distinctive geographical input to topic work. There was, nevertheless, by the mid-1980s a significant build-up of ideas and expertise in curriculum planning, at least in theory – for instance the GA's *Geographical Work in Primary and Middle Schools* (Mills, 1981, and the clear statement of aims and objectives for primary provided by HMI in *Geography from 5-16: Curriculum Matters 7* (DES, 1986).

What remained unresolved was how this experience should be used in the totally different context of centrally controlled curriculum planning, as established by the Education Reform Act 1988. The national curriculum was implicitly being formulated to a totally different model (Kelly, 1999), starting not from an overview of the purposes of education, but from a list of required subjects and pre-conceived views about their content. When geography was accepted as a foundation subject by Kenneth Baker in 1987, the strident New Right discourse, translated for geography into locational knowledge and map-skills, seemed already to have set the agenda for content selection. As Ball explains, at the heart of the New Right assertions was a firm belief that progressive curriculum development threatened to weaken and belittle traditional knowledge and skills, sacrificing these to 'opinionated vagueness' (1990, p. 46). The cultural restorationist mission was to restore the traditional grammar school curriculum, founded on solid content and well-established skills. School-based curriculum development did not feature in this vision.

Key ideas

Dissemination of the 'new geography' had encouraged teachers to identify spatial concepts and to use specific content to exemplify general theories. There are also strong echoes of Bruner's view, that meaningful learning depends on mastery of the structure or fundamental ideas behind the subject (1960), in the work of the projects. Rather than just list descriptive content GYSL set out key ideas for each of its major themes (Boardman, 1985); Geography 14-18 guided teachers to use some major organising concepts of geography (Tolley and Reynolds, 1977); and Geography 16-19 referred both to key organising concepts (Naish *et al.*, 1987) and, at course-planning level, to generalisations. The History, Geography and Social Science 8-13 Project drew attention to the 'big' concepts common to all contributory subjects. The HMI publication *The Teaching of Ideas in Geography* (DES, 1978) further disseminated this approach, giving consideration to primary geography as well, and Trevor Bennetts in 'Geography 5-16: a view from the inspectorate' in *Geography* confirmed the importance of developing 'important ideas and skills [which] should be reinforced and extended over the length of a course' (1985, p. 312).

The advantages of focusing on key ideas, concepts and principles was that it encouraged teachers to help pupils find pattern and meaning in their work and seemed a better way to proceed than to add continuing layers of place description and hope that some synthesis would result in pupils' minds. The unresolved issue about the key ideas approach was how to deal with the continuing need for pupils to build up a coherent and balanced framework of locational knowledge (i.e. to know where places are) and a knowledge of some specific places (i.e. to know and understand what some places, such as their own country, are like). In fact, the projects made some attempts to address the issue of place studies, providing matrices for plotting places used as exemplars and encouraging teachers to check that there was a balance of different scales, places and environments chosen for study. However, at the end of the 1980s, it was becoming clear that too many schools were failing to ensure a basic locational general knowledge among pupils. An International Gallup Survey (1988), for instance, made unflattering comparisons of Britain with many other countries in the world (Figure 3), while the press continually confirmed this picture by referring to their own horror stories about young peoples' ignorance of the world around them. A particularly trenchant critic was Michael Storm, the Inner London Education Authority's (ILEA) Inspector for Geography who, while championing the more conceptual and ideas-based geography in the 1970s, was, as a result of direct confrontation with some of its consequences in ILEA schools, becoming more disillusioned. In the ILEA Bulletin of summer 1987 (18 months before his appointment to the NC GWG), Storm suggested that 'most people would be concerned to discover school leavers who couldn't identify Britain on a map of Europe or London on a map of Britain' (1987). It was this aspect of school geography which was seized on by the New Right as a prime indicator of what was wrong with the subject.

British know little about the world and care even less
British adults have come near the bottom of an International Gallup survey on geographical knowledge, with only the Italians and the Mexicans scoring significantly worse.

Most Britons, given an outline map of the world, cannot identify correctly Central America, Japan, the Persian Gulf, Mexico, Sweden, Egypt or Vietnam. While this may be excused as ignorance of faraway countries of which we know little, 13% were apparently unable to locate the United Kingdom and 52% West Germany.

The survey, covering 10,000 adults in nine countries, was carried out last spring. It was commissioned by the National Geographic Society in America, which was concerned about the level of geographical knowledge in the United States. It did, indeed, find cause for American concern, but the results were equally disturbing for Britain.

Figure 3: British know little about the world and care even less.
Extract from article in *The Independent*, 29 December 1988.

Geography as an educational medium

The Schools Council curriculum projects all focused on the development of skills and abilities and on using the subject as a 'medium for education'. In pursuit of this end, they were selective about subject content, attempting to balance the traditional subject headings with material that would inspire and motivate students. In order to ensure that students could understand and apply their learning, the projects, and subsequent textbooks of the 1980s, emphasised concepts, ideas, skills and values rather than facts. All this was anathema to the New Right. Roger Scruton's complaints about the politicisation of subjects could easily have been written with the geography curriculum projects in mind:

> 'First difficult and disciplined parts of the subject are removed or downgraded, so that educational achievement can no longer be represented as mastery of a body of knowledge. Second, texts and subjects are chosen not for their intellectual or literary merit, or for their ability to further pupils' intellectual grasp, but for the political attitudes which are conveyed in them, and pupils are taught to consider the acquisition of such attitudes as the true mark of educational success' (Scruton et al., 1985, pp. 8-9).

And, as the contrasting quotation from Geography 16-19 reveals:

> 'The approach to geography focuses on questions, issues and problems arising from the inter-relationships of people with their varied environments ... It is an educational approach rather than a strictly academic one, and it is designed to permit selection of ideas and methods from across the range of academic approaches to the subject. In this way, it can offer a role for geography in the 16-9 curriculum which has appeal and relevance for a large cross-section of students' (Naish et al., 1987, p. 40).

The medium-for-learning approach had two wider consequences. First, school geography initially moved further away from academic geography as these new ways of viewing the subject generated feelings of confidence and of a distinctive purpose for schools as opposed to universities. This was potentially a dangerous situation, given the subject-based nature of the national curriculum and was to cause subsequent problems for the geography community. Second, the educational medium approach seemed to open up a whole range of new opportunities for geography to contribute to social and political purposes. *Geographical Education: Reflection and action* reflected this view. John Huckle (editor) claimed in his preface that: 'the "new geography" was a conservative and adaptive response to social realities and that subsequent developments in geography and education now allow geography teachers to make a more constructive contribution to human development and social justice' (1983, p. iv). However, such developments inevitably meant selective use of geographical content and the result was an increasing move into human geography and a growing concern with welfare approaches (who gains, who loses?), with humanistic ideas (different perceptions and viewpoints) and with political literacy (who decides what action can be taken?). A more critical geography was made possible by the newer active learning approaches promoted by curriculum development. *Geographical Education: Reflection and action* contained chapters on topics such as welfare approaches to geography, radical geography, political education, development education, environmental education and urban studies – authored by geographers who, in many cases, moved strongly into these areas of interest (David Hicks, John Fien, John Huckle). The 1980s was also the time when the urban and radically oriented *Bulletin of Environmental Education* was popular with geographers, the World Studies Project published materials, and geographers became involved in initiatives as diverse as the Royal Town Planning Institute's Environmental Education programme and the Royal Institute of British Architects' Art and Built Environment Project. The radical, new Association for Curriculum Development in Geography was launched in 1983 by a disenchanted London teacher, Dawn Gill, and its journal *Contemporary Issues in Geography* promoted, for a few years, radical perspectives on geography education. For many teachers such developments were exciting, but they were diametrically opposed to the traditional subject stance favoured by the cultural restorationists and were probably unsuited to a period in which curriculum justification lay in subject disciplines. The New Right abhorred 'isms' (such as multiculturalism) and 'studies' (such as World Studies or Peace Studies). Scruton argued that, for instance, World Studies masqueraded as a discipline: 'It is designed to close the child's mind to everything but the narrow passions of the radical' (1986, quoted in Ball, 1990, p. 47). Progressive geographers' involvement served to confirm the New Right's view that the subject had become political indoctrination or social studies. Similarly, the New Right was concerned about the growth of humanities, a loose amalgam of geography, history and, often, religious studies, which enjoyed popularity as a framework for teaching in lower secondary forms in the 1970s and 1980s, and was also represented in some GCSE syllabuses.

With hindsight, it may be said that it would have been most helpful if, at that particular time, the whole geographical community (school and higher education) had reaffirmed some basic principles about the core or heart of geography. In fact, not only were school teachers exploring new horizons but, as Stoddart explained, even in academic geography 'too many of our colleagues have either abandoned, or failed even to recognise, what I take to be our subject's central intent and indeed self-evident role in the community of knowledge' (1987, p. 329).

Geographical enquiry
One of the biggest impacts made by the curriculum development activities was in the area of pedagogy. It is certainly not the case that all geography classrooms prior to 1970 were dominated only by chalk-and-talk and note-taking. Marsden (1976) referrred to 'enlightened traditionalism' to identify those teachers who had already made attempts to vary teaching styles and appeal to the interests of the child through, for instance, the use of case studies, pictures and fieldwork. In the 1960s and early 1970s the gradual diffusion of new ideas about quantification, models and theories in geography was beginning to bring new possibilities into geography classrooms (e.g. publications by Cole and Beynon, 1968; Everson and Fitzgerald, 1969, 1972; and Briggs, 1979). However, it is true to say that the existence of the geography projects provided the opportunity for new teaching and learning strategies to be piloted and considered in the whole context of curriculum change:

■ What was the reason for introducing new strategies?

■ How did they contribute to pupils' development in geography?

■ What changes did they imply for the role of the teacher and how could they be assessed?

Of particular significance were the changes summarised as 'geographical enquiry'. Although all the secondary projects explored enquiry/active learning approaches, it was the Geography 16-19 Project which presented the most complete exposition. It defined enquiry-based learning as 'a range of teaching methods and approaches by which the teacher encourages students to enquire actively into questions, issues and problems rather than merely to accept passively the conclusions, research and opinions of others' (Naish et al., 1987, p. 45). The focus on active involvement of pupils derived partly from the projects' desire to motivate pupils (hence the stress placed by GYSL and Geography 16-19 on relevant enquiry questions) and partly on a belief that pupils would thus learn the methods and approaches of geographers. In addition, as Slater showed (1982), active enquiry-based learning, particularly the focus on questions, was legitimised by the educational literature (Collingwood, 1939; Gagne, 1965) and similar developments were occurring in other subjects such as history (Schools Council, 1976). Teachers were introduced to a much wider range of teaching and learning approaches, including strategies like group discussion, role-play, decision-making exercises and active practical and fieldwork tasks. Inevitably, greater attention was also given to attitudes and values, both as factors affecting geographical issues and in the sense of pupils developing their own values.

There was confidence in the geographical education world that these developments would lead to pupils with a wider range of skills and abilities, better prepared to participate in the world around them. However, to the New Right, now dominating educational discourse, geographical enquiry represented the previous era and seemed to represent all that was wrong with education – a lack of rigour, emphasis on woolly attitudes and general skills, and a lack of discipline and teacher control. Some critiques of active and discovery learning methods (see Bantock, 1969) stressed the dangers of open-ended learning situations when used uncritically and, in some respects, might have been aimed at the simulations, role-plays and decision-making exercises which featured in all the geography curriculum projects. Although every project explained the need for a balanced range of teaching approaches, classroom interpretation did not always attend to this advice. The idea of changing classroom relationships with the teacher sometimes acting as facilitator rather than always the 'fount of wisdom' was also an idea which featured in all the projects and was met with extreme hostility by the New Right. The whole national curriculum exercise, with its AT/PoS structure focused on 'what should be taught' and 'what children should know', was formulated to ensure that more traditional teaching methods and subject content would be given priority.

Two necessary corollaries of a commitment to enquiry-based learning were changes in assessment and changes to the role of the teacher.

Assessment

Prior to 1970, assessment for most secondary geography teachers referred to the summative or end-of-course public examinations (O-level or CSE) at 16+. As the Geography 14-18 Project found, the style of examination question (predominantly essay style for O-level) was the deciding factor in curriculum planning, leading to a limited range of teaching strategies – a case of 'the assessment tail wagging the curriculum dog'. Starting from the other direction and taking curriculum decisions first, the projects had established the need to develop, and so to test, a wider range of skills and abilities. Accordingly, project examinations promoted new styles of assessment, such as the use of resource-based questions, individual studies and decision making exercises. The projects highlighted the link between curriculum and assessment, helping teachers to appreciate that if enquiry skills were to be tested, then pupils would need to experience and develop them throughout the course. In addition, the introduction of coursework in project examinations began to blur the distinction between the formative process of assessment used by the teacher to diagnose strengths and weaknesses during the course, and summative assessment used to summarise achievement for more public purposes at the end of the course. Although such developments were taken up with enthusiasm, certainly in secondary education, by the limited number of initial pilot schools, there were a number of unresolved issues which quickly became apparent when the innovations were disseminated more widely. Some assessment results yielded a great deal of information about the capabilities of individual pupils and helped the teacher to plan improved learning (e.g. individual study, pupil interview, teacher-marked coursework test), but the methods were difficult to carry out or standardise for large numbers of schools if reliable and nationally comparable results were needed.

This tension between assessment for learning and assessment for public accountability became more visible as the curriculum debate was increasingly dominated by the New Right. Ball (1990) points out that, in the New Right discourse, concerns about formative assessment subsumed both the neo-liberals' desire to use examination and test results as the basis for market comparisons and consumer choice, and the neo-conservatives' distrust of teacher involvement in assessment. In fact, the TGAT Report (DES and WO, 1987) which provided the model for national curriculum assessment, did find a place for teacher assessment alongside national tests. In many ways, this was quite a progressive document (Daugherty, 1995). There is no doubt that, given the opportunity, the geography projects' experience could have fed into the production of a more balanced assessment system, recognising approaches suited to both formative and summative purposes. However, even some clearer thinking from the subject community might not have assisted discussions on the GWG, since the roles and functions of ATs, SoAs and PoS were neither well understood nor adequately explained to the subject working groups. As Daugherty explains, assessment policy was being developed as the working groups worked, with decisions made by one group often pre-empting decisions of the next. This was a recipe for inconsistency and confusion. He notes that the proposals for history and geography 'emerged at the same time but could hardly have been more contrasting in their interpretation of the central concepts of "attainment target", "statement of attainment" and "programme of study"' (Daugherty, 1995, p. 33).

The role of the teacher

Though differing in detailed approach and development model, all the projects, even those which produced packages of materials, laid great stress on the involvement of teachers in curriculum planning. The Geography 14-18 Project coined the term 'a new professionalism' (Tolley and Reynolds, 1977) to describe the responsibility which teachers now accepted for deciding not only what to teach but also how to teach it, what learning opportunities to provide and how to evaluate the success of all this. As the Project pointed out, in the past teachers had only been concerned with discussions about syllabus content. In planning a curriculum, they were as much 'concerned with what pupils can be led to think, feel and do and the outcomes of those learning experiences as opposed to the subject matter which the teacher transmits' (Tolley and Reynolds, 1977, p. 27). In the classroom, the projects encouraged teachers to share control of learning more with their pupils, so that sometimes the teacher was a co-researcher or facilitator, rather than always being the provider of structure and information. All this necessitated a stress on professional development and, particularly, opportunities for teachers to work with other teachers, reflect on their own practice and be active in innovating with content and teaching/learning approaches. For the New Right, such professional activities were unnecessary since 'to teach is an aptitude, and ... formal qualifications do little in themselves to develop it' (Hillgate Group, 1987, p. 36). Given this assumption, and the distrust of 'left wing teachers', most New Right literature was founded on the view that 'whole areas of decision-making about the curriculum, about pedagogy and about assessment which may previously have been the concern of teachers are now to be pre-empted by decisions lodged elsewhere'. It was therefore not surprising that, when the national curriculum structure was drawn up, it seemed to reject these new roles, providing not a national curriculum framework for teacher interpretation at school and classroom level, but a very prescriptive checklist to be delivered to pupils in its entirety. A national curriculum need not necessarily have ruled out school-based curriculum development. Even Margaret Thatcher seemed anxious to endorse a continuing role for teachers, remarking in a *Times Educational Supplement* interview in 1990 that if the prescribed curriculum took up too much time, it was likely that the benefits of the teacher's experience would be lost, including the enthusiasm and devotion to that subject.

What was needed in the late 1980s, as Kelly (1999) suggests, was time for deeper discussion within the subject community about the gains and losses implicit in the curriculum development period, and about ways of incorporating public concerns. The biggest issue, which should have been clarified prior to the pressurised conditions of the GWG, was how to deal with place and locational knowledge. Most of the project frameworks could have been adapted to incorporate a greater prescription of locational knowledge and a stronger emphasis on places while, at the same time, leaving scope for teacher involvement and active enquiry learning. Given a less pressurised situation, one strategy might have been to work with colleagues in higher education, where discussion was already focusing on topics such as the implications of the neglect of physical geography in schools (Worsley, 1985) and the possibility of a new regional geography (expounded by Johnston, 1991b). Johnston suggested that because of the heightened debate about the economy and the role of education, it was time for school and higher education geographers to talk to each other again – 'such questions are translated into "What should we be doing?" "What is geography about and what is its value?" "How do we ensure that its value – and ours – is appreciated?"' (1985, pp. 10-11). However, at school level, the increasing speed of such policy changes left no room for such debates and geography in higher education moved inexorably away from its school counterpart. The resulting discontinuity or 'gap' was noted as early as 1977 by Professor Michael Wise in his Presidential address at the GA Annual Conference. Sixteen years later, in even stronger language, Professor Andrew Goudie (President 1993-94) spoke of the 'chasm that has developed between those who teach at school and those who teach in universities' (1993, p. 338). The origins of the gap lay in the different paths followed in the early 1970s. Increasing dissatisfaction with the narrowness of the quantitative and positivist approaches of the new geography had led academics into exploration of humanistic, welfare and radical geography. These new ideas were hardly considered by schools, partly because the new breed of A-level syllabuses had only just taken on new geography and partly because many schools were coming under the influence of the Schools Council geography projects. School geography moved into a period of curriculum development (see Chapter 2). Although there was some attention given to the changing nature of geography at the research frontier (for example behavioural and welfare approaches in GYSL and Geography 16-19) there was an increasing feeling of separation. As the Geography 16-19 Project stated 'since geography is to be used as a medium for education there is no requirement that all new academic developments necessarily be translated into the school context' (Naish *et al.*, 1987, pp. 26-7). In any case, as Jackson shows (1996), the 1980s particularly was a period of increasing diversity of focus and approach in academic geography, with research specialisms, especially in human geography, reaching out to embrace neighbouring disciplines rather than developing internal links.

By the late 1980s, the school/academic relationship was showing signs of being discontinuous (Stengel's model 2, see page 21). The implications were that common aims and principles of the subject would be neglected as each sector dealt with its own particular political, social and economic pressures. Chapter 10 will return to this point and consider whether this separation is in the best interests of the subject, in the light of policy changes described in Chapters 2-8. For the moment, for school geography, the first and most pressing issue was whether geography would be recognised at all as one of the 'real subjects' in the new national curriculum.

Geography's response to the New Right

The GA had no doubt that geography was a real discipline, as its Presidents constantly re-iterated in the 1970s (Wise, 1977) and 1980s (Walford, 1984). The problem during the initial round of curriculum debate following Callaghan's speech was that the politicians and educational policy makers clearly did not recognise this. In the spate of discussion documents and DES statements arguing the case for a common curriculum between 1977 and 1981, geography was initially hardly mentioned (e.g. in *Curriculum 11-16*, DES, 1977c; *A View of the Curriculum*, DES, 1980b) and subsequently it was referred to only as an apparently minor subject, seemingly interchangeable with history or economics (e.g. in *A Framework for the School Curriculum*, DES, 1980a; *The School Curriculum*, DES, 1981b). To its credit, the GA moved straight into the battle. Major restructuring of the Association taking place in 1977 provided it with a committee focused solely on educational matters (Education Standing Committee) and a strong team of GA officers (Richard Daugherty, Honorary Secretary 1976-81, Michael Williams, Honorary Secretary 1981-85 and Rex Walford, Chair of Education Standing Committee 1976-82) rapidly learnt the skills of political campaigning. Throughout the late 1970s and early 1980s, a whole range of tools was used (Figure 4) to inform and persuade the politicians that, as well as being a real and distinctive subject, geography was essential to the government's aims of ensuring that pupils 'understand the local, national and international environments in which they live and which they will help to shape' (Walford and Williams, 1982,

p. 74). Submissions were made by the GA at every stage in the national curriculum debate, GA representatives visited the DES in 1980, and a GA representative (Richard Daugherty) attended a Parliamentary Select Committee in April 1981. Of particular significance was the organisation of a special conference to which the Secretary of State for Education (then Sir Keith Joseph) was invited and attended on 19 June 1985. Sir Keith's address posed the Association with seven key questions about geography's curriculum contribution, to which a task force promptly responded. The whole set of papers was submitted to Sir Keith and published as *The Case for Geography* (Bailey and Binns, 1987). Although these activities seemed to be well-received by the politicians, and geography was subsequently mentioned more directly in documentation, the publication of a proposed structure for the national curriculum (DES, 1987) still showed geography as an alternative to history among the foundation subjects at all key stages. One final strategy of the GA was to request a meeting with the new Secretary of State, Kenneth Baker. This was granted and took place on 30 June 1987. The delegation of eight GA representatives was delighted to be told that geography would definitely be a full foundation subject and that a GWG would shortly be established to draw up the details. This victory for geography was sealed by geography's inclusion in the draft Education Reform Bill placed before Parliament in autumn 1987 and eventually passed as the Education Reform Act (1988).

It is important to recognise this achievement. A decade of political campaigning (Figure 4) had resulted in the required solution – a 'place in the sun', as Bailey (1989) called it, although other writers have pointed out that Kenneth Baker was already committed to this particular ten-subject formula (Aldrich, 1990). It seems likely, too, that the government's dislike of humanities, particularly the lack of structure and content exposed by an HMI survey of humanities courses in 20 secondary schools (DES, 1989b), might have been stronger than its approval for geography *per se*. It is also important to consider the problems implicit in this victory. One difficulty in producing the justification for the subject had been, as the earlier part of this chapter has shown, that school geography was in a period of fundamental rethinking, poised between the traditional regional approaches, the challenge of the 'new' scientific geography and the wider claims of the more progressive child-centred approaches provided by the Schools Council projects. The problem for the GA was which ideological slant should be taken. Rex Walford, speaking at the 1980 Charney Manor Conference, made it clear that he felt it was time to recognise the political situation and 'to manoeuvre gently into the prevailing breezes and sail before the winds of change', accepting that 'survival of the subject on the school timetable may best be achieved by a return to a more moderate informational tradition' (1981, pp. 222). Others, however, did not see the issue as quite so clear-cut. The GA, representing as it did teachers with the full spectrum of views and ideological traditions, clearly hoped to maintain a compromise position between the 'hard' New Right position and the 'softer' liberal/progressive ideas currently dominant in geography education. Daugherty explained that:

> 'an alternative and more productive approach in an era when value for money is the popular cry, would be to work for acceptance of a more liberal interpretation of "value" or worthwhileness in relation to education. If geography can help pupils gain understanding of issues and problems as well as of places and people, must it not have a place in the education of all young people' (1981, p. 125-6).

This view was reflected particularly in the GA's own suggested formulation for the Geography National Curriculum, edited by Daugherty (1989b), and published even before the GWG met.

Not surprisingly, however, whatever the intentions, when it came to political campaigning there is no doubt that the GA played with the New Right's own weapons of 'real subject' and 'utilitarian value'. And it played these cards strongly in response to the mood of the times. All the GA submissions emphasised the body of factual knowledge about the world which geography could supply, and referred to the geography of the United Kingdom and Europe, and to specific geographical skills

1976	PM Callaghan stimulates the Great Debate (Ruskin College speech)
1977	*Educating Our Children*, DES, 1977a *Education in Schools: Consultative document*, DES, 1977b *Curriculum 11-16 Working Papers* (HMI), DES, 1977c GA responses to these including *Teaching Geography*, 3, 2
1980	*A View of the Curriculum*, DES, 1980b *A Framework for the School Curriculum*, DES, 1980a (consultative paper) – geography given a low priority GA responses including *Geography*, 65, 3 GA visit to DES officials
1981	*Geography in the School Curriculum 11-16* (HMI Working Paper), DES, 1981c *The School Curriculum*, DES, 1981b – geography given marginally greater status GA responses and evidence given to Parliamentary Select Committee
1985	*Better Schools*, DES, 1985a Secretary of State, Keith Joseph, addresses the special GA conference at King's College, 19 June – seven questions *The Curriculum from 5-16, Curriculum Matters 2* (HMI) – areas of experience idea explained. DES, 1985b
1986	GA responds to seven questions with *A Case for Geography*, later published in book form (1987) *Geography from 5-16, Curriculum Matters 7* (HMI), DES, 1986
1987	*The National Curriculum 5-16: A consultation document*, DES, 1987 – geography still alternative to history GA visits Secretary of State, Kenneth Baker Draft Education Reform Bill – geography a foundation subject.
1988	Education Reform Act – geography a full foundation subject 5-16

Figure 4: Geography: winning a curriculum place.

associated with mapwork and fieldwork. At the meeting of the Parliamentary Select Committee on the School Curriculum (April 1981), the GA's representative (Richard Daugherty) drew attention to the GA papers which listed 'map-reading and use and world knowledge as the two first special contributions of geography', but explained 'that does not mean we do them first before we come on to international understanding and environmental awareness'. He was, however, pressed by one MP: 'Would it not be a jolly good thing if they all did know at least where the capitals of the EEC countries are? I went to a school recently and nobody knew any of them' (Hansard, April 1981). The *Times Educational Supplement* reporter at the GA conference with Sir Keith Joseph clearly recognised the political deal which geographers were being asked to make. Her report read:

'Geographers have been warned by Sir Keith Joseph, the Education Secretary, that they must define their subject more carefully if geography is to remain available as a separate subject up to 16 ... His views, containing veiled criticisms of radical activists in the subject who have questioned the values behind traditional geographical approaches and resources, were welcomed by members whose main concern was the place of their own subject in the timetable' (Kirkman, 1985).

Later, when the GA delegation met Kenneth Baker in 1987, hoping to convince him to include geography in the national curriculum, not only did the briefing papers focus specifically on the dangers inherent in humanities and the advantages of these traditional elements of geography, but the pre-meeting held by GA officers agreed on the appropriate order with which to deal with these topics, so that those likely to appeal most to the Minister would receive greatest emphasis.

It is interesting to speculate why the geography education community failed to appreciate the deepening ideological conflicts or to recognise the corner into which it was being imprisoned. On the eve of the formation of the official GWG, the big dilemmas remained, but were being pushed into the background by the strident utilitarian discourse. If geographers had seen the need to play up the utilitarian aspects of their subject and to use the real subject identity, they had not followed this through and undertaken the serious debate which this required about the curriculum implications (Lambert, 1991). The question was how would some of the new progressive developments relate to or even survive the impact with the rest of the cultural restorationist ideas? In the history education community, debates about content and process were noisy and very public (Phillips, 1998). The geographers, seemingly united to find a 'place in the sun', allowed their differences to be glossed over – but the evidence for these was beginning to appear throughout the 1970s and 1980s. The real legacy of the new geography was never fully addressed, though issues were continually raised (e.g. Unwin, 1980); the differing applications and definitions of geographical enquiry and of active learning were never fully tackled, although Burkill (1980) pointed out that even the projects were not consistent about this; the problems of improving primary geography within the context of an anti-subject primary school culture were becoming more apparent (DES, 1989a). Probably most significantly, geographers never openly tackled the growing problem of how place and locational knowledge were to be ensured alongside the newer conceptual approaches. While alternative and tentative ideas are perfectly acceptable for developments in their pioneer stages, at this particular time they left geography dangerously exposed to attack from its critics in policy making and set the context for the ensuing hostility to progressive education.

Conclusion

There is no doubt that because of geography's generally low public profile compared with say history, the subject community focused its greatest efforts on winning the all-important place in the curriculum. Beyond that, however, it is difficult to avoid the suggestion that there was an air of complacency about the gains and developments made by the subject in the previous 20 years. There was a tendency to retreat back to classrooms, departments of education and subject publications and to maintain a belief that professional autonomy would be strong enough to overcome the pressures (e.g. in Robinson, 1992). After all, the geography curriculum projects had been remarkably successful and one of the geography projects was still seen as the 'jewel in the Schools Council's crown' (Macdonald and Walker, 1976). The new GCSE courses starting in 1986 had incorporated many of the innovative curriculum and assessment features of the 1970s and 1980s. Many HMI publications set the seal of approval on progressive developments of the 1970s (e.g. *The Teaching of Ideas in Geography*, DES, 1978). The HMI-led DES Short Courses had been instrumental in spreading the best of the liberal humanist and progressive educational ideas further. The geography HMI were perceived as part of the progressive educational establishment and, with support like this, geographers may have felt safe – assuming that a democratic process of National Curriculum Working Group activity and widespread consultation would ensure a sensible compromise between New Right ideology and progressive subject developments. What was not foreseen was the highly politicised process of national curriculum formulation 1989-91, the downgrading of HMI influence and, in geography's case, some unfortunate miscalculations and errors of judgement.

Having successfully won the first battle for a place in the curriculum, geography was unfortunately ill-prepared for the second battle for what should be in the curriculum. In particular, the lack of opportunity to debate some of the unresolved issues within the wider geography community, including higher education, was to prove a crucial issue as the events of the late 1980s and 1990s unfolded. In terms of Ball's 'context of influence', there were signs of an inevitable struggle between progressive geography education and the new forces of cultural restorationism, but the geography education community failed to appreciate the full strength and significance of this until too late.

Study 2

Spot the ideology

Ideology: A theory or set of beliefs or principles (*Cambridge International Dictionary of English*)

Educational ideologies: 1. Utilitarian/informational 2. Cultural restorationist 3. Liberal humanist 4. Progressive educationalist 5. Reconstructionist (Figure 1, page 32)

Can you match each of the nine quotations below with the educational ideology which seems to reflect its character most? Can you work out who said each? And/or when each was said?

1. '... to make sure that our young people learn some geography, not just vague concepts and attitudes ... and to emphasise learning about places and where they are.'

2. '... geography should help pupils to understand how societies are made and remade. Curriculum content should be based upon the realities to be transformed – such conditions as youth unemployment, technological change, environmental deterioration and lack of social justice which confront young people daily.'

3. 'The proposals for the geography curriculum should be withdrawn; its instigators removed from office. Knowledge-led programmes of study should be urgently substituted for each key stage, emphasising the features and effects of physical geography, study of globes and maps, with names of countries and places.'

4. 'It is an educational approach rather than an academic one, and it is designed to permit selection of ideas and materials from across the range of academic approaches to the subject ... The enquiry-based approach to learning has been established with its emphasis on the development of students as responsible and competent individuals capable of playing a participatory role in society.'

5. 'Teaching a committed geography involves learning experiences that challenge and empower students to work for social justice and ecological sustainability.'

6. 'Geography is a Los Angeles among academic cities in that it sprawls over a very large area and merges with its neighbours. It is also hard to find the central business district. This book has been written for newcomers to the city ... to introduce some of the basic concepts geographers use as well as some of the essential environmental facts that form the background to their work. The emphasis in the book is on ideas and concepts.'

continued

7. 'Using work-related contexts to support geography offers opportunities to help pupils develop their skills in communication, application of number, information technology, working with others, improving own learning and performance, and problem solving.'

8. 'Academic and formal methods of treatment have been rejected and extensive use has been made of material which brings before pupils first hand accounts of travel, actual trains, steamships, aeroplanes and airships, as well as real experiences of the life and work of people in the areas described.'

9. 'We have a vital responsibility to ensure that our subject is not superficial but is intellectually rigorous. Geography is at last attaining intellectual respectability in the academic streams of our secondary schools. But the battle is not quite over.'

Final comment:
'In modern times we have been plagued with a succession of short-lived ideologies in education ... The trouble with ideologies is that they faze the mind so that lots of otherwise sensible well-intentioned people fail to see clearly where they are going. They feel like marchers towards a new dawn, and no one has the slightest idea that it will turn out be an ugly morning ... But one cannot simply ditch all forms of ideology and assume that the system will continue to work equally well. These ideologies sustained teachers, helped them to get out of bed in the morning, to work up a sense of purpose and go cheerfully into school to face a room full of bustling conflicting youthful egos' (Chris Ormell, *Education Guardian*, 17 March 1992).

Note: The suggestions below, for ideologies represented, are the author's personal ideas. You may disagree!
Answers: 1. Kenneth Clarke, Secretary of State for Education, 1991 (utilitarian); 2. John Huckle, *Geographical Education: Reflection and action,* 1983 (reconstructionist); 3. Campaign for Real Education (New Right pressure group) commenting on national curriculum for 2000 (cultural restorationist); 4. Geography 16-19 Project explaining the project's approach, 1987 (Naish *et al.*) (progressive educationalist); 5. John Fien, *IRGEE* article 1999 (reconstructionist); 6. Peter Haggett, academic geographer in *Geography: A modern synthesis,* 1972 (textbook based on spatial analysis approach) (liberal humanist); 7. QCA guidance on *Learning through Work-related Contexts,* 1999b (industrial trainer); 8. Brooks and Finch, introduction to *Golden Hind* textbook series for secondary pupils, 1939 (progressive educationalist); 9. Presidential address to the GA by E.C. Marchant, HMI, 1967 (liberal humanist).

4

The Making of the Geography National Curriculum 1989-91

Introduction

In 1988, geography won acceptance as a national curriculum foundation subject. The subsequent history of school geography in the 1990s reveals some significant gains (see Rawling, 1999a), in particular the opportunity to re-instate geography at primary level. However in the short term, the subject paid a high price for this victory. Ashley Kent, David Lambert and Frances Slater, writing in *The Independent* on 24 January 1991, in their capacity as PGCE tutors at the Institute of Education, London, explained that 'details of how the government intends geography to be taught in schools under the national curriculum have alarmed geographers at all levels in the education system' (p. 19). They drew attention to the lack of geographical enquiry, of attitudes and values and of issue-based investigations in geography, all benefits gained from the previous 20 years of curriculum development. With its five traditionally focused attainment targets and 183 content-based statements of attainment, the 1991 Geography Order seemed to emphasise specific items of knowledge and information and a relatively narrow range of subject skills. Some saw this as a triumph for cultural restorationism:

> 'With its undertones of assimilation, nationalism and consensus around the regressive re-establishment of fictional past glories, restorationist national curriculum geography isolates students in time and space, cutting them off from the realities of the single European market, global economic dependencies and inequalities, and the ecological crisis' (Ball, 1994, p. 37).

However, as implementation got under way, it was clear that a faulty curriculum model was more significant, making planning difficult and assessment almost impossible. Other subjects, notably English and history (Phillips, 1998), generated considerable debate and conflict in the years that followed. Design and technology also represented a complete transformation in organisation of content, since the subject did not exist before 1988. However, it can be argued that geography, though less high-profile, suffered equally if not more severely from the national curriculum building exercise. Despite the ideological arguments, English, history and design and technology retained curriculum models in which specific content was not allocated to the statements of attainment, making implementation and later amendments easier to effect than has been the case for geography. The geography subject community has had to devote considerable creative energy to supporting teachers and to redressing the 1991 formulation (as Chapters 5 and 6 will show). In addition, it may be argued that one consequence of its residual image as merely a utilitarian and informational subject is that school geography in the 1990s has not been recognised as a significant 'frontline' contributor to the curriculum debates about broader initiatives, for example citizenship and thinking skills (see Chapter 8). At the time, it was tempting to find evidence for a political conspiracy, as indeed some geographers did. Robinson suggested that:

> 'Geography and geography teachers have been out-manoeuvred in the creation of the GNC [Geography National Curriculum]. We have been used and divided and in the final phases, dismissed as irrelevant.

The government had clear objectives from the start, from the briefing of Sir Leslie Fielding to the final censorship by Kenneth Clarke. The results of democratic consultation procedures were not allowed to interfere ... One may or may not be happy with the GNC, but all must agree that it was derived from a process of manipulation and authoritarian decree' (1992, p. 31).

The following analysis of the politics of curriculum change will focus particularly on the Geography Working Group (GWG). In terms of the policy cycle, described in Chapter 1, the 1989-91 period was the context of text production for the 1991 Geography Order. The analysis will explore whether geography was the victim of a political conspiracy in 1991, or whether the 1991 Order is at least partly explained by what Ball calls 'the messy realities of influence, pressure, dogma, expediency, conflict, compromise, intransigence, resistance, error, opposition and pragmatism in the policy process' (1990, p. 9).

The Geography National Curriculum takes shape

The establishment of the National Curriculum GWG was announced on 5 May 1989 and the Group worked throughout 1989-90 with a remit to outline the 'knowledge, skills and understanding which pupils of different abilities and maturities should be expected to have acquired by the end of the academic year in which they reach the ages of 7, 11, 14 and 16' (DES, 1989c, p. 1). In particular the GWG was expected to produce *attainment targets* (ATs), representing the targets or teaching objectives divided into ten different levels of attainment, and *programmes of study* (PoS), covering a description of the content, skills and processes to be taught sequentially to pupils through the four key stages (or age groups).

The GA's report *Geography in the National Curriculum* (Daugherty, 1989b) was tabled at the first meeting of the GWG on 18 May 1989. It attempted to combine traditional geographical emphases (e.g. maps, world knowledge) with current educational concerns about enquiry skills and issues-based teaching. In addition to identifying 14 ATs, the report gave much attention to 'those aspects of a national curriculum which will be for teachers to determine' (e.g. teaching and learning approaches, selection of specific content, teacher assessment), thus hinting at the crucial need to consider the complete curriculum system. This pre-emptive strategy reflected the mood of cautious optimism and confidence within the Association and the wider geography education community.

By contrast, for history (for which the Working Group had begun life in January 1989), the situation seemed far from optimistic as fierce debates about 'process' and 'content' were paraded in the educational press during 1989-90. Geography educators did not appear so divided at this politically sensitive moment though, in retrospect, the agreement may have been illusory.

The Interim Report of the GWG, appearing in mid-November 1989 (DES and WO, 1989), was greeted with considerable concern and even hostility from many teachers and educationalists. The GA's submission (January 1990), based on the reports from a series of consultation conferences held in 14 locations, unequivocally stated that 'the Geography Working Group must appreciate that in a number of ways the Interim Report is flawed'. Articles and letters in the educational press suggested that the GWG had 'lost its way' (Schofield, 1990, p. 33) or pleaded with members to 'rethink their distorted, divided and trivialised world' (Roberts, 1990, p. 35). Such reactions were a response to the eight content-led ATs proposed, four of which focused on particular areas or regions for study (the Home Area and Region, the UK, World Geography 1 and World Geography 2). Considerable prominence was given to prescribed places and to locational knowledge. Many did welcome the physical geography AT, particularly as the GA had been concerned that aspects of earth science and meteorology, traditionally taught in geography, were being claimed by the Science Working Group (GA response to SWG, March 1988). However, the report had virtually no PoS and was weak on broader enquiry approaches, on skills, attitudes and values and on geographical issues – all the characteristics valued so highly in GCSE experience and by the curriculum projects. For primary schools, many feared that the weight of prescription would prove overwhelming in relation to good primary practice (Catling, 1991).

Not all the submissions about the Interim Report were completely hostile or critical. However, what is significant is that, on the whole, those which welcomed the Interim Report were welcoming particular items or specific headings (e.g. places, mapwork, physical geography, environmental emphases) while those which were critical were looking at the proposals and seeing the dangers in the way that the new emphases were expressed. The responses from the School Examinations and Assessment Council (SEAC) and the Institute of Education, London, representatives of the curriculum development projects, and the Birmingham Development Education Centre were all of this nature. Such responses drew attention to the mismatch between the widely approved aims and the actual structure chosen for geography, to the lack of genuine progression in geographical ideas, to the marginal recognition given to enquiry and to the absence of a real function for the PoS.

The Working Group did not respond to these messages. The Final Report (DES and WO, 1990) was quite clearly a compromise, in which moves had been made to address some of the concerns raised by consultation – there was more enquiry, less prescription, a larger role for the PoS, for instance – but all this was held within the same limiting structure. The subsequent process of making limited changes and amendments to the document, which characterised the National Curriculum Council consultation exercise (NCC, 1990), and the setting out of Draft (January 1991) and Final Orders (March, DES, 1991a; WO, 1991) gave rise to much comment, particularly in relation to the Secretary of State's intervention and to his actions in striking out references to enquiry skills and to attitudes and values. More significant however, was that the 'iron grip' of the original GWG model survived throughout. By October 1989 (the Interim Report), the problematic formulation for the geography curriculum was in place; the problems were not added subsequently, as some commentators would prefer to believe. It is to the GWG that we must look for reasons.

The eventual outcome of the Group's work (i.e. the 1991 GNC) has provoked considerable concern and debate, both at the time and throughout the 1990s as implementation has taken place and revisions have been made. It is thus important to present a full picture of events. Primary sources of evidence about the Working Group process include the official GWG minutes and papers lodged in DES archives, but also accessible to all Group members. In addition, two of the participants in the process (myself and Rex Walford) have written accounts of their involvement (Rawling, 1992a; Walford 1992) and Graham Butt's PhD thesis (1997) provides a major source of information. Butt interviewed all the Group members during 1995-96, apart from Andrew Wye and Sir Leslie Fielding, both of whom refused to participate. There is also a full sequence of reports from the national press, which gives a more public perspective on the Group's work. All these have been used as sources of information for this chapter and are clearly identified where a direct reference or quotation has been made. Figures 1 (Group Membership), 2 (Terms of reference) and 3 (The construction of a national curriculum subject) may be used as reference alongside the analysis which follows. Study 3 – see pages 65-66 – provides further detailed information.

Conflict, compromise and control on the GWG

The GWG started four months later than the History Working Group (HWG) but its final proposals were ready for consultation earlier than those for the HWG, a result of the controversy and political delaying tactics over the HWG Final Report. This point is significant because, as will be shown, geography's fate was intricately bound up with that of history. The HWG started out with the same constraints and political controls on national curriculum text production (Figure 3) as did all other working groups, including geography. Significantly, HWG members managed to obtain a compromise position for the subject in which the views of professional educators were given weight, particularly in relation to curriculum and assessment matters, alongside the New Right influences. That this did not happen for geography can only be explained by reference to those features distinctive to the GWG (Figure 4) – the chance events, the accidents of timing, the particular personalities and personality clashes and the errors of judgement made on the GWG. This section will attempt to illuminate these issues.

From April 1989:	
Sir Leslie Fielding, Chairman	Long experience in Diplomatic Service and the European Commission before his appointment as Vice-Chancellor of Sussex University in 1987
Professor David Thomas, Vice Chairman	Pro-Vice Chancellor and Professor of Geography at the University of Birmingham
Roger Davies	Chaiman, Thomson Travel Group
Kay Edwards	Head of Geography, Penglais Comprehensive School, Aberystwyth
Richard Lethbridge	Former Chairman, Tower Steel (Holdings) plc, now a Branch Secretary of the Country Landowners' Association
Wendy Morgan	Recently retired headmistress of Elmsett Primary School, Suffolk
Dr Keith Paterson	Senior Lecturer in Geography, Liverpool Institute of Higher Education
Eleanor Rawling	National Co-ordinator, Geography Schools and Industry Project
Michael Storm	Staff Inspector for Geography and Environmental Studies, Inner London Education Authority
Rachel Thomas	Member of the Countryside Commission and Exmoor National Park Committee
Rex Walford	Lecturer in Geography and Education, University of Cambridge
From October 1989: Hugh Ward	Inspector for Geography, Kent Local Education Authority
Also:	DES Assessor: Andrew Wye DES Secretary to Group: Les Webb HMI Assessor: Staff Inspector, Trevor Bennetts

Figure 1: Membership of the Geography Working Group.

Working Group process and terms of reference
There was never any doubt that this was a political exercise steered from central government. As Barber points out, it gives the impression of being democratic and open to consultation while, in reality, 'both the DES and Ministers kept a firm hand on the process' (1996, p. 41). For geography, this control was important in several ways. First, the Secretary of State (initially Kenneth Baker) appointed the Chair and members of the Group, and agreed the terms of reference and briefing for the Chair and civil servants. It is tempting to look hard at the terms of reference and supplementary guidance for the GWG (Figure 2, DES, 1989c) to discover strong ideological pressure. In fact, as

From: terms of reference

Background

1. The Education Reform Act 1988 provides for the establishment of a national curriculum of core and other foundation subjects for pupils of compulsory school age in England and Wales. The Act empowers the Secretary of State to specify, as he considers appropriate for each foundation subject, including geography, that there should be clear objectives – attainment targets – for the knowledge, skills and understanding which pupils of different abilities and maturities should be expected to have acquired by the end of the academic year in which they reach the ages of 7, 11, 14 and 16; and to promote them, programmes of study describing the content, skills and processes which need to be covered during each key stage of compulsory education. Taken together, the attainment targets and programmes of study will provide the basis for assessing a pupil's performance, in relation both to expected attainment and to the next steps needed for the pupil's development.

2. Both the objectives (attainment targets divided into up to 10 levels of attainment) and the means of achieving them (programmes of study) should leave scope for teachers to use their professional talents and skills to develop their own schemes of work, within a statutory framework which is known to all. It is the task of the Geography Working Group to advise on that framework for geography.

The task

3. The Working Group is asked to submit an interim report to the Secretaries of State by 31 October 1989 outlining and, as far as possible, exemplifying:

   i.   the contribution which geography should make to the overall school curriculum and how that will inform the Group's thinking about attainment targets and programmes of study;
   ii. its provisional thinking about the knowledge, skills and understanding which pupils of different abilities and maturities should be expected to have attained and be able to demonstrate by reference to defined levels of attainment, at key ages; and the profile components into which attainment targets should be grouped; and
   iii. its thinking about the programmes of study which would be consistent with the attainment targets professionally identified.

From: supplementary guidance

4. The study of geography in schools should enable pupils to develop a sense of place, an understanding of the relationships between places and an appreciation of the value of maps. It should create a framework of knowledge and understanding about pupils' home areas and about other places within Great Britain. It should be related to wider perspectives – of the world as a whole, its continents and oceans, and the place of Britain and Europe within it – so that pupils are able to put information and experience in a geographical context. Overall, it should enable pupils to develop an informed appreciation and understanding of the world in which they live.

Figure 2: Extracts from the National Curriculum Geography Working Group terms of reference and supplementary guidance. Source: DES, 1989c.

other commentators have noted (Butt, 1997; Walford, 1992), although the terms of reference hinted strongly at areas of public concern – places, the value of maps, a framework of knowledge and understanding of the home area and other places in Great Britain and the wider world', the physical environment – they also included some surprisingly progressive references to, for example, 'ways of life and cultures other than their own', 'sense of place', 'progressive development of skills and processes of geographical enquiry'. In this sense, the terms of reference were not as constraining as some (e.g. Bailey, 1992) have suggested and need not have resulted in the 1991 Order. Butt points out that from his interview evidence, it is clear that Trevor Bennetts, the HMI Staff Inspector for Geography, had been instrumental in shaping the terms of reference.

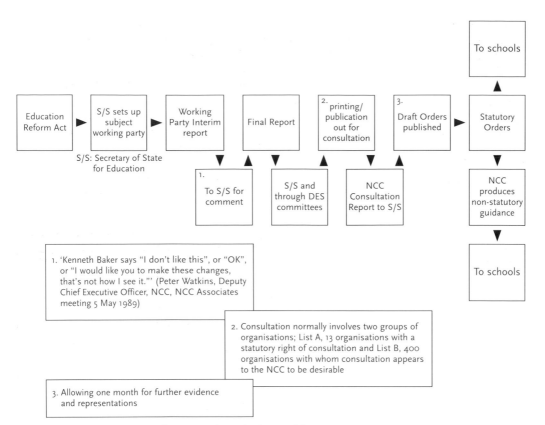

Figure 3: The construction of a national curriculum subject. After: Ball, 1990.

Power struggles within the GWG

Group appointments (Figure 1) were crucial and, in particular, the choice of the Chair, Sir Leslie Fielding, turned out to be highly significant. A former diplomat, then Vice Chancellor of Sussex University, Sir Leslie was not a geographer but brought to the task a 'common-sense, down-to-earth' experience of travelling and living in other parts of the world: 'there's got to be more mental discipline, facts, arguments and evidence rather than philosophy and opinion' Sir Leslie Fielding, quoted in *The Daily Telegraph*, 6 May 1989). In the absence of a clear New Right view of geography or of constraining terms of reference, it seems likely that the Minister (Kenneth Baker in May 1989) was happy to back this and to encourage Fielding to promote it strongly in the Group. Phillips suggests (1998, p. 55) that Baker's selection of Michael Saunders-Watson as Chair of HWG reflected a similar desire for a common-sense, non-academic view on the curriculum. However, whereas Saunders-Watson won the respect of HWG members by listening to the professional arguments and, where necessary, arguing the case for compromise with civil servants, Fielding managed the GWG in a much more domineering style. According to Butt's (1997) research, Group members were unanimous in describing Fielding as a strong Chair who threatened, cajoled and steered the proceedings, as appropriate, anxious to meet the timetable and provide a report acceptable to the Minister. For many on the Group, particularly those whose views were rejected, his approach frequently seemed arrogant and intolerant – though some saw this merely as effective chairing designed to reach a speedy outcome (Walford, 1992). There is no doubt that Fielding used a full range of control tactics to move the proceedings in the direction he believed acceptable to Ministers. Many of those interviewed by Butt referred to the way he marginalised potential trouble-makers by appealing to group loyalty or the shortage of time, and by refusing to allow time for discussion of difficult ideas. He was adept at using members of the Group against each other. At an early stage in the Group's work, two curriculum models were proposed. Model A placed specific content directly in the ATs and gave predominant emphasis to place and locational knowledge. Model B presented a mix of conceptually-based place and thematic ATs and allocated specific content to the PoS. Fielding saw model A as an appropriate model which would be acceptable to the Ministers and subsequently appealed to the teachers and lay people in a 'populist' way to support this common-sense view of geography. Butt explains that the lay members of the group were confused by the apparent disagreement between the professional educators in the early meetings (Butt, 1997). Unlike Saunders-Watson on the HWG, Fielding never allowed the kind of professional debate which would have illuminated matters for them. He allowed the debate to be over-simplified to a conflict between those who were for and those who were against place/locational knowledge. In so doing, he ensured that the bigger issues about curriculum design were ignored.

Mechanisms of control common to all working groups	Chance events, conflicts and compromises distinctive to Geography Working Group
The process of national curriculum construction for a subject, controlled strongly by the Secretary of State through: ■ terms of reference ■ appointment of Chair ■ appointment of Group members ■ hierarchical power structure ■ strong role for DES Assessor ■ lesser role for subject HMI ■ consultation highly controlled ■ intervention possible by Secretary of State for Education	Chance events, conflicts and compromises: ■ geography's position in the sequence of Working Groups ■ GWG's relationship to HWG ■ failure to consider full curriculum system of ATs/PoS ■ personality and style of Chair ■ group dynamics and relationships ■ failure of NCC to make professional input during the final stages ■ specific views about geography held by Kenneth Clarke and his political adviser

Figure 4: Factors influencing the outcome of the Geography Working Group's work.

On the GWG, it became clear at an early stage that the group was managed and controlled by a small secretariat or executive, consisting of the Chair, Vice-Chair (David Thomas), DES Assessor and HMI, together with the DES Secretary of the Group. This small group met frequently behind closed doors at key points in the proceedings and, as both Walford (1992) and Butt (1997) have confirmed, it exerted a tight hold on the Group's deliberations. What is interesting about this situation is that whereas for mathematics and English, or even history, there were existing views (often Black Paper promoted) for restoring and re-writing the subject, for geography, as noted, there was merely a vague feeling that physical geography, places and locational knowledge needed more stress and that common-sense should prevail. Thus the Chair, and in particular the DES Assessor, played a key role in interpreting what this common-sense view was and what might be acceptable to the Minister. Duncan Graham (NCC Chief Executive) suggests that the power of the civil servants was considerable, as he witnessed it on NCC committees, and that they were often arrogant and dictatorial (Graham with Tytler, 1993, p. 15). Certainly Andrew Wye, the DES Assessor to the GWG, made frequent, blunt interjections to the meeting, particularly when there was a danger that more progressive educational ideas might gain acceptance. Walford (1992) refers to Wye's 'laconic style' and intellectual sharpness, but the nature and style of his interventions were often perceived as rudeness by other members of the Working Group (Butt, 1997). As Walford explains 'the assessor also had a trump card to play – would things be acceptable to the Minister in the last resort' (Walford, 1992, p. 198). Such resort to Ministerial views was a civil service tactic – 'one could be fairly sure that the Minister had never been consulted or that he had displayed an unlikely and encyclopaedic grasp of detail' (Graham with Tytler, 1993, p. 18). Certainly, in Wye's case, he frequently intervened to question or criticise curriculum ideas, an area of understanding crucial for the translation of any geographical material into a workable curriculum but about which he and the Minister were not necessarily well-informed. At the fifth meeting of the Group when advice was being given that the content-packed ATs resulted in an impractical curriculum model, Wye interrupted to say that curriculum experience was not required. The exercise was not one of curriculum design (personal diary notes of fifth meeting). Advice from SEAC, the government's appointment assessment body (reinforced by a visit to the GWG by Philip Halsey, Chief Executive), raised exactly the same concerns several months later when this model (A) was enshrined in the Interim Report (SEAC Geography Committee submission to GWG, 25 January 1990).

It might have been expected that the HMI representative on the GWG would offset the more severe aspects of DES control and provide an informed and even progressive geography education perspective. In fact, as Ball points out (1994), HMI were perceived as part of the educational establishment by the New Right and hence part of the problem. On the GWG, HMI Staff Inspector for Geography, Trevor Bennetts, was rarely accorded the same status in decision making as was the DES Assessor, a situation which resulted in some open confrontations on the Working Group. Butts' (1997) interview data, derived from Group members, confirms that this was the case. Many members noted the tensions between Bennetts and Wye. Some noted that Bennetts openly supported the alternative curriculum model (model B) put forward in the early meetings of the Group, but that he was persuaded to accept the views of the majority by Wye and Fielding even before the Interim Report was published. The Minutes of the GWG for the third meeting, 8-10 July 1989, record that 'the Chair was concerned that SI Mr Bennetts' comments in support of a concept-based model of ATs with facts in the PoS might be construed to imply that facts were "second order" and that he feared "over-sophistication"'. My personal diary for that meeting records that:

> 'Trevor [Bennetts] supported my model for the ATs explaining that they should be at a higher level than specific knowledge or facts about regions and countries. Andrew Wye was annoyed at the idea that knowledge was a second order concern, misunderstanding the curriculum implications of Bennetts' point, and weighed in with sharp criticism. Trevor's input had the effect of raising the temperature of the debate and polarising the argument – eventually the Chair asked him to sit down!'

This particular anecdote is a good example of what Walford has called 'the struggle between the DES and HMI' (1992, p. 92) – a struggle weighted heavily in favour of the DES as far as GWG events were concerned.

Group members – geographers or curriculum people?

Membership of the Group reinforces the view that Ministers saw common-sense as the key to dealing with (or 'culturally restoring') the geography curriculum. In each case, appointment was a direct result of a tightly controlled process in which short-listed candidates were interviewed directly by the Minister, Angela Rumbold, presumably after DES vetting. Rex Walford, a teacher educator, and Michael Storm, ILEA geography inspector, were both past-Presidents of the GA and influential in geography education. Both had already expressed the view that geography should return to a stronger place focus and informational tradition (Walford, 1984; Storm, 1987). Walford also suggested that he was influenced by the views of E.D. Hirsch about 'cultural literacy' ('that it was both possible and desirable to specify a corpus of factual knowledge that ought to be learnt' (1992, p. 93)), a point picked up later by Dowgill and Lambert (1992). Of the remaining educational members of the Group, Kay Edwards was head of geography in a large Welsh comprehensive school, which had consistently achieved high standards. She provided a Welsh perspective, as unlike the situation for history, there was no separate Welsh Working Group. Wendy Morgan was an ex-primary headteacher well known for her advocacy of geography as opposed to integrated topic work in primary schools. Keith Paterson was a teacher educator best known for his research in physical geography and David Thomas, who became Vice Chairman, was a university professor of human geography with wide experience and relatively traditional views. Though my experience as associate director of one of the progressive Schools Council projects subsequently proved an unwelcome source of ideas for the Group, I was actually appointed in my capacity as co-ordinator of a school-industry initiative. Hugh Ward, LEA Inspector for Kent, joined the Group later (October 1989) in order to strengthen primary expertise. There was a general emphasis on safe, traditional positions and, through Walford and Storm, an implicit approval (though not shared by all) of a return to a more traditional curriculum.

For all national curriculum subjects the government had expressed its desire to balance the interests of teachers, advisers and educators with those of 'lay' members – Ball suggests that this was part of the New Right's strategy. As the Hillgate Group explained: 'we have no confidence in the educational establishment which has acted as an ideological interest group, and which is unlikely to further the government's aim of providing real education for all' (1987, p. 10). Lay members of the GWG included: Roger Davies, Managing Director of Thomson Travel (then one of Britain's leading holiday firms) and representative of an industry which had been publicly critical of pupils' knowledge of world geography (quoted in Storm, 1987); Richard Lethbridge, formerly director of a steel company but also secretary of the Country Landowners' Association and author of County Guide Books; and Rachel Thomas, a member of the Countryside Commission and Exmoor National Park Committee as well as a part-time teacher. If this selection is taken as significant, then there was a clear emphasis on travel, world knowledge, the British countryside – what might be regarded as a popular view of geography's content.

There was also representation within the geography educators of more progressive approaches to school geography. Walford's work on games and simulations was well known (in geography education circles), as was Storm's interest in development education and my own involvement in curriculum development. There was a high profile for the GA (nine GA members, two past and one future President). Ultimately, however, the professional educators on GWG failed to form an effective functioning opposition to off-set the cultural restorationist thrust or, more significantly, to ensure that at least a workable curriculum model resulted from the changed content emphases. In the pressurised conditions of the GWG, with the Chair stressing the shortage of time and the need to ensure geography a place in the curriculum by producing a politically acceptable report, Group members reacted in different ways. The lay members assumed they had done their duty by confirming the public concern about place knowledge and were content to leave more technical matters of curriculum construction to the 'experts' – failing to understand why in the early meetings these experts could not agree. Although many of the professional teachers and educators on the Group expressed support for the conceptual and skill-based model (model B) in the early GWG Meetings, they quickly realised the DES hostility to this. They then took the least confrontational route, supporting model A (content-based ATs) and arguing, as Butt's interviews (1997) reveal, that this was the price for getting geography into the curriculum. Some members felt that because enquiry was not seen by the DES to be uniquely geographical, it was not helpful to continue fighting for its inclusion. In this atmosphere, the Group closed ranks and, as Butt shows, became openly hostile to any who persisted in referring to curriculum planning principles or to model B. Butt suggests that events on the GWG can be understood by recognising the split in the Group's professional membership between supporters of the subject ('the geographers') and supporters of pedagogy (the 'educationalists or curriculum developers'). He points out that the Chair, because of the clear briefing from the DES, sided automatically with 'the geographers' and so used their backing to marginalise all curriculum input. While this may be one way of viewing the situation, what is crucial for the geographical education profession to recognise is that there should not have been this split. The curriculum projects may have moved school geography too far from its subject content roots, but it was possible to find a better balance. The previous two decades of curriculum development should have shown that 'curriculum' and 'subject' were not destined to pull in opposite directions but to be used as twin sources for a sound and meaningful school geography. That this point was not clarified, either before the GWG met or during the meetings (as happened with history), was a major cause of the problematic structure of the 1991 Geography Order.

So far, reference has been made in an abstract way to the professional interests of Working Group members. However, since all such bodies are actually collections of individuals, it would be foolish to deny the significance of personalities, relationships and the whole group psychology of the situation (Butt deals with this in some depth, 1997). For each member, there were the pressures of the meetings with long hours, tight deadlines and residential commitments, on top of their normal life and workload. There were great expectations from the world outside, new tensions and stresses within the Group and an over-riding cloak of confidentiality drawn round the whole proceedings. A psychologist would, no doubt, explain the range of approaches to be expected from an average group of individuals in these circumstances. There are always the dominant personalities who impose their will, the relationships that create conflict and aggression, the compromisers, the negotiators and the peacemakers. It is not possible to follow up these connections here, though interested readers might find parallels in Ian McEwan's account of life on a government appointed Committee (Figure 5) in *The Child in Time* (McEwan, 1987).

Extracts from *The Child in Time*

From pages 9-10:
The Official Commission on Childcare, known to be a pet concern of the Prime Minister's, had spawned fourteen sub-committees whose task was to make recommendations to the parent body. Their real function, it was said cynically, was to satisfy the disparate ideals of the myriad interest groups ... Stephen's was the sub-committee on Reading and Writing ...

From page 10:
The Committee divided between the theorists, who had done all their thinking long ago, or had it done for them, and the pragmatists, who hoped to discover what it was they thought in the process of saying it. Politeness was strained but never broke ...

From page 11:
Lord Parmenter presided with dignified and artful banality, indicating chosen speakers with a flickering swivel of his hooded, lashless eyes ... He had an aristocratic way with the commonplace. A long and fractious discussion concerning child development theory had been brought to a useful standstill by his weighty intervention – 'Boys will be boys' ...

From pages 22-23:
The academic who had proposed the phonetic alphabet began to talk dyslexia, the sale of state schools, the housing shortage. There were spontaneous groans. The mild-mannered fellow pressed on. Two thirds of eleven year olds in inner city schools, he said, were illiterate. Parmenter intervened with lizard-like alacrity. The needs of special groups were beyond the committee's terms of reference. At his side, Canham was nodding ...

From page 134:
So the committee took evidence, dull depositions from two experts, and Stephen gave himself over once more to the luxury of structured day-dreaming ...

Figure 5: Life on a government-appointed committee. Extracts from: McEwan, 1987.

Rejection of curriculum planning

In retrospect, the rejection of curriculum advice by some of the professional educators is surprising because it was a matter of crucial importance, as the HWG members realised at an early stage in their deliberations. Phillips explains (1998) that Saunders-Watson not only allowed discussion around the important question of whether the ATs should contain factual content, but was swayed by their arguments despite initial negative reactions from civil servants. In the end, even some of the civil servants came to see that, as one explained in correspondence to Phillips 'specific knowledge belonged in the programmes of study and not in the statements of attainment' (1998, p. 77). Yet on the GWG which, four months later, should have been able to benefit from HWG experience, content-based ATs were heavily promoted from the beginning.

Some commentators have laid the blame for the inadequacies of the 1991 Order squarely at the door of the framework provided by the TGAT (DES and WO, 1987). For example – 'the complexities of the 10 level framework complicated the task and led to another fateful decision – the inclusion of content in the SoAs' (Walford, 1992, p. 95). However, the TGAT framework, though cloaked in new jargon, only suggested the clarification of aims and coherence for the subject by recognising overarching themes (Profile Components, soon abandoned); the outline of more specific educational objectives (ATs) capable of being broken down into testable statements (the SoAs); and the establishment of clear procedures for selecting content and organising teaching and learning approaches (PoS). In this sense, it may be likened to many models of curriculum planning used by geography teachers and others in the 1970s and 1980s (e.g. Graves, 1979; Geography 16-19 Project, Naish *et al.*, 1987). If the Group had been allowed to draw on this experience, the task would still have been difficult (particularly the ten levels of attainment), but at least there would not have been the same confusion over curriculum outputs (the ATs) and curriculum inputs (the PoS).

The DES 'guidance' to the Group (Figure 6) contained no explanation of the TGAT model, only an exhortation to decide and agree on the definition and number of the attainment targets. Meetings 2-9, representing the first five months of the Group's work and taking it up to the Interim Report (see Study 3, pages 65-66), focused almost exclusively on the ATs. What should they be? What should be in them? PoS were not even mentioned until meeting 6 (briefly) and meeting 7 when there was a belated attempt to suggest that perhaps they should complement the ATs. Despite the wealth of curriculum development experience in geography education and the existence of one curriculum project representative on the Group, there was never any discussion of the TGAT framework as a whole or of how it might relate to the structure and characteristics of geography as a school subject. Significantly, there was already concern expressed by SEAC about the model taken by the Science Working Group, in which the ATs contained specific content. SEAC had warned that this would lead to curriculum and assessment problems later. The Group was pushed by the Chair to reach 'firm conclusions on the AT structure' as early as the 8 August (GWG minutes, meeting 4) despite misgivings from several members at that stage. Model A, which the Chair insisted should be 'trialled', comprised eight ATs containing everything which had been discussed and which seemed tangible enough to please the Minister – specific places, specific topics and themes in human, physical and environmental geography, particular skills and techniques. The major casualties in this 'attainment targets take all' approach were the process of geographical enquiry, a clear recognition of key ideas in geography and an outline of any genuine progression through the levels – failings which remained through to the Final Report. Model B never saw the light of day again, though at the time it was equally well developed as model A and showed that the desire to re-emphasise place knowledge and basic geographical facts and skills could have been met by specifying these directly in the PoS. It was the simple solution promoted by the Chair, that such knowledge had to be in the ATs which led to many of the subsequent problems with implementation.

Suggested approaches to planning the geography national curriculum
1. Decide on definition and number of ATs (in light of perceived structure of geography).
2. Consider how ATs group into profile components.
3. Develop ten levels for each AT and appropriate SoAs.
4. Give examples to illustrate each level, where appropriate.
5. Consider weighting of elements in SoAs at each level.
6. Provide arguments in support of range of levels chosen for pupils at each reporting age.
7. Consider how PoS should be constructed to enable level requirements to be met.
8. Indicate which aspects of performance at each level would be best assessed by SATs.

Figure 6: DES guidance on planning the Geography National Curriculum.
Derived from: DES GWG Paper (89)2.

The History Working Group and the debate about content

The place of GWG in the sequence of subjects and, in particular, its relationship with HWG was crucial. By the spring of 1989, when the GWG was established, the government had already struggled with a divided Mathematics Group and resignation of its Chair; difficulties over the place of grammar in the English National Curriculum; and controversy in science over scientific enquiry and the status of the three separate sciences. Many of the problems were related to difficulties in interpreting and translating the framework of ATs, PoS and levels of attainment provided for all Working Groups by the TGAT. However, beyond the technical problems lay the deeper ideological conflicts, between the New Right and the progressive educationalists in the different subject communities, over the definition and control of subject knowledge. By 1989, there was a strong desire from Ministers and the DES not to allow any further public airing of these differences and to keep a tight control on the process of national curriculum construction. Graham acknowledges that Ministers and civil servants were aware that 'both history and geography had considerable political overtones' (Graham with Tytler, 1993, p. 62) and, particularly for history, were determined to ensure that the working group process resulted in the appropriate outcome of a traditional and knowledge-led history curriculum. As early as May 1989 when the GWG was holding its first meeting, the historians had agreed to go for a model of ATs focused on skills of interpretation and critical awareness, with the content (historical knowledge of specific periods and events) being placed in the PoS. Rumours were circulating that the Minister was displeased with this approach and indeed when the History Interim Report was published in June 1989, Kenneth Baker told the HWG Chair in no uncertain terms (according to Graham, with Tytler, 1993) that the model would have to be changed, and the new Secretary of State (John MacGregor), though slightly less confrontational, confirmed that the Report did not 'put sufficient emphasis on the importance of acquiring factual knowledge' (MacGregor letter to HWG, August 1989). It is not surprising that the civil servants should have been keen to avoid a similar situation for geography. Accordingly, at the GWG second meeting (June), when the history proposals were briefly introduced, members were 'warned off' by the DES Assessor who confirmed that 'the approach being contemplated for history was untried and might prove controversial' (GWG minutes, meeting 2). Such was the DES concern about history, that one similar model presented for geography, as well as the fated model B, both elaborated at the third GWG meeting (July 1989), were quickly rejected by the Chair. At one stage model B had support from about half the group including the HMI. At a later stage, as originator of this model, I was explicitly asked not to produce any further papers promoting it (as Butt confirms, 1997), GWG members were explicitly warned not to meet and talk with HWG members and, as Rex Walford explains, this restriction was enforced: 'one member of the group sought some unauthorised consultation with HWG at one stage, but was admonished by the Chair for doing so' (1992, p. 97). Graham wonders why the HWG and GWG 'resolutely failed' to liaise as the NCC asked them to do – he was clearly unaware of the specific political context (Graham with Tytler, 1993, p. 74).

Consultation and public reaction

The lack of attention to the curriculum and assessment implications of the model chosen featured as one of the main criticisms of the Interim Report. The responses from the SEAC, the Institute of Education (London), and representatives of the curriculum development projects were all of this nature. Norman Graves, a well-respected figure in geographical education and past President of the GA, was one of many who urged the group to reconsider the model:

> 'if geography's justification in the curriculum is the intellectual development it can stimulate in pupils ... then it is the ideas, concepts, principles and skills of the subject which matter. The areal coverage provides the context within which skills and concepts are illustrated and applied. I have no quarrel with the areas chosen – but they should not form the ATs' (Submission to Interim Report, November 1989).

There is evidence in the GWG minutes and papers and from Butt's interviews that the Working Group rejected contrary advice, using techniques which Ball (1990) identifies as classic New Right. Those who disagreed were either 'not to be trusted' 'not one of us' – such as LEA advisers, curriculum project representatives or left wing teacher educators – or they had misunderstood the situation. Thus the GWG minutes of 5-8 January 1990, referring to criticisms of the Interim Report, state that 'some of the points were incompatible with our terms of reference'. The LEA advisers were accused of 'stage-managing their consultation meeting' held at Woolley Hall because 'their interests lay in the field of integrated humanities'. Even the GA was suspect in this respect – the hostility to the Interim Report experienced at some of the GA regional consultation meetings was explained because the 'key speaker [GA] turned the audience'. GWG Paper 90(9) entitled 'A Summary of Issues arising from Comments on the Interim Report' explained that:

> 'many commentators have sympathy with the Group's conception of the nature of geography and of the aims of geographical education set out in chapter 2, and they support the strengthening of geographical education by a re-emphasis on factual knowledge. There is, however, dissatisfaction with the ATs and outline of PoS offered in the Interim Report'.

Despite the mainly hostile reception from the geography education community, and advice from the GA and from the Geography Committee of SEAC (the government's own assessment advisory body) on how to make amendments, there was never any suggestion that the content-based model should be changed. The Group continued to operate in the same way during the second half of its life, with most GWG members having convinced themselves that model A offered the best hope of maintaining geography's curriculum survival. Those who were unhappy with the situation but wished to continue to influence events followed the slightly less confrontational strategy of trying to include some more progressive elements (e.g. enquiry, curriculum planning, cross-curricular themes) in the Final Report and so to leave signposts for later revision. At the end of the process, when the Final Report was published (June 1990) it was seen as an improvement over the Interim document, although many of those who commented (e.g. Graves et al., 1990; GA Consultation Response, 1990) noted with dismay: first, that the grand rhetoric of the aims was still not put into practice in the very prescriptive and narrowly focused curriculum; and second, that as the National Association of Humanities Advisers (NAHA) explained, in its 1990 response, 'despite the Working Group being given much "food for thought" by commentators, they appear to have been unable to address the fundamental and dire structural weaknesses which crippled the Interim Report' (1990, p. 1). It is significant that Leslie Fielding hailed the Final Report as a great personal achievement, seeming to enjoy the media interest and seeing himself as the saviour of school geography – 'Kids will have to work at geography in the future ... for too long the subject has been half taught, wrongly taught or not taught at all' (quoted in *The Daily Telegraph*, 7 June 1990).

From Final Report to Final Order

After publication of the Final Report of the Working Group, there was an opportunity for the NCC to make amendments to the curriculum model. Despite the strength of critical reaction revealed during consultation, the NCC was unable to wield real power. As Graham's book reveals (Graham with Tytler, 1993), the DES assumed that it was leading the national curriculum exercise and attempts by Graham to share responsibility were met with suspicion and hostility. The growing strength of the New Right eventually led to the resignation of Graham in July 1991 (as his position became increasingly untenable) and greater central control over the NCCs work. The timing of the geography work (June 1990-March 1991) must have been affected by this situation. Even more telling is the fact that Graham and the NCC were focusing attention on the controversial history proposals, particularly throughout 1990 when Nick Tate, then the NCC History Officer, was trying to rescue the controversial process-based model and to rewrite the history document. Graham, as a historian himself, was involved in this rewrite and in the delicate political manoeuvrings, so it is not surprising that he was less aware of GWG activities. He states that in his view 'the Group was working well' (Graham with Tytler, 1993, p. 71); he wonders why HWG and GWG did not liaise; and he wrongly identifies the key issue as being about aspects of geography rather than curriculum considerations. As Butt points out, 'Graham's account of the workings of GWG must be treated with a degree of circumspection and scepticism' (1997, p. 261) and the NCCs misunderstanding of the situation and pre-occupation with history go some way to explaining its failure to do more than tinker with the inadequate geography model.

Also significant is evidence that the NCC did not have as effective a subject team for geography as Nick Tate (then NCC's Professional Officer for History) and the NCC History Task Group proved to be for history (see Phillips, 1998). The NCC Professional Officer for Geography was only appointed in May 1990 – just as the Working Group was reaching conclusions. Little knowledge of the tensions on the GWG had reached NCC so it may be that the new officer assumed a less problematic situation than actually existed. The NCC Geography Task Group met between June 1990 and April 1991 with a brief to identify key issues from the consultation exercise, to make recommendations to the Secretary of State (Kenneth Clarke), and to advise about the development of non-statutory guidance for geography. According to the minutes of this Group, it was continually frustrated by wishing to make major structural changes to the geography proposals (which were also promoted by SEAC) but receiving little leadership from the NCC Geography Officer and positive rejection of this approach by the DES (minutes of NCC Task Group, June 1990-April 1991). As a result, although the NCC did reduce the number of ATs to five and make a token gesture to introducing enquiry, it made no attempt to redesign the curriculum model, to rewrite more meaningful PoS or fully to 'rescue' geographical enquiry from the marginal chapters of the Final Report by integrating it with the content. The NCC's hasty attempt to make the PoS more distinctive only resulted in an unhelpful level by level repetition of SoAs, creating more rather than fewer problems for teachers.

In January 1991, as part of a wider downgrading of foundation subjects, Clarke announced that geography and history should be options at KS4 (one or the other or short courses in both). This was a blow for the status of both subjects and for the Baker vision of a ten-subject entitlement curriculum, and it had severe implications for the history and geography proposals which had been designed on the assumption that both subjects would be compulsory. Kenneth Clarke also intervened in the details of the Draft Geography Order in January 1991, taking out the few remaining references to attitudes and values, enquiry and issues. Clarke explained, in the letter accompanying the Draft Order (January 1991), that he considered 'attainment targets should emphasise more strongly knowledge and understanding of aspects of geography and put less emphasis on assessment of skills – which however desirable are not particular to geography – and less emphasis on the exploration of attitudes and values'. One of his key advisers at this time was Tessa Keswick, identified by Callaghan

(1995) as one of the New Right 'Believers', and later to become head of the right wing Centre for Policy Studies. The geography community saw this as the final straw in political control over the school subject. Even bodies not normally given to effusive responses (such as the RGS and the CBI) expressed their concern at the way the action was taken as much as with the outcome. The GA attempted to make some capital out of the disturbance by offering Clarke a complete rewrite of the 'level by level' PoS (later published as Rawling, 1992b), about which he had expressed concern. In the end, all the activity resulted in only minor gains (e.g. the re-appearance of land use conflicts, some readjustment of PoS) but the faulty model and the hard New Right flavour remained. Lawrence describes Clarke as someone with the characteristics of full-blooded Thatcherism with its 'widely held view that everyone knows more about teaching than do professional teachers' (1992, p. 98). This analysis seems to fit Clarke's reactions to geography.

The GNC as 'Policy text'

Bowe and Ball with Gold point out (1992) that policy texts are often revealing items, and they frequently reflect in their format and wording the struggles and compromises which led to their production. Accordingly, it is valuable to look at the official policy documents and, in particular, to study the GWG Final Report as an example of a contested text. Figure 7 shows the sequence of text production.

The Interim Report of the GWG appeared at the end of 1989 (DES and WO, 1989) and comprised essentially an exposition of the eight new content-based ATs, four of which were place-specific. The widely approved aims for geography sat unhappily with the way in which the ATs were expressed;

GWG Interim Report, October 1989
- simple traditional view of geography – places and maps
- strong political control

- Eight content/skill-based ATs (1. Home Area and Region, 2. United Kingdom, 3. World Geography part 1, 4. World Geography part 2, 5. Physical Geography, 6. Human Geography, 7. Environmental Geography, 8. Geographical Skills)

GWG Final Report, June 1990
- 'report within a report' structure of document illustrates conflicting ideologies
- some professional educational influences (e.g. enquiry, curriculum planning) feature in main document but not in ATs

- Seven ATs focused on specific content and skills (1. Geographical Skills, 2. Home Area and Region, 3. UK and EU, 4. Wider World, 5. Physical Geography, 6. Human Geography, 7. Environmental Geography)

NCC Consultation Report, November 1990
- minimal 'tidying up' without changing faulty model
- awkward level-related PoS developed
- bureaucratic influence

- Five ATs (1. Geographical Skills, 2. Knowledge and Understanding of Places, 3. Physical Geography, 4. Human Geography, 5. Environmental Geography)

Draft and Final Orders, January-March 1991
- issues, values and general enquiry skills out, because 'not essential to geography' (Kenneth Clarke)
- stronger focus on knowledge
- re-assertion of strong political control

- Five ATs (1. Geographical Skills, 2. Knowledge and Understanding of Places 3. Physical geography, 4. Human Geography, 5. Environmental Geography)

Figure 7: Sequence of text production.

there was little development of the PoS; and the document was weak on broader enquiry approaches, on skills, attitudes and values and on geographical issues – all the characteristics valued so highly by the curriculum projects and in GCSE experience. At one level, the document may be read as a confident expression of the new culturally restored geography, with Chapter 2 setting the scene about all that was wrong – the deficit view of school geography. The confidence could not conceal the poor rationale and the underlying issues which the model raised – e.g. the difficulty of developing progression in the content-based ATs and the illogicality of relegating enquiry to a mere mention in the PoS when the argument had already been made that it was impossible to separate it from skills and content. The 'cube diagram' (DES and WO, 1989, p. 47) is often quoted as justification for the chosen curriculum model. In fact it merely confirms the way in which geographical work integrates areas (places), themes and skills, a characteristic which could be a feature of many different models.

The Final Report (DES, June 1990) was a more polished document, though the subject was held within the same limiting structure of content-led ATs. The Group's only direct response to the consultation issues had been to reduce by one the number of ATs, thus avoiding the awkward World Geography Part One and Part Two distinction. Some references to enquiry, to curriculum planning and to the wider contributions of geography were added to the Final Report but not to the main AT/PoS structure. I have referred elsewhere (Rawling, 1992a) to the GWG Final Report as a 'report within a report', because of the way conflicting ideologies are uncomfortably held within the one document. Figure 8 provides a detailed diagrammatic representation of the situation. Chapters 5 and 6 (The ATs and PoS) in the Final Report comprise the 'meat' of the proposals. These are the sections which eventually became statutory and, inevitably, the ATs reflect the required 'hard' statutory language – 'pupils should acquire knowledge and understanding', 'pupils should be able to'. The ATs are focused on specific areas of factual knowledge, 'The Home Area and Region', 'the UK within the European Community', 'Physical Geography', and the detailed SoAs focus mainly on hard information, e.g. 'describe the sources of energy in the USA, USSR or Japan' (AT2.6e), or on specific skills 'measure the straight line distance between two points on a plan, using a simple linear scale' (AT1.4c). For both the Interim and Final Reports, the locational map requirements and the prescriptive lists of regions and countries for study seemed to re-orient the subject back towards a traditional 'capes and bays' format, though in fact the amount of factual learning required was relatively minor compared with the demands of many early twentieth century regional texts (e.g. Pickles, 1935). More striking was the distorted 'world view' which they seemed to promote. Roberts (1990) and Ball (1994) both suggested that the choice of places seemed to reposition the UK in some mythical golden age of empire. Even AT 7, the heading of which (Environmental Geography) might suggest a more global viewpoint, is seen to comprise requirements for pupils to describe and explain particular environmental topics in a technocractic way, rather than to analyse and appreciate global links and inter-relationships in a critical way.

The contrast with the more progressive educational ideology incorporated in the 'soft surrounds' of Chapters 4, 7, 8 and 10, in particular, is striking (Figure 8). Chapter 4 outlines aims for geographical education in schools (para 4c) which were not only widely accepted in consultation but which also include statements such as – 'develop a sense of place and a feeling for the personality of a place and what it might be like to live there' – a far cry from the 'blow by blow accumulation of facts about places' which seems to be the approach represented in the ATs. Chapter 7 outlines geography's place in the wider curriculum, including the statement (para 7.21) that geography has an important role in developing the 'abilities to explore values and beliefs and to understand the views of other people'. Paragraph 7.30 suggests that 'by emphasising the process of enquiry in the study of places, themes and issues' geography can make an essential contribution to the development of citizenship – a strange comment in the light of the fact that enquiry never appears in the ATs. Finally, diagram 1 in Chapter 4 and paragraph 10.5 present a view of the proposals as a curriculum system from which teachers can plan and develop their own school-based curriculum, though the over-prescribed nature of the ATs does not support this interpretation. Throughout the additional chapters there is continual reference to aims, purposes, curriculum, the contribution of geography, enquiry, attitudes and values – all the terms that characterised the progressive educational movement and curriculum thinking. It was the hard core which became the legal requirement. The strange 'doughnut' shape of the GWG Final Report may be read as a reflection of what happened in the Group. The 'hard core' reflects the way in which the Group was controlled and steered towards an outcome which accorded more or less with the New Right's cultural restorationist ideology, i.e. geography as a 'real subject' with specific facts and skills to be learned and with a confident and uncritical view of Britain's place in the 'wider world'. In this vision, pupils are not encouraged to enquire critically; places, locations and distances are facts to be learned; 'development' is an economic matter; and environmental problems all have solutions. The 'softer surrounds' reveal that the battle was not completely one-sided and the professional geography educators did make some impact.

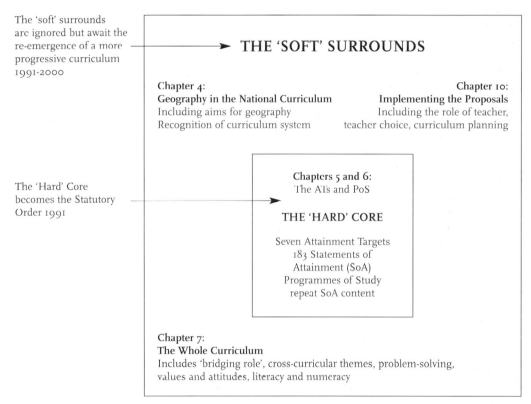

The 'soft' surrounds are ignored but await the re-emergence of a more progressive curriculum 1991-2000

THE 'SOFT' SURROUNDS

Chapter 4:
Geography in the National Curriculum
Including aims for geography
Recognition of curriculum system

Chapter 10:
Implementing the Proposals
Including the role of teacher,
teacher choice, curriculum planning

Chapters 5 and 6:
The ATs and PoS

THE 'HARD' CORE

Seven Attainment Targets
183 Statements of
Attainment (SoA)
Programmes of Study
repeat SoA content

The 'Hard' Core becomes the Statutory Order 1991

Chapter 7:
The Whole Curriculum
Includes 'bridging role', cross-curricular themes, problem-solving,
values and attitudes, literacy and numeracy

Figure 8: The Geography Working Group Final Report: a contested text.

The *Consultation Report for Geography* (NCC, 1990) reflected the bureaucratic confusions of 1990 and the failing influence of NCC. If some members of the GWG had attempted to leave signals and levers in the marginal chapters so that later amendments could be made to the proposals, in the short term they were disappointed. NCCs ineffectual changes produced minimum gain – an extra strand of enquiry in AT1 and reduction in number of ATs – at the expense of an even more unwieldy format for the PoS.

In the Draft (January 1991) and Final Orders (DES, 1991a; WO, 1991) for geography, strong political control was re-established. The intervention of the Secretary of State (Kenneth Clarke) in striking out any remaining references to attitudes and values or to broader enquiry skills gave rise to much comment from the profession and in the press (Rawling, 1991b; Kent *et al.*, 1991). More significant was the fact that the 'iron grip' of the original GWG model remained, resulting in an Order which was not only at fault structurally, but seemed to represent an educational ideology alien to that of most of the geography community. There were no 'frills' in the Orders – all that was legally required were the hard statutory requirements. From the introductory wording of the preamble through the legally correct items of 'pupils should be able to' to the final lists of content on prescribed maps, the 1991 Geography Order may be read as a statement of political control. As Kenneth Clarke explained during a parliamentary debate April 1991, its role was:

'to make sure our young people learn some geography not just vague concepts and attitudes which relate to various subjects, and to emphasis learning about places and where they are' (Hansard, 29 April, 1991).

It must be remembered, however, that the official text is not the curriculum which actually happens in schools. Teachers have considerable power in what Bowe and Ball with Gold (1992) call the 'context of practice', i.e. in implementing the curriculum. However, texts do carry with them material constraints and restrictions – for geography these seemed immense in 1991. The implementation of the GNC and its impact on teachers will be dealt with in Chapter 6.

Conclusion

The story of the making of the GNC 1989-91 undoubtedly illustrates the confident assertion of central control over curriculum content. The 1991 Geography Order was a political solution, resulting in what appeared to be a culturally restored geography curriculum. In this sense, Robinson's (1992) view that the subject community had been politically out-manoeuvred is correct. However, as the details of GWG activity show, the story is not simply one of an ideological take-over. Although, as Goodson (1998b) and Ross (2000) explain, New Right ideology saw both history and geography as playing a key role in reviving a traditional national identity, there was not a clear view of what this meant in detail. For geography, much of this interpretation was left to the Chair, with the DES ensuring the general direction of movement away from progressive education – perhaps not so much a case of the GWG being steered by a new ideology as being left to the common-sense views of an ex-diplomat. Many of the emphases in the Order (e.g. places, physical geography) were undoubtedly an attempt to balance some of the developments of the curriculum era (e.g. enquiry, issues) with a greater recognition of subject content. Handled differently, this might have worked. The mistake was for the professionals on the GWG to allow some of the gains of curriculum development to be totally rejected. The subject community, while accepting praise for winning the place in the curriculum, must also accept some blame for the way it handled the national curriculum exercise and failed to negotiate some compromise position on the GWG. In particular, the rejection of curriculum advice resulted in a model which caused immense difficulties for implementation, and this might have been avoided, to some extent, despite the New Right influence. The GWG episode revealed that there was not a clear and publicly acceptable view of school geography which would have prepared the subject community to participate in this more pressurised political curriculum 'game'. Finally, however, there is no doubt that the evidence reveals how unlucky the GWG was in the timing and sequencing of its work, choice of key personnel and the general political context within which it worked. The 'messy realities' referred to by Ball (see page 48) proved all too effective for geography.

Study 3

A Geography Working Group narrative

Date	Events	Selected comments/quotes
5 May 1989	**Establishment of GWG** announced and DES press release issued	Membership of the Group is well balanced and draws on a wide range of valuable expertise in geographical education – including two past-Presidents and one future President of the GA. The Group should produce a well-reasoned set of ATs for geography (GA press release, 8 May 1989).
18 May 1989	**First meeting of GWG –** procedures explained, and introduction to task	
15 June 1989	**Second meeting –** immediate focus on choice of ATs and warning to avoid history's approach	
8-10 July 1989	**Third meeting –** two approaches (models) to AT considered (A areal based and B concept/perspective based). Chair favours A	*The Chair personally considered geography fortunate to have been included in the national curriculum as a foundation subject; it could have gone either way. The subject was what its consumers perceived it to be as well as what its theorists wished it to be; geography was not the property of school teachers* (Chair, GWG minutes 8-10 July 1989).
8 August 1989	**Fourth meeting –** decision to continue work on model A only	*A small agenda committee of the Chairman, Vice-chairman, Secretary, DES Assessor and HMI Assessor often met before the main meetings, ostensibly to determine the order of business; some of us came to*
5-7 September 1989	**Fifth meeting –** criticisms of model A set to one side, key proponent of model B asked not to produce any more papers	*wonder if the ultimate decision making might not rest in such a conclave. It was a group notably light on the professional element of the Working Group and, perhaps, it was designed to be so* (Walford, 1992, p. 98).
23-25 September, 11 October, 16 October and 24 October 1989	**Sixth, seventh, eighth and ninth meetings –** attempts to provide an enquiry AT are rebuffed and a geographical skills AT is accepted instead, and work continues on factual content for SoAs of model A	*Persistence with the attainment target structure currently being explored (model A) would in my view be detrimental to the future of geography in school. In an attempt to satisfy the need to strengthen the regional locational knowledge of pupils (a need which I am not disputing) the Group has seen fit to allocate 4 or 5 ATs to specific factual and regional knowledge. There are other more appropriate ways to give emphasis to specific place knowledge* (Rawling, GWG Paper 89(18)).
30 October 1989	**Interim Report** based on model A (but with addition of some themes and skills ATs) is presented to Secretary of State	

continued

Date	Events	Selected comments/quotes
20 November	**Interim Report published for consultation**	
28 November, 5-7 December 1989 and 5-8 January 1990	**Tenth, eleventh and twelfth meetings** – responses to Interim Report being received. GA visits GWG and makes a critical response (6 December)	*The Interim Report's proposed attainment targets, with the exception of AT8 (geography skills), contain considerable content overlap in that ATs 1-4 are only different from ATs 5-7 in being located in particular places; the concepts and ideas which underpin the knowledge about and understanding of the key topics and issues are common to all seven ATs ... there must be doubt about whether the model, as developed in the report, would facilitate ease of assessment and assist clarity of reporting* (SEAC Geography Committee, note to GWG, January 1990).
23 January 1990	**Thirteenth meeting** – SEAC representatives, including Chief Executive, Philip Halsey, visit GWG and are critical about the model chosen	*The Geography Working Group must appreciate that in a number of ways the Interim Report is flawed. The GA does not believe that, as they stand, the draft proposals contained in the report will encourage forward looking and dynamic geographical study during the 1990s and into the twenty-first century. The Association believes that the Working Group must make several fundamental changes*
30 January 1990	**Duncan Graham, Chief Executive of NCC** meets Sir Leslie Fielding (GWG Chair) and expresses concern about content-led ATs	(GA Response to Interim Report, January 1990).
31 January 1990	**GA Response to Interim Report** published, very critical	
3-5 February, 21 February, 8-9 March, 21 March and 3-4 April 1990	**Fourteenth, fifteenth, sixteenth, seventeenth and eighteenth meetings** – Group reject any criticism of overall model, but attempt to take some content out of ATs, to reduce ATs by one and to improve the PoS	*The historians, who really did have a debate during the life of their Working Group, developed a strong framework and have been far more able to withstand attacks made by politicians and others on the shape of their proposals* (Lambert, *TES*, 29 March, 1991).
18-19 April 1990	**Nineteenth (final) meeting** – Report finalised and agreed by whole group with one Statement of Concern tabled by E. Rawling, referring to inadequate model, lack of progression and marginalisation of enquiry	*Some bemoan the fact that the idealism of whole curriculum planning was sacrificed to a realistic quick fix arrangement through separate subjects. Flawed though it is, I suspect it represents an acceptable first step that might otherwise never have been made* (Walford, 1992, p. 97).
27 April 1990	**Final Report submitted to Secretary of State** (published 6 June 1990 by DES)	

5

Contesting the Geography Curriculum 1991-2000: Two National Curriculum Reviews

Introduction

With the passing of the Statutory Order for Geography in 1991, one traumatic chapter in the history of the geography curriculum came to a close. Helsby and McCulloch (1997b) point out that the establishment of National Curriculum Orders did not mark the end of contestation of the curriculum for any subject, since continuing phases of what they call *bureaucratic control* and eventual *settlement* (in schools) resulted in further changes being made.

During the 1991-93 period, the New Right tightened its grip on educational policy making (Lawrence, 1992; Ball, 1994). Both Philip Halsey, Chair and Chief Executive of SEAC, and Duncan Graham, Chair and Chief Executive of NCC, had been seen by the cultural restorationists as part of the educational establishment (indeed Halsey had supported the SEAC Geography Committee's criticisms of the GWG Final Report, see page 53). They were replaced respectively by Lord Griffiths, former chair of the Centre for Policy Studies, hard-line restorationist and absolutely 'one of us' (Ball, 1994, p. 32), and David Pascal, a former adviser to Margaret Thatcher. For geography, the result of the new hard-line climate was, as will be seen, a continuing expansion of the tools of bureaucratic control, both at SEAC and NCC, and a continuing failure to recognise or address the real problems of geography implementation.

During 1991-93, the difficulties and pressures involved in implementing national testing arrangements for English and mathematics also came to a head in the teachers' boycott of tests, summer 1992. The Secretary of State, John Patten, called in Sir Ron Dearing (April 1993) to review the whole curriculum and assessment structure and the School Curriculum and Assessment Authority (SCAA) replaced the NCC and SEAC in October 1993. In many ways, then, 1993 may be seen as a decisive date marking a change in political discourse and the beginnings of national curriculum amendment.

Nevertheless, it will be shown that for geography the slow process of ameliorating the 1991 Order was really set in train in 1991, the minute that teachers were presented with the faulty and over-prescribed framework to implement. From that date, the practicalities of implementation made it inevitable that change would occur: the gradual realisation by schools and teachers of the impossibility of covering all the content; the conscious decision taken by the GA to develop and support good practice *despite* the National Curriculum Order; the steady accumulation of evidence from NCC, SEAC, and eventually SCAA and Ofsted, that the Geography National Curriculum (GNC) was causing immense problems – all these were responsible for a subtle change of discourse between 1991 and 1993 despite the continuing influence of the New Right. Indeed, such beginnings set the scene for the whole decade. The necessity to 'put right' the faults of the 1991 Order has been a key feature during the processes of change involved in both the Dearing Review (1993-95) and the QCA Review (1998-99) of the national curriculum.

In both cases, the emphasis has been on simplification and improving manageability and there has not been the opportunity for a major rethink, certainly for any non-core subject (though the Literacy and Numeracy Strategies have necessitated reformulation for English and mathematics). Much of the New Right ideology (subject-based curriculum, emphasis on content) has remained embedded in the national curriculum structure. Given this situation, it is tempting to assume that all subsequent curriculum changes have been minor. Indeed Kelly suggests that curriculum change in the 1990s has been 'no more than tinkering with content, attainment targets, profile components, levels and so on' (1999, p. 101). This chapter will continue using the policy cycle approach, explained in Chapter 1, to investigate whether the changes made to the GNC have been mere tinkering, or whether the politics of curriculum change has allowed genuine contestation of the principles and practices enshrined in the 1991 Geography Order. The analysis will be applied to the two reviews of the GNC (1993-95 and 1998-99), first examining the context of influence for both reviews and then comparing the contexts of text production. Finally, this chapter will draw out some key issues about curriculum policy making with respect to the national curriculum 1991-2000. Chapter 6 will deal with implementation (the context of practice) more thoroughly. Note that the overlapping nature of each context is significant – effectively the context of practice for one national curriculum is the context of influence for the next.

The context of influence for the Dearing Review 1991-93

Whereas for the core subjects of English and mathematics the biggest problems in the 1991-93 period were related to national assessment, for geography, discontent with the practicalities of curriculum implementation dominated the subject community debates. Initial reactions, both of the geography community as a whole and of individual teachers, focused on the sheer weight of prescription, on the limiting nature of the 'information about the world' view of geography, and on the apparently alien ideology it incorporated. The Order emphasised facts and knowledge and seemed to marginalise geographical enquiry, concepts and transferable skills. It seemed to 'present a situation strangely out of line with current concerns and with best educational practice' as understood by most geography teachers (Rawling, 1991b, p. 18). It was these features which caused the immediate problems, particularly in primary schools where Catling (1991) feared that the huge weight of content would overwhelm the many non-specialist teachers. However, as more evidence became available about implementation KS1-3, so deeper structural concerns assumed much greater significance than the traditional ATs and detailed prescription.

The 1991 Geography Order was essentially common to both England and Wales (though published in two separate documents). Both the NCC (1992) and the Curriculum Council for Wales (CCW) (1993a) carried out monitoring exercises, while Ofsted, England (1993a), and HMI Wales (1993) also published reports of the first years of the GNC. The main conclusions from these sources are strikingly similar. In each case, the responses from schools and LEAs showed that the broad emphases of the Order (skills, places, physical, human, environment) were generally agreed to provide an acceptable if somewhat traditional base from which to develop courses and schemes of work. However, 'the way in which the AT/PoS structure has been interpreted for geography makes it very difficult for teachers to plan and implement good quality work' (NCC, 1992, p. 1).

Despite this conclusion from its own monitoring, NCC failed to produce effective assistance for teachers, although the Non-Statutory Guidance (NSG) for Geography (NCC, 1991a) apparently provided the opportunity. The NCC's Geography Task Group, whose role it was to advise on the NSG, did not believe that the Order provided an appropriate basis for the work, because of its structural faults. The eventual NSG document produced in the spring of 1991 failed to meet their approval. At its penultimate meeting (6 March 1991) the Group gave its view that 'NSG and in-service training materials would be unable to overcome the problems of the statutory order' and they urged NCC to draw the attention of DES to 'the fundamental flaws' and to request 'a significant revision of the Order' (Task Group minutes, 6 March 1991). SEAC was also highly critical of the draft NSG, pointing out that it failed to recognise the difficulties of teaching 'across the levels' (internal SEAC memo of 12 March 1991). As a result, HMI Peter Smith and the editor of *Teaching Geography* (David Boardman, University of Birmingham School of Education) were called in to revise the NSG. However, their attempts to ameliorate the Order's failings, by re-introducing geographical enquiry and introducing a more curriculum-led approach, did not find favour with the right wing NCC Council members. The version which appeared in May 1991 (NCC, 1991a) did little more than confirm the traditional focus of the Order. An evaluation of all NCC's guidance materials carried out by Social Surveys (Gallup Poll) in 1992 found that 'the geography NSG was rated the least useful' and, not surprisingly among the things which they most needed, 40% of geography teachers said help with enquiry, one of the items which had caused the most debate in NCC Task Group meetings. Significantly, in Wales, the CCW under the chairmanship of GA ex-President, Richard Daugherty, was able to take a more progressive line on many curriculum issues (Daugherty and Jones, 1999). The Welsh NSG (CCW, 1991) took the direct approach of ameliorating and opening up the Geography Order and geographical enquiry, including a section from the GA's publication (Rawling, 1992b), featured dominantly in this advice. Not surprisingly, CCW's guidance material sold well in England.

In SEAC, under the chairmanship of Lord Griffiths, there was the same story of professional advice from geographic educators being constantly at odds with the framework provided by the Geography Order, and of a continuing push from the centre to extend bureaucratic control. Callaghan describes Griffiths as 'the consummate backroom boy to whom Mrs Thatcher ... devolved the responsibility to actually shape the policies into a workable format' (1995, p. 379). After Richard Daugherty finished his term of office as Chair of SEAC's Geography Committee in summer 1991, this position was taken by John Barnes, an academic from London School of Economics, recognised by Callaghan as being one of the New Right 'Believers'. Development work was established on KS1 optional geography SATs, on KS3 geography tests, and on preparation of KS4 national curriculum criteria and full/short course syllabuses. The irony of this situation was that all this assessment work was proceeding despite the SEAC Geography Committee's own severe criticisms of the Geography Order and its particular concerns that there were intractable problems for assessment. SEAC's geography officer was, nevertheless, able to ensure that the optional KS1 SATs incorporated geographical enquiry effectively (SEAC, 1992a). A number of SEAC publications in this period also emphasised the teachers' professional role in making formative assessment decisions (SEAC, 1991a,b, 1992a,b, 1993a,b), aiming to counter the 'tick-box' approach seemingly promoted by the Order. Fortunately for geography teachers, the KS3 tests were abandoned before implementation because of the Dearing Review, and the GCSE exercise was also dropped as a result of Sir Ron's recommendation to reduce the KS4 curriculum and make geography optional. Although a severe blow for geography's status (see Chapter 7), this did at least avoid the difficult task of merging GCSE good practice with national curriculum levels.

Given this situation of a difficult Order and restricted help from the curriculum and assessment agencies, much depended on teachers' understandings of these problems and their perceptions of how these difficulties might be addressed. In secondary schools, the inspection and monitoring exercises found a diversity of practice. Essentially, in those schools with curriculum development experience and with confident and creative leadership, it was possible to impose a more appropriate curriculum structure and to develop good quality teaching and learning despite the Order (Ofsted, 1993b; Roberts, 1995). The poorest quality of geographical experience was found by Ofsted to be in departments that had perceived the teacher's role in more narrow terms as merely 'delivering' the required content. In primary schools, non-specialist teachers generally struggled to manage the overlapping PoS and detailed SoAs. In comparison with the history 'study units', the geography requirements seemed confusing. Many primary schools inspected by Ofsted in the first few years of implementation had hardly begun to grapple with the problem (Ofsted, 1993a,b), implementing history first. They were helped by some further NCC material (NCC, 1993a, b, c, d) and by the gradual flow of high quality guidance materials from the GA.

It would have been difficult to ignore this mounting evidence in 1991-93 of the structural inadequacies of the Geography Order. The GA, while explicitly recognising these faults, took the line that constructive support to geography teachers on making the most of the national curriculum (Rawling, 1991c) was the best way to maintain and promote good geography, at the same time as campaigning for change. Discussions in GA Council meetings moved away from 'placing blame' and focused on strategies such as the establishment of a regional support and in-service training network (Rawling, 1992c, 1994), consolidation of the readership of the new primary journal *(Primary Geographer),* and the preparation of primary and secondary teacher guidance publications. Behind the scenes, however, senior GA officers took every opportunity to make known to policy makers the particular structural problems of the 1991 Order. In July 1992, a seminar at St Anne's College, Oxford, resulted in a chance meeting between myself (GA President, 1991-92) and Baroness Blatch, then Minister for Education. The Minister explained that she was aware of concerns about the geography curriculum. She requested and received a brief resumé of what was wrong and how it could be put right. Figure 1 presents an extract from the correspondence. This was followed up by an invitation from the next GA President, Simon Catling (1992-93), asking Baroness Blatch to speak at the GA's Annual Conference in Sheffield. In her speech to GA members (14 April 1993), Baroness Blatch made explicit reference to the difficulties caused by the structure and requirements of the Geography Order (Figure 1) – so confirming that policy makers had been influenced by (or at least recognised) the dominant discourse of concern (Blatch, 1993). Baroness Blatch also announced that Sir Ron Dearing had been appointed to review the national curriculum, and she urged the Association to make its concerns known. John Patten (Secretary of State for Education and formerly an academic geographer at Oxford) later attended the GA's Centenary Dinner in Oxford, July 1993, but made no substantive comment on the problems faced by school geography. As Lawton points out, Patten was desperate 'to convince the right wing that he was not "wet"' (1994, p. 82). Despite John Patten's background, it was not Patten himself but his junior Minister who publicly recognised the intractable problems of the 1991 Geography Order.

Both the GA and COBRIG did indeed make strong representations to Sir Ron Dearing, attempting to read the political climate by accepting that major change to content was not on offer. They focused their submissions on the fact that 'the central difficulties which teachers report relate to structural problems' (Carter, 1993, p. 155 for the GA) and explained that 'the problems of complexity and overload in the geography curriculum are intimately bound up with the way in which the AT/PoS structure has been interpreted' (COBRIG, 1993). Both suggested that reformulation of the AT/PoS relationship was a necessary first step, before slimming could be addressed. The RGS and IBG provided supportive submissions. Such lobbying, backed by Ofsted evidence, proved effective. The Final Dearing Report contained a separate paragraph which sanctioned major amendments to the Geography Order despite the fact that the whole exercise was publicised as merely 'slimming down':

> 'The structure and content of the Geography Order have been widely criticised. The proposals made above (i.e. about reduction and simplification) will lead to a radical reduction in statutory content and the proposals in paragraphs 4.43-4.45 below will lead to a reduction in the number of attainment targets at the lower levels. In making these reductions, the opportunity should be taken to address criticisms which have been made of the structure of the Order' (Dearing, 1993, p. 36, para 4.39).

The context of influence for the QCA Review 1995-98

By contrast with this negative focus on problems, the context of influence for the QCA Review (1995-98) was generally more positive as far as the subject community was concerned. The Dearing Review

1. Extract from Baroness Blatch's correspondence with Eleanor Rawling (the author), August 1992

'I was interested to read your comments about implementation of the Geography Order following our conversation at the seminar. The national curriculum is not set in stone. We are sensitive to the concerns expressed by interested parties about the Order. It is the job of the National Curriculum Council to keep all the national curriculum subject orders under scrutiny and to advise the Secretary of State accordingly. They are actively monitoring the implementation of the Geography Order and whilst we have no plans to review the Geography Order in the immediate future the need or otherwise to do so will become clearer as implementation – only the first year of which has been completed – progresses. I believe that you are in touch informally with NCC about implementation of the Order; no doubt you will be passing your concerns on to the Council.'

2. Extract from Baroness Blatch's speech to the Geographical Association Conference, April 1993

'... we do recognise that the Orders may not be perfect, and that experience may show that changes need to be made. We listen to teachers, and once we are sure that the problems are more than temporary, we set a review in hand, as we have done with technology. We also recognise, of course, that the national curriculum cannot be set in concrete. Inevitably changes will need to be made to bring the order up-to-date and, for instance, in geography to take account of world changes, such as those in the former USSR, or of new subject developments.'

Figure 1: Baroness Blatch: involvement with the Geography National Curriculum.
Source: Blatch, 1993, p. 364.

had made significant changes, producing a GNC with a clearer content entitlement for each key stage, a reduction in the overall content and a greater commitment to geographical enquiry (although, significantly, because of political sensitivity and the influence of New Right Council members such as John Marks, the term was never used!). The broad emphases of the 1991 curriculum (skills, places, physical, human, environmental) were retained as headings for content in the PoS and not as separate ATs. There was now a single AT (geography) and, as with all subjects, a set of eight level descriptions (plus exceptional performance), rather than SoAs, to be used to summarise and report on pupils' progress. The initial reaction of the geography education world to the new requirements was one of relief. Roger Carter, writing on behalf of the GA, wrote in the *TES*:

> 'The revised national curriculum for geography is good news. Most of the problems identified in the earlier Order have been addressed, although some with more success than others. Teachers will now be able to work with programmes of study that are more realistic in content terms, more straightforward in presentation, and clearer about the relationship between key stages' (Carter, 1994, p. III).

While there was general agreement that the revised curriculum offered more scope for teachers to exercise their professional skills, there was some doubt about whether this would happen on a large scale (Rawling, 1996). The 1991 curriculum had called into question the nature of teacher work; as Lambert explained 'the national curriculum is a device which some teachers imagine denies them certain kinds of decision. The direct response to these teachers seems to be less autonomy and more conformity' (1994, p. 70). Certainly, one particular textbook series (Waugh and Bushell, 1991), produced in the style of a manual covering all the SoAs from the 1991 Order, had sold strongly in the early 1990s. It lent immediate support to struggling teachers but, almost certainly, one consequence was the neglect of more creative and divergent responses, even after the Dearing revisions had made the situation more flexible. Unfortunately, despite the clear recognition that it would be crucial to effective implementation of the Dearing geography curriculum, non-statutory guidance was not produced by SCAA. This was partly because of the Department for Education's (DfE's) reluctance to overburden teachers with more paper, and civil servants failing to appreciate that guidance would be seen differently from statutory documents. It was also a reflection of the continuing influence of New Right thinkers on the SCAA Council. Dearing might have 'blown the winds of change' through the national curriculum, but policy decisions still had to be approved by Council members such as John Marks and Anthony O'Hear (as SCAA Council minutes reveal). They retained a suspicion (perhaps with some justification!) that the Dearing Review would be used by subject officers as a means of subverting the intentions of the original national curriculum.

After this initial setback, however, the role played by the curriculum and assessment authority was very different in the 1995-98 period than in 1991-93. SCAA was established in October 1993, as a direct result of the Dearing recommendations to bring curriculum and assessment advice under one body. The appointments of Sir Ron Dearing as its first Chair (April 1993), Gillian Shepherd as Secretary of State for Education (July 1994), and Nick Tate as Chief Executive of SCAA (from October 1994) signalled the beginning of a period in which the curriculum and assessment body was able to give greater stress to curriculum matters. As Lawton (1996) commented, it was clear that the Dearing Review had shifted the emphasis away from delivery of a fully prescribed entitlement curriculum and back to recognition of teachers' responsibilities for developing a balanced curriculum from a minimum national framework. Given this (and despite occasional blocking tactics from the more right wing members of Council), SCAA was able to interpret its role more creatively after 1994 and, as Dainton (1996) suggested, to operate more consultatively. Significantly, the Corporate Plan for 1995-98 (SCAA, 1995a) recognised, in Aim 1, the need to identify and undertake 'development work to support the national curriculum', in addition to its work in monitoring, commissioning tests and regulating the public examination system. In this developmental capacity, the SCAA (and later QCA) Geography Team was able to develop a strategy for subject support and an increasingly fruitful relationship with the subject associations and the geography teaching community. This was reflected during the 1994-99 period in regular up-dating meetings, publication of a termly subject 'Update', and involvement of subject experts and consultative groups in all its work. SCAA/QCA officers also attended subject association committee meetings as observers. Another result was the production of a whole range of curriculum-focused guidance publications: *Exemplification of Standards: Geography, KS3* (SCAA, 1996a), *Expectations in Geography at KS1/2* (SCAA, 1997a), and *Optional Tests and Tasks, Geography KS3* (SCAA, 1996b) all incorporated a strong element of curriculum planning and a framework of geographical enquiry, despite their rather unpromising assessment-focused titles. *Curriculum Planning at Key Stage 2* (SCAA, 1997b) and *Geographical Enquiry at Key Stages 1-3* (QCA, 1998a) were more directly focused on curriculum matters. The aim was to highlight and improve elements of good curriculum practice, particularly where the requirements were lacking. The most obvious examples are geographical enquiry and the four aspects of geography (Figure 2). The significance of these publications is that at national level they laid the groundwork for further necessary structural changes and more progressive features to be added to the GNC in the forthcoming review. Within the geography community they established a more productive and professional discourse about the geography curriculum. It is notable, for example, that throughout this period *Teaching Geography* (the GA's journal for secondary teachers) frequently followed up SCAA publications with favourable comment, more detailed discussion and practical advice on classroom use (e.g. on assessment, Butt *et al.*, 1998). Geography's high profile in more general SCAA publications (e.g. *Information Technology and the National Curriculum at Key Stages 1 and 2*, 1995b,c; *Teaching Environmental Matters*, 1996c; *Geography and Use of Language*, 1997c,d) also proved useful as a way of emphasising geography's wider contribution. The GA, and also to a lesser extent the RGS (since 1995 merged with the IBG), were able to redirect their energies into curriculum support (see, for example, the GA's *Geography Guidance* series and special issues of *Primary Geographer* and *Teaching Geography* and the institution of an annual teachers' in-service day by the RGS-IBG from 1993). They worked with the SCAA/QCA Geography Team to enhance a GNC which, from the subject community's point of view, was steadily improving. During this period, the GA's journal *Primary Geographer* was extended in size to create more room for ideas and resources about geography teaching, and primary membership of the GA continued to grow rapidly, until the growth was temporarily halted by the 1998 announcement which made teaching the full geography PoS optional at KS1 and 2.

SCAA/QCA publications	Characteristics
Exemplification of Standards KS3 (SCAA, 1996a) *Expectations in Geography KS1/2* (SCAA, 1997a) *Optional Tests and Tasks* (SCAA, 1996b)	Enquiry re-instated and four aspects of geography (i.e. underlying structure/ideas) introduced
Curriculum Planning at KS2 (SCAA, 1997b) *Geographical Enquiry KS1-3* (QCA, 1998a)	Explicit reference to curriculum planning and the role of the teacher
Geography and IT (SCAA, 1995b,c) *Geography and the Use of Language* (SCAA, 1997c,d) *Teaching Environmental Matters through the NC* (SCAA, 1996c)	Geography's wider contributions to skills and understandings, and its dependence on active enquiry teaching/learning

Figure 2: Re-emergence of more progressive educational features in SCAA/QCA publications in the 1990s.

Given the improved curriculum and the raised morale of the geography community after 1995, it is not surprising to find that SCAA monitoring activities and Ofsted inspection evidence charted a steady improvement in the implementation of school geography. The SCAA Monitoring Reports for 1995-96 and 1996-97 (SCAA, 1996d, 1997e) covered the first two years of implementation of the revised curriculum and were based on information gleaned from visits to schools, teacher meetings and liaison with subject associations. They revealed that teachers found the curriculum a more 'appropriate and manageable basis for planning at all key stages' and that this was reflected in more balanced geography curricula which gave attention to the full range of places, themes and skills required. Ofsted inspection evidence confirmed this picture. For primary schools over the 1995-96 period 'the introduction of the national curriculum and the revision of the Geography Order have noticeably improved the quality of curriculum provision and planning' (Smith, 1997a, p. 5), while the secondary findings for that year showed that 'teachers have certainly benefited from the changes brought about by the Dearing Review' (Smith, 1997b, p. 126). Throughout the 1995-98 period, Ofsted evidence presents a picture of steady improvement in standards of achievement at all key stages, although both SCAA and Ofsted point to similar remaining concerns; in particular a lack of common understanding of geographical enquiry, difficulties with interpreting subject knowledge at KS2 and problems in developing sound assessment practice at all key stages.

More worrying than these detailed points of concern were growing signs that geography's overall position in the curriculum was less secure. According to SCAA's 1997 Monitoring Report, geography's apparently declining status at KS4 was the key issue for secondary schools. However, in January 1998 David Blunkett, Labour's new Secretary of State for Education, announced the lifting of the requirement for primary schools to follow the PoS in six non-core subjects, including geography. Designed to focus schools' attention on literacy and numeracy, it had the immediate impact of reducing emphasis and commitment to the six foundation subjects. As a result, the 1997-98 QCA

Monitoring Report for Geography (unpublished, QCA, 1998b) explained that 'pupils' entitlement to a continuous and progressive education about places and environments is threatened by piecemeal changes to individual key stages, without sufficient consideration for the implications of such changes for the whole picture'. What is more, after 1996, the Ofsted inspections began to reveal that geography was not holding its position relative to other subjects with respect to quality of teaching and progress made by pupils. This was particularly noticeable at KS3, but there was also a recognisable dip in quality and progress in years 3 and 4 of KS2. Although the causes for this situation are undoubtedly complex (see Chapter 6) Ofsted reports hinted at the likely link between the general status of the subject and quality of implementation. The 1996-97 Ofsted findings (1998b) mention the infrequent nature of geographical study in the primary years causing continuing problems. The 1997-98 secondary leaflet (Ofsted, 1999b) suggests that disappointing standards at KS3 may be related to deployment of non-specialist staff and lack of short-term planning and clear aims for KS3. All in all the 1995-98 period began to reveal that although the Dearing Review had improved the curriculum framework for the subject and resulted in a changed political climate more conducive to professional educational discourse, ironically it and subsequent policy decisions had almost certainly led to a decline in geography's status in schools. This concern was expressed strongly at the joint QCA/Subject Associations Conference on Geography and History in the 14-19 Curriculum (see QCA, 1998c).

Since SCAA had been involving the education community in dialogue throughout the 1993-98 period, there was no need for its successor body, QCA, to conduct a major consultation prior to the establishment of the national curriculum review. In most cases, the key issues had already emerged from monitoring. Geography, similarly to most other subjects, held a pre-Review Consultation Conference for representatives of the subject community and subject associations, in July 1997. The messages from this were clear and were repeated in the Geography Team's submissions to the National Curriculum Review Team in SCAA. Manageability was no longer an issue for geography at any key stage: 'The key issue in a review of geography is its place in the curriculum rather than any demand for major review of the subject orders' (SCAA, 1997f). In 1998, geographers were concerned about the visibility of geography at KS1 and 2, declining status and numbers at KS4 and the unknown effects of forthcoming changes at 16-19 level. They were also anxious about the possible impact of the Labour government's desire to create room for its 'new agenda' of citizenship, personal, social and health education, education for sustainable development and creative and cultural education. These were the main elements of the context of influence for the second review of the national curriculum.

The context of text production: the Dearing and QCA reviews compared

Investigation of the process of policy text production is essential to understanding the impact and significance of the final texts. Policy texts such as National Curriculum Orders and requirements represent policy, but as several recent studies have shown (Bowe and Ball with Gold, 1992; Evans and Penney, 1995, 1999; Woods and Wenham, 1995), their production is not a straightforward matter. It always involves struggles and compromises, particularly when there are different official bodies competing for control of policy (NCC, SEAC, DfE in early 1990s and SCAA/QCA, DfEE in later 1990s) and interest groups such as subject associations with a strong stake in the outcomes. Although policy texts take various forms (e.g. there are official statutory requirements, official regulations and circulars and less formal non-statutory guidance), here the focus is on the statutory requirements formalised by the Geography Orders.

At first glance what is striking about text production for the Dearing and QCA Reviews is the contrast with the text production process in the 1989-91 period when the whole exercise was controlled and managed by ministers, with the curriculum and assessment bodies merely managing consultation and support. After 1993, SCAA and QCA were given responsibility for managing the reviews more directly, though with frequent reference back to the DfEE and ministers. However, on closer analysis, it will be seen that the Dearing and QCA Reviews differed in significant ways and that these differences can help to illuminate changes to the geography curriculum.

Whereas the formation of the 1991 Geography National Curriculum represented a brand new departure, a fresh start uninhibited by previous practice as the New Right saw it, both subsequent reviews had as their main aim simplification and amendment of an existing curriculum. The difference between the Dearing and QCA Review processes was that the Dearing Review was, in a sense, a single focus exercise. Teacher discontent meant that, for negative reasons, the brief was slimming down the over-weighted National Curriculum structure and enhancing flexibility for teachers. For geography, there was the added necessity for structural change. The QCA Review, on the other hand, had a multi-focus brief. Greater simplicity, reduction and flexibility were one strand, particularly at KS1/2 and 4, but the new Labour government which came to power in May 1997, also wished to add its own concerns to the list of aims. Thus, basic literacy and numeracy, key skills, and the 'new agenda' areas formed crucial additions, to some extent in conflict with the desire to keep the whole exercise manageable in schools.

A first significant point, about the differing processes of text production 1993-95 and 1998-99, is the short timescale available for the actual development work. In the Dearing Review only three months were available to undertake the major task of slimming and restructuring the geography curriculum, although it was building on earlier consultation and preparatory work. This compares with the more leisurely seven months development time allotted in the QCA Review and the 12 months available to the GWG, admittedly stepping out into the relatively unknown territory of ATs and PoS.

In SCAA, there was a determination to make the development work efficient and coherent. Subject advisory groups were set up to undertake the three-fold task of identifying essential knowledge, understanding and skills from the original subject Orders, redrafting the PoS more simply and writing the new level descriptions. However, SCAA was anxious to keep a tight rein on individual subject enthusiasms (seen by many as a problem of the original exercise) and to maintain overarching consistency and coherence (Figure 3). Hence there were powerful Key Stage Advisory Groups acting in a supervisory capacity at every stage of the work. Although subject officers were nominally in charge of the development work, control was exerted centrally from SCAA by means of: set guidelines for representation of subject associations and membership of the subject advisory groups; chairing of each subject advisory group by an assistant chief executive of SCAA (in geography's case, Keith Weller, also responsible for the science and KS4 groups); common proforma for undertaking and reporting the development work; the existence of a SCAA Council observer on each subject advisory group (for geography, Shawar Sadeque, someone with a strong interest in information technology). The work was all tightly managed and controlled within the short timescale, before the proposals went to the Secretary of State (April) and out for consultation in May 1994. Although some subjects may have chafed under these restrictions, for geography the situation could only improve from the low point of 1991. The subject advisory group, with strong GA and teacher representation, was fully supportive of the thrust towards simplification and may even be said to have gained from the tightly focused task, given the clear recognition of the problems for geography (Battersby, 1995).

By contrast, in the QCA Review, again handled by a newly formed body (QCA formed from the merger of SCAA and the National Council for Vocational Qualifications (NCVQ)), although the subject groups were given the more directive name of 'task groups', they were not as tightly constrained this time (Figure 3). QCA was as keen as SCAA had been to maintain consistency and

	1989-90 Working Group	1992-93 Advisory Group	1998-99 Task Group
Chair	Government appointed. Ex-diplomat and VC Sussex University, Sir Leslie Fielding, 'common-sense view'	SCAA senior officer – Deputy Chief Executive, Keith Weller. 'bureaucratic task'	QCA Geography Subject Officers – 'professional input'
Members	Government appointed. Business and lay people represented (3). Emphasis on relatively traditional and 'safe' membership from geography academics and educators. No explicit representation from subject associations or projects. DES – 'trouble shooter' and secretary	SCAA appointed. A mix of practising teachers, subject association representatives plus industrialist, SCAA Council member and DfEE observer	QCA subject team appointed. Practising teachers, geography educators, subject associations all represented plus academics, industry representative and DfEE observer
Remit	'A Working Group' 'to submit a final report to the Secretaries of State setting out and justifying its final recommendations on the attainment targets and programmes of study for Geography' (GWG Terms of reference, DES, 1989c)	'The role of the groups is an advisory one. They will receive proposals and make recommendations according to the criteria outlined' (SCAA, 1993a)	'to provide a way of drawing on the experience and expertise of practitioners and others' 'one group among many' (QCA, 1998d)
Other points	Geography subject community was allowed very little involvement in the process	Geography subject community had constrained influence within tight remit and schedule	Geography subject community was able to have considerable influence on details and to build on the groundwork laid 1995-98. Less influence on big issues (e.g. KS4)
	Intervention directly by Secretary of State in final stages (Kenneth Clarke, January 1991)	Powerful key stage groups existed to oversee the work of all subject groups	'the approach has been adopted to avoid the high profile subject and key stage advisory groups used in the previous review' (QCA, 1998d)

Figure 3: Comparison of subject groups creating and reviewing the national curriculum.

coherence across the whole exercise, but given the greater consultation and dialogue which had taken place with the subject communities and teaching unions in the 1995-98 period, it felt more able to involve and trust the subject communities to undertake the required work. Significantly too, QCA was a very different body from SCAA, much larger since it had taken over the vocational and general vocational qualifications work from NCVQ, and with a new Council. Not only did the QCA Council have reduced New Right influence (especially with John Marks' departure) but it also had stronger representation from the professional education community (e.g. Professor Ted Wragg, University of Exeter). It also played a very different and in many ways more distant role than its SCAA predecessor, since it was no longer possible after October 1997 to involve Council members in the minutiae of decisions about individual subjects. QCA's own subject officers were given responsibility for leading and managing the process. There were common proforma for outcomes and key stage/phase groups were established with a remit to overview the whole process, but the task groups were chaired by the QCA subject teams not by senior QCA officers and there were no QCA

Council observers on subject task groups. More significantly, despite their names, the groups did not represent one single high-profile group destined to carry out all the work. They were merely one part of a myriad of groups and individuals from whom the subject teams sought assistance. The difference between the Dearing and QCA Reviews in this respect is highlighted by the contrasting remits for the geography groups (Figure 3). In addition, the QCA development work included a period of 'informal consultation' or (as it was later re-named due to government sensitivity) involvement of the educational community in 'work in progress'. The geography community responded enthusiastically to this, the GA running several regional meetings so that members could comment on the work in hand. Most of the feedback was positive, with the main concerns being about possible further reductions at KS1 and 2.

For geography, again, the style of development suited the situation. The strong and positive relationship which the subject officers had established with the subject community, and the range of SCAA and GA guidance publications, provided a sound basis for further improvements to be made to the structure of the Geography Order. Greater subject solidarity also allowed geographers to make strong claims for inclusion in it of sustainable development education and a global citizenship dimension. Another positive point about the QCA Review is that the national curriculum, and the school curriculum as a whole, were finally provided with a statement of values and broad aims. For geography, as for other subjects, this was not only a major improvement presentationally, but gave the subject task group and subject officers a much clearer framework for their work.

Consultation is potentially an important element in text production, though the experience of the first national curriculum did not inspire confidence in the opportunity to make a real impact. For both reviews of the national curriculum, consultation was handled by the curriculum and assessment agency, i.e. the same body which was managing the development work. In both cases too there were clear steers from the government about desired outcomes (a more flexible curriculum, especially at KS4 in 1994; room for Labour's new agenda in 1999). In 1994 and 1999, consultation versions of the subject requirements were published together with summaries of changes proposed (SCAA, 1994a; QCA/DfEE, 1999a) and educationalists were asked for their views. Geographers' responses were largely positive about the changes to the structure and layout of the Order at both times, with the main criticisms reserved for bigger issues likely to affect the subject (in 1994 the future of KS4 and in 1999 the introduction of citizenship). As noted, these were both issues on which the government had strong counter views and the final decisions went against geography. However, one particular aspect of wider consultation did work in geography's favour in 1999. The consultation version of the GNC, distributed in May 1999, still retained the Dearing model, i.e. with key ideas and specific content mixed up together in the PoS. As a result of lobbying from primary teaching organisations at QCA meetings, there was a suggestion made that geography might be made consistent in structure with history, for the benefit of non-specialist KS1-2 teachers. Accordingly, in May-June it was possible for the QCA subject team to redraft the subject Order using a model which finally, ten years after the original national curriculum, distinguished key aspects from specific content and clarified the flexibility available to teachers. Since such amendments had frequently been discussed within the subject association meetings at QCA, the approval of the subject community was not likely to be an issue. Ironically, on this occasion, the often frustrating bureaucratic requirement of consistency worked in geography's favour in England.

One final factor to consider in terms of text production for the 1995 and 2000 reviews is the way in which presentational features were addressed (Figure 4). The 1995 requirements, though not as starkly presented as the original national curriculum ring binders, nevertheless still had a basic utilitarian feel to them, providing no friendly teacher introductions, no general aims and purposes for the school curriculum and no explanatory commentary. The text was business-like and brief, the only gestures towards assistance being the outline of common requirements (DfE, 1995) and the non-statutory examples given in italics throughout. It might be argued that the 1995 geography text reflects the character of the Dearing Review – a business-like attempt to sort out a problem and deliver the answer as efficiently and economically as possible. Earlier expectations (Bennetts, 1994) that the geography document would include a statement of aims, information about progression, and a matrix for choice of scales, areas of study and environments were not fulfilled. The decision was taken not to proceed with non-statutory guidance, though as explained, from 1995 onwards SCAA invested considerable time and effort in producing guidance publications which expanded and explained all the subject Orders. As some commentators noted, teachers would have found these helpful in 1995 at the same time as the new requirements. The SCAA geography team was also able to use its informal 'Update' publication (which did not have to be approved at higher levels) to make available some of the guidance which did not find its way into the Order (e.g. 'Updates' in 1994 and 1995 contained matrix for scales, ideas about curriculum planning). The special NC issues of *Teaching Geography* and *Primary Geographer* (April 1995) were another vehicle used to add extra detail by the SCAA and ACAC (the qualification and assessment authority for Wales) geography teams in co-operation with the GA.

Aspect	1991	1995	1999
Aims/rationale			■
Attainment Targets	■	■	■
Programmes of Study	■	■	■
Level Descriptions		■	■
Common requirements		■	■
Examples in PoS		■	■
Introductory paragraphs to PoS		■	■
Marginal text			■
Learning across curriculum			■
Quotations			■
Explanation of format			■
Children's work			■
Linked website			■
Implicit message	Requirements to be delivered, no negotiation	Requirements to be developed if you wish	A dialogue encouraged about how to develop the curriculum

Figure 4: The national curriculum requirements: presentational aspects.

The 2000 GNC provides a striking contrast. A conscious decision was taken by QCA in 1998 (QCA, 1998d) to produce a more user-friendly, curriculum-conscious document and, indeed, a design consultancy (EDIT) was commissioned to carry out market research with teachers and to make suggestions for presentation. Accordingly, the national curriculum requirements are now incorporated in the more informally named 'Handbooks' – one for primary (DfEE/QCA, 1999b) and one for secondary (DfEE/QCA, 1999c), together with individual subject handbooks. In each case, there is a foreword presenting the aims and rationale for the national curriculum and its place within the whole-school curriculum. Every subject document repeats the general information about 'learning across the national curriculum' and explains the format of the material. Each subject has an introductory paragraph about purpose and an informational commentary explaining the character and emphasis of the key stage, links with cross-curricular areas and other subjects, and any necessary explanatory notes (e.g. for geography about locational knowledge and the maps available on the website). Particularly significant is the use of children's work and quotations from the 'great and good' to personalise and illustrate the bare requirements. Another innovation possible for the 2000 curriculum was the launching of several linked websites in 2001 (e.g. the main national curriculum website; QCA's National Curriculum in Action website and the DfES Schemes of Work website), an opportunity not available to the previous versions of the national curriculum, and one which has immense potential to stimulate real interaction with and between teachers (see Appendix 1 for main website addresses). Such details are significant for a national curriculum text and for geography in particular. Given the increasing emphasis on dialogue between the policy makers and the professionals and given the re-emergence of a more progressive educational ideology in the geography requirements during the late 1990s, the new presentation seems to make explicit recognition that the professional role of the teachers is re-valued and re-instated. What is in doubt, however, is how this professionalism is to be defined. Does it signal the development of a more open and creative professionalism under a Labour government or is it the culmination of a brief period of greater openness and dialogue 1994-97, which is already coming to an end? Chapters 6 and 7 will examine this point.

Policy context	Original GNC (1991 version)	Dearing Review (1995 version)	QCA Review (1999 version)
Context of influence	■ New Right 'discourse of derision' ■ Geography gains a place in the curriculum but unresolved issues about process/content	■ Overwhelming evidence of faulty Order (NCC/Ofsted) ■ Political imperative to 'rescue' the NC and Dearing special para 3.49 about geography	■ Relief at structural changes and flexibility ■ Re-emergence of progressive educational influence via SCAA/QCA publications
Context of text production	■ Direct political control over GWG and interference by Secretary of State with Draft Order ■ Subject professional influence marginalised	■ Pragmatic single-focus exercise – 'simplify' ■ SCAA runs subject advisory groups, with strong central control of task and outcomes ■ Subject community has constrained influence	■ Multi-focus exercise – simplify and new agenda ■ QCA subject teams given freedom to draw on subject task groups and consultants ■ Labour's 'new agenda' is 'no-go' area for QCA
Context of practice	■ Severe implementation problems especially primary ■ KS4 curriculum never implemented and geography optional after 1994	■ Improvements in practice noted by SCAA/Ofsted ■ Subject associations raise profile and membership and work together	Big issues will be: ■ Re-establishing high quality geography at KS1-3 ■ Supply of geography teachers ■ Changing 14-19 context
Overall message	*An imposed political solution produces a 'culturally restored' geography curriculum.*	*A pragmatic solution results in an improved simplified geography curriculum framework.*	*Professional influence allows consolidation in curriculum detail but fails to improve status.*

Figure 5: The policy cycle approach applied to the Geography National Curriculum.
Note: The GNC was approved and became part of the statutory requirements in 1999, but it was not implemented until September 2000. It is therefore sometimes referred to as the Geography National Curriculum *for* 2000.

Cycles of change: some key issues 1991-2000

This chapter has focused on outlining and comparing the processes of curriculum change taking place in the two National Curriculum Reviews. However, just as striking as these detailed comparisons are some of the big differences between the 1991-99 period compared with the 1989-91 period of national curriculum development. Figure 5 summarises and compares the contexts of influence, contexts of text production and contexts of practice for the three different versions of the GNC. Key issues arising from the comparison are dealt with below.

The different scale and character of curriculum change in the 1990s compared with 1989-91

The 1989-91 period was an example of the 'big bang' approach to change, with a high-profile Working Group developing a completely new curriculum in relative secrecy and isolation from the rest of the subject community. The Conservative government had chosen this approach deliberately, in order to promote what it saw as a 'fresh start' to the school curriculum and to reject previously accepted professional expertise and wisdom about the subject. Lawton (1994) points out that these policies were a result of a genuine fear and suspicion by the New Right about the effect of progressive educational policies on British education. In this respect, the 1991 Order may be seen as an imposed political solution producing a culturally restored geography curriculum, as desired by the New Right. By contrast, both of the national curriculum reviews were necessarily smaller scale because they were starting from an existing Geography Order and attempting to simplify and reduce it. In addition (and also inevitably because of the problems caused both for the whole curriculum and for geography by the first attempt), the process was less secretive and involved the subject community more directly. The Dearing Review was constrained by being a rescue job. It is best described as a pragmatic solution, characterised by some increasing contribution to the policy-making process from the subject community, and resulting in an improved and simplified curriculum framework for geography, though not necessarily for other subjects. By the time of the QCA Review, it can be argued that for geography the development work was a more co-operative and professional venture between QCA and the subject associations representing geography teachers. Professional influence allowed consolidation of the improvements to curriculum detail, but the subject community was not able to make much impact on the continuing big curriculum issues, such as KS4 and the 14-19 curriculum.

The improved GNC framework

Despite the small-scale and constrained nature of the change process in both reviews, the changes have been very significant for school geography. Figure 6 compares the three sets of requirements (1991, 1995, 1999) against five criteria which experience has shown are essential if a national curriculum framework is to promote good practice and high quality geographical work.

■ Why are we teaching the subject? What can it contribute to the school curriculum? *(aims/rationale)*

■ What is the basic structure of important ideas in the subject which will enable it to make this contribution? *(key ideas/aspects)*

■ What is the minimum required content to be taught to each age group? And hence what is the scope for teacher choice? *(minimum content)*

■ What is the approach to learning and how is this integrated with the knowledge and skills *(approach to learning)*

■ What are the expected outcomes or expectations for pupil achievement after teaching and learning have taken place? *(outcomes)*

Criteria	1991 requirements	1995 requirements	1999 requirements
1. Aims/ rationale	No rationale for national curriculum and no aims provided for geography – though Geography Working Group did provide aims in its Final Report (1990)	No rationale for whole curriculum and still no explicit aims for geography, although para 1 of Order gives flavour of each key stage	Values, aims and purposes are given for the school curriculum and the national curriculum, and geography has an overall rationale ('the importance of geography') and aims/purposes for each key stage ('during the key stage...')
2. Key ideas/ aspects	ATs and SoAs focus predominantly on content. Key ideas/ aspects not drawn out, though hinted at in some SoAs	Places, themes, skills division of programmes of study gives greater coherence to the content, and general ideas receive some recognition in level descriptions	Four key aspects of geography are identified and the general ideas and areas of knowledge, understanding and skills to be developed are outlined in PoS
2. Minimum content	Content entitlement for each age range overlaps confusingly because PoS repeat content from SoAs	Each PoS more clearly identifies the content for the key stage, although specific topics and general ideas are still mixed up together	Specific topics/content to be studied (para 6) is clearly distinguished in each PoS from the general ideas/ understandings, skills to be developed (paras 1-5)
4. Integrated approach to learning	Geographical enquiry is mentioned at the beginning of each PoS, but not explained or integrated into SoAs or PoS	Geographical enquiry process is included as para 2 of each PoS and as a section in each level description, but it is not named	Geographical enquiry is clearly outlined as one of four key aspects of geography and explicitly described for each PoS. It is linked with skills and integrated with content
5. Outcomes for pupil achievement	SoAs are intended to be the basis for assessment but they are mainly factual content or specific skills, so broader outcomes (e.g. enquiry approach) or higher intellectual skills. (e.g. analysis, evaluation) are marginalised	Eight-level scale introduced. Geography level descriptions set out broad outcomes for pupil achievement. SCAA guidance explains 'best fit' process for summative assessment. Further implementation left to schools and LEAs	Eight-level scale retained and very minor changes made to level descriptions to emphasise sustainable development education and enquiry. Confusions about the distinction between summative and formative assessment remain

Figure 6: Comparison of the 1991, 1995 and 1999 requirements for the Geography National Curriculum.

The 1991 GNC did not answer any of these questions adequately. It failed to provide a rationale for the subject (although a generally accepted set of aims was given in the GWG report); it failed to provide a clear framework from which teachers could select and develop a school curriculum; key ideas were lost in the weight of specific facts; and it failed to integrate the geographical enquiry process with the knowledge and skills. The GNC for 2000, by contrast, presents a completely different curriculum model which recognises in the PoS four key aspects of the subject, including geographical enquiry and skills, provides a clear entitlement for pupils of different ages and allows sufficient flexibility so that teachers can develop their own school-based curriculum plans (Westaway and Jones, 2000a,b). In addition, sustainable development education, a global dimension and attitudes and values all receive explicit recognition, thus highlighting geography's wider contribution. Arguably, the 1999 model owes more to the curriculum development movement of the 1970s than it does to the 1991 Order. This is not to suggest that it provides a perfect solution. In particular, while the structure has improved, neither of the two reviews has allowed reconsideration of the changing nature of geography itself. Although the flexibility now exists for innovation to occur, the headings in the programmes of study do not actively encourage teachers to explore, for example, new approaches to place study, new aspects of cultural geography or issues about gender and identity.

Interestingly, the 1995 GNC can now be seen to occupy a kind of halfway stage in the re-emergence of a workable curriculum. The places, themes, skills framework allowed the imposition of some kind of order on the programmes of study and made it possible to make a better distinction between the content to be taught in the PoS and the expectations for achievement in the level descriptions. However, geographical enquiry was not named or adequately explained and scope for teacher flexibility was not fully identified.

The growing importance of professional educators active within policy-making arenas

In 1986, Lawton drew attention to the different kinds of people involved in policy making at the DES. He identified politicians, bureaucrats and professional educators (represented particularly by HMI in the mid-1980s) as holding different beliefs and values and hence making different impacts on educational policy. As a result, policy decisions at the DES were rarely the result of consensus but more often arose from compromise or negotiation within what Lawton called a 'tension system'. For geography pre-1988, HMI had been particularly supportive of some of the more progressive developments initiated by the curriculum projects and this may, in part, explain why the geography subject community failed to recognise the dangers in the national curriculum exercise.

During the construction of the first GNC, the impact of professional educators was seriously constrained even though by 1989 there was another group of professional educators active in the curriculum and assessment authorities – the subject officers. Chapter 4 shows that subject HMI were marginalised and subject officers in NCC and SEAC were not able to have much influence on the Working Group deliberations. The way in which the GWG functioned inhibited a genuine professional dialogue so that although professional educators were represented on the group, the dominant ideology was a form of cultural restorationism, promoted by politicians and political advisers. However, in the 1990s, one of the most significant features has been the re-emergence of a progressive educational influence on curriculum details. The changing political climate has enabled the subject officers in SCAA and QCA, and those HMI able to play a subject role (National Subject Adviser and Teacher Education Inspector), to work co-operatively rather than in conflict with the subject community. Too often it is assumed that politicians and bureaucrats are the key influences, whereas, certainly for geography, the 1990s show a rather different picture. It is interesting to note that, despite this, one of the most significant changes for geography (i.e. the changed model) resulted from a bureaucratic requirement for consistency, though it needed professional expertise to implement it in a helpful way.

Conclusion

During the 1990s, the geography curriculum has undergone phases of imposed political control, pragmatic amendment and a re-emergence of professional educational influence. Despite the traumatic beginnings, the GNC 2000 now provides a national framework for the subject which after ten years finally makes curriculum sense, highlights geography's wider contribution to the curriculum and leaves teachers considerable curriculum freedom to vary the content and develop varied teaching and learning approaches. These changes have been achieved by a slow process of incremental change; by the undertaking of unobtrusive amendments out of the political limelight; by the gradual 'winning of hearts and minds' among key people and organisations; and by assiduous attention to curriculum detail. Helsby and McCulloch note that:

'disputes over detail [of the NC] should not be seen as simply teething problems, as the sponsors of the national curriculum would no doubt have preferred to think, but as continuing contestation over the principles and practices involved' (1997b, p. 8).

This chapter has revealed the truth of this statement as applied to geography in the 1991-2000 period. Significantly, however, while the curriculum framework has improved, the GNC is still held within the traditional and now outdated shell of subject content. This rather than curriculum concerns remains the key area for continuing contestation.

Study 4

A distinctive Welsh perspective?

The 1988 Education Reform Act legislated for a national curriculum not for one nation but for two, England and Wales. It is interesting to note some key differences about the process of text production for England and Wales in the three periods of production and review. The original 1991 Geography Order was published in two virtually identical publications, one for England and one for Wales (DES, 1991a; WO, 1991). Daugherty and Jones have pointed out that although there was a separate Order for Wales, it was a result of 'no more than a copy editing exercise, in the course of which a few sentences in the Order for England were amended'. This was not surprising given that despite 'the smokescreen of consultation' all policy decisions were 'in the hands of government Ministers, officials and a government appointed Working Group, all of them London based' (Daugherty and Jones, 1999, p. 450). By the time of the Dearing Review, Wales had created for itself a stronger identity in educational matters, largely through the work and guidance publications of the Curriculum Council for Wales (CCW) (1988-93), chaired 1991-93 by Richard Daugherty, a former GA President (1989-90). CCW appointed a geography subject officer and the subject was given substantial support, a decidedly progressive pedagogical slant (e.g. CCW 1991, 1993b,c) and recognition as a significant contributory subject to the distinctive Welsh dimension or 'y Cwricwlwm Cymreig', being developed by CCW. Daugherty and Jones suggest that, in this respect, although cultural restorationism may have been the ideology influencing many curriculum decisions in England in the early 1990s, 'it would seem that the spirit of reconstructionism was alive and well in Wales' (1999, p. 451).

For geography in England, this situation was important during the process of Dearing amendments to the Geography Order. The Geography Officer for the Welsh Curriculum and Assessment Authority (later ACAC and now ACCAC) was included as an 'observer' on the English advisory group as well as managing a separate advisory group and process of revision in Wales. Although the two groups were separate, they were working on the same difficult Order, which had created the same problems for schools. The ACAC presence, backed by the context of a more impressive set of guidance publications, undoubtedly contributed to a general sense that professional educational input was more highly valued in this review, in both countries. It is significant, however, that geographical enquiry, which re-emerged in the English Order in 1995 but without being given a name, had featured strongly in the CCW non-statutory guidance and was therefore restored and named (and

continued

stated as the first aspect in the level descriptions) in the Welsh Order 1995. The naming of geographical enquiry had to wait for the 1998-99 review in England. Evidence about implementation of the Welsh National Curriculum 1995-2000 may be found in the reports of Estyn (Her Majesty's Inspectorate for Education and Training in Wales), particularly 2000 and 2001. In these reports, HMI note a significant geographical contribution to y Cwricwlwm Cymreig, especially in secondary geography in terms of knowledge about Wales. There seems to be less success in dealing with broader notions of identity or with Wales' relationship with other countries (see also Daugherty and Jones, 1999).

Between 1995 and 1997 when QCA was created, the English and Welsh subject officers were able to work closely together on guidance publications; thus for instance, the KS3 *Exemplification* booklets were planned co-operatively and the two publications can be used as complementary for geography. However, by the time of the QCA Review, wider political events – including the advent of a Labour government, the granting of a measure of devolution to Wales and the formation of a more powerful and individual Welsh Curriculum and Assessment Authority (ACCAC) – had resulted in curriculum and assessment decisions for Wales being taken independently. For geography, the effect has been a sudden cessation of co-operation between the subject officers and a totally separate review process. The English and Welsh Geography Orders for 2000, although bearing the signs of common origins and having similar broad themes, now show some significant differences (Copnall, 2000). The Welsh Order, not surprisingly, makes more of citizenship and community understanding as part of y Cwricwlwm Cymreig, although both English and Welsh documents focus on sustainable development education. Lack of dialogue has meant that the Welsh Order has not been able to undertake the change in structure made in the final stages to the English Order.

References

ACAC (1996) *Geography: Exemplification of standards key stage 3*. Cardiff: ACAC.

Copnall, G. (2000) 'Cwricwlwm Cymru 2000', *Teaching Geography*, 25, 1, pp. 24-7.

Curriculum Council for Wales (CCW) (1991) *Geography in the National Curriculum (Wales). Non-statutory guidance*. Cardiff: CCW.

CCW (1993b) *An Enquiry Approach to Learning Geography*. Cardiff: CCW.

CCW (1993c) *Approaches to Teaching and Learning about Wales*. Cardiff: CCW.

Daugherty, R. and Jones, S. (1999) 'Community, culture and identity: geography, the national curriculum and Wales', *The Curriculum Journal*, 10, 3, pp. 443-61.

Estyn (2000) *Aiming for Excellence in Geography: Standards and quality in primary schools*. Cardiff: Estyn (HMI for Education and Training in Wales).

Estyn (2001) *Good Practice in Geography: Standards and quality in secondary schools*. Cardiff: Estyn (HMI for Education and Training in Wales).

Jones, G.W. (1998) *Geography and y Cwricwlwm Cymreig*. Paper presented at the conference of the Council of British Geography, Oxford, July.

WO (1995) *Geography in the National Curriculum, Wales*. Cardiff: HMSO.

6

Policy Implementation 1991-2000: Empowerment and Professionalism

Introduction

The creation of the official policy text – in this case the Geography National Curriculum (GNC) – is by no means the end of the story. Bowe and Ball with Gold (1992), drawing on their research in schools, highlight the importance of the 'context of practice' in which the policy texts are translated and implemented. Not only do schools and teachers have to reassess the nature of their professional 'work' in implementing the requirements, but also, to some extent, they actively amend or re-create the meaning of the texts as they interpret them.

> 'The national curriculum remains both object and subject of struggles for meaning. It is not so much being implemented in schools as being recreated, not so much reproduced as produced. While schools are changing, so is the national curriculum' (Bowe and Ball with Gold, 1992, p. 120).

It should be remembered too, that at the beginning of the period in question, the geography education community had considerable experience in school-based curriculum development in geography. The curriculum development projects (particularly those operating in the secondary curriculum) had involved many teachers in planning the content and pedagogy of their geography courses. Even those not directly involved in projects were influenced by the profusion of books, articles, resources and professional development opportunities, all actively targeting curriculum development (see pages 25 27). The result was that most secondary geography teachers, even if they did not make full use of the opportunities, saw themselves as professionals undertaking a creative role within their schools. In primary schools by 1988, as Pollard et al. (1994) have shown, teachers' understanding of their professional roles was strongly rooted in what has been called the 'developmental tradition'. This emphasised developing the curriculum and teaching/learning experiences to suit the needs of individual children. The primary humanities curriculum projects reinforced this focus on the needs of the child and promoted collaborative curriculum planning, within and between schools.

The existence of a centralised national curriculum is not necessarily in conflict with continued professional creativity and involvement at the school and classroom levels of planning. Indeed the Conservative government always stressed that the NC was not intended to dictate how schools and teachers should deliver the curriculum (DES, 1989d). For geography, as Chapter 4 has shown, the particular circumstances surrounding the Geography Working Group (GWG) resulted in a faulty curriculum structure, an over-prescriptive set of requirements and an ideology alien to most of the geography teaching profession. Significantly, it also provided primary school teachers with a strongly subject-based framework, contrary to their normal topic-based approach. For many teachers and educationalists, it seemed that the GNC would result in a decline in school-based curriculum development, so that course planning and lesson planning would disappear as creative activities, while teachers would become mere technicians delivering central requirements (Schofield, 1990; Robinson, 1992).

This chapter will examine whether this fear was justified and what effect the two subsequent reviews have had on the balance between the levels of implementation. The reviews have, in general, resulted in a move away from a prescriptive set of course requirements towards a less detailed and more open curriculum framework. In the way that the NC text now seems to invite teachers to 'join in', to co-operate and to make sense of the text for themselves, it displays what Bowe and Ball with Gold (following Barthes) refer to as 'writerly' characteristics. This is in direct contrast with the 1991 Order which seemed to be more typical of a 'readerly' text, i.e. one which presents little opportunity for involvement and creative interpretation. However, there is evidence not only that teachers have not appreciated the significance of these changes, but also that a professional response has been constrained in other ways. This chapter will first consider the evidence available about implementation of each version of the GNC. The focus will then move to the context provided for professional activities throughout the 1990s, and to the changing nature of geography teachers' professional work. Special attention will be paid, as Bowe and Ball with Gold (1992) suggest, both to the way teachers have interpreted and changed the curriculum and to the way the experience has changed them.

Policy translation: implementing the Geography National Curriculum

In this section, substantial use has been made of the official sources of evidence about implementation of the national curriculum. Ofsted, the national inspection agency, began work in 1992 and one of its first tasks was to publish the HMI findings for implementation of the national curriculum during 1991-92, i.e. the first year of the GNC. There are Ofsted Annual Reports for the period 1991-2000, two five-year reviews (Ofsted, 1998a, 1999a), some more detailed geography subject reports and leaflets which exist for some years (e.g. Ofsted, 1993a,b, 1995, 1996a,b, 1998b, 1999b) and a range of specially focused reports (e.g. HMI Assessment Report for 1996-97) which sometimes have a bearing on geography. The NCC undertook a survey of LEAs implementing NC geography during 1992, while SCAA carried out monitoring activities after the Dearing Review, resulting in Monitoring Reports for 1995-96 (SCAA, 1996d), 1996-97 (SCAA, 1997e) and 1997-98 (QCA, 1998b). The Centre for Formative Assessment Studies (CFAS, 1999) also presented findings of the School Sampling Project to QCA during 1998-99. All these sources are listed in the References. Note that the figures do not provide comparisons before and after 1996 because the data is not strictly comparable. The lesson grading system was changed and the basis for expressing percentages was altered from percentage of lessons to percentage of schools.

The official sources inevitably have a strong focus on checking whether the required curriculum is being implemented (SCAA) and assessing how far national standards (as defined by NC levels) are being achieved (Ofsted), though both sources do also provide pointers to the factors which hinder or promote improvement. To extend and clarify the picture, reference is also made in the text to other available evidence – for example, a survey undertaken by the GA (Thomas and Grimwade, 1997), research carried out by individuals or groups (e.g. Daugherty and Lambert, 1994; Pollard *et al.*, 1994; Roberts, 1995, 1997; Galton, 2000), particular commentaries in the subject journals (e.g. Marsden, 1997b; Catling, 1999; Rawling, 1999a) and other evaluative publications (e.g. De Villiers, 1990-95; Marsden and Hughes, 1994; Blyth and Krause, 1995). It is helpful to consider 1991-95 and 1995-2000 as two separate implementation periods, relating to the first (1991) and the Dearing revised (1995) Order respectively.

Implementation 1991-95 (see Figure 1)
In the first four years of implementation of GNC 1991-95, Ofsted found considerable diversity of practice in both primary and secondary schools, but common difficulties deriving from the 1991 Order. Many primary schools were slow to take on the task of interpreting the difficult and weighty 1991 Order, preferring to deal with the core subjects and then, perhaps, to work from the more 'user-friendly' History Order with its clearly outlined history study units. Research into the experience of

	Percentage of lessons that were satisfactory or better				Key trends and issues (from Ofsted reports and SCAA monitoring)
	KS1&2		KS3		
Year	Standards	Teaching quality	Standards	Teaching quality	
1991-92	66	66	66	66	**KS1/2** National curriculum presenting considerable challenges and little evidence of detailed curriculum or assessment planning. KS1 lessons better than KS2. **KS3** Detailed planning only taken place for year 7. Difficulties with Order mean narrow focus on ATs and failure to integrate content and skills. Places neglected.
1992-93	66	66	66	66	**KS1/2** Lack of teacher expertise and subject competence hindering planning. Emphasis in teaching on physical topics and skills to neglect of places and human themes. **KS3** Significant number of schools finding difficulty in planning curriculum and assessment from the 1991 Order, especially small departments and those with non-specialists. Places and assessment neglected.
1993-94	80	74	83	83	**KS1** Standards rising though KS2 still lags behind. Considerable variation between schools in curriculum planning. Local area work now a strong feature but distant places poor. Lack of specialist geographical knowledge noted as a problem. **KS3** Most departments have KS3 schemes of work but complexity of Order still causing problems, especially for assessment. Failure to integrate geographical skills. Reliance on one textbook causes problems for some.
1994-95	80	80	80+	80+	**KS1/2** Geography still under-represented in many schools although distinct geography units appearing at KS2. Poor planning/lack of subject knowledge hinder progress. **KS3** Improvements in curriculum planning result in rising standards. But still problems with assessment. 1/10 lessons taught by non-specialists.

Figure 1: Implementation of the 1991 Geography National Curriculum: the first four years.

primary schools planning for the GNC (Naish, 1992) confirms the great variability in approaches in the early planning period. Ofsted reports found that the GNC presented considerable challenges, especially for the predominantly non-specialist primary teacher. Although by the end of the period standards of achievement and quality of teaching were found to be satisfactory or better in over 80% lessons, and this was a considerable improvement compared with a base of about 25% in the mid-1980s (DES, 1989a), further progress was being hindered by poor curriculum planning and lack of subject knowledge. While physical topics and skills were being addressed individually, many schools did not understand the need to integrate teaching across all ATs. As Keith Lloyd, HMI, reported in *Primary Geographer*:

> 'the three-dimensional conceptual model, with its dimensions of places, skills and themes, each making a contribution to the work, has not been well understood by many primary teachers. Consequently, skills are often taught in isolation and without the context of place studies; and coverage of ATs 4 and 5 (human and environmental geography) is uneven' (1994, p. 7).

In the subject reports for 1994-95 one conclusion was that 'most schools meet the Statutory Requirements for National Curriculum Geography in terms of documenting their intentions, but not always in more detailed implementation' (Ofsted, 1996a, p. 12). It seems that limited curriculum coverage was being achieved in primary schools rather than extensive curriculum interpretation. The role of the geography co-ordinator, not clearly identified in every school by 1995, was considered by Ofsted to be a vital factor in improving this situation.

Evidence for secondary schools shows a similar picture, though secondary teachers started from the supportive base of existing subject departments. Despite this, some schools did not plan an overall curriculum for the first few years but developed schemes of work for each term and year group, as the national curriculum worked its way through. Standards of work did improve steadily throughout the period with 80% lessons being judged satisfactory or better in 1994-95 as compared with 66% in 1991-92. According to Ofsted, weak areas in the early years were the development of place studies and of good assessment practice, both aspects which demanded a departure from previous practice. The Ofsted report on *The First Year 1991-92* (1993a) noted that the poorest quality of geography tended to be found in departments that had perceived the teacher's role in narrow terms as delivering the specifically defined content. Invariably such practice was characterised by focusing almost exclusively on ATs, neglecting the PoS and failing to consider any overall objectives for the course. Some departments relied almost exclusively on one textbook (in particular Waugh and Bushell, 1991) which offered comprehensive coverage of the AT requirements.

For the weaker primary and secondary schools, then, curriculum coverage seemed to be the prevailing philosophy – a classic response, perhaps, to a 'readerly' NC text. The NCC's own monitoring exercise made it clear that the structural problems of the Order were more to blame than the detail (NCC, 1992).

However, from the very beginning of implementation, there were strong indications that the geography subject community was promoting, and some teachers were attempting to implement, a more 'writerly' response to the 1991 Order. The GA explicitly took the line of recognising the structural faults but offering compensatory support so that teachers could 'make the most of the national curriculum' (Rawling, 1991c). Articles (e.g. Robinson, 1992) and GA publications (e.g. Rawling, 1992b; Fry and Schofield, 1993) exhorted teachers to adapt and develop the Order. Schofield, introducing the publication *Teachers' Experiences of National Curriculum Geography in Year 7*, stated that in his view it was essential that teachers 'make it work in line with advances in geographical education that have been made since the 1960s' – though he recognised that this was 'an immense task' (Fry and Schofield, 1993, p. 1) which would be made easier if structural amendments were made to the Geography Order. The DES Grants for Education Support and Training (GEST), available for foundation subjects from 1992, helped to increase LEA provision. These courses had to be targeted specifically on training teachers to 'deliver' the national curriculum and the GA attempted to co-ordinate and enhance the inevitably wide range in course quality. The GA Conferences of 1992, 1993 and 1994 each had a strong focus on presenting good past practice as an aid to implementing NC geography at all key stages, with particular support offered for primary teachers (see e.g. De Villiers, 1992, 1993, 1994, 1995). Articles in *Primary Geographer* and *Teaching Geography* between 1991 and 1995 show a strong emphasis on curriculum planning. The Ofsted reports for the first four years of GNC (1993a,b, 1995, 1996a,b) reinforced the value of this approach. The common factor in schools where high quality geography was found was that teachers had perceived the need to impose their own planning approach to compensate for the problems of the Order. In primary schools, it was suggested that the best teaching brought together work on all ATs 'good lessons are planned to develop skills and understanding within an increasing framework of knowledge in the study of places and themes' (Ofsted, 1996a, p. 12). The conclusion was that 'if the teaching of geography is to make consistent improvement, schools need to pay greater attention to providing guidelines for teachers and schemes of work from reception to year 6' (Ofsted, 1996a, p. 13). In secondary schools there was a similar need (identified by Ofsted) for curriculum thinking and for 'detailed discussions within departments, allowing geography specialists to contribute towards a team approach and reach a fully understood rationale and shared objectives' (1993a, p. 15). Good secondary practice, according to Ofsted was characterised by the preparation of curriculum plans for the whole key stage, making clear the integrated nature of places, themes and skills and 'having specific objectives in mind, usually in terms of key ideas, skills and attitudes' (1993a, p. 15).

Assessment was generally a weak feature in both primary and secondary schools 1991-95, but as with curriculum planning generally, schools' approaches to assessment showed a similar range from 'readerly' to 'writerly' interpretations. The best practice was found where primary schools and secondary departments had planned assessment tasks as an integral part of learning, including a variety of tests and tasks from which to gain evidence and concentrating on obtaining an overall view of the pupil's level in geography. This kind of curriculum-led approach was rare in the early years, more common reactions were either to make no reference to SoA at all, or to attempt to assess and record every SoA, these two representing 'the extremes of indifference and over-complexity in meeting NC requirements' (quote from HMI Wales report, 1993). A survey of KS3 teachers in South Wales and South East England, undertaken in 1992-93 by Daugherty and Lambert (1994), revealed that the existence of formal assessment arrangements (planned KS3 national tests and formally reported teacher assessment) had resulted in a tension for teachers between the internal formative purposes of assessment, previously promoted by the curriculum projects, and the newly imposed demands of external accountability. Daugherty and Lambert found that, despite some advice from SEAC (1992b) which encouraged geography teachers to use day-to-day assessment, most teachers were concentrating on the formal high stakes assessment purpose with an inevitable detrimental feedback onto the quality of teaching and learning experienced. As Desmond Nuttall explained:

> 'You cannot combine formative, summative and evaluative purposes in the same assessment system and expect them all to function unaffected by each other. By making the stakes so high we are making sure that the evaluative function predominates and that the pressure for comparability and rigid systems of moderation that will make the system as cheat-proof as possible, will drive out good formative practice and the facilitating conditions that allow pupils to put forward their best performance' (Nuttall, 1989, quoted in Lambert 1996, p. 276).

A KS3 research project undertaken by Margaret Roberts into curriculum planning (1995) extended understanding of what was happening in secondary schools. Roberts undertook a small-scale survey of three secondary schools in South Yorkshire, chosen for their distinctive pre-national curriculum philosophies. She found that differences in implementation were strongly linked to departmental philosophy and previous experience. Thus the department which believed the curriculum to be most concerned with transmitting content found least adjustment to make with the content-based Geography Order. Conversely, the other two, concerned more with the curriculum as a framework of ideas and skills on the one hand, or a process of pupil development on the other hand, made major efforts to retain their distinctive approaches, despite an apparently alien philosophy. Daugherty and Lambert (see above) found a similar relationship between pre-NC approach and post-NC implementation style. All in all, as Roberts summarised:

> 'deeply held beliefs about what it is to teach and learn are persistent. In these three schools, teachers' and students' roles have remained the same. Teachers frame the new curriculum according to the ways they have learned to frame the old curriculum' (1995, p. 203).

Although there is no direct research evidence for primary geography practice, the work undertaken during the first phase of the PACE Project (Primary Assessment Curriculum and Experience, an ESRC funded project based at the University of Bristol) seems to indicate a similar general conclusion. Pollard *et al.* (1994) suggest that on the basis of research in primary schools (KS1 particularly), it was apparent that the demands of a highly prescriptive subject-based National Curriculum led to considerable tensions and challenges for primary teachers, steeped in a non-subject-based 'developmental tradition'. The PACE data showed that primary teachers found it necessary to move towards a greater degree of subject teaching. Ofsted (1996a) confirms that discrete blocks of geography were more common by 1994-95 especially in KS2. Teachers felt inhibited in their planning by a greater number of external and knowledge constraints. However, many teachers worked hard to ensure that older cherished beliefs about curriculum and teaching/learning were retained. As Pollard *et al.* explain, they sought to ensure that the new practices (i.e. the national curriculum requirements), 'support rather than undermine their long-standing professional commitments' (1994, p. 227). Ofsted's list of good practice for primary geography teaching (1998b) – emphasising the existence of curriculum planning, the need to build on pupils' previous experiences, and the transformation of key ideas and skills into activities suitable for the age group – all seem to show that for geography, high quality work in the 1991-95 period was strongly linked with the kind of residual professionalism described by PACE.

The experience of implementing the 1991 GNC seems to confirm that the nature of the policy text is only one factor in explaining what happens in classrooms. The constraints of the national curriculum were very real, as Ofsted evidence reveals. However, also important are a whole range of other factors, as Bowe and Ball with Gold suggest (1992) in relation to secondary teachers. These include the past experience of teachers (their histories), the skills and background of members of the department (their capacities), the strongly held views of the department (their commitments) and the school contextual factors (contingencies) such as staffing and facilities. In primary schools the evidence suggests that it was whole-school philosophy and the existence of some geographical expertise, and in secondary schools departmental values and past innovation histories (i.e. in both cased teachers' commitments, capacities and histories) which helped teachers to translate rather than just cover the Geography Order. This seems to be in accord with the Bowe and Ball with Gold conclusions that 'high capacity, high commitment and a history of innovation may provide a basis for a greater sense of autonomy and "writerliness" with regard to policy texts' (1992, p. 118). Effectively, in the 1991-95 period, school-based curriculum development was 'hanging on', having given some teachers the ability to cope in their own way with the changed context of a prescriptive and badly structured national curriculum.

Implementation 1995-2000 (see Figures 2 and 3)

After 1995, the Dearing reviewed geography curriculum provided a much simplified and more flexible framework for curriculum development, a fact which the geography community tried hard to publicise. The April 1995 issues of *Primary Geographer* and *Teaching Geography* both contained a series of articles launching the curriculum and encouraging teachers to be more creative about implementation. In the years that followed, the geography community focused its efforts on support for this improved curriculum. Two GA Handbooks dealt comprehensively with curriculum planning, teaching/learning and resources for secondary (Bailey and Fox, 1996) and primary teachers (Carter, 1998). The GA launched an impressive programme of guidance and support, especially through its publications and journals. GA conferences began explicitly to provide a primary curriculum day, a secondary curriculum day and a geography-focused day and, from 1999, professional development pathways were offered through the conference programme. In 1993, an official annual Primary Geography Conference was also established and the RGS-IBG annual teachers' conference offered extra support for secondary teachers in raising quality at KS3, GCSE and A-level. As Chapter 5 explained (page 72), a range of publications from SCAA and, after 1997, QCA, also provided curriculum and assessment guidance with a strong progressive educational slant and compensation for national curriculum deficiencies (e.g. in promoting geographical enquiry). To support the second revision of the national curriculum (1998-99) QCA, jointly with the DfEE Standards and Effectiveness Unit, produced schemes of work for all NC subjects apart from mathematics and English. These are optional materials, designed to exemplify planning at long-, medium- and short-term. For geography, the KS1/2 guidance was available in time to be of use with the Dearing 1995 curriculum (QCA/DfEE, 1998) though the update and the KS3 pack only came out in 2000 (QCA/DfEE, 2000).

One of the most notable effects of the simplified Order and the improved support was an increase in the visibility of primary geography, at least in the first three years (1995-98) of the revised Order.

(a) (b)

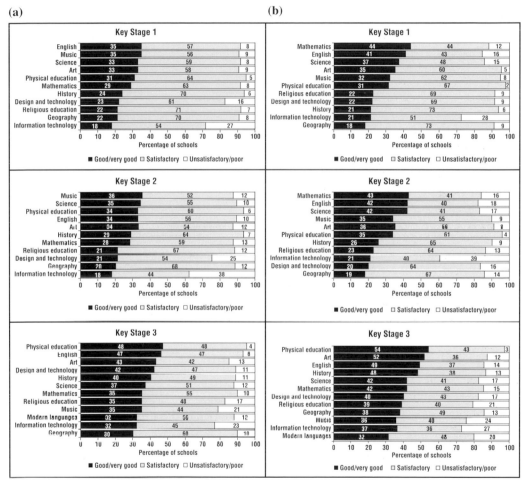

Figure 2: Progress and achievement of pupils by subject at key stages 1, 2 and 3:
(a) 1996-97, and (b) 1999-2000. Source: Ofsted Annual Reports.

Notes: 1. Due to changes in the inspection framework, the data is not exactly comparable for the periods. 1996-97 and 1999-2000. 1996-97 *progress* was defined as 'the gains pupils make in knowledge, skills and understanding' judged by lesson observations and written work, pupil interviews, test results. 1999-2000 *achievement* was defined as 'how well pupils achieve taking account of progress they have made and other relevant factors', especially levels of attainment on entry. 2. Percentages refer to percentages of schools having full inspections and that the figures have been rounded up so may not add up to 100%. 3. The rank order of subjects for 1999-2000 is based on the 'very good' grades, although they are not shown separately from 'good'.

(a) (b)

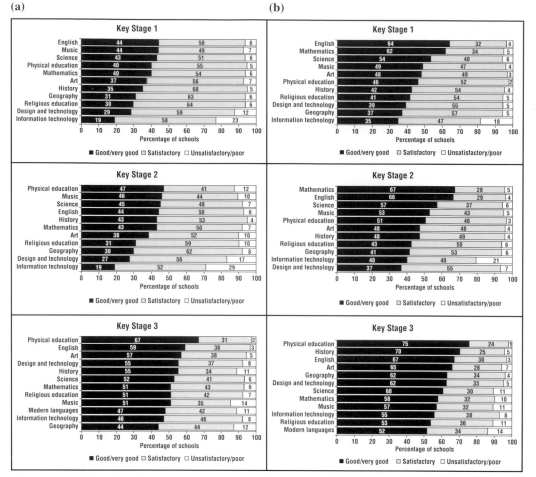

Figure 3: Quality of teaching at key stages 1, 2 and 3: (a) 1996-97, and (b) 1999-2000.
Source: Ofsted Annual Reports.

Note: 1. Percentages refer to percentages of schools having full inspections and the figures have been rounded up so may not add up to 100%.

The Review of Primary Schools in England 1994-98 commented that:

'at the beginning of the review period, many teachers were confused by the content and complexity of the initial Geography Order, and this was visible in the quality of work. The revised Order, simpler in structure and reduced in content, has allowed many schools to devise a scheme of work with a clearer focus' (Ofsted, 1999a, pp. 120-1).

GA primary members reached a peak in 1997-98, a clear sign of this increased interest in the subject, although, not surprisingly, the continued rise was halted after 1998 when the Secretary of State lifted the requirement for study of the geography PoS in primary schools. The achievement of pupils showed a steady improvement (Figure 2). The grading system in 1996 was the same as that used in 2000. However, because of changes to the inspection framework 'standards' were observed until 1995-96, 'progress' of pupils was being observed in 1996-97, while pupil 'achievement' was the measure 1999-2000. The data are not therefore strictly comparable for the 1996-97 and 1999-2000 period, but it is possible to pick out the general trends (Figures 1 and 2). By 1999-2000 pupils' achievement was deemed to be satisfactory or better in 91% schools at KS1 and 86% schools at KS2.

The Ofsted Review of Primary Education 1993-98 noted that quality of teaching (Figure 3) had also improved – 'in KS1 and 2, teaching is now good in one third of schools and satisfactory in most of the rest; a steady improvement in recent years' (Ofsted, 1999a, p. 120).

For KS3, Peter Smith, HMI and National Adviser for Geography, explained that secondary geography teachers had 'certainly benefited from the changes brought about by the Dearing Review' (1997b, p. 26). Individual yearly Ofsted reports (Figure 1) note improvements in curriculum planning, a gradual increase in progress made by pupils and steady improvements in quality of teaching. According to the geography report in Review of Secondary Schools in England 1993-97 (Ofsted, 1998b), the percentage of schools in which standards of achievement were good increased from 50% to 52% between 1993-94 and 1995-96, while the percentage of schools in which quality of teaching was good grew from 41% to 44% (and to 50% 1997-98). Reports for the 1996-97 to 1999-2000 period (though collected on a different basis) reveal that the overall trend of slow improvement has continued (Figures 1, 2 and 3).

However, these generally positive trends are replaced by a more disappointing picture when the most recent period 1998-2000 is brought fully into the picture and comparisons are made with other subjects. Pupils' achievement grading (Figure 2) and the quality of teaching (Figure 3) are not rising as fast as might be expected, compared to other subjects in primary schools. For both KS1 and 2, geography was second to last for pupils' achievement in the early period and last in 1999-2000. The Ofsted Annual Report for 1999-2000 stated that 'much work in geography is satisfactory but not enough is good or very good' (Ofsted, 2001, para 13, p. 26). For quality of teaching, the picture was also less than satisfactory for KS1 and 2, with geography ranking near the bottom of the table at eighth, ninth or tenth for both dates. The Review of Primary Education 1994-98 stated quite clearly that 'Although much geography teaching is now satisfactory there is less good teaching than in most other subjects taken by the same teacher', and what is more the quality of teaching is 'often variable within a school (often between key stages) as well as between schools' (Ofsted, 1999a, p. 120). The main reasons continually given by Ofsted for this poor performance are the lack of subject knowledge and consequent failure of teachers to understand the requirements of the subject PoS or to plan effectively. Targeted in-service training for geography co-ordinators was consistently suggested as a response. It was noted that 'where geography teachers have attended local education authority GEST courses or used other specialist consultants, there has been a noticeable and, at times, substantial improvement in planning and a better understanding of NC requirements' (Ofsted, 1999a, p. 120).

More significantly, however, the Ofsted findings suggest some of the deeper reasons for this lacklustre performance, compared with other subjects (Figures 2 and 3). Inspection evidence increasingly reveals what a common-sense view might suggest, i.e. that geography teaching is being adversely affected by the high-profile and time-consuming curriculum provision for Literacy and Numeracy. 'In some schools there are signs of a loss of depth and breadth of the curriculum, for example in design and technology and geography, in part as a result of a loss of time' (Ofsted, 2001, para 29, p. 29). This still does not adequately explain why geography consistently fails to rank as highly as history in primary teaching. Further evidence from the QCA Primary Monitoring Seminar, March 2001, and the Ofsted Report 2001 suggest that geography is frequently blocked against other subjects, so that it is taught only on alternate half terms or terms. Thus, pupils may suffer long gaps in their exposure to geography. In many schools, not only is less geography being taught but, what is probably just as significant, less geography is observed being taught. The regulations for a Section 10 short inspection do not require that the teaching of all foundation subjects must be observed as long as documentation and planning are seen. Informal evidence gleaned in some schools in South West England (by Margaret Mackintosh, teacher trainer and editor of *Primary Geographer*) revealed that when there was a Section 10 inspection, many schools and teachers preferred to teach history (with its well-defined study units) rather than geography (which demanded more interpretation). Schools adjusted the inspection week timetable accordingly. The low priority given to geography in many schools is, not surprisingly, being revealed in an inadequate time allowance, a low profile given to the post of geography co-ordinator and, consequently, a generally mediocre rather than high quality provision made for the subject.

The situation for KS3 geography is equally disappointing. The Review of Secondary Schools 1993-97 stated that 'KS3 is the weakest area of secondary geography teaching' (Ofsted, 1998b, para 7.6), although standards rose into KS4 and post-16. It was explained that, although there is a good deal of satisfactory work and some high quality investigative activities, overall geography compares unfavourably with most other subjects when standards, progress and quality of teaching are examined. Figures 2 and 3 provide an overview of this situation. The 1999-2000 Annual Report (Ofsted, 2001) shows a welcome improvement in quality of teaching, with geography moving up the ranking of subjects at KS3 (Figure 3), though in terms of pupil achievement (Figure 2), it still remains in the lower part of the table. For both quality of teaching and achievement, geography consistently performs less well than history (Figures 2 and 3), a subject with which it apparently shares similarities of status and resourcing in secondary schools. The reasons given, in all recent reports, for geography's mediocre performance include inadequate time available for geography in many schools; difficulties experienced by the significant number of non-specialist teachers (1 in 6 noted in Ofsted, 1998b); and a continuing failure to use assessment effectively to support teaching and learning. A stronger departmental focus on shared curriculum planning and creative teaching/ learning strategies is frequently offered as a strategy to address these problems. It should be noted that, despite these concerns, the geography KS3 teacher assessment results (see Appendix 2), with 63% pupils reaching level 5+, show remarkable consistency with other foundation subjects. However, this may only reveal the inadequacy of using the level descriptions for anything other than broad comparisons. As with the KS1/2 situation, one senses that behind the specific details lies a deeper sense that all is not well with KS3 geography. Many commentators (Dowgill, 1999; Rawling, 1999c, 2001a) have suggested that the key to raising quality and standards in secondary geography lies with creative and inspiring geography teachers ready to take on the new flexibility provided by the 2000 revisions. Reading between the lines of the recent Ofsted reports, however, it seems that there is no such spirit abroad. This situation may be both a partial cause and an effect of the declining candidature noted for GCSE and A-level geography. Certainly, given the significance of year 9 (14 year olds) choice of subjects for the 14-16 curriculum and beyond, geography's apparent inability to stimulate pupils to achieve higher standards, compared with other subjects, must be seen as a danger signal for the future.

Overall, despite the steady improvements, the overall picture is one of satisfactory coverage of the NC, not one of inspiring and imaginative teaching of geography. At its best, as the pages of *Primary Geographer* and *Teaching Geography* show, and as the 'good' lessons observed by Ofsted reveal, geographical work based on the 1995 Order can be stimulating and relevant to pupils' lives. The curriculum for 2000 provides even greater opportunities in this respect. But in large numbers of schools, if Ofsted is correct, the work is neither particularly well-taught nor inspiring pupils to achieve. In both primary and secondary schools, the direct result of curriculum policy, particularly in the years since 1997, has been to reduce the commitment of schools to geography and to diminish the opportunities for enhancing teacher capabilities. Even the past curriculum development experience which Roberts identified in secondary schools in 1994-95 may be hard to find still in existence, as older staff move on and the GNC itself becomes the past experience of most currently employed geography teachers. School-based curriculum development is still only 'hanging on' in 2000 despite the improving curriculum framework and the generally high level of support from the subject community.

The changing context for professional activities

The way in which teachers carry out their work (in this case geography teachers implementing the GNC) depends on the way they perceive their role as professionals. Prior to 1988, teachers of secondary geography had developed a relatively clear conception of what being professional meant. In a 1996 paper (Rawling), it was explained that the curriculum projects, in particular, had encouraged teachers to take on the full creative process of reviewing, designing and evaluating their own curricula from the base of broadly framed project guidelines. Five conditions were put forward as crucial to teacher professionalism and school-based curriculum development and all of these involved a strong element of trust:

1. Recognition and respect was awarded to all levels of curriculum planning in the education system.
2. Co-operative work with other teachers, within and between schools, was considered essential.
3. New developments drew on and recognised the value of existing good practice in the subject.
4. Curriculum content, teaching and learning and assessment were recognised as integral parts of the curriculum system.
5. Teacher development, including in-service professional development opportunities, was seen as an essential part of curriculum change.

It was assumed, mistakenly, by geography educators, that whatever the criticisms occurring of the particular project content, this kind of professionalism would be ideally suited to a period of national curriculum change (Naish, 1980) and that time would be built into the system for reflection and critical appraisal. This was not to be. Not only did the prescriptive NC framework seem to negate teacher involvement, but many of the other measures initiated by the Education Reform Act (ERA) ran counter to this wider concept of professionalism. The general ethos of ERA stressed the responsibilities of individual schools and teachers to deliver the detailed requirements. Other parts of ERA (e.g. local management of schools, opting out, city technology colleges) had the effect of dismantling many LEA structures which had given teachers the necessary support to work in curriculum groups. Another blow was given initially by the formation of Ofsted (1992) resulting in a powerful emphasis on accountability and inspection, which also diffused to LEAs. The number of geography-specific advisers progressively declined during the 1990s and their role has become increasingly managerial and inspectorial rather than concerned with advice and curriculum development. A NCC INSET Task Group reported in 1991 that 'the national curriculum has initiated a major curriculum development exercise in geography. The publication of the Statutory Order is only the first step, the follow-up is crucial' (NCC, 1991b, p. 1). It went on to suggest the establishment of local and regional support structures providing opportunities for teacher interaction and 'shared interpretation of the geography national curriculum'. Not surprisingly, given that Trevor Higginbottom, a former project director, chaired this group, this sounded too much like a 1970s style solution and the report was shelved by NCC. The GA did establish a regional support network from 1992, comprising seven regions each with a co-ordinator and a small budget (Rawling, 1992c, 1994). The DES showed considerable interest in supporting this venture in 1991-92 but eventually, after several meetings with the GA and a change in personnel at the Teachers' Branch, DES decided to limit its support to encouragement rather than funding. Between 1992 and 2000, the GA regional network has provided valuable support, particularly in the north-west and south-east regions, but its effectiveness has always been hindered by lack of resources. 'Dissemination and take-up' (as it was called in the 1970s) has never featured strongly in the thinking of any of the official agencies trying to establish the NC in the 1990s, although Schools Council publications evaluating the work of curriculum projects in the 1970s revealed the importance of this phase in any new curriculum development (Schools Council, 1974).

After 1995, despite the rhetoric about flexibility and the role of schools and teachers in implementing the curriculum, the focus has remained on individual schools and, with the Labour government after

1997, the emphasis has focused on performance against an increasing range of externally and internally set targets (Bell, 1999). Performance is inspected and checked by Ofsted and publicly disseminated by means of league tables. As many commentators have noted, such a system elevates a narrow view of teaching for performance above a broader view of teachers' work. In this situation, the old-style in-service training opportunities stressing teacher co-operation and teamwork become less relevant, the emphasis changing to a 'hard-nosed' swopping of 'tips for teachers' or learning how to address the latest statutory requirements. Even the Schemes of Work, though undoubtedly serving to raise the profile of the subject and to incorporate good practice, run the risk of being accepted uncritically as the 'government approved' interpretation of the curriculum. Early findings from QCA monitoring of the 2000 NC show that in the relatively small proportion of primary schools where geography has a significant presence, the tendency is to use the Schemes of Work as a 'ready-made' answer (QCA monitoring seminar, March 2001). At least this ensures a geography presence in some primary schools and others may follow, but it does not necessarily promote teacher development.

These changes are subtle but pervasive. For geography, for example, not only are in-service education opportunities less frequent at LEA and national level, but those that exist tend to focus on the technicalities of delivering or assessing a national requirement, rather than exploring exciting ways of teaching and learning or finding out about new developments in the academic subject. An analysis of articles appearing in *Primary Geographer* and *Teaching Geography* 1989-99 suggests that coping with national requirements (literacy, ICT, key skills, KS3 tests, inspections) is the main priority for teachers. This seemed to be confirmed at KS3 by the results of a GA survey carried out in 1996-97 (Thomas and Grimwade, 1997) which gave IT as the top priority for over 50% of the 274 schools surveyed. Marsden carried out an analysis of journal articles for 1989-96 which showed that, contrary to intentions, the NC framework has not fostered cross-phase liaison and co-operation in geography:

'Whilst the NC's stress on interdependence of geographical skills, places and themes offers a potentially helpful framework across the key stages, it would appear that a trend has evolved in which places (particularly at local scale) are emphasised in the primary phase and themes, often issue-based, in the secondary phase' (Marsden, 1997b, p. 70).

In addition, Marsden found that secondary schools generally have under-expectations of primary children's knowledge in geography but over-expectations in terms of the methods and techniques appropriate. All in all, the separate pressures affecting primary and secondary schools have resulted in a continuation rather than a reduction in the primary-secondary divide. One can postulate that one reason might be the decline in the kind of outgoing professionalism necessary to make cross-phase co-operation work.

Redefining professionalism: the wider context

A number of writers (Fullan, 1991; Helsby and McCullogh, 1997a; Coldron and Smith, 1999; Ball, 1999; Quicke, 2000) have noted that there seems to have been a re-definition of the concept of professionalism taking place during the 1990s. According to Lawton (1994), distrust and suspicion of educationalists was intense among the New Right and provided the motive force for many of the curriculum reforms of the early 1990s. The mid-1990s saw a relaxation of this approach for more pragmatic reasons with the Dearing reviewed curriculum recognising the need to involve teachers and schools more directly in implementation, though still within the confines of a strong national curriculum and assessment framework. Under New Labour, despite the rhetoric of professionalism and partnership which permeates documents like *Excellence in Schools* (see DfEE, 1997, para 20), it is clear from the emphasis on targets, performance indicators and implementation strategies that the government holds a quite restrictive view of professionalism. Ball, for example, referred to the 'managerial models and techniques which are being used to redesign teaching practices [and which] draw upon the low trust, Fordist model of regulation and control' (1999, p. 202). He found no evidence in government documentation of a clear conception of teaching and learning, but rather a simplistic input-output model which involves: defining the problem (e.g. poor literacy skills, poor performance at 16+); outlining the skills/knowledge and strategies needed to address this (e.g. the Literacy Strategy, school improvement and target setting); and then establishing procedures to check for achievement (e.g. national literacy targets, GCSE scores and league tables, all backed up by Ofsted inspection). In this model, the actual learning that takes place in the classroom and the teacher's role in developing this constitute a 'black box ... an absent presence, out of sight in this policy panopticon' (Ball, 1999, p. 201). Ball's analysis coincides with that of others (e.g. Quicke, 2000) by identifying a more bureaucratic/technical role now required of teachers as opposed to the more creative professional role previously considered appropriate. In the way that the black box is recognised as crucial to improving quality, Ball's work also confirms research into assessment practice undertaken by the Assessment Reform Group (Black and Wiliam, 1998; Assessment Reform Group, 1999).

It is easy to suggest how teachers of geography at KS1-3 might be affected by this changed definition of professionalism. The inputs are the national curriculum PoS (still perceived as restrictive, even though they have changed), the Schemes of Work and, to some extent, the extra demands placed on all subjects by literacy, numeracy and ICT requirements. The outputs are the necessity to produce an end-of-key-stage level for geography (particularly at KS3 where it is reported) and, powerfully in the background, the eventual need to reach school GCSE targets. As a result of national dictat, schools also impose their own output targets on teachers and departments of geography. A recent article in *Teaching Geography*, while very helpful to secondary teachers in picking their way through the minefield of requirements, information and advice provided to schools (Thompson, 2000a), nevertheless revealed the complexity of target setting and the increasing pressures now placed on subject teachers. It is not surprising that the average teacher of geography now has little creative time or energy to focus inside the black box of classroom planning and teaching/learning strategies. As Ball explains it: 'inside the black box, teachers are caught between the imperatives of prescription and the disciplines of performance' (1999, p. 202). A number of new initiatives seem to provide an opportunity to break into this black box. Geography is now (from April 2001) included in the second phase of QCA's Creativity Across the Curriculum Project, in which a small amount of funding is available to work with schools on identifying the subject's contribution to developing pupil's creativity. Jointly with history, geography has also been allocated funding for a small scale QCA curriculum development project investigating the contribution and future of both subjects at 3-19. The subject community is being involved and both pieces of work have the potential to recommend changes in classroom practice. Much larger sums of money are being put into the Department for Education and Skills (DfES) KS3 Strategy, managed by the Standards and Effectiveness Unit (SEU). This strategy has several strands (see Chapter 8, page 129) but one is the Teaching and Learning in the Foundation Subject Programme (TLF) being piloted from autumn 2000, before going national in 2002. It focuses on aspects such as planning and sequencing effective teaching and developing thinking skills. Geography departments are currently involved in the pilot work. All these initiatives are at an early stage and it remains to be seen how compatible and coherent the separate QCA and DfES initiatives will be, and what impact they will eventually make on geography classrooms.

It might be argued that the pressures on teachers of geography are not as great as for the core subjects. After all, it is English and mathematics KS1/2 test scores which are given priority, and for which David Blunkett threatened to resign as Secretary of State if targets were not reached, and it is English and mathematics which remain the focus of interest at KS3/4. Science, D&T, MFL and ICT can claim second rank because of their privileged position at KS4. However, in the very existence of such a curriculum hierarchy lies another blow to the professionalism of teachers of geography. Not only has professional identity been redefined to a 'targets and training for performance' model, but the targets and performances most valued do not seem to include geography. Arguably, one of the biggest factors currently affecting the professionalism of teachers of geography is the declining status of the subject in the school curriculum. Quicke argued that subject disciplines function as sources of power and identity in the school situation and that, using national signals about power and status, 'the school constructs teacher identities, giving them certain kinds of selves which can be readily managed by the school' (2000, p. 309). For teachers of mathematics and English, the selves so defined occupy a prominent position in the school hierarchy for pupils as well as teachers, but for geography the subject's identity has been progressively weakened (for primary schools, almost as soon as its place in the NC was confirmed). A graphic illustration of the consequences may be seen in Figure 4. This compares the ranking for English, a favoured core subject, and for geography, a more marginal foundation subject, in terms of quality of teaching in primary schools over the 1994-2000 period. Despite a common base in 1994-95 (fifth and sixth in rank for teaching quality), differences in performance and rank are striking by 1997-98 and 1999-2000, with geography retreating to the mediocrity its less favoured status ensures. Quicke (2000) also suggested that government strategies are under-estimating the importance of subject cultures in schools. The focus on basic literacy and numeracy and on generic skills may lead to an inadequate attention being given to subject-based professionalism. For school geography this could be the crucial factor in reviving professionalism. Interestingly, this same point about subject focus seems already to have been recognised in higher education where subject centres and networks are a central idea in the strategies promoted and funded by the Higher Education Funding Council for England (National Subject Centre for Geography, Earth and Environmental Sciences, GEES, 2001).

Subject	KS1 and 2 1994-95	KS1 and 2 1997-98	KS1 1999-2000	KS2
English	5 of 11	1 of 11	1 of 11	2 of 11
Geography	6 of 11	9 of 11	8 of 11	9 of 11

Figure 4: Subject ranking for teaching quality of English and geography at key stages 1 and 2: 1994-95, 1997-98 and 1999-2000. Source: Ofsted, 1999a.

From the high point of 1987 when geography was accepted as a national curriculum subject, the 1990s saw the gradual dismantling of the broad entitlement curriculum and the consequent downgrading of geography. In primary schools, geography's position has progressively been marginalised. The national inspection regime, national tests and the introduction of the national literacy and numeracy strategies have all reinforced the curriculum hierarchy. The latest Ofsted evidence (2001) confirms that the frequency and continuity of geographical work has suffered as a result. Not only that, but a link is made between the low priority awarded to geography in recent years and the adverse effects this has had on leadership of the subject and availability of in-service opportunities for teachers. At secondary level, successive structural decisions about KS4, the introduction of general national vocational courses and the establishment of citizenship KS3/4 are all combining to diminish access to geography, as the recent figures for GCSE and A-level seem to show (see Chapter 7, Figure 2, page 105). There are also hints of a declining commitment to geography, in the continuing Ofsted concern about use of non-specialists at KS3 and a need for in-service support. Further signs of status problems affecting the entire geography education system are apparent in the problems over teacher supply and the beginnings of a decline in applications to geography degree courses. There is evidence of 'curriculum distress' throughout the geography education system.

What is emerging is a picture of professionalism in crisis with teachers of geography not only sharing the professional tensions affecting all subject teachers, but also being exposed to a relentless downgrading of their subject's value and meaning in society. Might it be suggested that this situation may be the root cause of the lacklustre performance revealed in Ofsted data, despite the beneficial changes in curriculum and support? Ball suggested (1994) that we take up the positions constructed for us within policies. In a later article, Ball questioned whether what is being measured (in terms of core subject performance data and GCSE league tables) is really what is needed. He referred to the 'increased emphasis on preparation for the tests' and within these subjects 'the adaptation of pedagogies and curricula to the requirements of test performance' (1999, p. 204). As geographers, we might also ask whether what is not being measured is being undervalued in the school curriculum. Despite all the New Labour rhetoric of environmental concern, local and national identities and globalisation, geography – one of the subjects best able to deliver these – may be being reduced to a marginal offering, a 'bit part' on the wider educational stage.

Aspects of professionalism	Continuum of characteristics of professionalism	
	Fully-developed professionalism (reflexive practitioner?) ←——→	Restricted professionalism (skilled technician?)
How the teacher interacts with pupils	■ focusing on the needs of individuals and how to develop each to own potential ■ focusing on variety of teaching and learning strategies to fit each situation	■ focusing on the needs of the group to bring as many as possible to the required level/standard ■ focusing on transmission/direct teaching to ensure required detailed content is 'delivered'
How the teacher interacts with other teachers	■ working in co-operation, emphasis on team work at school and subject level ■ professional development activities focus on new ideas, creativity and reflecting on own classrooms	■ working as an individual teacher and/or subject department in competition with those in other schools ■ professional development focuses on 'tips for teaching' and how to manage and 'deliver' national curriculum/ assessment requirements
How the teacher values him/herself professionally	■ gaining enjoyment and satisfaction from finding out about new developments in educational, research and in society ■ seeing out of school hobbies and interests as feeding into personal development and professional creativity	■ finding no relevance in and/or time to follow up new developments in the wider educational context ■ seeing school and 'outside school' as separate existences with no beneficial overlap or creative interchange
How the teacher interacts with the wider subject community	■ participating in interchange and updating activities with subject colleagues at all levels from higher education to primary education ■ having an interest in the subject, its character and relevance to society	■ seeing the subject in school and in higher education as being separate systems and therefore no need for interchange ■ accepting the national requirements as the definition of the subject and seeing no need for debate
How the teacher interacts with the state and policy-making	■ making a valued contribution to discussions about the appropriate national frameworks for the subject (need to be creative) ■ seen as a creative professional who is trusted to make decisions about subject and classroom matters	■ seen as the 'technician' trained to deliver knowledge, understanding, skills prescribed by the state (need to be competent) ■ not envisaged as needing to make important decisions about subject or pedagogy and generally not trusted to do so

Figure 5: Being professional.

Conclusion

In the final chapter of his book, *Beyond the National Curriculum,* Lawton (1996) used the terms 'empowerment' and 'professionalism' against which to assess past, present and future opportunities for curriculum development by schools. I interpret 'empowerment' to mean the existence of an enabling and integrated curriculum framework for the subject with clear opportunities for schools to participate in decision making about curriculum content, pedagogy and assessment. 'Professionalism' refers to the extent to which the work of teachers, their role in planning and the status of the subject are valued within the education system.

Chapter 5 showed that the NC framework for geography has improved substantially and, in this respect, teachers of geography at primary and secondary level are now empowered to undertake the school-based curriculum development that is required, if geography is to contribute effectively to education. However, the analysis has also shown that the evidence of implementation so far is disappointing and that the parameters of professionalism have shifted dramatically. Figure 5 proposes five aspects of 'being professional':

- How the teacher interacts with the pupils
- How the teacher interacts with other teachers
- How the teacher values him/herself professionally
- How the teacher interacts with the wider subject community
- How the teacher interacts with the state and policy-making

For each of these, a continuum is identified, ranging from the characteristics shown in fully developed professionalism to those shown in a more restricted version of professionalism. Whitty *et al.* used the terms 'reflexive practitioner' and 'skilled technician' (1998, p. 65) which seem to link directly with these descriptions. The characteristics are designed to show the end points of the continuum, not to reflect a particular situation for any one time. However, it is striking that, from the evidence of this chapter, geography teaching in the 1990s seems to have moved towards the right hand (restricted professionalism) end of the diagram. This is the case even though monitoring and inspection evidence, from QCA, Ofsted and the subject community itself seem to point to the importance of a more fully developed professionalism for achieving high quality geographical education. It seems that the unintended consequences of a decade of New Right, followed by New Labour, educational policies have been to threaten geography's identity and reduce the creative professionalism of its teachers.

7

Discourse, Debate and Decisions About the 14-19 Curriculum 1980-2000

Introduction

This chapter provides an interlude from the national curriculum, which has been the main focus of attention in the preceding chapters. For a brief period between 1988 and 1994, geography was deemed to be part of the KS4 national curriculum but this was never implemented and, after 1994, geography was confirmed as an optional subject in a dynamically changing 14-19 curriculum. One chapter cannot do justice to the detailed changes in GCSE, A-level and general national vocational qualifications (GNVQs) that have taken place since 1988 (Figure 1), so the focus here is on some key 14-19 themes, as follows:

■ The move towards a 14-19 phase as opposed to separate 14-16 and 16-19 phases

■ Increasing regulation and control of curriculum and assessment

■ The retreat of curriculum discourse and the advance of an assessment and qualification discourse

■ The development of vocational qualifications and of the academic/vocational gap

■ The search for breadth, depth and progression

It should be noted that these refer to system-wide trends, resulting from the changing social, economic and political characteristics of the 1990s and 2000s. The intention is not to critique the changes themselves – others are involved in this task (Pring, 1995; Hodgson and Spours, 1999; Ecclestone, 2000; Ainley, 2000) – but to point up the consequences of these changes for subjects in general and geography in particular. This chapter will consider each theme in turn. There are strong links back to Chapters 2, 3, 4, 5 and 6 since many of the trends apparent in 5-14 education (such as increasing central control and decline of curriculum thinking) reappear in the 14-19 curriculum. Changes in 14-19 education have also been highly significant for geography as a whole, having a direct impact on the status and characteristics of the subject 1988-2000 and, consequently, a powerful feedback effect throughout the 5-14 curriculum, higher education and the wider geography community. Chapters 9 and 10 will draw together some of these interconnections. Note that Appendix 4 may be useful as a reference for this chapter.

The move towards a single 14-19 phase of education

Twenty years ago, there was no concept of a 14-19 curriculum. The 14-16 and 16-19 phases were both distinct, each comprising a self-contained curriculum ending in a publicly recognised qualification – GCE O-level or (from 1965) the CSE for 14-16 year olds, and A-level for 16-19 year olds. The merging of O-level and CSE into a single General Certificate of Secondary Education (GCSE) examination (first examination 1988) helped to make a more coherent and inclusive 14-16 curriculum, providing a subject-based qualification accessible to most of the age cohort. After 1987, the new AS qualification (the same standard but half the content of A-level) was intended to broaden and expand

Figure 1: 14-19 policy developments with special reference to geography.

Note: Details of all documents and reports referred to here are listed in the References, pages 187-202.

Year	14-16 developments	16-19 developments
1970s and 1980s	Continuing debate about the possibility of joint 16+ exams results in 1984 announcement of the merger of O-level and CSE in the new GCSE	Continuing debate about the need for greater breadth of studies post 16 results in a range of proposals (e.g. Q/F 1969, N/F 1973, I level 1980) but no change
1982	Introduction of *Technical and Vocational Education Initiative* for 14-19 year olds	
1983		■ *Certificate of Pre-vocational Education* introduced for those 16+ students for whom A-level is not suitable ■ A-level Common Core for Geography approved for voluntary implementation by examining boards
1984	GCSE announced	DES announces new AS (half A-level content but A standard)
1985	*GCSE Criteria for Geography* published (DES/WO) and syllabus preparation begins	
1986	Teaching of new GCSE courses begins	National Council for Vocational Qualifications established to rationalise vocational developments
1987		Teaching of new AS courses begins
1988	First GCSE examinations	Higginson Report (DES) proposes five leaner thinner A-levels, to encourage breadth and analytical thinking
1989		First AS examinations
1990	(June) National Curriculum Geography Working Group Report published, presenting a KS4 programme of study as an integral part of the 5-16 curriculum	(July) Institute for Public Policy Research proposes abolishing A-level and establishing a British Baccalaureat, a single advanced diploma for a range of academic/vocational qualifications
1991	(Jan) Secretary of State (K. Clarke) announces reductions in KS4 requirements, so that geography and history become alternates and full ten-subject NC ends at 14 years	(May) White Paper *Education and Training for the 21st Century* (DoE/WO) retains A-level and establishes the three pathways (academic, general vocational and vocational) and announces GNVQs
1992	(Nov) Joint GA/Historical Association conference takes place to clarify the KS4 situation and consider action	First five GNVQs (Advanced) launched, including Leisure & Tourism (L&T)
1993	(Jan) GCSE/KS4 GNC Criteria published, and during 1993, new NC-inspired GCSE courses prepared (April) Sir Ron Dearing's NC Review established (May) Decision taken not to use NC levels for GCSE but to add A* grade (Dec) Dearing Final Report recommends: 'reduction in the subjects which all students must study as a matter of law at KS4, with immediate action on history and geography' both of which become optional	■ New Geography A/AS Subject Core, mandatory and with a tighter control of content ■ During 1993-94 Foundation and Intermediate level GNVQs also developed and after 1994 made available to schools 14-19 as well as further education post-16

continued

Year	14-16 developments	16-19 developments
1994	(Jan) Dearing proposals all approved resulting in: ■ Geography and history now optional at KS4 ■ Geography KS4/GCSE syllabuses all abandoned and new GCSE criteria prepared ■ Work on KS3 geography tests stopped and formal KS3 testing requirement removed ■ Vocational pathway introduced at KS4 and work begins on GNVQ Part One	SCAA Code of Practice for GCE and A/AS-level
1995	(March) New GCSE Criteria for geography (Sept) GNVQ Part One introduced as national pilot including L&T from 1996	(April) Sir Ron Dearing Review of 16-19 qualifications established (Sept) Teaching of new A/AS syllabuses begins
1996	Teaching of new GCSE courses begins (including humanities, integrated courses and short courses)	(March) Dearing Report *Review of Qualifications for 16-19 Year Olds* confirms three pathways; also proposes new half AS, key skills qualification, work on overarching certificates and merging of SCAA/NCVQ
1997	(May) New Labour government	New Labour government (Autumn) Consultation on 16-19 proposals (*Qualifying for Success*)
1998	(July) First examination of new geography GCSE (Sept) GNVQ Part One made available nationally in six subjects including L&T and new model for specifications (closer to GCSE/A) introduced	(April) *Qualifying for Success* reforms set under way including: ■ New three-unit AS (first half A-level) ■ Revised A-levels incorporating key skills and linear/modular routes ■ New key skills qualification ■ Development of six-unit (vocational A-levels and three-unit advanced GNVQs
1999	(October) Revised National Curriculum published, making minimal changes to KS4 – extending possibilities for dis-application of subjects, but adding citizenship as a Subject Order compulsory from 2002	(March) New A/AS subject criteria published and development of new syllabuses set under way. Pilot work on Advanced Extension award for geography
2000	(April) New GCSE Criteria and development of new GCSE courses begins (Sept) Teaching of revised national curriculum begins. Dis-application opportunities for MFL, science and D&T. Geography could gain a little (Autumn) Consultation on vocational GCSEs (formerly GNVQ Part One (F & I))	(Sept) Teaching of new A/AS geography syllabuses begins Teaching of vocational A-levels (AVCEs) begins (formerly Advanced GNVQs, now available in six and three units as well as 12 units). Travel and Tourism is the title most relevant to geography departments
2001	Introduction of Vocational GCSEs announced Preparation of specifications begins for implementation in September 2002 (Sept) Teaching of new GCSE courses begins	(June) Labour government returned for second term Estelle Morris Secretary of State in new DfES announces intention to introduce a 'graduation certificate' for school leavers Review of AS announced

A-level participation. Despite the larger numbers of non-traditional sixth-formers staying on at school after 16, both the 14-16 and 16-19 phases continued along largely similar subject-based and predominantly academic lines. Some impact was made on the curriculum as a whole by newer developments like the Technical and Vocational Education Initiative (TVEI, from 1982) and the Certificate for Pre-Vocational Education (CPVE, from 1983).

Geography, by the late 1980s, was a popular subject at both levels, attracting substantial numbers of candidates. Content changes incorporating some aspects of the so-called 'new geography' in the 1970s, and the innovative developments inspired by the geography curriculum projects 1970-88 ensured that geography was seen as a relevant and dynamic school subject at this time. Walford (2000) shows how the candidate entry for 14-16 and 16-19 examinations grew steadily in the 1970s and 1980s. By 1989, geography was fourth in rank at GCSE with 276,740 candidates and exceeded only by English language, mathematics and English literature, and it was tenth in rank at A-level with 41,671 candidates. Geography was also closely involved in the 1980s in broader initiatives, evidenced by the Geography, Schools and Industry Project (GSIP) and the GYSL TVEI-related INSET Project (GYSL-TRIST).

In 1988, with the passing of the Education Reform Act, geography's growing status seemed to be confirmed since it was identified as one of the ten foundation subjects in the new national curriculum for pupils from ages 5 to 16. The Geography Working Group planned a KS4 programme of study, assuming that virtually all pupils would study a full course, but, under pressure from the DES, it also produced a KS4 Short Course covering only a selection of the content. Ultimately, neither of these subject Orders (DES, 1991a,b) was implemented. First Kenneth Clarke (1991) decreed that geography should be an alternative to history for 14-16 year olds and then John Patten (1992) announced that KS4 geography and history would not be implemented pending the Dearing Review. Finally, despite the preparation of GCSE courses based on the highly prescriptive national curriculum, the government's approval (1994) of Sir Ron Dearing's Review recommendations confirmed the optional status of geography and history as part of the attempt to reinstate curriculum flexibility. Subsequently, geography was again optional, but this time in the context of a substantial compulsory 'core'. Schools were required to teach the national curriculum subjects of English, mathematics, science, design and technology (D&T), information technology and modern foreign languages (MFL) and also to cover elements of religious education, physical education and careers education. Depending on decisions made by schools about science (double or single) and D&T and MFL (full or short courses), some pupils, after 1994, could find that up to 70% their time was taken up with the 'core'. As a consequence, although there are examples of individual schools and LEAs where geography has continued to flourish, it seems likely that the subject is not as accessible to pupils as pre-1994. The GCSE figures seem to bear this out (Figure 2). Between 1995 and 1999, geography candidature at GCSE declined by 12.85 % whereas the total cohort of students increased by 15.34 %.

Structural changes to the national curriculum must account for some of the decline shown on Figure 2, but there are other factors (Westaway and Rawling, 2001). In the small curriculum space left for options, geography was also faced with a growing range of other NC options (e.g. history, which had suffered the same fate as geography in 1991 and 1994), non-NC options (e.g. Business Studies) and, increasingly, vocational courses. The Dearing Review recognised that 'we should see 14 as the beginning of an educational continuum from 14 to 19' (1993, para 3.18). Accepted by the government in full in 1994, the Dearing proposals effectively re-launched the NC as a 5-14 framework and set in motion a range of other developments (in particular the GNVQ Part One courses, designed specifically for 14-16 year olds) which would make the 14-19 curriculum increasingly distinct from its NC counterpart. These trends were reinforced by the Dearing 16-19 Review proposals (1996) with their emphasis on a National Qualifications Framework (Figure 3) and recognition of three distinct

GCSE				A-LEVEL			
Year	Entry	Percentage total GCSE entries	Percentage change for geography	Year	Entry	Percentage total A-level entries	Percentage change for geography
2000	251,605	4.59	-2.2	2002	?	?	?
1999	257,294	4.69	-3.1	2001	?	?	?
1998	265,573	4.96	-8.5	2000	37,112	4.80	-12.0
1997	290,201	5.36	-4.0	1999	42,181	5.40	-6.0
1996	302,298	5.98	+0.8	1998	44,881	5.70	+2.8
1995	295,229	6.34	+11.7	1997	43,641	5.60	+1.9
1994	264,224	6.30	-0.3	1996	42,786	5.69	-2.0
1993	265,123	6.70	-1.2	1995	43,426	5.99	-6.3
1992	268,235	6.55	+0.1	1994	46,339	6.35	-0.1
1991	267,931	n/a	-2.1	1993	46,399	6.37	+1.7
1990	273,624	n/a	-1.1	1992	45,603	6.25	+7.4
1989	276,740	n/a	-9.4	1991	42,446	6.10	+1.9
1988	305,575	n/a	n/a	1990	41,671	6.09	+13.8

Figure 2: GCSE and A-level geography entries 1988-2000.

Notes: a. GCSE numbers are aligned with A-level numbers two years later so that numbers within the same cohort can be easily tracked through, and b. figures include entries for England, Wales and Northern Ireland. Source: QCA/Joint Council of General Qualifications (provisional figures).

pathways after 14 – the academic, the general vocational and the vocational. These policies impacted directly on geography because those schools which took on either the pilot Part One or the full GNVQ titles found that these required 20% or 40% curriculum blocks, thus adding directly to the pressures on curriculum choice. In many schools, geography struggled and failed to maintain its position post-14 (Figure 2) despite a sound report from Ofsted for the 1993-97 period:

> 'Standards in geography at GCSE and A-level have improved steadily since the beginning of the inspection cycle and could go higher still, given more substantial foundations in KS3. Some 50% candidates in maintained schools now achieve a higher grade (A*-C) at GCSE, and 80% a pass at A-level ... More generally, the study of geography appeals to pupils, particularly when the teaching has encouraged a questioning approach to the study of places and issues in human and physical geography and can be seen to be relevant to topical geographical matters. When the time comes to choose options in KS4, geography is the most popular non-statutory GCSE subject, taken by almost half of pupils. Progress improves in KS4 and post-16, reflecting more good teaching and the greater use of specialist geographers' (Ofsted, 1998a, para 7.6).

Even with revisions of the GCSE Criteria (SCAA/ACAC, 1995b), a new generation of GCSE syllabuses (from 1996) and a revised and simplified national curriculum after 1995, there was a perception of some continuing discontinuity in philosophy and approach between the 5-14 national curriculum and the pre-NC 14-16 curriculum. Whatever combination of factors is preferred, the overall result has been a decline in the take-up of geography post 14. By 1997, then, the government's policies designed to create a coherent and accessible 14-19 curriculum had, for geography, resulted in curriculum insecurity.

After 1997, the Labour government has continued with similar 14-19 policies. It has endorsed the National Curriculum Review set under way by the Conservative government and 'played safe' by making little change to KS4. Geography has remained optional and may be subject to even greater pressures as a result of the establishment of the Citizenship Subject Order. The QCA geography team, in a list of issues for geography in the NC Review (July 1997), explained that the key problem was no longer the structure of the NC Order but the declining security and status of the subject at KS4. In its Progress Report to the Secretary of State in December 1998, QCA proposed various models for greater flexibility at KS4. However, in his 9 February 1999 letter back to QCA, the Secretary of State made it quite clear that no subjects were to be removed from the compulsory KS4 curriculum. He thus effectively confirmed one of the biggest blockages to a more flexible 14-19 phase, even before the NC Review consultation had taken place (May-July 1999). The decline in numbers of candidates for GCSE and A-level geography continued 1998-2000, even while Ofsted reports confirmed the steady improvements in quality of teaching and standards of attainment at KS4 and post-16.

Aiming Higher: Labour's proposals for the reform of the 14-19 curriculum (Labour Party, 1996) argued the case for more radical change and for a completely unified qualifications system at this level. Despite this rhetoric, in government New Labour has been more cautious (see Hodgson and Spours, 1999, pp. 109-27). A consultation was held about the Dearing 16-19 proposals in the autumn of 1997. As a result, the government decided to endorse the concept of a national qualifications framework (Figure 5) and go ahead with essentially the same programme of limited change to A-levels, improvements to GNVQs/NVQs and the introduction of key skills and entry level qualifications. As Hodgson and Spours point out, these did mark a small first step in the direction of the more flexible, coherent and inclusive 14-19 qualification system described in *Aiming Higher*. However, they did not (for the moment) encompass the more radical overarching certificate at Advanced Level, nor did they include any more innovative changes to GCSE and A-level.

The new AS and A-level arrangements came into operation in September 2000, allowing schools to offer students potentially five new one-year AS courses and to continue some of these (normally two or three) for the second (A2) year, in order to complete full A-level courses. The new AS/A2 syllabuses (now called specifications) were prepared in relation to minimally modified subject criteria, and they are now all modular in structure (unitised) and include direct reference to key skills. GNVQs were been modified to bring them closer to GCSE and A-level in format, in assessment style and in grading. From September 2000, six-unit vocational A-levels (or Advanced Vocational Certificates of Education (AVCEs)) replaced the 12-unit GNVQ Advanced levels as the main general vocational offering (though a double AVCE award is still available). From September 2002, it is intended that Foundation and Intermediate Part One GNVQs will become three-unit Vocational GCSEs (DfEE/QCA, 2000a), opening the way to a more flexible 14-19 curriculum. If schools do indeed encourage students to broaden their sixth-form curriculum, as was intended, then geography could benefit, providing a useful AS-level to broaden either an academic or a vocationally oriented programme. Geography teachers are also likely to be involved more directly, at least in some schools and colleges, in general vocational developments. Also, the subject has a good track record in addressing developments such as key skills, citizenship and sustainable development education. During the 2000-01 academic year, it became clear that difficulties of timetabling and staffing mean that most schools/colleges cannot offer five subjects at AS-level nor a full range of GNVQ options. Four AS subjects is becoming the norm. A Universities and Colleges Admissions Service (UCAS) survey of 3500 schools and colleges, carried out in the autumn of 2000, found that 66% students taking the new AS were studying four AS subjects and 30% were studying three or fewer (source: UCAS website). What is more, the combined difficulties of preparation for AS module tests, addressing a new 'one-year A-level' standard, coping with key skills and timetabling four or five rather than three A-level subjects led to growing concerns in schools by May-June 2001. This reached a peak during and immediately after the summer examination period 2001, so that one of the first tasks for Estelle Morris (newly appointed as Secretary of State for Education after the June election) was to invite David Hargreaves (QCA Chief Executive) to conduct an immediate review of the new AS. Initial recommendations were to be made by early July and some longer term proposals by December 2001. In July, the government drew on the Hargreaves

Report (QCA, 2001) to propose some short term solutions, including the possibility of, a three hour, end-of-year examination for AS, providing a linear route to AS and a potential reduction in the assessment burden throughout the year. It is not clear how this solution 'squares' with the modular structure of AS subject specifications, nor what timetable will be introduced for any changes. For the longer term, however, the Hargreaves Report made clear that solutions to AS/A-level overloading will necessarily involve a wider look at GCSE and other features such as key skills.

It is difficult to make firm predictions abut the implications for geography of all the potential changes. Geography may benefit in the short term from an increase in AS students but whether this will translate into larger numbers at A-level is still unknown – the same UCAS survey found that 60% of the institutions questioned had a higher student drop-out rate after the introduction of the curriculum 2000 reforms. What is clear is that these new opportunities for geography are built on the shaky foundations of quality concerns at KS3, shrinking 14-16 representation, declining GCSE and A-level candidature in recent years, and a persistent problem of teacher supply at secondary level. A geography curriculum system beginning to show signs of distress in this way (Gardner and Craig, 2001) is not the best basis from which to plan a creative contribution to the 14-19 curriculum of the future.

New thinking is under way. The 14-19 curriculum was one of the 'projects' given government approval for consideration after the latest NC Review. In QCA some quite radical ideas are being explored. For example, a 14-19 'entitlement model' was put forward for informal consultation (QCA, 2000b), requiring all pupils to have learning experiences in each of the following areas: general learning in a range of academic subjects; vocational learning related to the world of work; learning for citizenship; and learning for independence (building on PSHE). But all these developments are still in the early stages and the plethora of organisations which have a stake in the 14-19 area (e.g. DfES, QCA, awarding bodies, employers' training organisations and the new Learning and Skills Council) mean that agreement is unlikely to take place quickly. Before the 2001 election, the Labour government seemed set on the more limited goal of extending vocational opportunities rather than on redesigning the 14-19 curriculum. However, concerns about AS may 'force its hand' and the second Hargreaves report, expected in December 2001, may suggest more significant change. For geography, the questions are – will more radical change be of benefit to geography? and will it happen in time, before the quality and status of geography are further diminished by the existing arrangements?

Increasing control and regulation of the curriculum and assessment

It is tempting to assume that increasing central control and regulation of the curriculum and assessment began with the national curriculum in 1988. However, even as early as 1983 with the formation of the Secondary Examinations Council (SEC) the 14-16 and 16-19 phases of education became more tightly controlled from the centre. Throughout the 1970s and early 1980s, public examinations had been monitored and scrutinised by the Schools Council but both the examining boards (especially for GCSE) and the teachers (especially for CSE) were able to exert considerable influence on the style and content of examinations, and so on the curriculum. There are many examples of innovative geography syllabuses and schemes of assessment from this period – notably the GYSL/Avery Hill CSE and O level syllabuses, the Geography 14-18 Project O-level and the Geography 16-19 Project A-level. All three provided scope for school-devised optional units and a high percentage of coursework, assessed by teachers.

With the establishment of the GCSE examination (1986-88) the Secretary of State set in place a range of new controls. All syllabuses had now to adhere to both general and subject-specific GCSE criteria. Examining boards had to submit all syllabuses for approval and to follow a code of practice to ensure that syllabuses, question papers and the whole marking and grading process were submitted to the central agency (SEC 1983-88 and SEAC 1988-93) for regular scrutiny. GCSE was generally seen as a beneficial development by the education world. Many of the progressive developments of the 1970s were incorporated in the subject criteria and the new syllabuses. The use of coursework, for instance, was one of the defining features of the new system (Daugherty, 1994) and, across all subjects with few exceptions, syllabuses were required to make provision for a minimum of 20% coursework. There was initially no upper limit placed on coursework – for example English presented the opportunity for 100% school-based assessment. Many of the new geography syllabuses launched in 1986 contained high percentages of coursework (see Carhart *et al.*, 1986) and included such innovations as key concepts and issue-based content. Despite the initial retention of innovative curriculum aspects for geography, these systems of increasing control and regulation were changing the nature of the process. Pring (1995) suggests that whereas before about 1980 assessment and examinations were the servants of the curriculum, after this time they assumed a key role in government policy as masters of the curriculum. As governments realised the potential of examinations to determine what is taught, so they sought a greater degree of power. Despite the HMI's favourable verdict in its first report on GCSE, identifying coursework as a means of promoting quality and improving feedback to pupils (DES, 1988), Ministers succumbed to right wing pressure in the late 1980s. First coursework was restricted to a 70% maximum and then (November 1991) further reductions were announced so that the minimum of 20% now became a maximum for most subjects (for geography, a 20% minimum and 25% maximum) from September 1994.

During the 1980s, there was little desire to regulate A-level, although a joint initiative by the GCE boards resulted in voluntary agreement over A-level 'subject cores' in the major subjects. The geography subject core (GCE examining boards, 1983) was influenced by the work of the Geography 16-19 Project, setting out broad principles to which all A-level syllabuses had to adhere rather than outlining specific content. The principles included such items as 'an awareness of the contribution which geography can make to an understanding of contemporary issues'. It was agreed by all but one of the examining boards (see Appendix 4).

Eventually, in the early 1990s, a greater degree of control was exerted over A-level, producing a set of *Principles for GCE A and AS Examinations* (SEAC, 1992c), which included a 20% coursework maximum. A more prescribed subject core was also produced (SCAA, 1993b). Extensions to the codification and regulation of syllabuses and assessment was enforced by means of the Mandatory Code of Practice for GCSE (SCAA/ACAC, 1995a) and for A/AS-level (SCAA, 1994b). In 1998, for the first time the codes of practice and regulations for GCSE and GCE A/AS were brought together (QCA/ACCAC/CCEA, 1998). The establishment of the NCVQ in 1986 extended regulation and control across the growing area of vocational qualifications and, after 1997, the QCA brought together the SCAA and NCVQ regulatory systems into one body.

Given the huge range of qualifications and NC tests for which QCA is responsible in the early 2000s, it is not surprising to find that assessment, qualifications and testing predominate in the organisation and that curriculum assumes a relatively small place (Figure 3). The emphasis has changed significantly since the Schools Council days. A large number of QCA employees and consultants now administer the various procedures and systems of control. Codes of practice now regulate the way all awarding bodies function for all qualifications; there are general and subject-specific criteria for all syllabuses (or specifications, as they are now called) in all pathways; and there are regular scrutinising and monitoring procedures including five-yearly reviews of GCSE and A/AS-levels (The Arrangements for the Statutory Regulation of External Qualifications in England and Wales (QCA/ACCAC/CCEA, 2000) sets out the full system). Regulation has also resulted in a declining number of examining boards (now called awarding bodies) and a smaller range of syllabuses (specifications). There are five awarding bodies, each dealing with academic and vocational qualifications (effectively three for England and one each for Wales and Northern Ireland,

QCA objectives 1999-2000:
1. Develop the national curriculum as part of a broad and balanced curriculum for 3-19 year olds
2. Create a clear, coherent and well-regulated framework of national qualifications
3. Support the development of national occupational standards as the basis for high quality vocational qualifications
4. Secure a rigorous and fair system of national curriculum assessment
5. Inform policy and practice through research and evaluation
6. Provide national data, information, guidance and support to those in education and training
7. Communicate and work effectively with partners
8. Make best use of resources

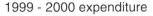

1999 - 2000 expenditure

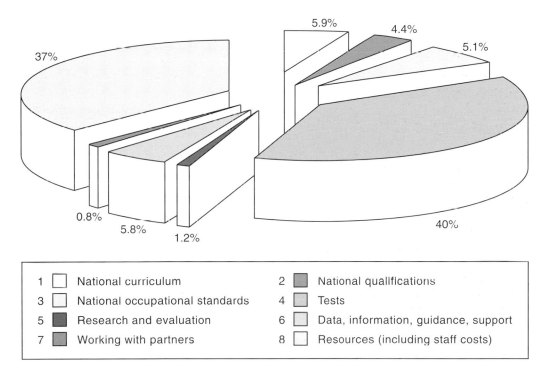

1 ☐	National curriculum	2 ■	National qualifications
3 ☐	National occupational standards	4 ■	Tests
5 ■	Research and evaluation	6 ☐	Data, information, guidance, support
7 ■	Working with partners	8 ☐	Resources (including staff costs)

Key objective	Cost £ (million)	Percentage	Percentage[a]
1. National curriculum [b]	3.8	5.9	9.4
2. National qualifications	2.8	4.4	6.9
3. National occupational standards	3.3	5.1	8.1
4. Tests	25.7	40.0	63.5
5. Research and evaluation	0.8	1.2	1.8
6. Data, information, guidance, support	3.7	5.8	9.1
7. Working with partners	0.5	0.8	1.2
8. Resources (including staff costs)	23.7	37.0	-
Total [c]	64.3	100	100

Figure 3: QCA: key objectives and distribution of budget. Source: QCA website.

Notes: a. Percentage values calculated excluding resources; b. The figures for key objective 1 include the National Curriculum Review, accounting for a higher percentage of total spending than will be the case in 2000-01; c. Values have been rounded, and so do not total correctly.

though they are not closed systems). The number of geography GCSE specifications has declined from 16 in 1986 to 10 in 2001, while the number of geography A-level specifications has declined from 12 in 1989 to 8 in 2000. Qualifications administration has become such a 'high stakes' operation that society rightly demands an accountable and transparent system, but the increasingly managerial features inevitably have impacts back upon the curriculum and classrooms.

To some extent, the GCSE and A-level examining systems have become closed systems (Figure 4), operating at a high level of complexity and detail to service the massive public examination programme. In this environment, experienced officers of the regulatory authority, dedicated awarding body professionals and trusted teams of examiners and markers operate in a tightly organised fashion to ensure that the reliability and accountability of the system is upheld. It is a system focused on what Broadfoot (1999) has called 'performativity'. Missing from this system is any major representation from the academic subject community who, for geography in the 1960s and 1970s, ensured that new ideas and trends in the subject were gradually incorporated into 14-19 examinations. A relatively small number of higher education geographers now sit on awarding body subject committees. Also absent (despite the highly developed procedures for schools to appeal about grades) is the opportunity for any more creative intervention from teachers. Teachers have the system applied to them and 'deliver the results', i.e. the percentage of high GCSE grades to add to league tables and young people trained to pass examinations. Lauder *et al.*, referring to school and national curriculum policies in general, argued that 'if we are not careful, policy settings which emphasise results at the expense of methods will lead to a trained incapacity to think openly and critically about problems that will confront us in ten or twenty years time throughout the system' (1998, p. 15). The experience of geography reveals that the 14-19 examination system may be drawing us nearer to such a trained incapacity to think clearly about the subject.

The retreat of curriculum discourse

In the mid-1980s, the 14-19 system moved from being curriculum led to being assessment and qualifications led. The characteristics of a curriculum-led system may be illustrated by reference to the work of the Geography 16-19 Project. The '16-19' approach (Naish *et al.*, 1987) was to start with the 16-19 student population, to assess their needs, to consider the potential contribution of geography to those needs and then to design an overarching 16-19 curriculum framework. This curriculum framework was used to design a range of academic and pre-vocational courses for different groups of 16-19 year olds, with the assessment system being used to reinforce the curriculum decisions. Thus for the project's A-level syllabus, the original 1980-83 (pilot) assessment scheme comprised 55% terminal or examining board assessment and 45% coursework assessed by teachers. The project team explained that each element of the assessment had been planned to assess some particular aspect of student attainment.

> 'The assessment as a whole is representative of the project's approach to geography and to learning, and in this capacity, acts as a continuing catalyst to curriculum development, not least through its impact on classroom strategies' (Naish et al., 1987, p. 136).

The 14-16 geography projects (GYSL/Avery Hill and Geography 14-18) followed a similar approach, recognising that assessment was a powerful tool to use in the service of the curriculum. Not all A-level, O-level and CSE syllabuses were as innovative as the project ones. Many were very traditional and some were influenced more directly by changes in academic geography. However, even the Q/F and N/F experiments and the A-level changes in the 1970s were motivated (certainly on the part of geographers) as much by a desire to see new kinds of content and skills taught in the classroom (e.g. quantitative techniques and systems models) as by the external pressures for structural change.

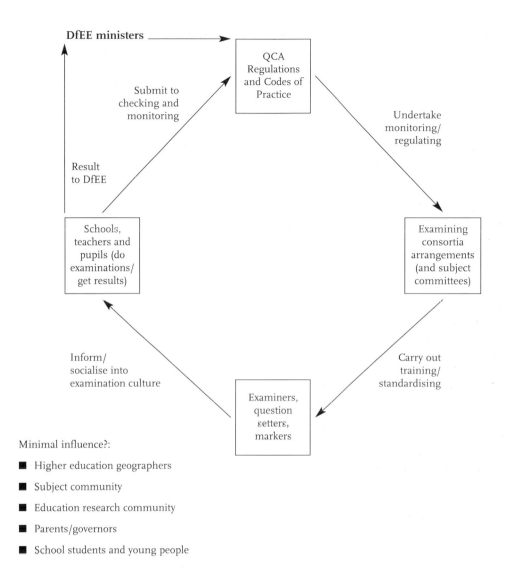

DfEE ministers

QCA
Regulations
and Codes of
Practice

Submit to
checking and
monitoring

Undertake
monitoring/
regulating

Result
to DfEE

Schools,
teachers and
pupils (do
examinations/
get results)

Examining
consortia
arrangements
(and subject
committees)

Inform/
socialise into
examination culture

Carry out
training/
standardising

Examiners,
question
setters,
markers

Minimal influence?:

■ Higher education geographers

■ Subject community

■ Education research community

■ Parents/governors

■ School students and young people

Figure 4: The 'closed system' of 14-19 examining.

The establishment of GCSE from 1986 is interesting because ostensibly it incorporated many of the curriculum innovations. For example, most syllabuses set out the required knowledge and understanding using key concepts or generalisations, and allowed teachers to choose the specific topics for study within constraints of scale and environment. All syllabuses required fieldwork and coursework and some included an issue-based approach. However, as Daugherty (1987) pointed out, they were not curriculum documents but examination requirements. They happened, because of the accident of GCSE timing, to incorporate the accepted fashions in curriculum and assessment. Inevitably opportunities were missed to resolve some of the big issues which the work of the projects, in particular, had thrown up (see Chapter 3, page 34). The nature of geographical enquiry was never fully addressed. All the new GCSE syllabuses, apart from the two project ones, turned enquiry into 'an enquiry' or piece of investigative work to be tested separately, rather than an overarching approach to learning underlying all assessment activities. Values and attitudes were treated cautiously in most syllabuses and the whole question of specific place and locational knowledge, one of the burning issues raised (but not resolved) at the joint projects conference (Rawling, 1980) was postponed. Teachers were left to make these decisions with no sense of any basic locational entitlement. As Daugherty commented in his survey of the new GCSE syllabuses 'a knowledge of particular places is no longer something which public examinations in geography require' (1987, p. 53). None of the 1986 crop of syllabuses attempted to design a full regional or place-based approach (although MEG B did require exemplification of themes in a West African or British context).

As time went on, each new policy development reinforced the need for a managerial and administrative response and reduced the opportunities for curriculum and professional activity. Thus the decline in coursework percentages, the use of grade descriptions and the increase in regulatory controls all required more technical examining expertise and allowed less subject and teacher input. There never was a chance to sort out geographical enquiry or to question the predominance of thematic and issue-based syllabuses, although the 1995 GCSE criteria (SCAA/ACAC, 1995b) were sufficiently open to allow this. With the removal of school-based curriculum units, teachers no longer had any incentive to undertake creative interpretation of examining board guidelines in the way that Pring (1995) noted brought such benefits in the 1970s. The 2000 GCSE criteria (QCA, 2000g) are very similar to the previous version – after all they build on a national curriculum which has hardly changed in content. The specifications (Weeden and Wilson, 2001; Westaway and Jones, 2001) consequently show little real innovation in subject terms, though some quick responses to current policy requirements – e.g. reference to sustainable development, global citizenship and interdependence, key skills, and ICT use – which might present opportunities for innovation. There is only one specification which claims to be place-based and there is still no consistent interpretation of geographical enquiry. Despite the hours of awarding body time put into changing the structures of specifications and question papers, and addressing new accountability procedures, the GCSE specifications seem 'frozen' in a late 1980s content and curriculum style.

The retreat of curriculum may be similarly described for A/AS-level. Greater specificity of syllabus content in the 1970s and 1980s made more explicit the standards required, but also increased the gap between teachers and examiners and reduced the scope for teacher creativity (Hall, 1996). In the 1994-95 revisions, the opportunities for rethinking content and approach (regularly needed if a subject is to remain dynamic) were inhibited by the tight timetable. The 1993 A/AS geography subject core (SEAC, 1993d) was influenced by the people-environment approach and the emphasis on active investigative work (see Appendix 4) and so many of the resulting 1995 syllabuses picked up this '16-19 flavour'. However, as Bradford noted (1995) in his survey of the new syllabuses, although there were many good features there was some evidence of hasty work. Substantial remnants of earlier positivist and quantitative paradigms remained in some syllabuses while others had experienced difficulties in interpreting the rather restrictive 'chosen environments' requirement of the core. Of greater significance than content developments was the need to meet structural changes – in particular the decline in coursework assessment (now 20% maximum), the availability of modular as well as linear assessment schemes and the requirement for synoptic assessment (Butt and Lambert, 1993). Modular assessment was adopted by all the boards. Only the University of Cambridge Local Examinations Syndicate (UCLES) and the Oxford and Cambridge Schools Examination Board (OCSEB) retained syllabuses which offered linear-only routes in 1995. Most boards did not radically change their existing syllabuses to design modular curriculum units afresh. In most cases, pre-existing content was divided into units of suitable size, approximate to one-sixth of the course, and one of a limited number of assessment types (resource-based questions, structured questions, an occasional decision-making paper) allocated to each. Enquiry/investigative work was in most courses allocated to coursework. The imperative to meet all the new regulations and requirements meant that wider curriculum considerations were not on the agenda.

Changes to A-level, resulting from the Dearing 16-19 Review and the subsequent 'Qualifying for Success' initiatives promoted by the Labour government, have continued this trend in the 1990s. Although there are new A/AS subject criteria (QCA, 1999a), they are very similar to the old subject core in content terms. The main changes are either structural, to allow for the new one-year AS, or extra additions to promote government initiatives such as key skills, ICT and use of extended prose. Inevitably given the constraints, the eight new specifications (each with its AS counterpart) now look remarkably similar in content, style and assessment opportunities (see Palôt, 2000). As Bradford (2001) has commented, the awarding bodies have 'played it safe', minimising change to that required by the regulations and focusing efforts on protecting their market share of schools. For this reason, few specifications have taken opportunities to introduce new and relevant ideas from academic geography. Lack of innovation is particularly notable for the new AS courses. Each AS represents a basic rather traditional introduction to its corresponding A-level course. No awarding body has followed up the possibility of providing a more specialised AS course – focused, for example, on physical/environmental issues, place, community and identity, economic geography and work-related issues, or cultural aspects, linking directly with art and literature – though all these and others might have provided ways of attracting students back to geography and of complementing or broadening the year 12-13 diet. The forces of conservatism are similarly in evidence in relation to geographical enquiry. It seems that little progress has been made in outlining what makes enquiry distinctive post-16, or how assessment of enquiry skills may be undertaken other than through pieces of personal investigative work (and this despite innovative thinking being undertaken on teaching and learning in higher education (GDN, 1998)). None of these comments is aimed at decrying the 'day-to-day' work of the examining boards and their subject committees which endeavour to respond to each new central edict, nor to suggest that there is not scope for some innovation if teachers had the time to find it (e.g. mention might be made of the OCR GCSE syllabuses B and C, and the EdExcel A-level syllabus B (former project syllabuses)), but awarding bodies are not designed to undertake curriculum development. As with the new NC framework, new developments in geography are not positively encouraged by the latest specifications. The stimulus for change needs to come from the subject community. Where are signals to incorporate, for example, new ideas from the 'cultural turn', gender issues, locality studies and the regional work, all now featuring in academic geography and relevant to current societal concerns? After 10-15 years of 'regulation without curriculum development', the geography specifications at all levels have become relatively static and technical documents.

Academic versus vocational: opening or closing the gap?

A key feature of the last 20 years has been the development of vocational opportunities within the 14-19 curriculum. Prior to 1980, the curriculum for 14-16 and 16-19 year olds in schools was still predominantly academic and subject based. It was assumed that only those who were successful in the academic GCE O-level and A-level examinations (a relatively small elite) would move on to higher education or professional training. Those who were less successful or less motivated left education early and undertook vocational training or unskilled employment. By 1980, global economic, social and technological changes meant that it was no longer appropriate to educate only an elite 'thinking class'. In order for Britain to remain competitive in the world economy, it was deemed necessary to ensure widening participation rates in education and to provide a wider range of knowledge, skills and understanding for all young people. This direct link between education, training and the economy became a main theme for education policy after 1976, signalled in Prime Minister Callaghan's 'Ruskin speech' in Oxford and followed up by governments of all political persuasions thereafter. A number of dilemmas have characterised policy debates. In particular, there are the linked issues of whether academic depth and high standards can be preserved at the same time as adding general and vocational breadth to the curriculum, and whether widening participation rates in education will result in a more or less divisive curriculum. Several commentators (Pring, 1995;

Tomlinson, 1997, 2001) have suggested that these dilemmas have been tackled in a piecemeal way and without the benefit of an overarching philosophy as a framework for each individual initiative.

In the 1980s, there were individual initiatives aimed at broadening the curriculum. TVEI was a comprehensive education and training programme from 1982, intended originally for all 14-19 year olds. CPVE (1983) was a qualification based on subjects and broad vocational areas the aim of which was to provide courses for young people who wished to stay beyond 16, but for whom academic A-levels were not appropriate (Joint Board, 1985). There was also a range of more directly vocational courses developed by bodies like the Business and Technical Education Council (BTEC) and the Royal Society of Arts (RSA). Many of these initiatives allowed schools (and LEAs in the case of TVEI) some freedom and the chance to draw on curriculum thinking. Geographers were closely involved in CPVE via the Geography 16-19 Project schools (see Hart, 1982) and TVEI via the GYSL Project and its associated GYSL-TRIST development work (Ash and Mobbs, 1987). There was also a BTEC module for 16-19 students, focusing on the relevance of geography to planning, business and the environment (Morrish, 1981). Pring suggested (1995) that these pre-vocational developments, and TVEI in particular, contained within them the seeds of an educational philosophy which could bridge the academic/vocational divide.

The NCVQ was created in 1986 to rationalise all vocational and general vocational developments. The White Paper on *Education and Training for the 21st Century* (DES, DoE and WO, 1991) introduced the idea of three distinct qualifications pathways post-14, and GNVQs were established to confirm the middle pathway and to provide an answer to broadening the curriculum. In addition, several decades of attempts to broaden the A-level curriculum seemed to be terminated by the decision not to introduce the Higginson model (DES, 1988) of five leaner AS-levels, despite widespread approval from the professional educational community. The Dearing Review of 16-19 qualifications confirmed the existence of the three pathways as the basic structure of the National Qualifications Framework and highlighted their distinctiveness (Figure 5). The academic pathway, incorporating A/AS-levels and GCSEs, was designed to 'develop knowledge, understanding and skills associated with a subject or discipline'. The vocational pathway covering all NVQs and work-related learning was intended to 'develop and recognise mastery of a trade or profession at the relevant level'. The newly created general vocational pathway, incorporated GNVQs, and was designed to 'develop and apply knowledge, understanding and skills relevant to broad areas of employment' though, as Sir Ron Dearing recognised, its distinctiveness was always less apparent: 'the problem comes at the interface between A-levels and the GNVQ ... it is difficult for people to understand the difference' (Dearing, 1996, para 3.16).

Categories	General qualifications	Vocationally-related qualifications	Occupational qualifications
Broad characteristics	Attainment in a subject	Attainment in a vocational area	Competence in the workplace
Level of attainment (Higher) level/5 (Higher) level/4	Responsibility shared with QAA		Level 5 NVQ Level 4 NVQ
Advanced level/3	A-level	Vocational A-level (AVCE)	Level 3 NVQ
Intermediate level/2	GCSE A*-C	(Intermediate GNVQ)	Level 2 NVQ
Foundation level/1	GCSE D-G	Vocational GCSE (all grades)	Level 1 NVQ
Entry level	Entry level qualifications recognise achievement, competence or skills which can lead towards qualifications at Foundation level across the framework		

Figure 5: The national qualifications framework (2000). Source: QCA.

Throughout the 1990s, while policies for the academic and vocational pathways, on the whole, focused on rationalising and regulating the examining system and ensuring accountability, in the general vocational pathway, there was rapid development work. The introduction of GNVQ was announced in 1991. By 1992, the first five subjects were launched at Advanced level with a radically different competency-based assessment system. A full suite of Foundation, Intermediate and Advanced-level courses were under way by 1995, covering vocational areas such as Engineering, Business, Health and Social Care and Leisure and Tourism (L&T). Although originally intended for post-16 students in further education, GNVQs were made available to schools in 1994. After 1995, Part One GNVQ was also introduced specifically for 14-16 year old pupils and offering a 20% curriculum block roughly equivalent to two GCSEs in time and in status. By July 1996, a total of 6784 students were involved in GNVQ Part One pilot activity at Intermediate and Foundation levels. In the same year, a total of 159,780 students were classed as 'active candidates' (i.e. intending to complete in that academic year) for the full GNVQ at the three levels. A majority of these would have been in further education colleges where vocational options were successful competitors with academic subjects. (Source of data: QCA.)

For geography, this new situation created dilemmas which, it will be argued, are representative of the wider problems resulting from the development of separate pathways (Rawling, 1997a,b). In retrospect, the two Dearing Reviews took away from geography with one hand (NC status at KS4) but gave back with the other hand (new opportunities to contribute to general vocational courses). Leisure, recreation and tourism were topics well-established in GCSE and A-level courses and so some school geography departments were persuaded to offer full Foundation, Intermediate or Part One L&T options. Benefits were clear from the start (Grimwade, 1997), including the opportunity to stress active and practical approaches to learning, a continuous portfolio style of mainly internal assessment and the possibility of building up strong links with the local community and the world of work. All these were features of the kind of learning developed in pre-national curriculum days and now somewhat restricted. On the other hand, there were concerns that L&T GNVQ was rather superficially focused on business and management in a leisure and tourism context, without providing students with a proper underpinning of knowledge and understanding about these industries (Ofsted, 1994). Early reports from schools suggested that take-up of full academic courses (Geography A and GCSE) was suffering in some schools because some students were choosing the vocational options instead. Key stage 4 timetable arrangements made to accommodate 20% (Part One) or even 40% (full GNVQ) blocks were of necessity restricting access to other option columns. In addition, there was evidence that some geography department staff were persuaded to move partially or wholly out of geography teaching to become L&T or GNVQ co-ordinators (Rawling, 1997a), with potentially negative impacts on the staffing and status of mainstream geography courses. Overall, then, the dilemma was one of identity and of the appropriate subject response. What exactly was the GNVQ? Should geography teachers embrace the rapidly expanding vocational pathway and develop geographical contributions to it? Or should they retreat to the academic pathway and seek only to strengthen and preserve the subject in this context? The difficulty lay not in the potential of geography – it has always been possible to use geography as a vehicle for understanding work related situations, for exploring social and economic issues and for developing transferable skills, as the GSIP experience in particular had shown (Corney, 1992). Rather it lay in the apparent need to make a choice between these kinds of characteristics in the general vocational pathway and in-depth academic study in the academic pathway.

Many educators do not believe that the separation of pathways is defensible on educational grounds. Pring (1995) argued for 'closing the gap' between the traditional liberal education exemplified in the academic pathway of GCSEs and A-levels, and the vocational educational pathway characterised by GNVQs and NVQs. He envisaged that both sides of the divide would benefit. Academic courses in schools had too often missed opportunities to illuminate practical situations in an intellectually sound way. Also, as a result of a narrow concentration on intellectual development they had, on the whole, ignored important areas of skills, understanding and practical 'know-how', particularly those concerned with human relationships and moral qualities. The pre-vocational curriculum, on the other hand, had:

> 'tended to overlook the distinctive contribution to personal development of public traditions of criticism and enquiry. To learn to think effectively or to feel sensitively or to reason correctly requires immersion into how others have done so and into how they have tackled the scientific and moral and aesthetic questions that concern us' (Pring, 1995, p. 102).

Too often the GNVQ specifications, as in the original GNVQ performance criteria, stressed the process of learning (how to do a task, as in promoting a tourist attraction) as if this were possible without the products of previous learning (understanding the meaning and context of the task, as in understanding the geographical characteristics of the tourist attraction and the economic, political and social factors affecting its attraction and availability).

Educational policy decisions since 1997 have actually resulted in the distinctions between the pathways becoming more blurred – but this has happened because of administrative and regulatory concerns (parity of esteem) rather than for curriculum reasons. Continuing criticisms of the competence-based model of assessment (Wolf, 1993, 1995) and of the lack of clarity in the specifications (Ofsted, 1994) led to a major review of all GNVQs (Capey, 1995). Subject professionals from SCAA and HMI also raised the issue of 'underpinning knowledge' and intellectual depth. Ecclestone (2000), in her policy analysis of the GNVQ assessment regime, recognised that there was a clash of philosophies in the review period and that the narrowly vocational GNVQ vision was effectively challenged. The 2000 model for GNVQ specifications and for the vocational A-levels moved much nearer to the GCSE format. Each unit contained a rationale accompanied by evidence of achievement, assessment criteria, content and guidance on delivery. The new assessment model reduced the amount of internal unit-based assessment and portfolio work, placed more emphasis on externally set tests and reverted to a GCSE-style A-E grading system. Key skills have also become detached units, available for certification alongside (but not integral to) any vocational or academic courses. From 2002, the pathways will become even less distinct as Vocational GCSEs take their place in the national qualification framework. As Marvell (2000) has explained, these changes bring greater clarity and assist geographers in picking up vocational opportunities. It is also the case that they reveal even more strikingly the lack of real distinctiveness between the academic and general vocational pathways.

Breadth, depth and progression

Exploring 14-19 developments from the point of view of one subject (geography) has highlighted two problems with the way that breadth, depth and progression have been addressed. First, these themes have not been addressed from a curriculum point of view – that is by starting from first principles about why breadth, depth and progression are needed and whose needs they are serving. Second, insufficient attention has been paid, at a policy level, to the subject viewpoint.

In the search for breadth, which has been pursued by governments over the past 30 years or more in relation to A-levels, most of the proposals have assumed that adding qualifications will add breadth. The history of this search for breadth is littered with the acronyms of intended qualifications – Q and F levels (1969), N and F levels (1973), I levels (1980) and the various AS proposals which have preceded the present system. In the 1990s, concerns about the lack of general skills have led to the addition of discrete items such as key skills and citizenship. Similarly, the recent expansion of vocational and general vocational qualifications has been a direct response to the perceived need to give greater emphasis to work-related experiences and to training for the workplace. Crombie-White *et al.* (1995) have argued that adding vocational courses to the curriculum does not necessarily produce the kind of adaptable, creative young people who are needed by society for the future, unless serious thought is given to the whole curriculum experience provided.

In the 1970s and 1980s, it was recognised that much could be achieved within subjects as far as the educational breadth of a course of study is concerned. The Schools Council projects of the 1970s were all interested in the development of a wide range of general skills and abilities, attitudes and values as well as the furtherance of subject-specific knowledge and skills. The Geography 16-19 Project, for instance, saw its main aim as that of using the subject as a medium to help satisfy the educational needs of 16-19 year olds in the society of the time (see Naish *et al.*, 1987). The NCC tried to encourage a broader view of subject teaching in the early 1990s, by promoting the need for schools and all subjects to address cross-curricular dimensions, themes and skills. The government of the day saw this as an addition to, and unwelcome distraction from, the task of teaching national curriculum subjects and accorded it lower priority (see Graham with Tytler, 1993).

Since that time, National Curriculum Orders, vocational and general vocational specifications, GCSE and A/AS criteria and official curriculum guidance have all focused on subject-specific content and skills. NC test arrangements, public examination requirements and the associated league tables of results, which publish the achievements of schools in subject examinations, have all tended to reinforce this narrow viewpoint. For geography, as for other subjects, this situation is frustrating because as school subjects have become narrower so policy-makers have begun to demand curriculum breadth from schools as a whole (see Study 5, pages 121-122) SCAA and QCA have produced guidance on, for example, careers education, information technology, literacy, key skills, environmental education and most recently PSHE and citizenship, and further support (often web-based) is planned for citizenship, creativity across the curriculum, inclusion issues and sustainable development education. Effectively, cross-curricular aspects have been resurrected, but without the corresponding attention given to breadth in subject disciplines, so that schools might respond without just adding ever more 'things' to their over-crowded timetables. Figure 6 provides a broad overview of the potential contribution of geography to the 14-19 curriculum; other subjects could provide similar statements. Although such an approach cannot achieve all the desired objectives for an education for the twenty-first century, some degree of greater breadth can be addressed within, as well as beyond, subject disciplines. Recent education policy has proceeded as if this is not the case.

While searching for breadth, policy makers have been anxious not to reduce the requirement for in-depth study and so the opportunity for students to develop high standards of intellectual achievement. The academic A-level has been seen as the 'gold standard' and the long and heated debates over A-level reform since about 1960 have all revolved round this balance between depth and breadth. Policy-makers have responded by, for example, adding another grade (A* to GCSE, 1993, Advanced Extension Awards from 2002) or creating further layers of regulation and checking (the five-yearly reviews of standards, the international review of A-level standards established by QCA, 2000). These technical and administrative responses might be necessary for reasons of accountability because GCSE and A-level grades are crucial selecting mechanisms for higher education. However, more grades and more regulations do not add immediately to our understanding of what a high standard of intellectual achievement would look like in any one subject area – i.e. depth in a curriculum sense. An examination of the highest level or grade descriptions for geography at national curriculum KS3, GCSE and A-level, for example (and even the university degree level descriptor in the Benchmarking statement (QAA, 2000)), not surprisingly, reveals broad similarities. The progression in knowledge, skills and understanding is closely related to the context

14-19 students need to:	Geography can provide:
Develop the distinctive knowledge, understanding, skills and perspectives of a subject discipline *(in-depth study)*	Knowledge and understanding of: ■ people/places, landscapes, changing environments ■ localities, regions, nations and international relationships ■ locations, distributions, patterns and spatial connections ■ global matters and sustainable development (e.g. food supply, resources, climate changes) Skills of: ■ using and making maps, diagrams and photographs ■ undertaking fieldwork investigations ■ using GIS, satellite imagery and the internet Values: ■ sense of identity and place in the world ■ awareness and understanding of other cultures ■ understanding of different views about the environment ■ clarification of own responsibility to people and environment ■ enjoyment and sense of wonder and beauty of the Earth
Apply the distinctive knowledge, understanding and skills in a meaningful way to their own lives and to important issues *(application of learning)*	Insight into: ■ issues about environment and resources ■ issues about society, culture and place ■ issues about work, industry and economic matters ■ issues of global significance and about sustainable development Practical experiences of: ■ the local area and local community matters ■ decision making about places and environments ■ work-places and work-related activities ■ rural and urban environments at different scales ■ issues which present strongly conflicting viewpoints
Find situations in which to enhance their own personal and social development *(personal/social development)*	Learning situations which provide: ■ the need to make decisions about matters affecting people, place and environment ■ the opportunity to disentangle different points of view and formulate their own moral dilemmas and the chance to resolve them to personal satisfaction ■ exposure to different people, cultures and responses to varied environments ■ opportunities to work individually or in teams on geographical enquiries ■ the need to use organisational skills to undertake investigative work ■ opportunities for making a creative or imaginative response to environments and places (e.g. poem, drawing)
Have opportunities to practice basic/key skills of communications, numeracy and application of IT *(basic/key skills)*	Contexts for: *Communication skills* ■ talking and listening about people, place and environmental matters ■ reading about places and environments in formal texts and in newspapers, literary sources, etc. ■ writing a wide variety of reports, articles, essays and creative writing *Number skills* ■ handling, manipulating and presenting data about environments, resources and places *ICT skills* ■ using ICT to explore relationships, handle and present data, gain access to information and images ■ using new developments (GIS and the internet) to explore geographical issues and problems ■ using ICT to communicate with people in different parts of the world and from different cultures to gain new perspectives on geographical matters

Figure 6: One view of geography's potential contribution to the educational needs of 14-19 students.
Source: Rawling, 1997a,b.

and complexity of the content for each age group. In 1996, Daugherty referred to the 'incomplete nature of the notions of progression' (p. 213) and argued that geographers did not have enough empirical research evidence on which to base any clear view of progression and achievement in the subject. The proliferation of examination regulations and criteria has confirmed this problem and highlighted the need for the subject community to undertake some well-targeted research. Work on pupils' understanding of environmental issues, concepts of place, identity and scale and development of enquiry skills might be good starting points.

Progression and continuity are two themes which are also referred to in a qualifications context in 14-19 policy documents. The Dearing Review, for example, explained that the national qualifications framework outlined in the report 'should facilitate understanding, progression within and between qualifications pathways, economy in teaching, recognition of all achievements and the building up of a portfolio of qualifications from different pathways' (1996, p. 11, para 3.6). The policy makers have looked for a neat and tidy system of qualifications. They have seen progression and continuity predominantly in the sequence of steps (e.g. Foundation, Intermediate, Advanced levels of GNVQs, the overarching levels of the National Qualifications framework) or in the creation of convenient sized units of vocational and A/AS courses (in 3-, 6- and 12-unit groups) which will allow mixing and matching between pathways. Such practical considerations are important. However, 'unitisation' or modularisation raises many further questions for curriculum planning and for teaching and learning. The rapidity of change has not allowed these to be thought through. All geography AS/A specifications now provide AS and A2 modules which give schools some degree of freedom within each year. However, inspection of the specifications and assessment arrangements reveals that it is difficult to do justice to progression of key ideas, skills and abilities within the syllabuses as a whole, and assessment has actually become more standardised for each unit. Though it is too early to obtain hard evidence about the impact, there are signs (e.g. Morrish, 2000) to suggest that, of necessity, teaching and learning have become more fragmented and more narrowly focused on each module at a time. Pupils learn the module content, are tested on it and then move on – without having the time or encouragement to make connections or extend their interest into related current issues or other areas of geography. Specific module content and skills may thus be emphasised at the expense of overarching concepts and ideas in the subject. It is not clear how the 2001 AS review will tackle this conflict between curricular and assessment imperatives. Linear and modular experiences of a subject may not amount to the same thing. The synoptic module and assessment represent an attempt to address the need for an overview, but teachers will need help to implement teaching and learning for synoptic capabilities within a more fragmented framework.

One issue which has perhaps not been given sufficient consideration in the move towards a more flexible National Qualification Framework is the curriculum experience resulting for an individual pupil. The QCA work on alternative models for 14-19 and the government's renewed interest in a 'graduation certificate' reiterated by Estelle Morris immediately after Labour's election victory, are encouraging in this respect, giving recognition to the idea of a wide-ranging educational entitlement for individual pupils whatever pathways they are following. As soon as the discussion focuses on individual entitlement, different issues are raised. What, for instance, might constitute a geographic entitlement for all young people, quite separately from the attainments measured by a GCSE, AS/A-level or GNVQ qualification? Might it include, for example: some knowledge and understanding of their own community and country; some introduction to global issues and to the responsibilities implicit in sustainable development; skills of map reading and ICT use necessary to handle spatial data: and some framework of locational knowledge? Concern about the decline of examination entries at GCSE, A-level and beyond should not just be seen as a defensive response from a subject community under threat. It is, or should be, registering a wider concern about young people growing up in the twenty-first century without such a geographic entitlement.

Conclusion

The period of dynamic change in 14-19 education since the mid-1980s has, for all subjects, raised major issues about their contribution and relevance in a period of rapid social and economic change and widening educational participation rates. Traditional subject disciplines still lie at the heart of the academic route within the National Qualifications Framework, and geography has gained from being a well-established subject at 14-19 level. However, subjects cannot 'rest on their laurels'. Walford points out that geography's rise to prominence as an examination subject through the twentieth century is a notable one. But that, in terms of candidate numbers, 'the high water mark of geography's examination success seems to have been 1994-96' (2000, p. 309). Since then, although there have been rises as well as falls (Westaway and Rawling, 2001) the overall picture, so far, is one of steady decline. This chapter has shown that policies since 1986 in particular have been one cause of this decline, destabilising an existing 14-19 system within which geography was a valued and favoured option. It is not just a question of reduced access to the subject and declining numbers. Geography 14-19 is in a 'double-bind'. Factors such as increasing central control and regulation and the retreat of curriculum discourse have also reduced the opportunities within geography for creative outward looking approaches to education, i.e. the kind of responses which might ensure its contribution to current initiatives.

It is important, however, not to overstate the external constraints. Some kind of system-wide response to changing social and economic conditions was inevitable for 14-19 education and many of the changes are now picking up appropriate themes – flexibility, entitlement, personal/social development of the individual and sustainable development education. The way that some of the changes have occurred have not been beneficial to geography but there are still opportunities for creative and innovative responses at the levels of specification preparation and assessment arrangements, textbook production and guidance, and, most importantly, classroom implementation. One of the remaining barriers to this kind of response from geography teachers is the lack of a dynamic and creative link with the subject in higher education (see Chapter 10). The renewal of this dialogue, and some ensuing clarity about geographic entitlement at all ages, may be seen as crucial for school geography to strengthen and extend its contribution to 14-19 education.

Study 5

The geography 16-19 A-level syllabus (1980-2000):
the changing fortunes of a curriculum innovation

The Geography 16-19 A-level syllabus is probably the best known of the many courses developed by the Schools Council Geography 16-19 Project. Its original characteristics derived from the Geography 16-19 Curriculum Framework, from which all '16-19' innovations were developed.

Three features of the '16-19' curriculum framework stand out:

1. The incorporation of a complete **philosophy** about geography and its contribution to the education of young people, i.e. the **people-environment approach to geography** which was seen as the basis for helping young people understand and enjoy the world around them, and to play their part effectively as citizens.

2. The incorporation of an active participatory **pedagogy** - the **enquiry-based learning approach** which the project believed should infuse all work. Teachers would focus work on 'questions, issues and problems' and aim to use a balanced mix of teaching strategies, ranging from expository methods, through structured skill-based work, to decision making and more open-ended problem solving and creative activities.

3. A belief in the **professionalism** of teachers. The project believed that teachers were the key to effective change, able to translate and develop the syllabus guidelines into a curriculum appropriate to the students, and to assess the significance of newer ideas in the subject.

The 1980 version of the Geography 16-19 A-level syllabus, produced initially for trialling by a relatively small number of pilot schools (about 55), provided six core modules representing the four major people-environment themes – Challenge of Natural Environments, Use and Misuse of Resources, Issues of Global Concern and Managing Human Environments. Teachers could also choose three option modules from the 24 identified, or choose two and develop one of their own. In addition, students could identify a people-environment topic for investigation in their individual study. The assessment structure was chosen to enhance and support the curriculum, resulting in two externally assessed examination papers (55%) (decision-making and resource-based questions); three different pieces of teacher assessed coursework (30%); and the student's individual study (15%), externally marked and with an interview undertaken by each student. The syllabus presented a coherent curriculum but also ample scope for teacher and student involvement.

The first set of changes occurring for the 1984 syllabus were minor and were a direct result of opening up the syllabus to a larger customer base (177 centres and 1680 examination entries for 1985-87 cycle). The syllabus was made available to any schools via the University of London Schools Examination Board. Option module assessment was streamlined and the individual study interview was withdrawn. The key features of the Project's philosophy and approach remained intact. The most significant changes occurred in the 1990s, as regulations and procedures enforced by the government's regulatory authorities (SEAC, SCAA and QCA) took effect. For 1995, the Geography 16-19 A-level syllabus was already the biggest syllabus with a candidate entry of over 12,000 in 1994 (27.6% of total entry).

continued

It had to meet the demands of the new A/AS-level Subject Core (SEAC, 1993), the new arrangements which allowed for modularisation and the 20% restriction on coursework. Although Geography 16-19 was one of the first syllabuses to be modular in a curriculum sense, the new game was modularity in assessment. The need for six single module tests conflicted with the carefully designed and varying weightings of the 16-19 assessment, while the imperative to reduce coursework to 20% meant that the coursework assessment items had to be reconsidered. An attempt was made to preserve the 16-19 people-environment and issues-based framework – thus the four themes were still apparent and a teacher assessed individual study was required (20%). However, the range of assessment types (and hence the range of enquiry-based learning strategies promoted) and the degree of teacher involvement in course design and assessment were both dramatically reduced.

By 2000, the syllabus (now 'specification') had changed again to meet the demands of the Qualifying for Success programme - yet another set of A/AS Subject Criteria, an increased number of regulations and procedures about assessment and the constraints of having to devise an AS to represent the first half of the A-level. A tightly controlled set of six-module (now 'unit') tests has become the curriculum. The issues-based people-environment approach still features in the specification aims and in the units, but the four themes have been merged with module titles and very little choice of content remains. Although enquiry skills are required, there does seem to have been some retreat from it being seen as an overarching teaching/learning approach developed and assessed throughout the course. It now seems to reside in specific units (e.g. the environmental investigation and the coursework). Neither the approach to geography nor to enquiry seem to have developed much beyond the mid-1980s definition, although continuous development of both by teachers and the subject community was a vital part of the 16-19 vision. It was never envisaged that the syllabus would remain the same; a healthy curriculum system would continually reinvent the 16-19 framework. The EdEcxel examining team has introduced some new topics during the 1990s (e.g. health), and has used the synoptic unit as the opportunity to maintain a decision-making activity. However, the short timescales allowed for each major rewrite, and the pressures of QCA regulatory procedures, have not been conducive to curriculum rethinking.

Most strikingly, the Geography 16-19 A-level teacher has changed roles from being the curriculum designer, orchestrating and developing the student learning experience, to become the deliverer and administrator of tightly prescribed module packages. The distinctive features of 16-19 philosophy, pedagogy and professionalism outlined above are no longer so apparent. It might be argued that, as the Labour government (2001) requires attention to key skills, citizenship, personal and social education, thinking skills and creativity, so the ability of EdExcel B (formerly Geography 16-19) to provide all these contributions has been constrained.

References

Naish, M., Rawling, E. and Hart, E. (1987) Geography 16-19: *The contribution of a curriculum development project to 16-19 education.* London: Longman for SCDC.
SEAC (1993d) *GCE A and AS Examinations: Subject core for geography.* London: SEAC.

8

Developing the Third Way: The Impact of Curriculum Policies on Geography after 1997

Introduction

The analysis so far has covered the changing Geography National Curriculum (GNC), up to and including the two National Curriculum Reviews, and developments and trends in 14-19 geography. Effectively, it ends with the implementation of the GNC requirements and the introduction of the new A/AS-levels in 2000. It has been argued that changes in policy making and policy management throughout the 1990s allowed amendments to be made to the Geography Order. These have weakened the grip of the cultural restorationist ideology and substituted a more workable curriculum model. Conversely, GCSE and A/AS-level geography, though not initially so strongly affected by New Right influences, have become increasingly constrained by regulations and structural changes. Neither GCSE, A/AS-level nor the GNC have undergone any reconsideration of subject content appropriate for the twenty-first century.

However, while 2000 was a key date in relation to immediate changes in schools, 1997 was far more significant for educational policy as a whole. Since May 1997 and the election of a New Labour government, the educational discourse has been moving away from the details of subject curriculum frameworks. Bell (1999) referred to the post-1997 period as a distinctive 'excellence phase' in educational policy making. According to Bell the five themes listed in the Conservative White Paper *Choice and Diversity* (DfE, 1992) have all been retained but remoulded to give a specific New Labour 'spin'. The emphasis remains, for instance, on market forces, on accountability and on improving standards of pupils' performance. What is more the Labour government has enforced a greater degree of control and direction in implementing these policies than the Conservatives did, through the use of targets and performance measures for LEAs, schools and even individual teachers (as in the performance-related pay). In this sense, New Labour's educational policies give a greater stress on the responsibility of schools and teachers to deliver excellence at all costs. 'Pressure and support go hand in hand' (Blair, 1998, p. 30). Power and Whitty (1999) remain to be convinced, however, that it is a new approach. They suggest that New Labour educational policies do not so much present 'a Third Way' as a continuation of right wing policies with an even harder line approach to implementation, apparent in targets, performance indicators and specific curriculum strategies (e.g. the Literacy and Numeracy Strategies). The 2001 Labour election victory may result in some changes of emphasis but it seems unlikely that there will be major changes in direction overall.

In the short term, geography has not gained from these approaches. The stress on literacy and numeracy has served to marginalise geography in primary schools. The KS4 Review decision leaves geography as an optional subject alongside an ever-expanding compulsory curriculum. Geographers are also anxious about new initiatives like Citizenship, which ought to provide opportunities for their subject but which seem to be increasing the curriculum pressure to geography's disadvantage.

This chapter will examine the policies and control structures created by New Labour and will explore how geography has fared and how far it may be expected to gain or lose in the future. In effect, the chapter will assess the context of influence for the next set of curriculum changes, both 5-14 and 14-19, and the likely impact on geography as a school subject.

The 'Third Way': national education policies and geography

In order to provide an accurate representation of the 'Third Way', reference has been made not only to Labour Party documentation (e.g. manifestos and annual reports) and DfEE, DfES and QCA policy papers (e.g. national curriculum guidance), but also to the writings of Anthony Giddens, one of the original architects of Third Way thinking. In *The Third Way and its Critics* Giddens (2000) denies the claim that it is not a distinctive approach, arguing that it is concerned with restructuring social democratic doctrines to respond to the twin revolutions of globalisation and the knowledge economy. In this respect it is not just 'an attempt to occupy a middle ground between top-down socialism and free-market philosophy' (Giddens, 2000, p. 163) but a genuinely new response to a changing world. Implementation of a Third Way will involve recognising a new balance between three key areas of power – government, the economy and the communities of civil society. 'A democratic state, as well as an effective market economy, depends upon a flourishing civil society. Civil society, in turn, needs to be limited by the other two' (Giddens, 2000, p. 163). All this needs to take place within the context of an increasingly globalised society.

In its pursuit of these aims, the Labour government has presented a combination of policies designed to foster enterprise (following closely in the footsteps of Conservative's neo-liberals) and policies designed to re-establish social welfare and individual responsibility. Education has been seen as a central part of the social and economic agenda. In this respect, unlike the New Right-dominated Conservative governments of the late 1980s and 1990s, Labour 'is pragmatic, willing to incorporate ideas from a range of ideological perspectives' (Bell, 1999, p. 221).

The initial foci of its policies were on school improvement and standards in the basics, but the attention of Ministers and the DfEE/DfES has already moved on to wider, more apparently radical aspects of education: 'as well as securing our economic future, learning helps us make ours a civilised society, develops the spiritual side of our lives and promotes active citizenship' (DfEE, 1998a, p. 7). Such aspirations were reflected in the so-called 'new agenda' topics, identified in and added to the National Curriculum Review – PSHE; citizenship; sustainable development education and creativity and cultural education. Each was the subject of a Task Group report and significantly for geography, some were given special backing from other government departments (e.g. Department for International Development – global citizenship; Department for Environment, Transport and the Regions – sustainable development; Department for Culture, Media and Sports – creativity and culture). The government also (perhaps selectively) listened to educational researchers and was impressed with new initiatives such as assessment for learning (Black and Wiliam, 1998) and thinking skills (McGuiness, 1999). Geography could claim to be ready to address many of these. The new national curriculum (DfEE/QCA, 1999b, c) is less dominated by one utilitarian ideology. Although many of the content headings (especially at KS3) still sound like a traditional outdated view of the subject, there are signposts in the text which open up different ideologies. Their existence reflects the confused curriculum history of the subject since 1988, but they do provide possibilities for the creative teacher. Environmental change and sustainable development is one of the four key aspects of geography (para 5 in PoS); geographical enquiry has been re-instated and reference to values and attitudes incorporated (para 1 in PoS); there is a requirement to study all scales including global (para 7 in PoS); and there are specific references to geography's role in citizenship, PSHE and thinking skills (in Learning Across the Curriculum, p. 8 and the 'importance of geography' statement (DfEE/QCA, 1999a, p. 14)).

What is striking in reading Giddens' book is that the broad sweep of understanding he brings to this conception of a changing world – with his emphasis on new technologies, the inter-relationship between local and global, the significance of place, community and identity, and the twin aspects of individual rights and responsibilities – all reflect many of the same issues with which academic geographers are involved (e.g. Johnston *et al.,* 1995; Barnes and Gregory, 1997; Massey, 1998). In particular, New Labour's vision of a Third Way seems implicitly to recognise the role of space and time. It is the regeneration of these concepts, according to Gregory and Urry (1985), which lies at the heart of the newly dynamic discipline of academic geography, helping to reposition a previously marginal geography towards the centre of the realm of social sciences. Creative curriculum development, starting from the national curriculum signposts and addressing the minimal content requirements, could enable geography to address some of these initiatives. The new GCSE and A/AS-level specifications, while having missed opportunities to make newer approaches more explicit (see Chapter 7), nevertheless do present some possibilities for the innovative teacher. In this sense, the central curriculum guidelines for geography 5-19 do, theoretically, give geographers the freedom to make an effective contribution to the curriculum of the twenty-first century. But though academic geography may be re-emerging as a frontline contributor to new thinking, its school counterpart does not seem to be central to New Labour's educational vision. Why is this?

Figure 1 outlines three characteristics of the Third Way:

■ Promotion of a dynamic economy and skilled workforce

■ Development of a cohesive and inclusive civil society

■ Taking globalisation seriously

For each, the associated curriculum policies are listed in the first column, the potential contribution of geography identified in the second column and a comment made in relation to its actual contribution in the final column. This figure should be used alongside the discussion which follows. It attempts to tease out what it is about the translation of Third Way ideas into educational policy which has been disadvantageous to school geography.

The promotion of a dynamic economy and skilled workforce

The promotion of a dynamic economy and skilled workforce is a crucial feature of the Third Way. Market forces are no longer rejected; as Giddens sees it, they are seen as a necessary evil: 'There is no known alternative to the market economy any longer; market competition generates gains that no other system can match. The chance of economic prosperity is one of these' (2000, p. 164). A dynamic economy is thus essential to the social and civil reforms that Labour wishes to make and, in this analysis, a highly skilled and productive workforce is therefore a vital requirement from the education sector.

Education policies since 1997 have continued the New Right tendency to link educational improvement directly with economic growth and to emphasis skills for employment. The KS1 and 2 Literacy and Numeracy Strategies and Targets reflect a desire to ensure the necessary levels of 'basic skills' in all pupils before they reach secondary school. Having achieved some success by 2000 (measured by the percentage of children reaching the targets set), these developments are now being extended into secondary schools through the KS3 Strategy. The promotion of 'key skills' represents a more direct attempt to focus learning on the kinds of skills employers want. The DfEE's booklet *Key Skills Explained* explains that basic skills provide the foundation on which to build key skills. The key skills which have received immediate promotion are communication, application of number and information technology, since these are 'those essential skills which people need in order to be effective members of a flexible, adaptable and competitive workforce' (DfEE, 1999a, p. 4). It is these

Characteristics of Third Way	Curriculum policies relevant to Third Way	Potential contribution of geography KS1-4	Constraints on geography's contribution
Promotion of dynamic economy and skilled workforce	■ Literacy/Numeracy Strategies ■ Key skills ■ National Grid for Learning and ICT ■ Financial capability/ Enterprise in 'learning across curriculum' (NC) ■ Work-related learning initiatives ■ Thinking skills ■ Vocational courses ■ National Qualifications Framework ■ KS3 Strategy ■ (Specialists schools?)	**Content:** emphasis on industry, work, economic development, settlement at all key stages **Skills:** geography as vehicle for literacy, numeracy, ICT and for wider key skills via, e.g. fieldwork, problem solving, investigations **Values:** recognition of changing attitudes/values to work and impact of ICT on people's lives and environments	**Constrained by:** ■ Marginal position in KS1/2 curriculum and priority given to core subjects ■ Relatively low status and variable time allocation given to geography at KS3 which prevents full development of, e.g. fieldwork, local community links and investigative work
Development of a cohesive and inclusive civil society	■ PSHE and citizenship framework at KS1/2 ■ PSHE framework at KS3 ■ Citizenship Order at KS3/4 ■ Values statements in NC handbooks ■ Education Action Zones ■ Social Exclusion Unit	**Content:** emphasis on place, community, identity, nation – especially via real places (locality and country studies) and social/ economic issues **Skills:** critical analysis of evidence, decision making **Values:** realising people value places differently and have different views on social/economic issues	■ Teachers' perceptions that NC is still highly prescriptive and traditional ■ Geography's declining status and position at 14-19 which inhibits significant contribution to citizenship and key skills, and impacts back on KS3 ■ Tension over the role of geography teachers in relation to general vocational courses such as L&T
Taking globalisation seriously	■ Values/purposes of school curriculum (in NC handbooks) ■ Sustainable development education (in NC handbooks) ■ Citizenship framework (KS1/2) and Citizenship Order (KS3/4)	**Content:** emphasis on local-global relationships and on environmental change and sustainable development at all key stages, locational knowledge and place studies at different scales **Skills:** critical enquiry and problem solving, use of ICT and internet, map skills including GIS **Values:** recognise and value diversity, clarify and develop own values about other places and people	■ Utilitarian/marginal image of geography held by policy makers and failure to include geography in key policies, e.g. specialist schools

Figure 1: Curriculum policies associated with the Third Way.

which from 2000, will form the basis of the key skills qualification, available to young people in full-time education or training. They are incorporated and signposted in national curriculum subject requirements, in Schemes of Work for KS3 and in all appropriate GCSE and A/AS-level specifications.

Significantly, the wider more personal and social aspects of key skills (working with others, planning ones own learning, problem solving) appear to have been left for a later stage of development, although many employers see these as the crucial competencies. The government's strong support for the National Grid for Learning, with grants available for hardware, and lottery money being used extensively to fund in-service training for all teachers, is another sign of the importance attached to creating a computer literate workforce.

Geography, like most other non-core subjects, has not been seen as a frontline contributor to these initiatives. Certainly at primary level, it is quite clear that English and mathematics are the priority subjects. Hence the rewriting of the English and Mathematics National Curriculum requirements to fit with the Literacy and Numeracy Strategies, and the substantial funding focused on training teachers in these aspects. Geography can be a useful vehicle for both literacy and numeracy. Indeed this role is promoted in many LEAs, in articles in *Primary Geographer* and by GA publications (e.g. the Barnaby Bear series, Jackson, 2000) and it is recognised by the significant involvement of geographical educationalists in the KS3 literacy pilot schemes and publications (2000-01). Nevertheless, the subject's role is, and probably should remain, a complementary one. What is more worrying about the emphasis on basic skills is the unintended impact on access to geography for pupils, particularly in the primary school.

In January 1998, eight months after taking office as Secretary of State for Education, David Blunkett announced that primary schools need no longer teach the full PoS in the 'non-core six' subjects of geography, history, art, music, PE and D&T (QCA, 1998f). This reduction in requirements was justified on the grounds that it allowed schools to give greater emphasis to literacy and numeracy. It was quickly followed by the introduction of the Literacy Strategy from September 1998 (DfEE, 1998b), and the Numeracy Strategy from September 1999 (DfEE, 1999b). In each case these strategies are highly prescriptive, giving details of content and timing of teaching sessions, and they are well supported with training and materials for teachers. Although the adoption of these strategies is notionally voluntary, in fact they have become requirements which few schools can avoid, given the literacy and numeracy targets to be reached and the threat of Ofsted inspectors checking on this aspect of work. Labour's first Secretary of State for Education (David Blunkett) staked his political reputation on the achievement of these targets, pledging to resign if 80% (English) and 75% (mathematics) of 11 year-olds did not reach level 4 by 2002. It was always clear that the humanities (history and geography) were likely to suffer from this policy. *The Independent's* correspondent (Figure 2) described the initial reaction as 'the Humanities get that sinking feeling' (Walker, 1998). Since then, Ofsted evidence (2001) and anecdotal evidence at the GA conferences reveal that, in some schools, geographical work was considerably reduced 1998-99, surviving only in the occasional afternoon's work on the school locality at KS1 or in the residential trip to another locality at the end of year 6. What has suffered is any in-depth work on people, places and environments and any consistent and progressive development of knowledge and skills. There is also evidence, however, that some schools and LEA advisers were creative about using geography as the vehicle for some literacy work (Caistor, 1999). As Ball (1999) points out, the pressures on schools to perform in the narrowly defined aspects of literacy and numeracy are acting back on both curriculum and pedagogy. Pupils' classroom experience is narrowed to a more restricted range of subjects and teaching/ learning approaches are narrowed to set strategies.

The national curriculum PoS for geography (and other non-core subjects) were re-instated from September 2000. As explained, the requirements, though slightly reduced, do provide greater clarity for primary planning (Westaway and Jones, 2000a) and there is an update to the Schemes of Work (QCA/DfEE, 1998, revised 2000). However, QCA monitoring suggests that, as yet, there is no evidence that curriculum priorities have changed in geography's favour, although the upsurge in GA primary membership 2000-01 may suggest that improvements will follow as schools become more comfortable with literacy and numeracy.

Mayday! Humanities get that sinking feeling
A couple of months ago, the Education Secretary, David Blunkett, made them shiver when he proposed to 'relax' the non-core subjects in the national curriculum – history and geography prime specimens – in order to allow primary school children to concentrate on attaining the official targets for literacy and numeracy. The national curriculum at large is to be reviewed. This fact was announced by the Tories three years ago. Labour is now consulting on the principles that should underpin the revision which is to be carried out by the Qualifications and Curriculum Authority, starting this summer, with a view to putting the new construction in place by the year 2000. By Easter, the scope and timetable of the revision should be clear. The mood music says the government wants – non-prescriptive, you understand – the basics plus technology and a foreign language – and if, sadly, that means less room for history, geography, art and music, so be it!

Figure 2: The humanities get that sinking feeling. Source: Walker, 1998.

In the secondary curriculum, geography can claim to be as well-represented as most other NC subjects in its potential contribution to key skills. The KS3 GNC, the criteria for GCSE courses and the A/AS criteria all make substantial reference to these skills, particularly to communications skills and to information technology. Geography has a strong background in ICT developments. Following on from its choice as one of the four subjects to be included in the DfE-funded IT projects of the mid-1990s, the publication of the 'minimum entitlement' statements for geography (GA/NCET, 1994, 1995), and an impressive range of GA publications, geography is now seen as one of the leading contributors to this aspect of education. Involvement in production of the initial teacher training guidance for ICT (TTA, 1999a,b) and in the joint BECTa/QCA web-based project on effective use of ICT in the National Curriculum (2000-01) reinforce this view. However, as with literacy and numeracy, the frustrations for geographers are that any attempts to foster continuous exposure or progression in geography and ICT are hindered by geography's fragile curriculum position 5-14 and optional status at 14-16.

Whatever the difficulties of maintaining its significant contribution to the three main key skills, the situation with respect to the wider key skills is equally worrying for geography. As a subject dealing with real world issues and with a focus on fieldwork, group work and planning investigations which cross the science/humanities divide, geography is well placed to help pupils improve their own performance and study skills, to work with others and to solve problems. Unfortunately, these key skills have, as yet, received lower priority. The Labour government has shown considerable interest in the related area of 'thinking skills' – an initiative which has grown out of the work on Cognitive Acceleration in Science Education (Adey and Shayer, 1994), but has been extended to cover newer subject areas including geography. Considerable work has in fact been done in geography, originally under the heading geographical enquiry, by the geography curriculum projects in the 1970s and more recently by the University of Newcastle Consortium (Leat, 1998; Nichols with Kinninment, 2001), which has also been involved in the government's KS3 Strategy. The KS3 Strategy handled by the Standards and Effectiveness Unit (SEU) at the DfES (Figure 3) includes a number of different emphases, one of which is entitled Teaching and Learning in the Foundation subjects (TLF). In this, funding has been provided for pilot training and in-service work for some teachers of foundation subjects in secondary schools in selected LEAs. TLF will cover four strands – planning and sequencing effective teaching; thinking skills linked to subject objectives; engaging and motivating pupils; and ensuring continuity into and across KS3. There are signs that geography departments are being chosen for involvement by schools and certainly there is scope to improve teaching and learning at

KS3 as Ofsted evidence shows. However, whether the TLF Progarmme will be sufficient to raise the quality and profile of the subject when it is implemented nationally in 2002 is another matter. Potential opportunities for geography also result from the report of the Task Group on creativity and culture, *All Our Futures* (DfEE/DCMS, 1999). This made much of the need to value and promote broader aspects of creativity in the curriculum, as a direct response to changing workplaces and needs of the economy. Geography and the other humanities subjects were specifically mentioned ('the humanities have key roles in creative and cultural education ... we are concerned too that children in KS4 are allowed to drop subjects such as arts and humanities, and then sacrifice breadth in favour of specialisation' (para 120)). Initially, the recommendations of this report were not given high priority, but during 2000 some small-scale development work on 'Creativity across the curriculum' was established by QCA and, from April 2001, geography is included in this work. As explained in Chapter 6, unlike the TLF Programme, funding is small for the QCA Creativity Initiative and it is as yet unclear how any creativity guidance will eventually relate to the TLF materials in schools. The lack of clarification about these initiatives mirrors the uneasy and ill-defined QCA/SEU relationship – a point explored further later in this chapter.

Main strands of KS3 Strategy	Potential in the Geography National Curriculum (GNC)
English and literacy across the curriculum	GNC has links to English in marginal text; Scheme of Work makes explicit reference; Geography and Literacy pilot materials are being prepared
Mathematics and numeracy across the curriculum	GNC has links to mathematics in marginal text; Scheme of Work makes explicit reference (a KS2 unit of work focuses on numeracy and geography)
Science	Geography/science linkages in relation to environment and sustainable development will feature on QCA website
ICT	GNC has links to ICT in marginal text and in the POS; Scheme of Work makes explicit reference to ICT; QCA and BECTa are producing case study materials
Teaching and learning in the foundation subjects, including: ■ Planning and sequence teaching ■ Thinking skills (subject based) ■ Engaging and motivating pupils ■ Ensuring continuity	Scheme of Work has a section on thinking skills, and work in geography has been undertaken by a Newcastle University consortium (Leat, 1998; Nichols with Kinninment, 2001); GNC is more flexible, allowing more creative interpretation, and the Scheme of Work suggests ways of planning and sequencing; Scheme of Work Unit 1 emphasises KS2/3 continuity; some Scheme of Work units provide possibilities for more motivating work (e.g. Unit 6 world sport, Unit 18 global fashion)

Figure 3: The KS3 Strategy (from 2000) DfES Standards and Effectiveness Unit.

Finally, mention should be made of the many initiatives aimed at re-emphasising the direct contribution of vocational education and training to the creation of a well-skilled and employable workforce. The impact of these on school geography has been elaborated in Chapter 7. Here it is important to note that despite geography's long-established inputs to an understanding of industry, and preparation for work and employment, the new developments have brought more dilemmas for secondary geography teachers (Rawling, 1997a).

Development of a cohesive and inclusive society

New Labour's vision of a well-developed civil society, according to Giddens (2000), is one in which individuals understand and act upon both their rights and responsibilities. In this view, government and state institutions play an important role in ameliorating the detrimental effects of the market and in regulating crime and anti-social behaviour, but not at the expense of inhibiting individual action. Highly important to this vision is recognition of different levels of community to which individuals belong – the family, the local community, the nation – and the roles expected in each situation. It is recognised that inequalities will exist in such a society, but the emphasis is on promoting equality of opportunity, by taking positive action (ensuring access to work or to education for all). Equality of opportunity, it is stated, will not necessarily lead to equality of outcome – indeed plurality and diversity are desirable and should be recognised as such.

A whole range of welfare and social policies emanate from these ideas but education is seen as crucial to producing informed and responsible citizens, and to raising life chances for those otherwise excluded or marginal in society. Curriculum policies reflecting these emphases include the PSHE and citizenship education frameworks which have been established for KS1/2, the PSHE frameworks for KS3/4, and the Citizenship Subject Order for KS3/4. The main strands of these initiatives highlight responsibilities, relationships, respecting difference and taking action. The advisory Statement of Values, outlined in the national curriculum handbooks (DfEE/QCA, 1999b,c), also has a stress on the individual as an active participatory member of civil society.

As with other subjects in the national curriculum, geography can only claim to contribute to some aspects of these cross-curricular initiatives. However, it can be argued that its contribution could be substantial given the emphasis on place, community, identity and nation, and particularly on the need to place all these within a global context. Goodson (1998b) and Ross (2000) show that both history and geography have been called on in the past to serve particular visions of the nation (most recently in the 1991 National Curriculum). The recent rhetoric has not, however, led to any re-evaluation of their curriculum status at KS3 and 4. For geography there are many new ideas and approaches to draw on in academic geography where, according to Goodwin (1999) issues of citizenship and identity are offering fertile ground for geographical research. Geography at KS1 and 2 deals specifically with the local area and locality-scale studies, giving children the opportunity to explore their own community and to understand its diversity and its coherence. They are also asked to relate all this to its location in Britain and the wider world. At KS3, scales of study are widened and there are opportunities to delve more deeply into economic, social and environmental issues arising from studies of space and place. Although the thematic headings, particularly at KS3, still present a rather traditional and static view of the subject, in fact there is ample scope for the kind of dynamic community – or local area-based initiatives which would allow pupils to address many of the PSHE and citizenship requirements. The Schemes of Work for Geography at KS3 (DfEE/QCA, 2000b) make hints in this direction. For instance, Unit 15, Crime and the Local Community, explains patterns of criminal activity within the local area. Unit 16, What is Development, analyses the meaning of development in both familiar (e.g. school locality) and unfamiliar places, and in Unit 5, Exploring England, pupils examine their perceptions and the perceptions of other people about what England is and how it relates to the UK and British Isles. Most GCSE specifications allow further work of this nature and given the greater maturity of pupils could lead to exciting participatory work in the local community or liaison with local employers. The Geography, Schools and Industry Project pioneered work of this kind in the 1980s (Corney, 1992). At present, a new GA-supported project, GeoVisions (Robinson *et al.*, 1999; GeoVisions, 1999) is developing innovative approaches to geography at KS3 and 4. Unfortunately, the lack of real encouragement in the topic headings of KS3 GNC, combined with the optional nature of geography at KS4, may make it difficult to provide for all pupils a continuous contribution to PSHE and citizenship. Initial PSHE and citizenship guidance has been produced by QCA for KS1 and 2 (QCA, 2000d) and for KS3 and 4 (QCA, 2000e). A Scheme of Work has also been published for KS3 (QCA/DfEE, 2001) and similar material is expected for KS4 (autumn 2001) and KS1 and 2 (spring 2002).

The biggest constraint remains that of curriculum time, particularly at KS4, where geography is in a highly competitive situation and having difficulty in maintaining numbers (Chapter 7). Dis-application possibilities are now available, originally allowing individual pupils to give up the study of science, a modern foreign language or technology in order to take up work-related learning opportunities. These have been extended (QCA, 2000f) to cover disapplication of MFL and D&T for individual pupils to consolidate learning in specific areas of weakness or to give emphasis to a particular curriculum area. Geography has gained from this initiative, according to the limited evidence available so far (QCA internal monitoring paper 2001), but not dramatically. Work-related learning and curriculum consolidation (often extra English and mathematics) were the most common reasons for dis-application of subjects in the 1100 schools which had so far used the regulations. Even where the 'curriculum emphasis' reason has been used, the arts and ICT are the most popular subjects to be emphasised. Geography and history fall somewhere in the middle of the list. Early in 2001, David Blunkett declared his intention to extend flexibility even further at KS4, but this was to allow more vocational emphasis rather than to widen choice generally for pupils.

Two other initiatives need to be mentioned. Educational Action Zones (EAZs) were established with a remit to tackle broader social issues from an educational perspective. The EAZ initiative was set up in 1997 and concerns relatively small-scale areas or zones identified mainly in cities, although there are also some in rural areas (e.g. Shropshire). Each of the original 73 EAZs was chosen to reflect significant under-achievement and deprivation in the local community. The emphasis is on initiatives which will raise educational standards, extend opportunities and promote greater diversity in what is offered. The EAZs are locally run and receive significant levels of funding from the DfES (DfES/Standards website).

The Social Exclusion Unit covers an even wider remit. This was established in 1997 as a cross-departmental unit located within the Cabinet Office and reporting directly to the Prime Minister. The Unit aims to reduce social exclusion, defined as the situation in which individuals and areas are marginalised in society because of poor skills, low incomes, poor housing, bad health and family breakdown. Most of the work is based on specific projects which cross other departments (e.g. Neighbourhood Renewal). It is meant to provide 'joined-up solutions to joined-up problems' and most of the projects have some educational dimension. Both initiatives allow a certain amount of curriculum innovation – schools involved in EAZs or social exclusion initiatives are not required to follow the national curriculum. Despite this, the signs are that few EAZ or Social Exclusion Unit projects have made major curriculum changes. The Annual Report of HMCI noted that 'some useful, though not necessarily ground-breaking, developments were being pursued in most of the Education Action Zones' (Ofsted, 2001, para 254, p. 68). If anything, the tendency has been to narrow the curriculum in the sense of focusing more on basic literacy, numeracy and work-related skills rather than to broaden it. While this might be appropriate for the initial phases of such projects, it could be argued that more innovative curriculum thinking might now begin to happen. However, there seems to have been little attempt to reconsider the content of a curriculum addressing social issues. Subjects like geography, art, design and technology and music, which might claim to justify a place in a curriculum seeking to regenerate deprived communities, restore a sense of identity and promote inclusion (see DfEE/DCMS, 1999), do not appear to feature in the thinking so far. Excellence in Cities is another initiative (from 1999) which aims to improve the education of urban children, but with a particular focus on gifted children, learning support and access to higher education. A recent report from the Runnymede Trust (2000) suggested (among other things) that the contribution of education to promoting a cohesive and inclusive society remains under-developed and that Labour's existing initiatives do not go far enough, despite the rhetoric and substantial efforts.

Taking globalisation seriously

As far as Giddens is concerned 'taking globalisation seriously' is one of the key characteristics of the Third Way, and this is in direct comparison to the narrower more nationalistic policies of the right wing governments in the 1980s and early 1990s. As Tony Blair explained, speaking in Chicago, April 1999:

'we cannot refuse to participate in global markets if we want to prosper. We cannot ignore new political ideas in other countries if we want to innovate. We cannot turn our backs on conflicts and the violation of human rights if we still want to be secure' (quoted in Giddens, 2000, p. 123).

Taking globalisation seriously would mean integrating national policies with global perspectives whether in the realms of economics, human rights, social policy, cultural change, environmental issues or education.

In educational policy terms, the Labour government has made a lot of 'noise' in relation to globalisation and, accordingly, has raised expectations. However, arguably, despite Giddens' clarity in this area, it is probably the least well-developed as an educational project in England. For geography, the GCSE criteria refer directly to the global scale, interdependence and global citizenship, but it is not quite so explicit in the A/AS-level criteria. Although there is potential for the awarding bodies to extend a global dimension, it has only been developed significantly in a small number of specifications. In the national curriculum, references to globalisation seem to have been tacked on to the requirements, without the benefit of clear thinking about how such a concept would be recognised and addressed in a curriculum. Thus the words 'continued globalisation of the economy and society' have been added to the paragraph about education responding to a rapidly changing world (DfEE/QCA, 1999a, p. 10). The need to develop awareness and understanding of sustainable development is also stated in the Aims for the school curriculum and as an 'other aspect of the school curriculum' in the section on Learning across the curriculum (DfEE/QCA, 1999a, p. 25). But it is as if sustainable development is a new topic which needs to be studied because of the impact of globalising economies on the environment. Even the subjects which are given special mention as promoting sustainable development education (SDE) treat this idea in different ways, probably not surprisingly since such references were only added at a late stage in the National Curriculum Review process (see Rawling, 2001c). In PSHE, citizenship and science, for example, environmental matters and global perspectives are added topics or extra criteria for breadth. Only in geography is there at least a recognition (if teachers are able to appreciate this) that global is a scale *and* a perspective, and that sustainable development issues underlie all the topics to be studied. The QCA/DfES SDE website (being prepared 2001-02) provides examples of school planning and subject-based pieces of work and will assist with developing this broader understanding.

It is significant that it is citizenship which has been established as a separate framework and national curriculum subject rather than either 'global citizenship' or 'SDE'. The Task Group on SDE, chaired by Sir Geoffrey Holland, had a distinctly lower profile than the Citizenship Task Group chaired by Professor Bernard Crick (though both reported at the same time, September 1998) (CEE, 1998; QCA, 1998g). The citizenship proposals had a markedly national tone to them focusing on laws, the constitution and local/national communities. It was clear, even during the early stages of NC Review, that the Secretary of State favoured the separate citizenship solution rather than the formation of any over-arching framework for all the cross-curricular 'new agenda' themes. An early paper from the QCA Preparation for Adult Life Working Group did recommend this approach. Arguably, SDE might have provided the required global perspective as well as an umbrella framework for PSHE, citizenship, creativity and cultural education and even for key skills and work-related learning, with the NC subjects lying underneath this as sources of knowledge, understanding, skills and values. As Jonathan Porritt describes it 'SD is not a single issue. It is essentially a different model of progress, balancing the social and economic needs of the human species with the non-negotiable imperative of living with Planet Earth's natural limits' (1999). This is the kind of vision which Giddens' book seems to have in mind for the Third Way. An education geared to such a model of society would be unlikely to create the kind of separate Citizenship Order now in existence. It would also (I suggest) be more likely to find a more secure place for geography as a subject whose core is the interactions between the human and natural worlds at all scales. As it is, geographers find that they have limited access to the area in which they could make one of the biggest contributions to school education. They are constrained by the outdated topic headings and consequent image of the national curriculum, by curriculum policies which see globalisation as a separate issue, and by the subject's insecure place in the 14-19 curriculum.

Guidance on the cross-curricular areas, being prepared by QCA, may be seen as perfectly appropriate in each individual case, but they may, paradoxically, prolong the confusion for schools about how to deal with the whole set. There are separate documents which have been produced for PSHE and citizenship (QCA, 2000d,e), there are Schemes of Work for Citizenship (QCA/DfEE, 2001) and web-based guidance for SDE. There are existing QCA documents about key skills (QCA, 2000c) and Work-Related Learning (QCA, 1999b). Added to this is the growing range of subject guidance materials. A range of individual solutions has thus been provided rather than any over-arching guidance on planning a curriculum which would develop responsible global citizens. The QCA document entitled *Flexibility in the Secondary Curriculum* (QCA, 1999c) does not attempt this larger task, but focuses on guiding schools through the technicalities of organising national curriculum subject blocks and coping with dis-application. The awaited primary version of this guidance is expected to focus, in a similar way, on helping schools to manage the expanding time demands of literacy and numeracy. A more radical approach to curriculum guidance might have provided an explanatory framework for the contribution of all subjects to the cross-curricular areas, and placed the greatest emphasis on facilitating active, participatory teaching and learning strategies. In this respect it would also have drawn on thinking skills and assessment for learning – i.e. a real joined-up solution. Note that a report from Professor Crick (2000) makes recommendations for citizenship post-16. If there is ensuing research or development work, then geography may be able to contribute, given its popularity as an A/AS subject.

Overall the treatment of globalisation provides a clue to the characteristics of New Labour's curriculum policies and to how they have provided problems for geography (and perhaps other subjects). The approach has been to make amendments to the existing national curriculum (e.g. mathematics and English to accommodate literacy and numeracy), to add new non-subject-based aspects (e.g. citizenship, SDE) or to create whole new initiatives outside the national curriculum (e.g. EAZs, social exclusion projects). Significantly, the 2001 education Green Paper (DfEE, 2001) proposed to extend the number of specialist schools to 50% all schools – i.e. effectively extending both funding for implementation and the possibility for many schools to opt out of some of the constraints of the existing national curriculum. What has not been done is to think afresh what kind of curriculum might be appropriate for a society at the beginning of the twenty-first century. As Quicke points out (2000) it is strange that the content (and specifically subject content) of the national curriculum has not been given any critique although it may be the one element which holds the clue to effective societal change. Significantly, there are no plans to provide a full National Curriculum Review in 2005. The government seems to have committed itself instead to a rolling programme of curriculum 'projects' – the first four of which were signalled in the QCA Report following consultation on the national curriculum (QCA/DfEE, 1999b). These include science for the twenty-first century, the 14-19 phase, MFL at KS2 and mathematics at KS3/4. PE and school sport and creativity and the arts are two projects which have been added subsequently, and from 2001 some limited funding has been made available for a humanities (geography and history) curriculum rethink. Although the project approach does allow in-depth reconsideration of curriculum content and teaching and learning approaches in individual areas, it fails to provide any overall review of the whole curriculum experience appropriate to young people. The Labour government has not evolved, and does not, it seems, intend to evolve, a curriculum vision to match the Third Way vision as a whole.

Structures of control

If it is difficult to find a genuine Third Way in curriculum policies, it may be easier to identify a distinct approach to the way policies are made and managed. The Labour government has brought new groups of people into policy making and policy management since 1997 – for example, the special advisers, task forces, advisory groups, literacy and numeracy teams and new policy units. Their involvement seems to represent an attempt to stimulate dialogue with education professionals. High profile educationalists such as Tim Brighouse (until 1999 Vice Chair of the Standards Task Force), David Hargreaves (also Vice Chair of the Standards Task Force from 1999 and, since his appointment in September 2000, Chief Executive of QCA) and David Reynolds (School Improvement Adviser) have been given positions where their voices can be heard. The creation of a National Educational Forum (1999) and the establishment of the Evidence for Policy and Practice Information and Co-ordinating Centre at the Institute of Education, London (2000) are other initiatives which aim to extend the debate about the relationship between research findings and policy. There is, however, some suspicion from educationalists (e.g. Pring, 2000b) about whether the agenda is genuinely one of drawing on current research in an open-ended way or whether the aim is to find research evidence to justify already agreed strategies.

During the National Curriculum Review, the government appointed a series of task groups to make recommendations about its 'new agenda' topics (citizenship, PSHE, SDE and creativity and cultural education). Although these eventually fed into a joint QCA/DfEE Preparation for Adult Life overview group and so into the review of NC subjects, they were not an integral part of the review process, but assumed an importance and influence of their own. Significantly, the QCA subject teams were held back from feeding appropriate curriculum requirements into the revised subject Orders until a very late stage (e.g. citizenship and SDE into geography after May 1999). In some cases, an independent decision was taken (e.g. to create a separate Citizenship Subject Order) instead of considering what existing subject formulations had to offer.

Other initiatives demonstrate a more direct attempt to implement already agreed strategies. The National Literacy and Numeracy Strategies both involve dedicated teams of professionals, producing quite directive guidelines for schools. In each case, as already explained, although the adoption of these strategies is notionally voluntary, in fact it has become a requirement which few schools can avoid. Although the suggestion is that once the content is familiar, teachers will use the strategies more flexibly (Barber and Sebba, 1999) there is little evidence yet that this is occurring on a wide scale. The actual effect is to produce the required short-term rise in measured standards of literacy and numeracy, but almost certainly (as Ball points out, 1999) at the long-term expense of more creative contributions of the whole curriculum to a wider set of curriculum objectives.

Also significant is the Standards and Effectiveness Unit itself (SEU), established in 1997 as a separate unit at the DfEE. The SEU is large and influential (in numbers, SEU staff roughly equal numbers in SCAA pre-1997). It now has five divisions (LEA Improvement, School Improvement, Pupils' Standards, Diversity and Best Practice, and Excellence in Cities). Professional educators are well represented on its staff, though not as independent advisers but more in the role of implementers of the government's stated objectives. This has impacted directly on the core subjects of English and mathematics – witness the decision that QCA should not produce KS1/2 Schemes of Work for these subjects because of potential conflict with the Literacy and Numeracy Strategies. So far the direct impact on geography has been slight but significant, involving debates over the extent to which the joint SEU/QCA Schemes of Work for Geography were to be directive (the approved interpretation) or exemplary (a model for curriculum development). However, the KS3 Strategy with its Teaching and Learning in the Foundation Subjects Programme will have a direct impact on secondary geography over the next few years. Indirectly too much of SEU's new work has implications for the future of geography in schools, whether it is about developing thinking skills, reconsidering urban education or creating more specialist schools. In most cases, each new initiative is managed by a separate SEU team, with a clearly defined strategy and advisers and, significantly, no geographers (identified as such) in the SEU hierarchy.

What is important about all these new developments is that they collectively represent a move to a more managerial and technocratic approach to curriculum matters. Ball suggests that the prescriptive strategies (e.g. literacy) and tightly managed systems of accountability (e.g. targets, performance indicators) reveal 'a model of schooling which is essentially Fordist and micro-managed' (1999, p. 203). Ball sees this as partly a local (English) response to shifts in global policy paradigms since the same kind of changes are seen in other developed countries (e.g. Australia). However, what is striking in the English context is that this managerialism seems strangely out of line with the rhetoric of the Third Way which, according to Giddens, places a big emphasis on creativity and flexibility.

Identifying some key issues

Three key issues arise from this discussion of the changing educational policy conditions existing under New Labour. Between them, they effectively define the 'context of influence' for the next set of curriculum changes.

i. Changing sites for struggles over subject knowledge

The 1989-91 period was characterised by a focus on subject disciplines, reflecting the Conservative government's desire to re-instate a subject-based curriculum and traditional subject knowledge and skills. The Dearing Review was also a subject-based exercise because it was focused primarily on rescuing the first version of the national curriculum. Most of the battles took place within subjects (e.g. English and grammar; history and dates/famous people). For geography, the implementation difficulties caused by the 1991 Order dominated the debate, so that the review concentrated on structural change, and content issues such as world knowledge and maps hardly featured (apart from in the national press!). In comparison, the QCA Review was a more multi-focused exercise, encompassing both continuing amendment and consolidation of the 'old' subject-based curriculum (inherited from the previous government), but more significantly, the introduction of New Labour's distinctive interests (e.g. citizenship) which tended to cut across the old subject framework. Some NC subjects benefited from this clash of interests – in geography's case there were gains in the curriculum framework but losses in curriculum status.

The Dearing and QCA Reviews now seem to represent the end of 'sorting out' the old curriculum. The signs are that New Labour's policy emphases and ways of working herald a new era in which there is less interest in the details of curriculum input by subject (e.g. the geography curriculum details), and more interest in curriculum output in certain defined areas (literacy targets, GCSE league tables, TLF objectives, percentage specialist schools). If the analysis is correct, then the 1990s saw a significant shift in the location of subject power struggles. The 1990s for geography were all about amending the detail of the 1991 Order to produce a workable curriculum framework and, in this respect, the 1994-2000 climate was favourable to change. Within the subject community it is now essential to support teachers in creatively implementing this framework and so to continue to be concerned with subject content details. However, at national level, the sites for promotion of and maintenance of the subject perspective have changed. Geography's future status and the contribution it will be allowed to make to the future curriculum will partly depend, as for other subjects, on how it is seen to address the newer policy initiatives emerging since 1997. These, as has been shown, include raising literacy and numeracy standards, developing thinking skills and promoting citizenship and SDE and contributing to assessment for learning. For many of these, geography has relevant experience to share (e.g. Leat, 1998; Nichols with Kinninment, 2001), is already being asked to contribute (e.g. GA involvement in the literacy strategy at KS3), or can draw on new aspects of the geography curriculum (e.g. environmental change and sustainable development, enquiry). However, there is a danger that this new discourse will encourage the subject community to promote geography as a servicing agent for continually changing national priorities. In fact, power struggles over subject knowledge will continue, even in an increasingly non-subject based educational policy framework and it is vital that geographers can argue their case from the base of a distinctive subject identity. Counsell, referring to history and literacy, explained the situation succinctly:

> 'subjects matter. They are not just the settings for the deployment of someone else's skills. The more we think clearly about the boundaries and distinctive purposes of our subjects the more we will be able to make the curriculum bigger than the sum of its parts' (2000, p. 21).

At present geography does not feature as a particularly distinctive or key subject in the minds of policy makers. This observation is confirmed by the fact that geography, the humanities and the environmental sciences seem to be the only significant curriculum areas not identified as appropriate for specialist school focus.

ii. A new breed of policy managers or 'technocrats'?
The Labour administration, as explained, has brought new groups of professionals into policy making and policy management since 1997. While these attempts at dialogue should perhaps be welcomed because they bring a larger group of professional educators into the policy-making circle, they do raise wider issues about control. For example, how should some, at least, of these people be identified in Lawton's classification of politicians, bureaucrats and professionals (Chapter 5, page 82)? As a number of commentators have pointed out (Bell, 1999; Power and Whitty, 1999) the Labour government's approach promotes a strange mixture of autonomy and control. It is pragmatic and willing initially to incorporate ideas from different perspectives but, having decided on policy, then detailed implementation is set within a directive framework of targets and strategies. Thus the definition and promotion of particular initiatives now under way (e.g. raising standards, school improvement, social exclusion, specialist schools) all use the government's own interpretation of how this is to be pursued and, significantly for geography, of which subjects will be included or excluded. It is noticeable, for instance, that neither the school improvement programme (Quicke, 2000) nor the thinking skills activites, nor initiatives like citizenship and PSHE suggest a radical critique of the whole national curriculum now being offered in schools. What mix of subjects, for example, would best address the needs of young people in the twenty-first century? Do subject disciplines any longer provide the best framework for such a curriculum? All that seems to be offered is a more technical concern with the details of implementation (literacy, numeracy, new-look science, a new subject called citizenship), within the existing NC shell. The big questions are not being asked, as one would expect of independent professionals. For the moment, it might be more correct to see this group as 'technocrats' acting in a tightly controlled policy management role, rather than as professional educators commenting on and influencing policy direction. Task groups and advisory groups may be less directed, and it is not yet clear, for instance, how much freedom will be exercised by the National Educational Research Forum and whether it will have the genuine ability to influence rather than react to the policy agenda (Pring, 2000b; BERA, 2001).

iii. Changing power structures inside the educational state

In the endnote to his book about *Politics and Policy-making in Education*, Ball (1990) presented a diagrammatic representation of the contending influences inside the educational state. It illustrates the predominantly ideological struggles over school knowledge played out between the New Right 'cultural restorationists', who strongly influenced number 10 and the Secretary of State's office, and the more progressive educationalists with their power base in the NCC and HMI. The DES, with its more traditional 'reforming humanist' ideology and openness to 'industrial trainer' ideas from business and industry lobbies, acted as a moderating influence.

The politics of the changing geography curriculum throughout the 1990s suggests that this representation now needs to be amended (Figure 4). The lines of ideological conflict are not so easily drawn in 2000. New Labour does not define itself in old ideological terms, but draws on a mixture of ideas from across the full ideological spectrum. Targets, performance indicators and the basic and key skills represent a continuation of right-wing curriculum policies. Measures to promote citizenship, SDE, PSHE and values borrow from more radical left-wing agendas. It might be

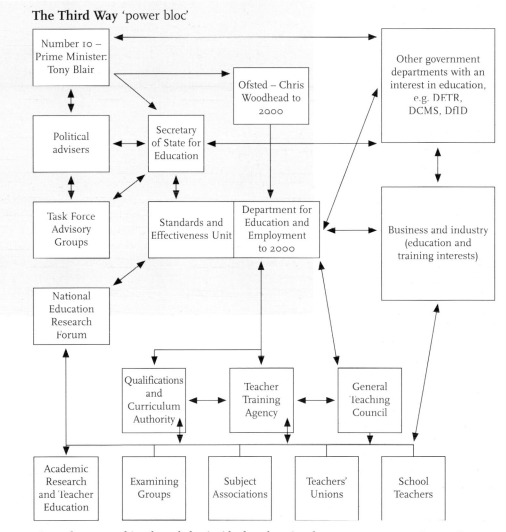

Figure 4: Struggles over subject knowledge inside the educational state, 2000. Derived from: Ball, 1990.

suggested that it is not the curriculum policies themselves which represent New Labour's Third Way, but the managerialist approach and structures of control which have been introduced to implement these policies (Rawling, 2001b). The centre of gravity of curriculum policy making and implementation is changing. The older model, of QCA providing curriculum and assessment advice direct to government, is being replaced by one in which politically appointed individuals and groups are focused on implementing stated government educational policies on a direct line from number 10. In this sense New Labour has built up a new educational 'power bloc' (Figure 4). Several political commentators have noted the growing influence and strong control exerted by the Prime Minister (Kavanagh and Seldon, 1999; Hennessy, 2000). Kavanagh and Seldon (1999) note that Tony Blair increased the number of political advisers in Whitehall from 38 under John Major to 64 by January 1998 (recent newspaper speculations suggest the number is nearer 78 in 2000). He has taken a more direct approach to setting and overseeing strategy, which frequently sidelines government departments. This is what Hennessy (2000) calls the 'command premiership'. Although designed to make things happen and to promote 'joined up policy' this strong control has implications for education, and specifically for curriculum policy making.

In the six years between 1993 and 1999, professional geography educators have been given considerable freedom within broad policy frameworks to manage the detail and make amendments to the subject Order. This was true for SCAA and also in the first two years of QCA. However, once the official NC Review was finished and Labour's own actions started to take effect, QCA's role began to change. As Chapter 7 has shown, its qualifications and assessment functions are ever-expanding and it is now faced with a whole range of new political advisers and a rival body. The SEU not only provides advice to Ministers on QCA's policy management role, but it actually implements new policy initiatives (e.g. the Literacy Strategy, the KS3 Strategy). So far the greatest impact of this has been felt by the core subjects. The SEU staff responsible for literacy and numeracy already duplicate to some extent the work of QCA subject officers, with consequences for the latters' independence. The appointment of a SEU Science Director for KS3 may overlap with the work of the QCA Science Team (indeed the person appointed to the post was originally part of the QCA Science Team). New initiatives such as thinking skills and the KS3 Strategy with its TLF programme will make more impact on the foundation subjects and are clearly being led from SEU, though they could easily have been allocated to QCA's curriculum division. There is not necessarily any greater merit in QCA being the curriculum policy management body as compared to SEU; what is significant is that the government has not redefined QCA's curriculum role but created new structures which are under its direct influence and which, judging by the overlapping initiatives in 2000 (QCA's Creativity and curriculum development projects and SEU's TLF programme) are operating independently rather than in close co-operation with QCA. These more restricted approaches to curriculum policy management might be termed the 'command curriculum'. They are already bringing criticism from academics (e.g. Ball, 1999; Goldstein and Woodhouse, 2000). For geography, the danger seems to be that, in the 2000s, there will be more prescriptive curriculum strategies and less involvement from professional geography educators.

Conclusion

An attempt has been made to identify the context of influence underlying the next set of changes to the curriculum and, specifically, to assess the implications for geography. Given the rhetoric of the Third Way and the initial suggestion that attention should be given to cross-curricular aspects like sustainable development education and citizenship, it might have seemed in 1997 that geography would be provided with opportunities to play an increasingly substantial curriculum role. However, as Labour's policies have emerged, these expectations have not, so far, been fulfilled, though some of the opportunities remain.

The government has not taken the opportunity, either for 2000 (which is understandable because it inherited a review from the previous government) or apparently for 2005, to undertake a full review of the kind of curriculum appropriate to the twenty-first century. In this sense, it has not developed a curriculum vision to match the Third Way vision propounded by thinkers like Giddens (2000). Instead, curriculum priorities are predominantly non-subject based, characterised by amendments to existing subjects, additions to the whole NC framework or changes to school structures (as in specialist schools). Geography is disadvantaged – first, because it does not feature significantly in the prescriptive solutions being put forward; second because teachers still feel constrained by the subject content headings of the national curriculum and 14-19 specifications; and third because of its insecure status, particularly at 14-19. On the other hand, this chapter has also shown that there are some opportunities for breaking into the policy discourse. Mention might be made of the SEU's TLF programme, the QCA creativity and geography/history curriculum projects, and the citizenship/social exclusion agendas, all of which might provide the possibility of developing a stronger geographical contribution, particularly to issues of community, identity, environment and sustainable development.

Finally, however, one of the biggest constraints for geography (and, arguably, for other subjects) is the 'command curriculum' with its highly controlled approach to policy management and implementation. During the 1990s, some freedom of movement developed in relation to the interpretation of the GNC, and this allowed a more open dialogue between geography educators within and outside the official agencies. It seems that this greater freedom is now threatened by the more rigid and managerialist approach of the Third Way. Prescriptive and centralised curriculum solutions might leave little room for creative professionalism at national or school level.

9

Ideology and Policy-Making: The Experience of School Geography

Introduction

In Chapter 1 it was explained that the intention was to undertake a case study of school geography 1980-2000. The aims were two-fold: first, and most directly, to examine the impact of changing curriculum policies on the character and status of geography in schools; and second, to highlight key points about curriculum change, school subjects and the impact of policy making in general. Drawing on the analysis in Chapters 2-8, this chapter puts forward some conclusions.

The impact and significance of ideology is a topic which has engaged educationalists over the past decade and still leads to heated debates. I hope this book has shown that this ideology, though significant, has not been as important to the curriculum history of this school subject as many of us, myself included, would like to have believed. Ideology is an easy scapegoat, but it may be time to get a more balanced view. The next section is an attempt to do this.

The analytical approach used in this book has been inspired by the work of Ball and, as explained in Chapter 1, the study of the Geography National Curriculum (GNC) has made use of the policy cycle approach, investigating the contexts of influence, text production and practice for geography. Although Ball's work stressed the powerful influence of the state on the changing curriculum, it also highlighted the fact that the educational policy process is unpredictable and open to conflict, compromise and re-interpretation (Ball, 1990; Bowe and Ball with Gold, 1992). This point has been borne out by the experience of geography, particularly in the formation and revisions of the original national curriculum and in the changes which have occurred in the 14-19 curriculum. Others have challenged this view, suggesting that Ball has underestimated the role of the central state in the determination of policy even at micro-level (Dale, 1989; Hatcher and Troyna, 1994). The discussions in Chapter 9 will address this issue, attempting to highlight for geography both the extent and the limits of state control and hence the 'spaces' left for action by geography educators.

Although the detailed analysis of geography's curriculum history in Chapters 3-7 has focused on 1980-2000, it is important to understand these changes in a broader context. Hence Chapters 1 and 2 provided historical background and this chapter will use a longer-term 'model' to place the 1980-2000 period in its chronological sequence. Throughout the period, it is possible to recognise key decision makers and interest groups influential in changing the subject. This will be addressed, with special attention given to ministers, political advisers, civil servants and government appointees (i.e. those who represent the state) and to the national media, which plays a key role in image formation. An attempt will also be made to assess the changing role of the subject associations in defending and promoting the subject at different times.

Changing ideologies

Chapter 3 explained the importance of understanding different ideological positions and their influence on the school curriculum, and Figure 1 in Chapter 3 (page 32) outlined a simplified view of the significant educational ideologies which have affected school geography in England over the past 100 years. Reference may be made back to this diagram, remembering that, at any one time, the curriculum is likely to be a mixture of different ideologies. During the last 30 years, school geography has been strongly affected by ideological swings. Marsden (1989) reminds us that it is not unusual for the curriculum to be used for socio-political purposes, referring in particular to the promotion of geography as an 'Empire' subject in the inter-war years. However, with increasing centralisation of curriculum policy making in the 1980s and 1990s, the scope for such politicisation and the resultant likelihood of ideological conflict have increased.

Chapter 3 explained that geography pre-national curriculum had expanded from an earlier informational/utilitarian tradition and had built up a strong claim to be included in the liberal humanist tradition as a rigorous academic discipline with a university base. Curriculum development activity in the 1970s promoted a more progressive educational ideology, revealing that the subject could also be a vehicle for the development of general educational skills and abilities and the exploration of values. Some developments opened up the possibility for more radical, reconstructionist interpretations (see Huckle, 1983, 1997). It is true to say that only a minority of schools took on a progressive ideology, and even fewer explored radical ideas, but as Chapter 3 explained, the curriculum development movement did change the discourse and it promoted a period of greater debate. These developments were overturned in the late 1980s with the establishment of the GNC. The process of change 1991-2000 makes a good case study of the impact of changing ideologies. Chapters 3 and 4 show how geography gained its place in the national curriculum but in so doing was strongly influenced by the thrust towards more utilitarian and informational purposes. This seemed to represent a triumph for the New Right, and specifically for those described as 'cultural restorationists' active in policy making at the time (Ball, 1990; Callaghan, 1995), although Chapter 4 reveals that there was more 'ad hoc-ery' than conspiracy about the process. The key features of a 'culturally restored' geography curriculum as seen in the 1991 curriculum were the stress on factual knowledge at the expense of key ideas, the emphasis on place study and locational knowledge, the marginalisation of enquiry and active learning methods, and the general ethos of a curriculum concerned with Britain and Empire. However, Chapter 4 noted that the more progressive features were not extinguished, merely pushed, for the moment, to the outer edges of the picture.

The changes made in the two National Curriculum Reviews were substantial and ideologically significant, despite the constrained nature of the change process in both cases. All the features referred to above have now been amended to give a very different balance of content, even within the same content shell provided by the 1991 Order. The Dearing Review adjusted the weighting so that place study was more obviously balanced by thematic studies and environmental work, and so that teachers had more flexibility to choose their own place examples within set criteria. If anything, because the rather dated details of human and physical geography themes tended to dominate the look of the programmes of study, and because geographical enquiry was still 'low key' compared with the long list of specific skills, the Dearing geography curriculum seemed set in a positivist theoretical mode, possibly more akin to liberal humanist ideology. The QCA Review arguably moved the geography curriculum further towards a progressive educational ideology. It has re-instated geographical enquiry and values and attitudes, and made direct reference to geography's wider contributions to sustainable development education, citizenship and understanding global issues. Most significantly perhaps, with a change in model emphasising four key aspects of geography (enquiry and skills, places, patterns and processes, environmental change and sustainable development) teachers are provided with the tools for curriculum planning and choice of appropriate content, all opportunities denied by the original Order.

The GNC has, then, undergone quite a dramatic ideological journey since 1991, perhaps a surprising outcome from the constrained and politically controlled processes of National Curriculum Review. It should be noted that evidence of implementation (Chapter 6) suggests that national level battles are less significant at school level. Roberts' (1995) research reveals that many schools carry on using the style and emphases inherited from previous eras. This is not to say that national level frameworks do not matter since they present the image of the subject accepted by the public and politicians and, ultimately, form the boundaries for possible future action.

Looking ahead, it is not so easy to plot the next move in terms of ideological influences. As Chapter 7 has explained, the Labour government is not ideologically driven. There are some radical-looking 'new agenda' initiatives – sustainable development education (SDE), citizenship, creativity and cultural education, thinking skills. However, the more pragmatic approach of Third Way policy control, apparently continuing after the 2001 election, is resulting in fragmented schemes added to the existing national curriculum, and to controlled strategies and guidance materials for implementation. Although geography has undoubted potential to contribute, these approaches may not suit a subject still trapped inside a traditional looking NC shell and still holding a relatively marginal status in schools. Geography also continues to be constrained in national debates by the old utilitarian image, an image which the press plays a significant role in promoting. Articles about school geography are normally prefaced by concern about pupils' locational knowledge and focus on the mistaken view that there is a conflict between knowing where places are and gaining deeper awareness and understanding of the complexity of places, environmental issues and global change. Indeed, the national newspapers appear to enjoy the idea of ideological conflict over the curriculum. *The Independent,* for instance, presented the issues for English, history, geography and citizenship as a polarised 'battle of the ideologies', taking place between the progressives and the traditionalists (Figure 1). It is certainly too simplistic a response, but it is tempting to place some of the blame on the 1991 GNC for the inability of geographical education to throw off the utilitarian image as a marginal servicing subject. This seems to have led geography teachers directly into utilitarian- and employment-driven initiatives with which they ideally would prefer to have only passing involvement (e.g. vocational courses) or into laying stress on developments in which they would hope only to play a supporting role (e.g. ICT, literacy). At the same time, it denies them full involvement in initiatives such as citizenship and SDE, with which they more closely identify.

Ross (2000) provided a useful model (Figure 2) which attempts to summarise the relationship between political positions/ideologies and the curricular types in the period of formation and implementation of the national curriculum. In this diagram the New Right take up positions on the surface between the academic and the utilitarian axes. The neo-conservatives are more strongly academic but with a measure of utility, and the neo-liberals are more utilitarian but with some regard for the subject-based, traditional liberal humanist position. These two were the strongest influence on the NC debates in the 1980s and it is notable that they are polar opposites to the progressive, process-driven position more characteristic of the curriculum project movements in the 1970s. New Labour is not easy to place on the diagram but may, according to Ross, lie at position 'G' with a strong industrial trainer/vocational orientation. The movements of the GNC have been predominantly bi-polar, the debate taking place along a line stretching between the utilitarian and progressive poles, i.e. 1980s cultural restorationism conflicting with 1970s curriculum development. Although New Right cultural restorationist influence has declined in the late 1990s, it is still in existence, as the submissions of the Campaign for Real Education made clear during the consultation on the 1999 Review of the Geography NC (see Study 3, pages 45-46). Little movement has taken place towards the academic pole, thus illustrating visually the gap which has been referred to as existing between school and academic geography.

	English (Jane Austen)	History (Henry VIII)	Geography	Citizenship/social and sex
The claim	Literary classics to be ditched in favour of modern books about drugs and football. Nick Seaton of the Campaign for Real Education says reading classics will become optional	Kings, queens, heroes, battles and dates 'eliminated' from national curriculum, claims History Curriculum Association. Chris McGovern said proposals will 'destroy history as a subject'	Maps to be removed from the curriculum; children no longer have to learn locations of towns and cities. Claims that weather will be removed	The government is 'subverting' the curriculum to create Blairite, politically-correct Britain, says the Campaign for Real Education. Churches attack lack of reference to marriage
The proposal	Compulsory to study two Shakespeare plays, two 'major playwrights'. Two pre-1914 authors and two post-14 authors	Primary and secondary pupils have to study six topics chosen from detailed government list of chronological periods in history	Pupils required to use maps to develop 'locational knowledge'. Courses to include the environment, physical geography and weather	Citizenship classes to teach social, moral and cultural issues, rights and responsibilities
The result	Extended choice but teachers banned from using figures from before 1914 outside the government list	Romans, Anglo-Saxons and Vikings compulsory for primary schools. Detailed guidelines will emphasise personalities, dates and events	Children must use maps, photographs and text. Must know location of 'key places and features'	Non-statutory guidelines amended to include explicit references to marriage, parents and the dangers of early sex

Figure 1: **Battle of the ideologies in the classroom.** Source: *The Independent,* 10 September 1999.

Marsden (1997a) provided a similar analysis (Figure 2), but using a slightly different model. He argued that the curriculum should contain a balance of three critical components – subject content, educational processes and social purposes (which may be matched with Ross's three poles). Without a balance of each, the curriculum is likely to be unduly narrowed or distorted and to offer an inferior quality of education for young people. Throughout the last century, geography has at various times exhibited imbalance. Marsden quoted the over emphasis on subject content in the old grammar school tradition and the dominance of the educational tradition in progressive primary ideology in the 1960s. The social purpose component was dominant in the inter-war years (world citizenship) and in some of the integrated studies/humanities movements in the new comprehensive schools of the 1960s. Significantly, Marsden (1997a) believed that by the mid-1970s, the school geography curriculum in England was reaching a reasonable balance. Sufficient of the new geography had disseminated from the universities to enliven and re-invigorate school work, the Schools Council geography projects were bringing fresh ideas about curriculum planning and pedagogy, and the interest in environmental education and in welfare approaches was ensuring that social purposes were not neglected. At the present time, according to Marsden, the curriculum is out of balance again. As a result of the dominant debates and conflicts being between the New Right and the progressive educational movement, links with academic geography have been neglected. Marsden referred to 'a debilitating anti-intellectualism' (1997a, p. 249) now apparent and threatening to take the geography out of geography education (title to Marsden's article). Referring to Marsden's diagram, it seems that policy debates in the late 1990s have still been taking place along the social purposes/educational processes axis. In fact, because New Labour's priorities are not subject-based, the danger is that the debates will gravitate even more strongly to this area, leaving subject content out of the action. It is not just the

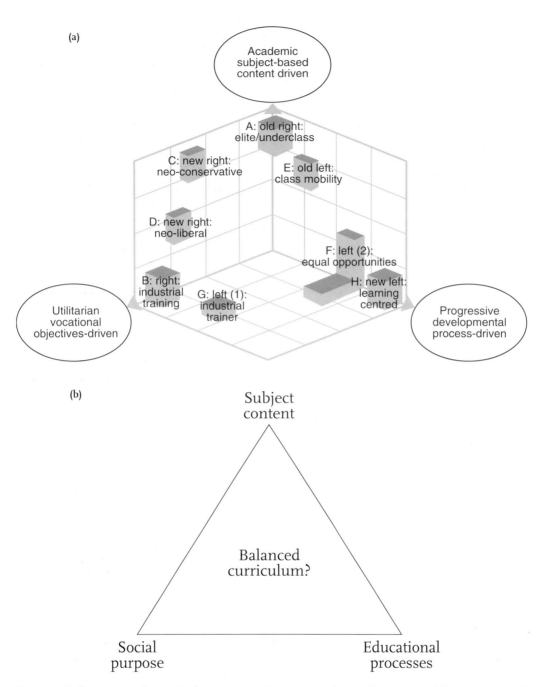

(a)

(b)

Figure 2: Influences on the curriculum: (a) political positions and curriculum types, and (b) components of a balanced curriculum. After: Ross, 2000; Marsden, 1997a.

national curriculum which seems to be frozen into a traditional and outdated framework. Chapter 7 has shown how GCSE and AS/A-level syllabuses have also failed to reflect recent developments in the academic subject and, in the push to address government initiatives such as key skills and modularisation/unitisation, have become more utilitarian and technical.

In order to go forward, it is crucial to recognise this recent curriculum history. As Alexander stated 'ideologies do not come in single file, one replacing the other, but compete, interact and continue in juxtaposition' (1985, p. 158). Writing about the first national curriculum, John Bale suggested that rather than imposing a retrogressive form of geography, he saw the requirements as 'a strange mixture of geographic paradigms and an equally eclectic mix of educational philosophies from utilitarian to reconstructionist' (1994, p. 97). In this sense, he viewed the 1991 curriculum as a reflection of post-modernism with ample opportunities for wide-ranging interpretations. Whether or not one agrees with this use of the term 'post-modernism', how much more is this flexibility the case for the national curriculum for 2000? In the current national curriculum, for instance (Figure 3), it is possible to recognise a utilitarian influence in the basic map skills and a continuing requirement for locational knowledge; the cultural restorationist concerns in the traditional theme titles and emphasis on knowledge of Britain and the world; some representation of the liberal humanist agenda in the separate strands of physical and human geography and spatial analysis; increasing representation of progressive educational opportunities through enquiry, values and issues-based work; and, as a result of the Labour government's new agenda, token recognition at least of more radical emphases. We cannot start with a clean slate.

Element of the geography curriculum 2000	Ideological tradition	Status
Map Skills Locational knowledge Literacy/numeracy references	Utilitarian and cultural restorationist	Residual
Physical and human geography – patterns, processes and spatial analysis	Liberal humanism	Residual
Geographical enquiry Values and attitudes Issues and questions	Progressive educationalist	Re-emergent
Sustainable development education Citizenship Global perspectives	Reconstructionist (or New Labour's more utilitarian agenda)?	Emergent (or residual)?
Key skills	Vocational/industrial trainer	Re-emergent in a different style

Figure 3: The Geography National Curriculum in England, 2000
     – a mixture of residual and emergent ideologies?

The main lesson from the ideological swings of the past 20 years appears to be that ideologies are powerful influences on the curriculum, but it is important not to overstress this. The most negative effects have resulted not from the existence of different ideologies (arguably they can be a stimulus to critical engagement with the discipline), but from the extreme polarisation of the discourse at national level since about 1980, and the resultant impact on geography's image and status. What is now required is a more balanced debate and, specifically a greater input from the academic discipline. The GNC now provides a very minimal framework and thus the possibility, through implementation, of reaching a more genuine balance between the social, educational and academic components. This is also true of the GCSE and A/AS-level subject criteria, though it is not yet reflected in the specifications. Macro-level struggles may have resulted in less than perfect curriculum frameworks at all levels in school geography, but creative curriculum development at micro-level is still a feasible strategy.

Bell's phases of educational policy making	Curriculum characteristics of Bell's phases	School geography phases of curriculum policy making	Characteristics of each phase for geography
1960-73 Social democratic phase	▪ Emphasis on growth and expansion ▪ Teachers exercised considerable autonomy over the curriculum ▪ Little conflict between interest groups ▪ Aspirations and expectations rising	**1970-80** Curriculum development and innovation	▪ Geography teachers have freedom to innovate at school level, with support from LEAs ▪ New ideas from geography and from education ▪ Strong influence of curriculum projects, teacher educators and some examining boards
1973-87 Resource-constrained phase	▪ Emphasis on cost effectiveness and resource management with declining pupil numbers ▪ Fundamental questions raised about the nature, purpose and control of education ▪ Manpower Services Commission is a key player in curriculum/pedagogy	**1980-87** Changing discourse and unresolved dilemmas	▪ Increasing central interest in the curriculum ▪ Fewer resources for curriculum and innovation ▪ Unresolved issues about pedagogy/content ▪ New Right 'deficit' view of geography
1987-97 Market phase	▪ Emphasis on the market as the dominant force through accountability and choice ▪ Power shifts away from teachers who are deprofessionalised and lose curriculum control ▪ The school system fragments and schools take bigger management role	**1987-93** Strong centralised control	▪ Establishment of GNC ▪ Prescriptive content and utilitarian image ▪ Minimal dialogue with higher education
		1993-97 Pragmatic accommodation and negotiation	▪ Reviewed GNC provides greater flexibility ▪ Re-emergence of progressive educational agenda at national level ▪ Continued constraints on professionalism ▪ Slow revival of dialogue with higher education
1997 onwards Excellence phase	▪ Emphasis on pupil performance, standards and accountability ▪ Some teacher autonomy, but constrained by targets and strategies	**1997-2000+** Command curriculum (Labour election victory suggests similar trends will continue from 2001?)	▪ GNC for 2000 provides even greater flexibility but still no changes in content ▪ Less ideology but more control over curriculum and assessment ▪ Decline in entries for GCSE and A-level geography ▪ Increasing opportunities to revive subject dialogue

Figure 4: Curriculum policy making and school geography in England.

Phases of curriculum policy making

In an article in the *Journal of Educational Administration* (1999), Bell recognised four phases of educational policy making in England between 1960 and the present. Figure 4 is based on the experience of school geography 1970-2000 and suggests a close correlation with the last three of Bell's phases (1973-99) but with a slightly different division of the 1990s (see also Rawling, 2001b). The difference is not surprising since the geography study has focused on curriculum policy whereas Bell's work covered all educational policy, including management and funding issues. Five phases of curriculum policy making are recognised for geography and may well be applicable to other school subjects:

1. 1970-80 Curriculum Development and Innovation
2. 1980-87 Changing Discourse and Unresolved Dilemmas
3. 1987-93 Strong Centralised Control
4. 1993-97 Pragmatic Accommodation and Negotiation
5. 1997-2000+ The Command Curriculum

Before examining the characteristics of school geography for each phase, it is worth drawing attention to the three different but overlapping systems which have implicitly lain behind the discussion so far. The questions are those which arise for any school subject, but are here applied to school geography in 2000 (Figure 5):

1. *The school curriculum system:* Do teachers have access to a curriculum framework for the subject which is workable and capable of being developed into good quality geography teaching and learning?
2. *The geography education system:* Do teachers perceive themselves as part of a wider community of geography and geography educators at all levels, so that the subject base is continually being renewed?
3. *The national education system:* Does geography have an appropriate public image and a firm place and assured status in the national education system?

These three systems are closely interconnected, though, as revealed above, frequently the fortunes of geography in one system have been inversely related to its well-being in another system. Note, for example, the irony of winning a place at national level in the 1988 National Curriculum only to be presented three years later with the narrow curriculum focus and faulty structure of the 1991 Geography Order. Figure 5 also presents a simple 'score-card' approach to identifying the gains and losses within these three systems over the last 30 years, using the five phases of curriculum policy making outlined above. Inevitably this is an over-simplified view but it does allow recognition of broad trends which might otherwise be obscured by the detail. Curriculum and educational developments were dominant in the 1970s, but links with the subject in higher education were slowly allowed to fade and the subject community did not give sufficient attention to geography's identity and public image. The 1988 Education Reform Act provided status and a higher profile for the subject. However, throughout the 1990s, while the geography education community focused its attention on ameliorating the faulty 1991 curriculum system and on re-engaging in cross-sectoral dialogue, the subject began progressively to lose status and prestige at national level.

A summary outline of each of the five curriculum policy phases will now be provided for school geography. Further information for each phase is given in the table at the end of the chapter (Study 6, pages 161-166).

1970-80: curriculum development and innovation
This was a period during which teachers exercised considerable autonomy in curriculum matters,

Phase	School geography curriculum system	Geography education system	National educational system
1970-80 Curriculum development and innovation	+++	+	+/−
1980-87 Changing discourse and unresolved dilemmas	+/−	−	++
1987-93 Strong centralised control	− −	− −	++
1993-97 Pragmatic accommod-ation and negotiation	+	+	−
1997-2000+ Command curriculum	+ +	++	− −

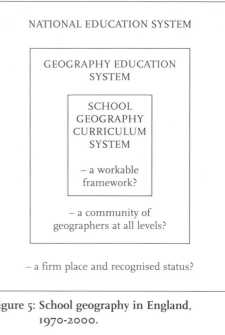

Figure 5: School geography in England, 1970-2000.

Key: + is a positive and improving position; − is a negative and declining position; number of + or − signs indicates strengths of influence.

and education was seen as a major mechanism for social improvement (the 'medium of education' idea expressed by the projects). A great deal of beneficial development work took place on the school geography curriculum system, notably but not only through the work of the curriculum projects. Local authority advisers and the HMI geography team provided strong support for the professional development of teachers. At the beginning of the period, relationships with higher education focused on dissemination of the so-called 'new geography' from universities into schools, although there was already some concern about the applicability of models and quantitative techniques to the school situation. Later in the 1970s, some geography educators began to consider more humanistic and radical approaches but these were never fully developed in schools. In this sense, the close but paternalistic relationship of the late 1960s and early 1970s was already beginning to fade by the end of the period. Membership figures for the GA and RGS showed a steady increase throughout most of the 1970s (see Appendix 2). At national level, geography was poorly represented in primary schools, but a popular subject at GCE O- and A-level. However, despite this popularity with secondary pupils, the subject failed to feature very prominently in initial debates about the school curriculum. In the spate of DES and HMI discussion papers and documents arguing the case for a common (core) curriculum, geography was hardly mentioned.

1980-87: changing discourse and unresolved dilemmas
In this phase, there was increasing central interest in the curriculum, a decline in funding for innovation and professional development and a more polarised and politicised debate about the curriculum. After 1980, the GA, in particular, took the lead in making greater inputs to national debates. Geography began to appear in official documents (e.g. *The School Curriculum* – DES, 1981). Appearance of GA officers at a Parliamentary Select Committee in 1981 raised the profile of the

subject, and attendance by Sir Keith Joseph (Secretary of State for Education) at a GA conference in 1985 seemed to confirm the subject's greater visibility. Finally, in 1987, the GA delegation visiting the new Secretary of State (Kenneth Baker) was informed that geography was to be part of the new ten-subject national curriculum. However, the 1980-87 period was characterised by a paucity of curriculum thinking and development work at the school level. Geography educators failed to undertake a full analysis of the positive and negative effects of the curriculum development movement, although this debate had been begun at the 'Geography into the 1980s' joint project conference and at the Charney Manor Conference of 1980. Curriculum activities did not cease entirely, but those that survived often had to suggest a more utilitarian flavour in order to gain funding (e.g. Geography, Schools and Industry Project). The establishment of GCSE in 1986 was one encouraging development, allowing some of the innovations of the previous decade to be officially recognised. During this period, dialogue with higher education colleagues declined even further, as academic geography explored the new opportunities offered by welfare approaches, humanistic geography, and radical/structuralist approaches, none of which was taken up seriously by the A-level syllabuses. Significantly, the first research assessment exercise for geography took place in 1986, ensuring that the attention of academics was necessarily diverted away from school geography.

1987-93: strong centralised control of the curriculum

This was the phase during which the details of the national curriculum content were formulated with strong influence from the New Right and little involvement by teachers and professional educators. The gains, arising from the relatively progressive formulation of geography GCSE criteria and syllabuses, were offset by events emanating from the Education Reform Act 1988. While geography won its place in the national curriculum and so gained much desired national status, the over prescriptive and structurally faulty 1991 GNC revealed that this was at the expense of a workable curriculum framework for teachers. Monitoring by Ofsted and the NCC in the 1991-93 period showed that teachers found implementation very difficult, meanwhile the SEAC initiated development work on tests for KS1/2 and KS3, despite growing evidence that the 1991 curriculum was virtually unassessable. Academic geographers were hardly involved at all in the development of the national curriculum and were gradually moving out of influential positions in examining board committees and textbook writing. Much has been made of the apparent ideological take-over of the GNC in this period. In fact, as Chapters 4 and 5 have shown, this was never as clear cut nor as constraining for teachers as many would have liked to believe. What was significant, however, was that the utilitarian and informational image, accepted by both teachers and the general public, inhibited geography's subsequent participation in creative dialogue about its contribution to the curriculum. Links with higher education reached a low point since teachers found little encouragement in the new curriculum to explore the possibilities raised by new developments in academic geography. The 1991 GNC also created huge dilemmas for teacher educators, since in its rejection of a role for teachers, it seemed to require a very different 'technician training' model, alien to the professional development model promoted by most geography teacher educators.

1993-97: pragmatic accommodation and negotiation

This phase was one in which the influence of the New Right diminished and, because of the need to involve teachers more co-operatively in implementation, professional educators within and beyond the central agencies participated more in policy making and management. Gradual but significant improvements took place to the school geography curriculum system. Recognition of the difficulties teachers were finding with implementing the 1991 requirements provided one of the main justifications for geography to undergo more extensive change, despite the fact that both National Curriculum Reviews (Dearing 1993-95 and QCA 1998-99) were publicised as involving minimal change. Many of the progressive features of curriculum development in the 1970s and 1980s (e.g. geographical enquiry, attitudes and values, curriculum planning) reappeared in this period, particularly through the publications and co-operative activities of both SCAA and the GA. Ofsted evidence suggests, however, that KS3 teachers were not necessarily receptive to these opportunities because of all the other pressures in schools and the changing definition of professionalism. Interestingly, some of the biggest advances in geography teaching and learning were probably made in primary schools at this time, as schools had now finished the immediate task of coping with English, mathematics and science and benefited from SCAA support materials. The 1993-2000 period saw the gradual revival of dialogue between different parts of the geography education community, promoted in particular by the subject associations, which was increasingly aware of the need for curriculum continuity and an improved public image. The merger of the RGS with the IBG in 1995 gave a stimulus to broader co-operation. Also influential was the Council of British Geography (COBRIG) with its biennial seminars beginning in 1994. Other factors contributing to cross-sectoral dialogue were the greater flexibility provided by the national curriculum and the increased interest from higher education in teaching and learning – partly as a result of the teaching quality audit. Ominously, a decline in geography GCSE numbers appeared in 1997, a 4% decrease and the first signs that the Dearing core and options formula for KS4 might be having a detrimental effect on geography.

1997- 2000+: the command curriculum

This phase, beginning with the election of a New Labour government, was characterised by less ideology but more control. New Labour's so-called Third Way was recognisable in the greater direction over outcomes and implementation strategies, with a new breed of technocrats managing policy and even classroom interventions (as in the Literacy Strategy). For geography, the 1998-2000 National Curriculum Review provided even greater clarity and flexibility within the GNC though still no opportunity to reconsider the now outdated subject content headings. However, high quality implementation has been hindered by constraints on teacher professionalism and by geography's declining status in schools. The dis-application of the KS1/2 PoS 1998-2000 dealt the fragile state of primary geography a blow from which it may take a long time to recover, given the prevailing emphasis on literacy and numeracy strategies. The decision not to make KS4 more flexible but to add the 'subject of citizenship' has provided further problems for geography's status, while major structural changes to A-level mean that teachers' attention has been drawn away from innovation with subject content. A decline in candidate numbers appeared at A/AS-level after 1998 and fears for the impact on higher education seemed to be confirmed by falling applications for degree courses. The new standards for teacher training introduced in 1998 and the growing concerns about teacher recruitment threaten to make it more difficult for teacher educators to respond to the new opportunities for teacher professionalism presented in the curriculum for 2000. There have been notable successes in reviving dialogue within the subject community, especially through the activities of the subject associations and COBRIG, and through the growing involvement of higher education geographers in pedagogical matters. Some of the government's initiatives aimed at raising standards (e.g. teaching and learning in the foundation subjects, creativity across the curriculum) and the QCA geography/history curriculum project provide opportunities to refocus on curriculum and on learning. It is, as yet, unclear how constrained these developments will be. The 2001 election victory ensures a second term for the Labour government with a new Secretary of State (Estelle Morris) at the renamed Department for Education and Skills (DfES). As yet it seems unlikely that there will be major changes of policy direction or any reason to recognise a new policy-making phase.

Who controls the curriculum?

Another interesting way of analysing the five identified phases is to consider the key people and groups that have been influential in the policy process and in curriculum change. Marsh (1997) classifies these as decision makers, stakeholders and influences (or interest groups). Decision-makers are those individuals or groups who because of their professional status or position are able to make specific decisions about what is to be taught, when, how and to whom. Examples from geography's curriculum history include the Schools Council funded projects and examining boards in the 1970s, the Secretary of State for Education and the DES after 1988, and professional officers with the various curriculum and assessment agencies in the 1990s. Stakeholders are those who have a right to comment on, and have an input into, the school curriculum. Some will have official powers to do so, e.g. headteachers, heads of geography, parents and governors (particularly after 1988). Others have no official power but rely on their modes of persuasion, for example newspaper editors. Interest groups hold common views and endeavour to persuade and convince the authorities that certain changes should occur. Examples for geography include the subject associations (RGS-IBG, GA, COBRIG), voluntary agencies like the Council for Environmental Education, educational researchers, textbook publishers and writers. To some extent these categories overlap. For example, subject associations are on the official list of consultees used by the curriculum and assessment agency and so to some extent are stakeholders as well as an interest group. However, this list is rather rigid because one of the most interesting points is the way that key influences change over time.

Figure 6 therefore summarises what were the key influences on curriculum change in each of the five phases of policy making. The last two columns on Figure 6 suggest at what level the curriculum discourse was being conducted and at what level curriculum decisions were being made. The distinction between discourse and decision making is important because, at some stages (e.g. 1993-97 and 1997-2000), the subject community was let back into the discourse but only made a minor (though significant) contribution to decision making. What is significant about the trends shown on Figure 6 is not, as might be thought, the growing influence of ministers and politicians on decision making – the most striking period of direct ministerial control was 1987-93. It is, more specifically, the predominant movement of decision making since 1987 to the national level, seen in the influence of a range of political advisers and appointed bodies as well as of ministers directly. At the beginning of the period (1970-87), decisions about the curriculum were predominantly taken at the level of the subject community, the school and the classroom. In the 1987-91 period, this situation changed, so that even the smallest decisions about the curriculum framework for geography (places to study, particular map techniques and skills) were taken at a national level of control, i.e. by political advisors or officers in the curriculum and assessment authorities. This effectively disempowered teachers and schools, and also to some extent textbook writers and subject associations. In fact, as this book has shown, the subject curriculum frameworks (NC, GCSE and A/AS criteria) have become progressively more minimal in the 1990s. However, the Labour government has retained the power over detail at national level by taking greater control over implementation (e.g. Literacy and Numeracy Strategies, Schemes of Work, performance targets). It may have moved slightly further away from 'what to teach' but it is certainly moving closer to 'how to teach'. In its rhetoric and consultation techniques, it has opened doors to greater involvement by educational professionals (e.g. the National Educational Research Forum, the TTA's teacher research grants, the attempts to involve subject associations more in producing materials and in-service support). But it is not clear yet whether this will lead to a greater sharing of control. Geography educators may welcome the increasing participation in debates but should be aware that this does not necessarily provide them with greater power over the curriculum.

A useful way of considering the curriculum is to envisage the different levels at which it operates, as suggested by Harland et al. (1999). The curriculum as specified refers to the statutory requirements, agreed nationally and, as explained, now comprising a minimal framework as far as subjects are concerned. The curriculum as planned describes the interpretation of the national frameworks by, for example, examining boards/awarding bodies, non-statutory guidance, textbook writers, subject associations and subject departments in schools. This is a level into which the government and political appointees have moved significantly 1997-2000, not only to exemplify standards (e.g. web-based exemplification) but also to give an interpretation of the curriculum (e.g. Schemes of Work). In 1996-97 SCAA also undertook a survey of KS3 textbooks aiming to evaluate how effective they were in covering the national curriculum (SCAA, 1997g), a move which some feared (wrongly) might be a forerunner of the government-approved textbook. The *curriculum as implemented* refers to the detailed course and lesson plans prepared by teachers to suit their own context. The Labour government seems to have been moving into this area too, with its prescriptive Literacy and Numeracy Strategies. It is not yet clear whether the TLF initiative will follow a prescriptive or a more open professional development route. Two levels of curriculum operation which are less frequently considered are *curriculum as experienced* and *curriculum as retained*. These are levels in which the pupils' needs and experiences are apparent because they focus on classroom interactions and on the knowledge, skills and attitudes which pupils then take away. To some extent, the national tests and public examinations reach into this area, but only partially because the term 'what is retained' suggests a far wider concern than the relatively narrow focused tests. There is scope for further research into *curriculum as experienced* and *curriculum as retained*, as a guide to improving the specifications and plans made at other levels. The work on formative assessment (Black and Wiliam, 1998; Assessment Reform Group, 1999) has this emphasis. For geography the thinking skills programme (Leat, 1998; Nichols with Kinninment, 2001) is directly concerned with these classroom levels of operation and so, also, is much of GeoVisions work. Thompson (2000b) reported on a GeoVisions exercise which studied young people's views and learning preferences in geography as a basis for designing more meaningful curriculum materials. Dowgill (1996) has also carried out work on pupils' experience of GNC.

Phase	Key influences on curriculum change	Level of operation for:	
		discourse	decisions
1970-80	Academic geographers Curriculum project teams Textbook writers	Subject community School and classroom	Subject community School and classroom
1980-87	LEA advisers/Inspectors Subject associations Examining boards	Moving away from subject/school to national level	Subject community School and classroom
1987-93	Politicians/ministers Political appointees (e.g. Chair GWG) Lay members of Working Group Curriculum/assessment agencies	National level	National level
1993-97	Curriculum/assessment agencies Ministers Subject associations	Subject community moving back into the discourse	National level
1997-2000	Political appointees, e.g. task groups, strategy teams Ministers Curriculum/assessment agencies	Subject community and national level	National level
2000+	Need to draw schools and teachers more directly into curriculum discourse and into decision making at subject, school/classroom level?	Subject community and schools/teachers and national level?	National level for strategic decisions? Subject community/school teacher for subject and teaching detail

Figure 6: Who controls the curriculum?

This analysis of curriculum levels is valuable because it can highlight the spaces for action by subject communities. The analysis in this book has shown that for the GNC, there is now considerable potential for action, particularly at the levels of implementation and classroom experience. Teachers do have, and can use, their power to develop the curriculum to suit their school and to reflect advances in the discipline. Chapter 10 will consider this potential further. Overall, if the school curriculum is to fulfil the kind of aims outlined in the Education Reform Act and the National Curriculum Handbooks (DfEE/QCA, 1999b,c), then it is crucial that subject communities are involved not only in the curriculum discourse but also the curriculum decision making at the appropriate levels. Ministers, political advisers and curriculum/assessment authorities are justifiably involved in decisions about the statutory specifications and to some extent in planning guidance. It may be suggested, on the basis of geography's curriculum history, that they do not belong in the lower levels of curriculum operation.

The role of the media (see Figure 7)

It is increasingly recognised that the mass media plays a significant role in the educational policy making process. Wallace (1993) suggested that, at the time he was writing, this role may have been underplayed. Since then, advances in technology and the proliferation of means of communication (particularly the internet, e-mail, videos and mobile phones) mean that media messages shape and recreate images of the world more than ever before. The way in which the media reports, for instance, standards in the basics, GCSE and A/AS-level examination results or teacher supply shortages can effectively constrain the options which policy makers have (as events in 2000-01 showed). In academic geography, the so-called 'cultural turn' currently finds the media fertile ground for study, examining the way in which newspapers, film, television, music and the internet mediate landscapes and environment (e.g. Crang, 1998). However, while academic geographers have taken on the media, the media still does not appear to have taken on more than a narrow utilitarian view of school geography.

Before the mid-1980s, school geography rarely appeared in the national press. This is not to say that the general public was not interested in people, places and landscapes. Walford suggests that, for example, the popular *I-Spy* series of books, although not labelled as geography, 'probably made a greater contribution to the geographical and environmental education of children than any other teacher of the 1950s and 1960s' (2001, p. 154). However, as Richard Daugherty, GA president 1989-90, pointed out: 'apart from the shock/horror headlining of a survey showing how few people know their capital cities, geography is perceived as neither important enough (compared with say mathematics) or controversial enough (compared with say history) to prompt much public debate' (1989b, p. 146). During the build-up to the national curriculum, the national newspapers were powerful in setting the scene. The educational press (e.g. *TES*, *THES*) was full of articles expressing the concern of educationalists about centralisation, while the general press made more of the deficiencies in school education which the reforms were supposed to address. For geography, the most obvious deficiency was world and place knowledge — the shock/horror stories of pupils' ignorance. An International Gallup Survey, commissioned by the National Geographic Society of America, handed the press its main story – 'British know little about the world and care even less' (see Chapter 3, Figure 4) ran the headline in *The Independent* in December 1988, just four months before the Geography Working Group (GWG) started its work. It was perfectly acceptable that geography educators should be made aware of an issue that undoubtedly needed addressing after a decade of experimentation with new geography and new pedagogy. The problem was that place/locational knowledge became *the* issue for the GWG and *the* story for the next decade, even when the context had changed. Press reaction to the Interim and Final Reports of the GWG and to the Geography Order focused on welcoming the greater stress on these elements of factual knowledge, though there was also take-up of the GWG's attempt to claim a strong environmental dimension for geography. Notably, too, the editor of *The Times*, Simon Jenkins, seemed to be fighting a lonely battle to have geography recognised as a core subject:

The Descent of Humanities

The most puzzling feature of the DES's new proposals on the 5-16 curriculum is paragraph 22 on the place of the humanities in secondary schooling. It runs: *'Some pupils are bound to devote less time to the humanities (giving that term a broad meaning) than others. During the five secondary years, every pupil should study, on a worthwhile scale, history, geography, and, under whatever guise (which may in some cases be history or geography) the principals underlying a free society and some basic economic awareness. But choices will have to be made in years 4 and 5. Is it acceptable that any of these three elements can be dropped in these two years?'*

The DES is not exactly going overboard, then for the humanities. There is none of the certainty found in the terse paragraph 17:

'There can be no question that English and mathematics should be compulsory for all pupils', or in the statement in paragraph 19 on science:

'Pupils suffer a particular loss of subsequent opportunity if at the end of year 3 they cease to study any important element of a broad science curriculum'.

No hint here that choice will have to be made in later years or that some pupils will spend less time than others on these subjects, no invitation here to suggest which elements might be dropped, science and 'basics' are unquestionable.

From: *Times Educational Supplement,* 19 October 1984.

Downgrading alarms geographers

The nation's geographers are incensed by the Education Secretary's proposal that their subject might be dropped by some pupils at the age of 14.

Mr John MacGregor told the Professional Association of Teachers' annual conference in Nottingham last month that he had asked the National Curriculum Council to review the 14-16 curriculum framework and 'not to rule out the possibility that some subjects might be dropped by more pupils than I envisaged'.

Professor Richard Lawton, secretary of the Council of British Geography, an umbrella organization for geographical societies, has written to Mr MacGregor 'deploring any suggestion that geography should be further downgraded' and asking him to clarify his position.

From: *Times Education Supplement,* 17 August 1990.

Teach pupils to save world

by James Meikle, Education Correspondent

SCHOOLS are set to bring green politics into the classroom – with the Government's blessing.

Education experts want to give pupils compulsory geography lessons highlighting man-made threats to the planet and rows over how to save it.

The classes, to be phased in over the next four years, will take up at least three periods a week for all children between 5 and 14.

Topics discussed will include soil erosion, water pollution, acid rain and global warming.

The new studies will be combined with a back-to-basics approach to ensure pupils can reel off world capitals, rivers and seas.

A survey last year showed nearly one in six 11 year-olds could not find Britain on a map.

The scheme is part of a new drive to step up geography teaching, which curriculum advisers yesterday claimed had been seriously neglected.

From: *The Mirror,* 7 June 1990.

Quote

'If Parliament had not reserved the final decision on the shape of each subject to the Secretary of State, we would have seen history defined as current affairs, geography covering politics but not places, and English shorn of grammar but including Monty Python' *(Michael Fallon, former education minister, reviewing 'A lesson for us all' by Duncan Graham, the former chairman of the NCC, in this week's* Times).

'I did not want the Government to stand accused of introducing a narrow, utilitarian, Gradgrind curriculum' *(Kenneth Baker, Education Secretary 1986-89, defending the national curriculum in* The Guardian).

From: *Times Education Supplement,* 27 January 1992.

What they must know

AGE 7
- *Identify land and sea on maps*
- *Tell north, south, east and west*
- *Recognise seasonal weather patterns*

AGE 11
- *Use four-figure map co-ordinates*
- *Identify countries and cities*
- *Discuss how humans affect natural resources*

AGE 14
- *Understand environmental problems in Europe*
- *Compare development around world*
- *Say why some rivers are polluted*

AGE 16
- *Say how residents and developers change areas*
- *Understand global warming*
- *Explain impact of industries on environment*

Ken gets lost in a fo[g]

The news that Kenneth Clarke had gone up to the North-east and congratulated Consett on the splendid productivity record of its steel works, which had in fact been closed down several years ago surprised nobody who remembered his impeccable knowledge of education when he was Secretary of State. Not reading his North-east brief properly could be added to a huge list of other things he never read, like the Plowden Report, when he claimed to have buried it; his own national curriculum levels, when he asserted, wrongly, that large numbers of seven year-olds could

not recognise three letters in [the] alphabet; and the Maast[richt] Treaty, when he was suppose[d to] be debating it.

His observation that Cons[ett's] magnificent steel production [is] actually it's zero, Clarkie) [had] been achieved with fe[wer] employees than previously [that is, none at the last count) w[e] have crowned another immacu[late] performance from the ro[ving] maestro, had he not trumped [his] own ace by admitting that he [had] confused Consett with Red[car]. One hoped in vain that he w[ould] don his swimming trunks [and] plunge fearlessly into a s[ea of] breaststroke across the nea[...]

Geography 'too foreign'

Curriculum adviser yearns for traditional values of Britishness

John Carvel

After stalwart work trying to put the British heroes back into school history, the Government's chief curriculum adviser yesterday tackled the undue emphasis on foreign parts of the world afflicting the study of geography.

Nick Tate, the Anglo-centric chief executive of the School Curriculum and Assessement Authority, complained about the lack 'of a specific requirement to study the geography of England or the United Kingdom as an entity in itself'.

From: *Daily Telegraph,* 10 April 1996.

Florence! Where's that then?

I realised just how far things had slipped when I tried to book a flight to Florence and the chirpy girl in the travel agent asked me what country it was in. I expect she has passed GCSE geography and has probably done the ubiquitous GNVQ in travel and tourism. Yet she doesn't know facts about the world in which her customers are travelling that she should have been taught at about the age of eight.

Ignorance of elementary geography is rife and becoming worse. And now that David Blunkett has decreed that primary school children need no longer follow even the rudimentary requirements of the national curriculum for geography there is no hope whatever of any improvement. Children need not learn anything about the layout of the world until they are at secondary school. Then, after only three years, it becomes optional.

From: *Sunday Times,* 8 March 1998.

Geography loses the place in new PC lessons

Geography is set to become the new battleground for political correctness. In a move that will infuriate supporters of traditional education, children will no longer have to be taught the location of the Pennines or the capital of Germany but will instead be educated in 'environmental awareness and sustainable development'.

Even requirements such as knowing how to measure distance on a map and 'locating and naming on a map the constituent countries of the United Kingdom' may go.

The proposals by the Qualifications and Curriculum Authority, a watchdog body, are being considered by David Blunkett, education secretary, as part of a broader package of changes to the national curriculum. He is likely to announce the reforms soon after this week's local elections.

From: *Sunday Times,* 2 May 1999.

Figure 7: Geography in the news.

Revenge of the progressives

As David Blunkett relaxed in his flat in Sheffield on a sunny bank holiday morning, he was startled to hear an official from Britain's most powerful education quango declare on national radio that schoolchildren need not know exactly where Paris was.

Here was Tony Millns, the public face of the Qualifications and Curriculum Authority (QCA), the body responsible for deciding what the nation's children are taught, apparently downgrading a basic geographical principle; the knowledge of maps and the location of capital cities.

Instead, Millns underlined the importance of economic geography. 'What we are saying is that you only need a certain number of facts before you can move on to interpretation, understanding, hypothesis and the real skills which grow out of geography,' he said.

For traditionalists, such disregard for 'facts' is anathema; the QCA, it had been revealed, was proposing that maps showing capital cities and the locations of rivers and mountains should be dropped from the curriculum. For Blunkett, the education secretary, who is now a staunch supporter of traditional teaching methods, such a move was too much.

He authorised an official statement that the removal of maps from the curriculum would not be tolerated by the government.

From: *Sunday Times,* 16 May 1999

the Tees

...ty field, believing it to be the ...th Sea. He never did know his ...side from his Elstree.

...st think of the post-Dearing ...onal curriculum levels that ...kie failed to achieve. Take ...graphy for a start. There is ...e doubt whether he could ...n be given a tick in his level 1 ...: 'Pupils ... express their views ...features of the environment of ...cality that they find attractive ...unattractive. They use ...urces provided and their own ...ervations to respond to ...stions about places'

...m: 'Last word' by Ted Wragg, ...es Education Supplement, ...March 1995.

Have I got news for you?

Ian Hislop: Children trade cards and have a fantastic knowledge of 150 monsters. They can't remember five countries and their capital cities.
[Audience laughter]
Angus Deayton: One school in Berkshire has banned Pokeman after instances of bullying to obtain the rarer cards. The bullying has finally stopped though, now that Mr Hunt, the geography teacher has the complete set.
[Audience laughter]
BBC 2, October 2000

Comic relief

Forget geography.
These are your neighbours.
This is your doorstep.
Please help.

From: Lenny Henry, television advert, March 2001.

'Geography should be encouraged to seize the central fortress, ejecting both pure science and that grossly over-promoted intellectual exercise called mathematics. Geography should stand alone with its one educational equal, the study of the human spirit in English Language and Literature. Geography is queen of the sciences, parent to chemistry, geology, physics and biology, parent also to history and economics. Without a clear grounding in the known characteristics of the earth, the physical sciences are mere game playing, the social sciences mere ideology' (1990, p. 13).

In the period surrounding the Dearing Review, the big stories in the newspapers and on television and radio were about English, mathematics, history, the teachers' boycott of testing arrangements and the resultant curriculum slimming exercise. Geography, not surprisingly, did not feature significantly – although one newsworthy story was inspired by Nick Tate, Chief Executive of SCAA, who (at the GA Conference in April 1996) questioned why, despite the review, school children were not expected to study the geography of England or the UK as an entity in itself (Figure 7). It was a reasonable question and the answer partly went back to the GWG's level-related content which had fragmented references to the geography of England or the UK across different age groups, and partly to NCC's merging of three place ATs into one. However, it was reported by the press as being purely about place knowledge, whereas Tate was also raising bigger issues about national identity in a globalising world.

During the 1998-99 QCA Review, the main foci for the GNC were pruning the content and amending the curriculum model. The new model allowed a much clearer definition of the four aspects of geography, in one of which (knowledge and understanding of places), locational knowledge was finally given a secure and manageable place. There was some flexibility for teachers to amend the details of what should be taught as the world changed. The national press, however, happily returned to the same story, the tabloids in particular seeing the changes as a threat to place knowledge. A QCA public relations officer was even interviewed by Radio 4 on Bank Holiday Monday (May 1999) and asked was it true that children need not know the location of Paris (Figure 7). Interestingly, too, many newspapers re-excavated the 'ideological battles' theme (Figure 1) – revenge of the progressives against the traditionalists – though as Chapters 5 and 8 show, for geography this was yesterday's story. Elwyn Jones, in his study of the role of the press in the formation of History National Curriculum (2000), explained that the press over-simplified issues and tended to miss the larger underlying debates, an observation which seems to be confirmed by the experience of geography. The place knowledge story forced David Blunkett (Secretary of State) to make a public show of taking action – 'Labour backs down over curriculum' was the heading in *The Independent*, September 1999. While there was a real story for English (classic literary texts) and history (famous people) the geography story was a media-generated event (Figure 1). Neither maps nor locational knowledge were in danger of being removed from the curriculum, though there was a change to the curriculum model, some increased teacher choice and the significant addition of values, sustainable development education and a global dimension. The media debate thus made little real impact on policy outcomes, but it may have confirmed public perception that the subject was only of utilitarian and informational value.

It is impossible to be sure how influential this utilitarian image is with the general public and policy makers. If the newspapers and television/radio reporting are anything to go by, then it is remarkably persistent. Occasionally reference is made to geography's role as a subject which develops a deeper understanding of social and economic change, environmental understanding, global awareness and critical enquiry skills. Significantly, this is often in January at the time of the RGS/IBG Annual Research Conference, publicised effectively by higher education geographers. More often, for schools, if these things are mentioned, they are seen as separate and in competition with the task of developing locational knowledge. At the time of the national curriculum consultation exercise (May 1999), most newspapers set out the two positions as if they were competing visions. For example, *The Sunday Times* (2 May 1999) claimed that 'children will no longer have to be taught the location of the Pennines ... but instead will be educated in environmental awareness and sustainable development'. It was not recognised that, as Rita Gardner, Director of the RGS explained (1999), these are twin aspects of the modern school subject. Whenever geography is referred to in popular parlance, it is the old 'capes and bays' image (probably never accurate) which prevails. Ian Hislop and Angus Deayton, exchanging witticisms on the quiz show 'Have I Got News for You' (October 2000) made a joke about geography's inadequacies (Figure 7). Lenny Henry, advertising the 2001 Comic Relief effort (March 2001) exhorted listeners to 'forget geography' as being irrelevant to problems in the developing world. Distressingly, given modern geography's central concern with local to global connections, an executive with the media communications company, Spectramind, recently affirmed that 'geography is history. Distance is irrelevant' (*The Guardian*, 9 March 2001).

It seems, then, that the role of the media in the 1990s has been to confirm and even extend the traditional cultural restorationist view of geography which was enshrined in the 1991 Geography Order. Geography educationalists may have been successful in changing the details of the national framework, but they have not managed to change the public image as represented in the media. This is one big space that the subject community needs to occupy. The media views of school geography are not just a mild irritation. They are, or could be, crucial weapons in the policy debates. If school geography is to find a role in developing understanding of environmental issues, sustainable development, cultural diversity and global change, *as well* as place knowledge, then it needs to use the media to change its image.

The changing role of the subject associations (see Figure 8)

Subject associations play several different roles on behalf of the subject. They provide support for teachers by means of resources and professional development opportunities; they ensure continued renewal of the subject through educational and subject-based research and dialogue; and they promote the subject's status and contribution at national level. Goodson (1983, 1988a) and Walford (2001) have highlighted the promotional role, played particularly by the RGS in the late nineteenth century and by the GA in the early twentieth century, in ensuring geography's acceptance as a secondary and university level subject. Since the late 1970s, the conditions for such activities have changed dramatically with the centralisation of curriculum decision making and the more significant role played by ministers, political advisers and civil servants. There is a need to talk directly to these people rather than to focus only on influencing awarding bodies and universities and, as the previous section has shown, to ensure an accurate and coherent public image.

For geography, as Chapter 3 shows, the GA quickly took on a more political campaigning role in the 1976-88 period, benefiting from its new constitutional structure (1977) and financial stability, the result partly of publication sales. As Catling explained: 'It is the responsibility of subject associations to seek to influence those who wield power ... The skills of the lobbyist and promoter will be needed. Such is the future for every "other" foundation subject' (1990, p. 77). The GA took the initiative in arranging meetings with two Ministers (Joseph and Baker) and producing a range of well-argued curriculum submissions (see Daugherty, 1989a), including its own version of the ATs and PoS for geography before the official Working Group had even met. The GA was rewarded with the satisfaction of seeing geography claim its 'place in the sun'. Despite its campaigning strength, the GA's influence on the GWG was minimal since, as Chapter 4 reveals, there were major issues about content, approach and responses to the New Right agenda which had not been addressed. Knight (1996), in an interesting article comparing the roles of the Home Economics Association and the GA, points out that subject associations generally experience difficulty at times of crisis in accommodating the diversity of views represented by their members. Phillips, talking about the role of the Historical Association in NC debates (1998) explained that the HA had difficulty in playing an effective campaigning role because it found itself cast in the role of arbiter between different views

Phase	Detailed characteristics
1970-1980 Active curriculum support and dissemination role	GA active via committees, working groups and branches. Also publications beginning to develop. RGS and IBG provide background support but not active in curriculum matters.
1980-87 Mainly campaigning/policy role at national level	GA – the key player. Successful in getting geography into the curriculum but less successful in influencing discourse about content and character of the new curriculum.
1987-93 Mainly support role at school level; marginalised at national level	GA still the key player but supported by RGS, IBG and (after 1988) COBRIG. Minimal influence on the content/format of the 1991 National Curriculum or, later, on KS4. Supporting implementation and compensating for the faults of the 1991 GNC.
1993-1997 More subtle and effective policy role; strong support role	Close relationship with professionals in SCAA/QCA over changes to curriculum. Greater co-operation between organisations, especially after 1995 RGS-IBG merger. Strategies to influence the subject's status.
1997-2000 Greater involvement in national discourse but declining impact on key policy decisions. Strong support role.	Increasing and formalised co-operation between the subject associations. Extension of support activities and strategies (e.g. RGS-IBG/TTA initiatives). Changing power structures at national level result in difficulties in influencing key policy decisions (e.g. 14-19).
2000+ Effective response needs; understanding of new power structures and promotion/support for the subject at different levels; national, subject community and school curriculum	Need: High degree of co-operation ('subject tribe') with common aims/priorities at national level, active/creative subject dialogue and playing to organisational strengths.

Figure 8: School geography: The changing impact of the subject associations.

about the subject (content-based v skills-based). In the period leading up to the GWG, the GA was successful in taking a middle line between the traditional and the progressive educational groups but inevitably this meant glossing over some of the difficult questions about place knowledge and regional geography alongside enquiry and issues. The GA even played up the 'utilitarian card' strongly (Rawling, 1992a) in negotiations with policy makers. It was the right strategy to get geography into the curriculum, but as the detail of Chapter 4 shows, the professional membership of the GWG failed to form a coherent unit to resist the pressure of cultural restorationism and DES control. Ironically, as the events of the GWG unfolded, the GA found itself re-cast as a dangerously progressive educational force, threatening the more traditional line prevailing on the Group, and so its increasingly critical submissions were ignored. The amendments by Kenneth Clarke over Christmas/New Year 1990-91, made despite protestations from the GA, seemed to highlight the powerlessness of the Association. The tone of the response by the Honorary Secretary (Education) in an article in the TES illustrated the frustration felt by some senior officers:

'Billy Connolly expressed concern that the Scud missile was the only missile that could miss a country. As education secretary of the GA, I have found dealing with the Secretary of State for Education a bit like that ... Kenneth Clarke is big but awfully difficult to hit, even with better targeted and universally supported points and opinions' (Burtenshaw, 1991, p. 31).

Knight claims (1996) that after 1991 the GA retreated from its involvement in curriculum making, reverting to a curriculum support role. It is certainly true that the Association invested considerable effort in producing materials, in-service activity and a regional support network, and that this played a valuable role in interpreting the initially narrow requirements and to some extent re-skilling teachers. However, as Chapter 4 has shown, what Knight neglects is first the significant impact this support activity made in changing the context of influence for the two NC Reviews, and second, the subtle change in GA tactics after 1991-92. While accepting the benefits of some aspects of the new curriculum (e.g. locational knowledge, place study), Association officers found ways of working with the curriculum and assessment authority not only to change the discourse but also to influence decisions to reinstate important elements that had been marginalised (e.g. enquiry, teacher choice, values). After 1993, the situation was certainly helped by the changed political climate and the increased opportunities for subject communities to liaise with SCAA/QCA subject officers – but the GA took full advantage of this. It was not so successful at changing the status of geography at KS4 because this was a whole-curriculum matter, beyond the immediate influence of a subject team.

It should be noted that COBRIG has played a strong supporting role to the GA since 1988. The first two chairs of COBRIG (Rex Walford (1988-93) and myself (1993-95)) were both former GA Presidents and gave a strong lead on educational matters, an emphasis continued by subsequent Chairs. COBRIG submissions were full of curriculum detail. Through the Seminars established from 1994, COBRIG also began the process of renewing links between geography in schools and in higher education. The seminars have continued 1996, 1998 and 2000 and the proceedings (Rawling and Daugherty, 1996; Daugherty and Rawling, 1998) have helped to stimulate debate more widely. COBRIG's role is significantly different from the other subject associations in that it is able to bring together the experiences and voices of all the countries of the UK. From 1996-98, an informal 'Future of Geography' group brought together key people from across the associations, meeting at the RGS to start a dialogue about how to influence policy makers. The GA took up the same issue from the mid-1990s. A letter from its Education Standing Committee to QCA (December 1995) referred to concerns about the decoupling of higher education geography from school geography, with special reference to A-level. Subsequently a Schools/Higher Education Working Group was established (1996-99).

The new series of GA publications, *Changing Geography* (edited by John Bale, 2000) are one result, designed to 'introduce A-level students to concepts and ideas from current research in higher education' (GA catalogue). The annual conference of the Association has, since the early 1990s, been making efforts to include more substantial inputs from academic geographers. The GA has also taken over the funding of GeoVisions, a project originally established by the Birmingham Development Education Centre, which aims to reconsider the content and approaches of school geography 11-16.

All this has been helped by the greater involvement of the merged RGS IBG. In the 1980s and early 1990s, the RGS played an important but supporting role in the politics of the school curriculum. It was not concerned with curriculum detail, but restricted its input to brief, often traditional, but supportive submissions about geography's wider contribution to society and schooling. In 1995, the RGS merged with the IBG and, under its new Director (Rita Gardner, a former University of London geography academic) took on a more pro-active and outgoing approach to the school curriculum. A restructuring of the Society gave it a stronger and more representative Education Committee, a programme of in-service training events targeted at teachers was launched, and the Society took the initiative in links with the Teacher Training Agency over teacher supply issues. While this policy might have led it into conflict with the GA, both organisations were mature enough to realise that given the politics of the curriculum and the growing threats to geography's status, co-operation was more likely to be effective. During the late 1990s, the two organisations have undertaken regular meetings to discuss complementary activities, consider common threats and plan joint actions and responses. Two striking examples were: the Education for Life Seminar for key policy makers and influential people, held in July 1997 and resulting in the well-disseminated leaflet *Education for Life* (RGS-IBG/GA, 1998); and the formation of a joint RGS-IBG/GA task group (2000) to consider the issue of declining entries for GCSE and A/AS-level.

The close working of the geography subject organisations has resulted in a more united subject community in the 1990s and also allowed the voice of academic geographers to be heard more effectively in school curriculum matters (Figure 8). It could be argued that the subject associations are in a stronger position now and also more skilled to make an effective input into the policy process as well as to continue their support roles. Recognition of the strengths of each organisation and of the levels of curriculum operation will allow the whole system to work more effectively. The RGS-IBG, with its contacts among the powerful and famous, provides a platform for political lobbying, public education and support for the academic community. It has had notable successes on behalf of the higher education community, managing the benchmarking work (1999-2000) and unifying the views of geographers, earth scientists and environmental scientists in order to gain the HEFCE Subject Centre funding (2000). In the GA, there is the strength and expertise in school curriculum and pedagogical matters, teacher education, educational research, in-service support and teacher publications to continue the detailed work of amending national frameworks, supporting implementation and influencing classroom pedagogy. Both organisations have national policy matters as part of their strategic aims. Whether or not consideration is eventually given to an even closer relationship between the two organisations, it is essential that this wide range of activities continues, and particularly the attention to national discourse. The important remaining task, which will demand a shared view of the broad aims and principles of the subject, in schools and in higher education, is the promotion of a stronger and more balanced public image. This is a crucial weapon for the subject community to use in the policy-making process.

Conclusion

In 1991, it seemed as if the subject battles were predominantly ideological. It seemed that the future would consist of polarised debates and conflict between the professional geographical educators and the policy makers at national level, with teachers reduced to 'delivering' the outcomes of the struggles. It is now clear that this was always too simple and dramatic a picture. National policy and the processes of policy making have made a direct impact on the content, character and structure of school geography, particularly the national curriculum. However, as this chapter has explained, at school level the national curriculum frameworks are now and probably always were a mixture of ideologies with ample scope for creative development but too little contact with the parent discipline. More subtle and more damaging than the effect on curriculum detail has been the impact on the status and image of the subject and on the conditions for teacher professionalism. This chapter has explained this and identified five significantly different phases of curriculum policy making for school geography 1970-2000+. The phases in curriculum policy making have derived from the admittedly limited evidence base of school geography but there are almost certainly similarities to be found with other foundation subjects. It is hoped that this study might stimulate further research about their experience.

For the geography subject community, the analysis has highlighted possibilities for action. An understanding of the different levels at which curriculum decision making operates makes it clear that there is ample scope for subject-based professional input at school, classroom and pupil level. There are undoubtedly still battles to fight over curriculum specifications and future curriculum changes at 5-14 and 14-19. The big opportunities at all levels, however, lie in the hands of the subject community. Given this, a united subject community, with a coherent vision of the subject's contribution to education, is likely to be the strongest weapon in future struggles for subject knowledge inside the educational state.

Study 6	A timeline for school geography 1970-2001		
Year	School geography curriculum system	Geography education system	National education system
1970-80 – Curriculum Development and Innovation			
1970	■ Establishment of GYSL and Geography 14-18 projects ■ First Charney Manor Conference	Radical journal *Antipode* founded	*Black Paper 3* published by Critical Quarterly (Cox and Dyson)
1972		*Geography: A modern synthesis* published by Harper & Row (Haggett)	Raising of the school leaving age
1973		*Social Justice and the City* published by Edward Arnold (Harvey) (welfare approach)	
1974	*Oxford Geography Project* published		
1975	*Teaching Geography* launched by GA		
1976	Geography 16-19 Project established	*Geographies of the Mind* published by Oxford University Press (Lowenthal and Bowden)	James Callaghan's 'Ruskin speech' launching the Great Debate in education
1977	New constitution and structure for the GA	■ *Progress in Geography* splits to become *Progress in Human Geography* and *Progress in Physical Geography* ■ *Human Geography: A welfare approach* published by Edward Arnold (Smith)	■ *Curriculum 11-16* published by HMI ■ *Black Paper 3* published by Critical Quarterly (Cox and Boyson)
1978	*The Teaching of Ideas in Geography* published (DES)		
1979	*Curriculum Planning in Geography* published (Graves)		Conservative government elected, Margaret Thatcher as PM
1980	Charney Manor Conference		*A View of the Curriculum* published by (DES/HMI)
Changeover: 1980 a framework for the school curriculum, DES 1980-1987 – Changing Discourse and Unresolved Issues			
1980	■ GA Response to *Framework for the School Curriculum* ■ Geography into the 1980s joint project conference in Oxford		*A Framework for the School Curriculum* published by DES

continued

Year	School geography curriculum system	Geography education system	National education system
1981	*Geography in the School Curriculum 11-16* published (DES)	Women and geography Study Group of IBG formed	*The School Curriculum* published by DES
1982			TVEI initiative launched
1983			Schools Council disbanded and SCDC and SEC formed in its place
1984		25th IGU Congress in Paris	
1985		*Social Relations and Spatial Structures* published by Macmillan (Gregory and Urry)	▪ *Better Schools,* White Paper DES ▪ *Curriculum 5-16* published by DES
1986	▪ Sir Keith Joseph addresses special conference called by GA ▪ *Handbook for Geography Teachers* published by GA (ed, Boardman)	▪ First research assessment exercise for geography in higher education ▪ *On Geography and its History* published by Blackwell (Stoddart)	▪ *Geography from 5-16* published by DES ▪ GCSE launched and intention to introduce national curriculum announced
Changeover: 1987 GA meets Kenneth Baker *1987-93 – Strong Centralised Control*			
1987	▪ *A Case for Geography* published by GA (eds, Bailey and Binns) ▪ GA delegation meet Kenneth Baker	*Journal of Geography in Higher Education* launched	*The National Curriculum 5-16: A consultation document* published by DES
1988			*National Curriculum Task Group on Assessment and Testing,* Published (Jan) ▪ Education Reform Act ▪ NCC and SEAC formed to replace SCDC and SEC
1989	▪ NC GWG established (April) ▪ Interim Report of group (Oct)	▪ *Post Modern Geographies* published by Verso (Soja) ▪ *The Condition of Post-Modernity* published by Blackwell (Harvey)	*The National Curriculum: From policy to practice* published by DES
1990	▪ Final Report of GWG, *Geography for Ages 5-16* published by DES/ WO (June) ▪ *Consultation Report; Geography* published by NCC (Nov)		Kenneth Clarke becomes Secretary of State for Education (Oct)

continued

Ideology and Policy-Making: The Experience of School Geography

Year	School geography curriculum system	Geography education system	National education system
1991	■ Implementation of geography NC for KS1-3 ■ *Non-statutory Guidance for Geography* published by NCC ■ *Key Geography* published by Thornes (Waugh and Bushell)	*Teaching Geography in Higher Education* published by Blackwell (Gold *et al.*)	■ K. Clarke makes amendments to the Draft Geography Order (Jan/Feb) ■ Statutory Order for Geography published (March) ■ *Education and Training for the 21st Century*, White Paper on post-16 education
1992	Optional SATs material for KS1 geography published by SEAC	■ *The Geographical Tradition* published by Blackwell (Livingstone) ■ *International Journal of Research in Geography and Environmental Education* launched	■ John Patten, former geography academic, becomes Secretary of State for Education ■ *Choice and Diversity: A new framework for schools* by DfE (July) ■ Education (Schools) Act stresses opting out, selection, private sector and establishes Ofsted
1993		*Geography and Feminism* published by Polity (Rose)	Ron Dearing invited to review the national curriculum (April)
Changeover 1993: Dearing Review of national curriculum *1993-1997 – Pragmatic Accommodation and Negotiation*			
1993	■ GA centenary ■ Geography/ICT Conference funded by DfE and grant given to GA for Geography/ICT Project		■ Dearing Interim Report (July) and Final Report (Dec) ■ Ofsted inspection system starts (Sept) ■ SCAA formed from SEAC and NCC (Oct)
1994	SCAA Geography Advisory Group established to review the GNC	■ First COBRIG Seminar: *New Perspectives for Geography in Schools and in Higher Education* ■ Teaching Quality Assessment for geography in higher education	
1995	Revised NC for geography to schools (Jan) and implemented (from Sept)	Merger of RGS with Institute of British Geographers	Dearing Review of 16-19 qualifications established
1996	*Geography Teachers' Handbook* published by GA (eds, Bailey and Fox)	Second COBRIG Seminar: *Quality and Standards in Geographical Education*	*Qualifying for Success* (Dearing Report on 16-19 qualifications) published

continued

Year	School geography curriculum system	Geography education system	National education system
1997	SCAA geography guidance, produced in co-operation with subject community, re-asserts curriculum planning and progressive educational ideas		Election of Labour government (May)
Changeover 1997: Election of Labour government 1997 *1997-2000+ – Command Curriculum*			
1997	*Handbook of Post-16 Geography* published by GA (ed, Powell)	*Reading Human Geography: The poetics and politics of inquiry* published by Hodder (Barnes and Gregory)	■ David Blunkett appointed as Secretary of State for Education ■ *Excellence in Schools,* White Paper (New Labour's agenda) ■ Consultation on *Qualifying for Success* (autumn) ■ Standards and Effectiveness Unit established and Standards Task Force
1998	■ *Handbook of Primary Geography* published by GA (ed, Carter) ■ *Bibliography of Geographical Education* published by GA (eds, Foskett and Marsden) ■ *Schemes of Work for Geography at KS1 and 2* published by QCA	■ QCA Conference: *Geography and History in the 14-19 Curriculum* ■ QAA establishes geography benchmarking exercise (RGS-IBG co-ordinated) ■ Third COBRIG Seminar: *Why Geography Matters* ■ Geography Discipline Network *Teaching and Learning Guides* published (HEFCE funded)	■ Dis-application of non-core six subjects in primary schools to allow greater focus on literacy and numeracy ■ NC Review gets under way ■ Circular 4/98 established teacher education competence framework ■ National Literacy Strategy in schools (Sept)
1999	Consultation on GNC proposals	International Network for Learning and Teaching Geography in higher education inaugural conference in Hawaii	*Handbooks for National Curriculum* published by DfEE/QCA (include statutory provision for citizenship and PSHE)
2000	■ *Schemes of Work for Geography at KS3* published by QCA/DfEE ■ Implementation of reviewed NC for geography	■ Geography benchmarking statement approved and begins piloting ■ National Subject Centre for Geography, Earth and Environmental Sciences (GEES) is established	■ New A/AS-level specifications implemented (from Sept) and key skills qualification becomes available ■ KS3 Strategy launched. Pilot work for TLF begins
2001	■ National curriculum website launched with linked sites ■ Geography included in QCA's creativity and curriculum development projects	Research Assessment Exercises 2001	■ Election (June) returns Labour for second term. Secretary of State for Education and Skills is Estelle Morris ■ Review of AS-levels announced

10

Subject Knowledge, the Subject Tribe and the State: Identifying Strategies for School Geography

Introduction

In the analysis so far, I have tried to maintain some distance from the evidence, to tell the curriculum story and to analyse the significant factors in, as far as possible, a detached way. In this chapter, I will engage more directly with the study, presenting my own views on how the geography education community should respond to the situation in 2001 and beyond.

In his 1994 book, Ball talks about a fifth policy context – the context of political strategy – and describes it as the identification of a set of political and social activities which might change the situation and tackle inequalities. Ball was referring to the injustices and inequalities in the education system as a whole and it may be somewhat naïve to extend this idea to the school geography curriculum alone. However, I am attracted to the idea of rounding off the more objective analysis in this book by proposing strategies for action. I believe that this is appropriate for the critical educational research stance that I have attempted to take. I also hope that it will be of some value to the geography subject community.

This chapter looks again at the school/higher education gap described in Chapters 1 (page 18) and 9 (page 147) explaining why I believe this to be a crucial matter to address if geography is to participate effectively in policy matters. It then evaluates the possibilities and priorities for geography and geographers, gives a brief summary of 'where we are now', and highlights strategies for action by the subject community in the immediate future.

Subject knowledge and the subject community

Chapter 2 referred to Stengel's models of the relationship between the academic subject and the school subject (page 21). It was suggested that on the basis of its place in the structure of knowledge and its curriculum history to about 1980, geography most closely fitted the third model. This is that the academic subject and the school subject were related by broad aims and common principles, although developing differently in detailed content and structure. The analysis so far, however, has shown that the bi-polar nature of the debate over the past 10-15 years has resulted in a relative neglect of the academic subject content by school geography and the appearance of the gap, mentioned in Chapters 1, 2 and 9. In this sense, the geography education system is now showing signs of a discontinuous relationship (as in Stengel's model 2) rather than a loose structural relationship (as in model 3). It is now useful to look at the characteristics of the gap in more detail, in order to see why it matters.

Neither the Geography National Curriculum (GNC) (Chapter 5) nor the GCSE and A/AS-level specifications (Chapter 7) show much evidence of influences from geography as it is currently developing in universities. Bradford, referring to the A/AS-level specifications for 2000 regretted missed opportunities to bridge the school-higher education gap:

'While the majority of developments in university geography are not appropriate for use at A-level, the inclusion of some would be beneficial for students. Geography could have been made a more relevant and popular subject and perhaps increased the numbers entering degree course programmes involving geography ... Unfortunately neither opportunity has been taken' (2001, p. 7).

In particular, mention could be made of the failure to pick up possibilities inherent in the 'cultural turn'. Cloke *et al.* describe this term as signifying 'the ways in which questions of meaning, language, discourse and representation have become central not just to the longstanding discipline of Cultural Geography but to Geographers' studies of environmental, economic, political, social and historical processes' (1999, p. xii). Chapter 8 has shown that a critical questioning approach to current societal concerns (e.g. national identity, social exclusion, youth culture, countryside issues) need not be just a way of updating the school subject for those going on to further advanced study. It could place geography centrally within some of New Labour's social policies. Morgan (2000) explains, for instance, how such perspectives provide an ideal starting point for geography's contribution to citizenship in schools, and a publication edited by Lambert and Machon (2001) gives further advice. Similarly, recent new work in physical and environmental geography, particularly in areas of environmental modelling, use of GIS and the global politics of environmental change do not seem to have penetrated school studies significantly. These often remain rooted in positivist models harking back to the 1970s. It is ironic that while the Prime Minister is moving environmental matters back up the agenda (6 March 2001 environmental speech) and the press is full of reports about flood management, climatic change and agricultural practices (winter 2000-01), geography, a subject centrally concerned with environmental change, is still not in a position to take full advantage of this in schools. The Third Report of the government's own Sustainable Development Education (SDE) Panel (DETR, 2001) argues for a continuing effort to support SDE and claims that geography is the national curriculum subject in which the potential is most explicit. One encouraging sign is that geography will play a strong role in the QCA/DfEE website of exemplar materials being developed (2001) to support environmental and SDE.

Arguably, the last big dialogue between school and university geographers took place in the 1960s and 1970s with the new quantitative geography. Since then, although there has been a trickle of ideas (from e.g. welfare geography, behavioural approaches, radical geography) influencing to some extent GCSE and A/AS specifications, this has never swelled to a full dialogue. School geography has picked up remnants and oddments as favoured by individual textbook writers and examiners. The school curriculum and the higher education curriculum have become separate components, each influenced more by the socio-political contexts of their production and by the need to address government priorities than by any sense of a common disciplinary base. In higher education, diversity is the picture, and particularly a division between physical and human geographers. At school level, geography has become a relatively static vehicle for social and educational purposes.

So far, universities and schools have been referred to as if they are the only components in the geography education system. Another very significant element is teacher education. Trainee geography teachers, particularly those undertaking the one year PGCE course (primary and secondary) who are predominantly graduate geographers, provide a direct link between the other two systems. They have the opportunity to build on their degree work as they reflect how to use it in the school context. In the 1970s and 1980s, such a link was a stimulus to innovation and change. However, teacher education has been caught up in the same moves towards accountability, central direction and utilitarianism (Furlong *et al.*, 2000). The increasing amount of time spent by students in schools rather than in the university base has produced benefits in terms of practical classroom skills but, arguably, it has reduced the time available for deeper consideration of either the educational theory base or the academic subject base. What is more the introduction of the competence-based standards for teacher education via Circulars 10/97 and 4/98 (DfEE/TTA, 1997, 1998) have forced the geography education courses to become both more prescriptive and more tightly linked to the national curriculum and public examination syllabuses. As Roberts explained, the statements which make up the standards for both primary and secondary 'present a model of learning guided by the outcomes of learning (what students must know, be aware of, understand and be able to do)' (2000, p. 39). It does not encourage questioning and dialogue with the subject. Lambert suggests that the problems with all this are two-fold:

> *'first, the lack of explicit reference to disciplinary expertise in its own right rather than how it relates to the classroom, syllabuses or programmes of study; and second, the rather mechanistic view that suggests students acquire knowledge and then just apply it' (2001, p. 3).*

What is missing, if these standards are followed literally, seems to be any deeper and more critical view of the discipline which recognises the dynamic and contested nature of the knowledge and skills, and the equally dynamic and creative processes required to translate this into teaching and learning situations.

Evidence for a discontinuity between students' degree-level experience and their teacher education activities is beginning to appear. Small-scale research done by Barratt Hacking revealed that novice teachers feel that they have to 'suspend' what she called their 'geographical persuasion' when planning national curriculum geography. They 'assume they should conform to the content and approaches of the school geography department, their mentor or the national curriculum for geography' (1996, p. 84). Rynne and Lambert (1997) found from their research that while most trainees felt competent to deliver the required material, they often felt disempowered and frustrated because they could not draw creatively on their degree work. The RGS-IBG/TTA Report on Teacher Supply and Geography (Rawling, 2000) noted that, although recruitment problems were bound up with bigger issues of finance and image, there was a significant disincentive provided by the perception that school geography lacked status and opportunities for creativity. Most of the concern noted above has been about secondary teacher education. Primary geography teacher education is equally subjected to regulations, and experiences greater difficulty (particularly via the dominant three-year, six-subject BEd route) in providing anything more than an introduction to the national curriculum packages. As in the other parts of the system, subject knowledge in teacher education seems to have been redefined by national policies. Evidence from Ofsted (presentation at the University Departments of Education (UDE) conference, Liverpool, 2001) suggests that, on the basis of a small sample of primary geography providers, the actual geographical content of teacher education courses is only sufficient to be a 'taster'. The point is also made that many students with geography degrees do not choose to take geography as their specialist subject for primary teaching because the subject is perceived to have low status. Mathematics or English training are seen to provide a better career move, a point confirmed by the experience of the UDE tutors at the QCA monitoring seminar in March 2001. Given the potential of teacher educators to play a mediating role between school geography and academic geography, such issues are of crucial concern in any attempts to revive the school-higher education dialogue.

It is important to recognise another, often neglected, part of the geography education system – geography in adult and continuing education, or lifelong learning. Since the early 1990s, governments have been keen to promote this aspect of the system, seeing it as a way of making learning more flexible and accessible for those who have missed earlier opportunities (Fryer, 1997). Lifelong learning is difficult to define, involving those returning to education or interested in leisure and recreation activities at a variety of stages in life and in a range of different institutions. Thus some adult learners will be in universities or university extra mural courses, many in further education and others in employer-funded training. The DfEE Green Paper, *The Learning Age: A renaissance for a New Britain*, recommended a significant expansion of funding and opportunities, suggesting that this was the key to maintaining economic prosperity and to promoting citizenship in the new age 'of information and global competition' (DfEE, 1998a, p. 9). Geography is a significant contributor to further education and to the Open University's academic courses. In 2000, the Open University, whose academic geography courses are already highly acclaimed, agreed to run a secondary geography PGCE course. In various guises of landscape studies, local studies, travel and outdoor activities, geography is one of the most popular areas of leisure/recreational courses (though not rivalling the dominant position of history). Geography's attractions are also apparent, though often not formally recognised, in the great increase in popularity of travel writing, regional tourist guides and books which explore the landscape, literature and poetry connections. Lifelong learning is, or could be, a more explicit part of the geography education system with a crucial role in public education and image making, though too often it is seen as a separate and marginal activity.

What is being revealed is not one 'gap' in the subject community, between schools and higher education, but a multiplicity of gaps within the whole geography education system. In an era of centralised control, it is crucial that the subject label 'geography' has an immediate, relevant and distinctive meaning to policy makers. Individual parts of the system should not seem to be heading in different directions. A school geography which is believed only to be concerned with trivial world knowledge will not gain entry to debates about critical thinking and citizenship; an academic subject which is fragmented between physical and human geography specialists will find it difficult to capitalise on the subject's contribution to environmental issues. As Johnston explains: 'geographers must demonstrate that their understanding of the world is knowledge that others need; people must be convinced that they want geography – that indeed they cannot do without it' (1993, p. viii). In addition, although academic research is the source of most new ideas and approaches, equally there are new perspectives about pedagogy and interpretation to be shared from the different experiences of implementing geography in different parts of the system. Subject knowledge and subject identity are important weapons in the struggles for curriculum status and this is something which must involve the whole subject community.

Closing the gaps in the geography education system

Action during the past few years has concentrated on opening the lines of communication between the different levels of the geography education system and on updating and exchanging information. But it is probably now time to be clearer about some of the big issues for discussion, agreement and strategic action. One priority, an essential pre-cursor to further initiatives, is a joint agreement about common broad aims and principles for geography as a discipline, as a basis for restoring Stengel's continuous school-academic relationship. Shaw and Matthews (1998) argued that any attempt to impose a common viewpoint on the disparate interests of academic geography is doomed to failure. Indeed attention has been drawn to this point by other writers. Johnston (1991b) and Unwin (1992) both referred to the fragmentation of academic geography as a feature which makes communication and joint objectives difficult, even without the complications of communicating with the school sector. However, much thought has also been given to ways of recognising unifying principles amongst academic geographers. These efforts are no doubt stimulated as much by the need to make strong arguments for disciplinary funding and status in higher education institutions as by concerns for public image (though this may in the end amount to the same thing!). Unwin (1992) explained that physical geography had become set in a positivist mode of operation, while human geography was increasingly developing its links with the social sciences. While this was leading to fruitful exchanges with other disciplines, an unfortunate result was that geography and geographers were failing to capitalise on the subject's contribution to environmental debates. O'Riordan made the same point in his paper for the COBRIG Seminar 1994, warning that geographers should grasp the opportunities presented by environmentalism 'or let the world pass by. Now is the time to take action' (1996, p. 126). There are echoes in both these of Stoddart's exhortation to geographers to 'claim the high ground' by drawing physical and human geography back together. Similar integrating motives lie behind the new interest in place 'as a focus for understanding the human world of experience and the physical world of existence' (Unwin, 1992, p. 21; see also Johnston, 1991b; Massey 1999a,b). To some extent, the benchmarking exercise (Chalkley and Craig, 2000) outlining a common framework for degree level geography, has encouraged geographers to consider an overview of the whole subject but, to the relief of most academics, this is only a loose teaching framework. It is not, as feared, a national curriculum for higher education 'institutions offering degree programmes must be free to decide upon the details of content and organisation' (QAA, 2000, para 1.6).

The benchmarking statement serves to remind us that, although it may seem a long way from the frontier debates of academic geography to the school geography curriculum, at the level of broad aims and principles it may not be so far. The widely accepted aims for the GNC (as outlined in the 1990 GWG Final Report) chime closely with the broad outlines of areas of achievement identified for degree-level geography, including a desire to restore the balance of physical and human geography, to claim environmental issues and to incorporate distinctive subject-specific skills, intellectual and key skills and active enquiry-based learning (see QAA, 2000). It was the curriculum structure and over-prescription which made realisation of these aims impossible at school level. So far, higher education geographers appear to have avoided this trap. Now, in the 2000s, the GNC is a genuinely minimal framework and the GCSE, A- and AS-level criteria are equally open to the kind of interpretation which could re-open the lines of dialogue with academic geography. Massey (for instance) has already explained lucidly some of the ideas about place for both primary teachers (in *Primary Geographer*, 1999c) and for secondary/higher education teachers (in *Geography*, 1999a). In both cases she makes clear how a new dynamism and relevance can be brought to the study of localities, regions and countries by starting from an awareness that social interactions are crucial in forming their identities and characteristics. The GA has been quick to direct teachers to the opportunities present in the NC emphasis given to environmental education and sustainable development (Grimwade, 2000a,b) and the Geography Discipline Network series on *Teaching and Learning Geography* (GDN, 1998) seems to have stimulated considerable interest among school teachers.

The important point is that common aims and principles need not be a totally constraining framework but can easily allow diversity of content and approach in each sector and dynamic interchange at appropriate contact points. In any case, the other advantage of recognising common aims is that it makes communication easier with the wider world and this should be seen as the second priority for the subject community. For the purposes of communicating with the general public and policy makers, a succinct statement is likely to be more effective. Existing statements, such as the GA's (1999a) Position Statement, the joint RGS-IBG/GA leaflet *Education for Life* (1998) and official documentation, such as NC Orders and the QAA benchmarking statement, might provide starters for discussion. A vital task will then be to use the common aims and principles to disseminate a more appropriate public image for geography. According to the national press, geography is a subject mainly concerned with knowledge of states, capitals, rivers and mountain names and, even this, they perceive as not well done. Changing the image to encompass both locational knowledge and deeper critical understanding of space, place and environment is a task which must involve all levels of education. Unwin states that for an image change to be effective, academic geographers must accept the need for change and become more involved in non-academic as well as academic writing, a point taken up by Martin (2001). Figures like Norman Davies (history), Simon Schama (history), Susan Greenfield (science), Richard Dawkins (science), and Lisa Jardine (history), for instance, have become household names, with almost celebrity status. Geographers have been active in specialist research and academic writing, but as Martin points out 'the fact remains that we lack the path-breaking popular best-sellers that could do much to raise the image of geography amongst the wider public. Herein, it seems to me, resides a major challenge for the subject' (2001, p. 5).

Communicating with policy makers is dependent on a positive public image but it also goes much deeper than that. Geographers and geography educationalists will be judged as much by what the subject does as by what it claims. This has been a topic of critical debate in academic geography circles, exposing different views about the way in which academic geographers might engage with policy makers (Shaw and Matthews, 1998; Peck, 1999; Massey, 2000; Pollard *et al.*, 2000; Martin, 2001) but no disagreement that they should undertake the task. Peck argues that in order to make an impact on social, economic and environmental policies, academic geographers need to be careful not to retreat from the 'big picture'. Although policy makers need specifically targeted proposals for the detailed follow-up of issues (in, for example, agriculture, local economic activity, environmental planning), they also need to recognise the bigger issues about the way these things inter-relate. Geography is one subject that has the special attribute of making connections and drawing together understanding across the physical, human and environmental divides. Peck concludes:

> 'In this era of "joined-up" thinking, strategic policy co-ordination and local/flexible delivery, geographers have a potentially important – one might even say unique – contribution to make. Perhaps things really are moving in our direction, but paradoxically, this may be occurring at precisely the same time as we abandon the terrain' (1999, p. 135).

Educationalists have also been exercised by the proper relationship between research and policy (Pring, 2000a,b; Sylva, 2000), particularly as a result of the criticisms that much research has been obtuse or insignificant (e.g. Hillage *et al.*, 1998). There has also been debate about whether the government's professed interest in evidence-informed policy is more than an exercise in justifying already selected policy lines. However, most educationalists agree that a positive approach is most productive (Pring, 2000b). While geography educators have been giving growing attention to research and to publishing the findings (e.g. Foskett and Marsden, 1998; Scoffham, 1998; Bowles, 2000), in the policy context it is probably sensible to heed the same warning given by Peck, namely that while it is important to produce research about teaching and learning or about contributions to citizenship and literacy, it is equally important, as Chapter 8 shows, that these smaller scale inputs do not detract our attention from explaining the bigger picture. Geography may have many and varied contributions to cross-curricular concerns and other initiatives but its claim for a place in the curriculum must be based on much bigger ideas about its distinctiveness in giving unique insights into the realities of place, space and environment. As Chapter 8 shows, these characteristics will directly 'hit' some of New Labour's key policies but, as this chapter explains, our success in this endeavour will depend on our restoring a lively school-higher education dialogue. For school geography educators this project will be crucial to future quality and status.

Scholarship, professionalism and curriculum development

A third priority for the subject community is signalled by the finding that geography subject knowledge at school and in teacher training seems to have been redefined in a static, lifeless way. The answer may lie in the concept of scholarship. Healey (2000a,b) has explored this notion as applied to teaching and learning geography in higher education. He believes that there is a need to move away from an emphasis on disciplinary research (i.e. in this case, research into geography *per se*) as the single most prestigious form of scholarship and to embrace similar notions of excellence in relation to teaching and learning. Quoting Martin *et al.* (1999) he suggests that scholarship would involve engagement with the scholarly contributions of others, reflection on one's own teaching practice and the learning of students, and dissemination of aspects of practice and of theoretical ideas about teaching and learning. The recent recognition of pedagogical research as a category for research assessment exercise submission may help to promote this work. This idea of scholarship may be eminently applicable to the school situation. Lambert (2001) draws on Rice (1992) to identify three elements of the scholarship of teaching and learning relevant to teaching geography at school level:

■ synoptic capacity or the ability to draw together the strands of a field in a way that provides coherence and meaning

■ pedagogical content knowledge or the ability to represent the subject in ways that transcend subject and teaching knowledge

■ knowledge of learning or the ability to investigate at first and second hand how students learn.

He suggests that, applied to teacher education, this notion of scholarship, particularly the synoptic capacity, could allow students' own experiences of geography to be better used and encourage a re-interpretation of subject knowledge in the national curriculum and the public examination syllabuses. Such a critical, questioning approach is also consistent with Roberts' plea (2000) for teacher education to become more research-based, despite the restrictive nature of the ITT standards. One might argue that a similar approach to teacher in-service training, involving secondary teachers working with academic geographers to re-interpret and question the central school frameworks, could equally open up the school curriculum.

The promotion of discipline-based scholarship in teaching and learning seems to be one 'big idea' with potential to revive cross-sectoral dialogue as well as to redefine school subject knowledge. It also introduces the fourth priority for subject community action, which is the redefinition of professionalism. Chapter 6 suggests that older conceptions of professionalism have been particularly hard-hit by developments since 1988. It is no longer the NC framework which is a serious constraint but the wider context of school management, funding and performance targets. Early findings from QCA monitoring of the 2000 NC show, for instance, that most secondary teachers are envisaging minimal change to their KS3 courses because of other school pressures, including the structural re-arrangements consequent on introduction of the new A/AS-level specifications. In primary schools where geography features significantly at all, the tendency is to take the KS1/2 Scheme of Work as a ready-made answer. (At least this ensures a geographical presence in some primary schools!) However, curriculum development '2001 style' need not involve a complete rewrite of the whole course. Much can be done with small-scale but creative restructuring of the NC framework (some units in the KS3 Scheme of Work give hints to the possibilities) and with changes to teaching and learning. Roberts (2000) suggests that the way PGCE students are taught and learn provides them with a model for their own classrooms. Critical enquiry approaches in ITT lead to open enquiring classrooms in the future and to opportunities for rethinking the curriculum. The GA's interpretation of the 'National Standards for Subject Leaders' (Leading Geography, GA, 1999b,c) makes a start in this direction, with a section of each publication (primary and secondary) focused on the 'direction and development of the subject'. Similarly, enquiry-based in-service training for practising teachers could encourage them to be innovative with national guidelines and support materials and to allow their pupils to see subject knowledge as tentative and dynamic. The work of the Thinking Skills consortium based at the University of Newcastle is based on this kind of two-way approach; the publicity blurb for the Thinking Skills series states that 'the Thinking Skills series is as much about professional development as it is about providing direct teaching resources' – the kind of claim that was frequently made by the geography curriculum projects 30 years ago. It will be interesting to see if the government's programme to improve teaching and learning in the foundation subjects (TLF, part of the KS3 Strategy, see pages 128-129) promotes this kind of critical enquiry for teachers or whether it is tempted to offer more managed and controlled solutions. There may be opportunities in the two areas of work, beginning in 2001 at QCA – the Geography and History Curriculum Project and the Creativity across the Curriculum initiative. The intention is to work closely with schools and subject specialists. Some kind of link between the various QCA and DfES projects concerned with learning and standards would also be useful!

Further encouragement for curriculum development can come directly from higher education, where innovation has been helped by the establishment of the Institute for Learning and Teaching, with its associated funding for institutional projects. Geographers have been at the forefront of new developments (see Healey, 2000a,b), notably through the activities of the Higher Education Study Group of the RGS-IBG, the GDN, the formation of the International Network for Learning and Teaching Geography in higher education (INLT) in 1999 and the setting up of the subject centre for geography, earth and environmental sciences (GEES) in 2000 at the University of Plymouth. Some results of all this activity are the series of GDN curriculum guides (1998) and the booklets from the Key Skills in Geography Project (Gravestock and Healey, 2000). These publications cover topics such as assessment, teaching and learning, work-related learning, problem solving and curriculum planning. Many of them have potential for school geography, drawing on theory as well as giving practical examples. Most importantly the guides will serve to remind school geography teachers that teaching and learning, at all levels, is not just about implementing national prescriptions. It is about creativity, innovation and developing new ideas to fit the students and the institutions. Indeed, in some ways, the buzz of innovation (admittedly only in a section of the higher education community) has similarities with the 1970s curriculum development movement which took place in school geography. School educators have been involved in a small way in all these initiatives so far, notable examples being the joint school/higher education seminar on pedagogical research in geography education held in Coventry in May 1999 (see Rawling, 1999b) and the school education contribution to the INLT Symposium in Hawaii (Bednarz *et al.*, 2000). But there is ample scope, and every reason, for school educators to be more involved in this kind of curriculum development. Faced in the 1990s with common threats to the subject arising from centralisation and accountability, it can be seen as a subject community activity with potential to revitalise the subject at all levels.

The subject and the state: strategies

This section should be read after studying Figure 1, which identifies opportunities and threats facing school geography in 2001. A stronger and more coherent subject community will be better placed to 'make the case' and to 'fight the battles' necessary within the educational state of the twenty-first century – i.e. to progress the subject as well as to make progress within the subject, to use a distinction introduced by Lowe and Short (1990). Stengel's model of the relationship between the academic subject and the school subject might be extended (Figure 2) to take in all parts of the subject education system. The broad definition of subject knowledge at the level of common aims and principles is essential to all. It presents the public image of the subject, it provides policy makers with the reasons to include or exclude the subject from current initiatives, and it provides the foundation from which to share research and discussion. Becher drew attention to the fact that disciplinary groups provided a powerful organising structure and social cohesion for disciplinary researchers and teachers. He argued that, in higher education institutions, 'disciplinary groups can usefully be regarded as academic tribes each with their own set of intellectual values and patch of cognitive territory' (1994, p. 151). It might be suggested that geography educationalists at all levels should now begin to consider themselves as part of a bigger 'subject tribe' as an explicit response to the changing context of the 2000s.

Where are we now? Opportunities and threats

Level	Opportunities	Threats
School geography curriculum system (SGCS)	1. National frameworks and criteria 3-19 provide a continuous sequence (entitlement?) throughout school education. 2. GNC now provides an acceptable model for curriculum planning and scope for teacher input. 3. The GCSE and AS/A-level criteria are flexible enough to allow for more innovative specifications (syllabuses). 4. Geography is a popular subject with pupils at most ages. At GCSE it is still the most popular optional subject. 5. Given time and resources some teachers are keen to participate in professional activities (e.g. GeoVisions, Best Practice Research).	The national framework may not be as strong as it appears – weak at KS1/2; highly competitive situation at 14-19; decline in examination entries GCSE and AS/A-level. Teachers do not always perceive the flexibility and are constrained by a residual 1991 image and a restricted view of professionalism. The awarding bodies will not move into more innovative specifications unless a strong lead for change and development is given by the subject community. If school geography does not shake off lacklustre image and problems with quality at KS3, pupils may be attracted to other more 'exciting' subjects (e.g. media studies). If centralised solutions to professional development remain prescriptive and managerial, then there is unlikely to be a genuine revival of professionalism.
Geography education system (GES)	1. Geographers in teacher education provide a base for good practice and educational research. They can also be mediators between academic geography and school geography. 2. Academic geography is well-respected for its innovative ideas and sound research, especially in human geography with a re-emphasis on place/space. 3. Geographers in higher education have a new interest in pedagogy with exciting practical developments and growing strength in research to share with schools. 4. The subject associations have grown in strength and maturity over the past decade, providing a good base to make a more pro-active input to policy matters.	The ITT standards do not seem to promote the idea of a research-based profession. Time/institutional arrangements often make links with higher education colleagues difficult. Teacher recruitment problems. The necessity for dialogue with school educators is not always clear. Higher education audit exercises are only just beginning to recognise and give status to publications and activities involving schools. Higher education geographers may construct their own new structures, organisations and journals, leaving little room for participation by school educators. If competition rather than co-operation results over, for example, membership, access to government funds and initiatives, then the impact will be weakened
National education system (NES)	1. Geography has a place and recognition in the national education system, particularly for its wider contribution to, e.g. ICT, literacy, citizenship. 2. As indicated by interest in travel, different places and cultures, landscapes and environmental issues, geography is popular with the public. 3. Recent policy initiatives seem to provide opportunities for geography, e.g. SDE, the TLF programme, creativity and thinking skills. 4. The subject associations have built up strong links with policy through the QCA subject team and subject HMI.	If policy makers see these as geography's main contribution, the subject could end up acting only as servicing agent for other priorities. Neither the public nor policy makers seem to connect these interests directly with school geography. A more traditional and utilitarian image of the subject prevails. The Labour government's controlled approach to policy making (the command curriculum) may make it less easy for geography to bring out its full contribution. The centres of power are shifting towards a more diffuse range of political advisers, strategy teams and policy units (e.g. SEU).

Figure 1: Opportunities and threats facing school geography, 2001.

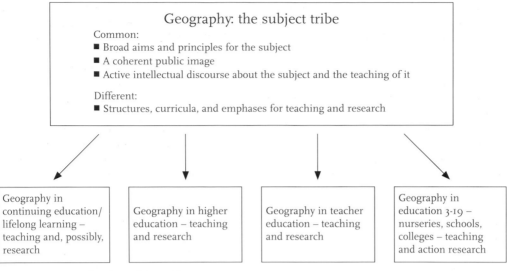

Figure 2: **Geography: the subject tribe.**

The school subject community also needs to have a clear understanding of the levels of curriculum operation identified in Chapter 9, to understand where power lies in relation to curriculum policy making and policy implementation, and to recognise where action is feasible and appropriate. This is not merely an interesting exercise; the experience of geography 1980-2000 has shown how policies constrain our actions. As Ball explains it: 'we do not speak the discourse, it speaks us' (1994, p. 22). Given the pressures of the command curriculum, the scope for action is limited but this section will use the levels of curriculum operation to highlight some of the possibilities (Figure 3). The references in italics are to the numbered items in Figure 1, to indicate which opportunities/ threats are being addressed.

Curriculum as specified

This is the macro-level in which national government, the DfES, the political advisers, the various agencies of government (e.g. TTA, QCA, QAA) hold sway and, given the strong control exerted by the Labour government, there is not a great deal of room for manoeuvre by a subject community, perceived as relatively marginal to current priorities. The aim should be to move out from the base of an improved public image and stronger identity for the subject, to focus on a small number of priorities – for example, the 14-19 curriculum and new ideas for the national curriculum framework. Co-operation between the subject associations will be crucial for this strategy. The 14-19 curriculum is already the subject of alternative proposals, discontent with implementation of the new AS has grown (hence the 2001 AS-level Review), and the moves to further vocationalise the curriculum may re-open debates about flexibility. All these may lead to a major restructuring in the near future. Geographers should argue for a more balanced and flexible curriculum in which geography can: contribute a distinctive geographic entitlement (not necessarily always linked to existing qualifications, perhaps relating to the pre- and post-16 citizenship proposals); provide a range of subject-specific courses and qualifications; make selective inputs to vocational courses; and contribute to general skills, abilities and experiences (*NES 1, SGCS 1*).

Rethinking of the existing national curriculum framework is already under way and given official credence by the existence of the QCA geography and history 'curriculum project'. This is only a small-scale initiative, with minimal funding, and it is not clear how the resulting proposals will be received and acted upon. It is already intended that this work will involve the subject community and draw on existing research in geographical education and geography. On the basis of the past 20 years of curriculum history, it is vital that the distinctive contribution of the subject is stressed, rather than its role as a servicing agent for other priorities. Any changes to the national frameworks should draw out the spatial and environmental perspectives and discipline-based skills which geography provides – why its place in the curriculum is necessary in the changing world of the twenty-first century. It would also be valuable to consider defining a geographic entitlement, i.e. an absolute minimum level of geographical knowledge, understanding and skills necessary for young people in the different age groups throughout the 5-19 (or 3-19) curriculum (not necessarily linked to qualifications). This may be particularly important for the 14-19 phase, as mentioned above. The recommendations should not shrink from making reference to structures and arrangements that inhibit a continuous entitlement to geography 5-19, as well as to details of curriculum content and skills (*SGCS 1, NES 1*).

The KS3 Strategy, through the TLF programme, is another opportunity in which geography educationalists are already involved as consultants and advisers. The overall impact is still uncertain but there is scope for influencing some schools and teachers, and possibly for improving geography's image and standing in policy making circles. Finally, mention might be made of the specialist schools and proposals (DfEE, 2001) to increase their number to 50% all schools. The humanities seem to be the one major curriculum area not recognised for special attention. Whether or not one

Curriculum level	What it includes	Focus for action	Reference to Figure 1 (page 173)
Curriculum as specified	Statutory/legal/mandatory requirements, e.g. NC Orders, GCSE and AS/A-level Criteria	■ More flexible, balanced 14-19 curriculum ■ Rethinking NC content ■ Entitlement to geographical education for all age groups Also ■ Humanities/environment role in specialist schools?	NES 3, 4
Curriculum as planned	National advice/guidance for planning, public examinations specifications, textbooks, support materials, teacher education strategies and school level plans	■ Rethinking content/approach of some GCSE and AS/A-level specifications ■ Use of internet and new technologies to open up curriculum Also ■ Support/promote role of teacher educators	GES 4 NES 1, 2 SGCS 1, 5
Curriculum as implemented	Teachers' course plans and lesson plans (what they intend to teach)	■ Classroom-based curriculum development and professionalism ■ Scholarship of teaching and learning ■ Exchange and dialogue with higher education	GES 4 NES 1, 2, 3 GES 2, 3
Curriculum as experienced and retained	Realities of the classroom interactions, especially from the pupils' viewpoint. (What is actually experienced and retained by pupils)	■ Potential of 'assessment for learning' ■ Further research into the perceptions, experiences and existing knowledge which pupils bring to their geography	SGCS 2, 4 GES 1, 2, 3

Figure 3: School geography: suggested foci for action. Derived from an idea in Harland *et al.*, 1999.

agrees with the policy, geography and history stand to lose status even more, without recognition of their special curriculum contribution and, accordingly, a role in this initiative. It may be necessary to enlist support from outside geography education (*NES 1 and 2*).

Curriculum as planned

At this level, government agencies, subject associations, educational publishers, awarding bodies and schools themselves all play a part, as they translate statutory requirements into curriculum plans, support materials and examination specifications. For school geography, one priority is the examination specifications for GCSE and AS/A-levels which, as Chapter 7 has shown, are in need of some curriculum rethinking. The national criteria are not a major constraint, but the awarding bodies need clear encouragement and guidance from the subject community. As Bradford pointed out (2001), it is in the subject community's interest to ensure that there are ample and innovative interpretations rather than many versions of the same traditional line (*SGCS 3*).

The GA is already producing a range of guidance publications and resources and promoting the diffusion of newer ideas from the academic subject (e.g. *Changing Geography* series, Bale, 2000). There is also scope, as the GA has realised, to produce alternative interpretations of the national curriculum – Schemes of Work do not necessarily rule. In this respect, recent textbook series closely following the KS3 Schemes of Work (e.g. *Geog 1 2 3 Series,* Gallagher *et al.,* 2000-01) may be in danger of reinforcing the image that these are the only interpretation. In the GA's work with QCA on national guidance, there are some new and interesting opportunities becoming apparent – the creativity work, the sustainable development initiative and a new programme (Respect for All) intending to exemplify the 'inclusion' statement in the national curriculum. One significant point about the future of curriculum planning at this level is that the internet and the whole range of new communications and information technologies have a huge potential to open up debate and interaction. Already the agreed approach for government agencies is now to disseminate material electronically rather than on paper. Most of QCA's new materials will be in this format, including via the high profile 'National Curriculum in Action' website. For geography a whole range of new informational and exemplification materials will shortly be available – the geography exemplification materials (part of NC in Action); the education for sustainable development website; the joint BECTa/QCA geography/ICT examples; and eventually the materials from the 'Respect for All' and creativity work. Particularly significant is the fact that most of these websites have potential for interaction, i.e. teachers/educators can download, amend, comment on and submit their own materials. Such developments may radically change the nature of curriculum planning and the GA should continue to encourage teacher awareness of and confidence in these new developments. They will, arguably, make it more difficult for there to be one centralised interpretation of a national curriculum (*SGCS 2 and 5*).

Teacher educators have been identified as an important influence on the 'curriculum as planned'. It is recognised that there are immense pressures on the teacher education community, promoting standardisation rather than reflection or individualism. Also there are fewer teacher educators who can encompass both the research and teaching roles. Wider extension of their potential role as mediators may not happen immediately, but it is important for the subject associations and higher education colleagues (e.g. teaching and learning networks) to give them as much support as possible (*GES 1, 2 and 3*).

Curriculum as implemented

Arguably, this is the level with most potential for change. As explained in earlier chapters, the national curriculum in particular is no longer a prescriptive, constraining framework. There is ample room, though not yet full encouragement, for innovation within the framework of the four aspects of geography. This is where the notion of scholarship is relevant to asserting that the teacher's task of interpreting and expanding national frameworks is, or should be, seen as an essential part of the professional role. Exchange with higher education colleagues will be of mutual benefit, producing a livelier, more relevant school subject and, potentially, more secure recruitment to degree courses. A more professional and critical approach to the school subject is implicit in the work of the GeoVisions project, the Thinking through Geography consortium and a host of smaller teacher research-, teacher education- and local authority-inspired initiatives. Given the constraints and pressures surrounding the work of teachers (Chapter 6) this is unlikely to involve major curriculum development projects '1970s style'. On the other hand, there are now some centrally organised initiatives which can allow school geography to be more expansive (e.g. the QCA creativity initiative and geography/history curriculum project – the TLF programme) which should be seized. Whatever the eventual impact on national policies, they do have the potential, by their very existence, to stimulate a rethink of classroom practice. Teachers of geography need to be ready to use these initiatives as starters for school-based development and not as national prescriptions to be implemented. Smaller scale school- and classroom-based curriculum development founded on the confident basis of a more coherent and interactive geography community and linked by e-mail and internet could provide a powerful force for change. A renewed professionalism may ultimately be the best way to balance and moderate the demands of a centralised curriculum (*SGCS 2, NES 1 and 2*).

While innovation and diversity are to be welcomed in geography classrooms, it is important to heed the warnings of curriculum history. Whatever image is sold to the public and policy makers must be delivered. If there is a distinctive core (or entitlement) to geographical education – and if it includes (as I believe it should) world knowledge, maps and essential locational knowledge as well as critical geographical enquiry skills, understanding of environmental issues and of global interdependence, then the school subject must address these. In this sense, a genuine appreciation of our common aims with other parts of the geography community will be a crucial aid, as will the subject community's involvement in and respect for the national framework (*GES 2 and 3, NES 2*).

Curriculum as experienced and retained

This may be one of the most exciting areas for further exploration and development by all subject communities and by educationalists in general. It is crucial for geography's status in an increasingly flexible NC and 14-19 framework, that pupils' experience of the subject is meaningful, relevant to their lives and encourages them to take the subject further in some way (*SGCS 4*). More than this, however, pupils are not, and never have been, passive recipients of a planned curriculum. The range of influences, attitudes and competing information now brought to classrooms by school children and young people is massive and growing. It is not just a question of how to plan the next stages in their learning, aspects which the 'assessment for learning' initiatives are exploring. For a subject like geography, with its diverse content and roots in the wider world, it is also about learning from and building on pupils' experience, seeing them as integral parts of geographical enquiry, and blurring the distinction between in-classroom and out-of-classroom learning. There is not space here for further discussion – but this is undoubtedly a topic for investigation in the medium and longer term, and it may well turn out to be *the* most crucial factor in changing the curriculum in the twenty-first century (*SGCS 4, NES 2*).

Conclusion

In many ways, the latest phase of curriculum policy making in England is posing some of the most difficult issues for school geography. Not only do many current policies, whether in terms of literacy, 14-16 structures, vocational developments or specialists schools, seem to marginalise geography's contribution and question its identity, but the structures of the 'command curriculum' make it difficult for the subject community to respond in a creative professional manner. One response would be to 'batten down the hatches' and to retreat behind the utilitarian image that the policy makers still seem to hold of us. I do not believe that this is the way forward, as I hope the preceding curriculum history of geography has shown. As a subject community we still hold in our power many of the weapons to use in the battles ahead – although as this chapter has explained, we do need to sharpen and polish them!

For the geography subject tribe, the political strategy must include:

■ clarifying an essential 'geographical entitlement' (i.e. what aspects of geographical knowledge, understanding, skills and approaches might be considered essential for all young people by the end of compulsory education?)

■ reviving and extending notions of disciplinary-based professionalism and curriculum development, to suit the twenty-first century

■ recognising and using the opportunities becoming apparent within current policy frameworks

■ maintaining an awareness and understanding of the curriculum policy process, the locations of decision making and power, and the possibilities for action.

These are not luxuries to be left until quieter times. The linked questions of subject definition, subject professionalism, scholarship and curriculum development are crucial elements in the macro-level policy equation as well as in the micro-level arenas of teaching and learning.

Appendices

Appendix 1: Abbreviations used in the text

ACAC	Curriculum and Assessment Authority for Wales (from 1994 to 1997)
ACCAC	Curriculum and Assessment Authority for Wales (from 1997)
A-level	GCE Advanced level
AS	Advanced Supplementary 1987-2000 (half the content/same standard as A-level) Advanced Subsidiary 2000+ (equivalent to first half of an A-level course)
AT	Attainment Target – specific objectives or goals for pupils' attainment in a subject
AVCE	Advanced Vocational Certificate of Education – the vocational A-level
BERA	British Educational Research Association
BGRG	British Geomorphology Research Group – affiliated to RGS-IBG
BTEC	Business and Technical Education Council
CCEA	Northern Ireland Awarding Body (www.ccea.org.uk)
CCW	Curriculum Council for Wales (1988-1994)
COBRIG	Council of British Geography (from 1988)
CPVE	Certificate of Pre-Vocational Education
CSE	Certificate of Secondary Education (1965-88)
DCMS	Department for Culture Media and Sports (1997 onwards)
DES	Department of Education and Science (to 1992)
DETR	Department for Environment, Transport and the Regions (1997-2001) From June 2001 it is divided into two new departments.
DfE	Department for Education (1992-1995)
DfEE	Department for Education and Employment (1995-2001)
DfES	Department for Education and Skills (from 2001) http://www.dfes.gov.uk (The Schemes of Work website is http://www.standards.dfes.gov.uk/schemes/)
DTI	Department of Trade and Industry
ERA	Education Reform Act 1988
GA	Geographical Association http://www.geography.org.uk and http://www.geographyshop.org.uk
GCSE	General Certificate of Secondary Education (from 1986)
GDN	Geography Discipline Network http://www.chelt.ac.uk/gdn
GEES	National Subject Centre for Geography, Earth and Environmental Sciences http://www.gees.ac.uk
GNC	Geography National Curriculum
GNVQ	General National Vocational Qualifications (from 1992) Part One GNVQs specifically for 14-16 pupils (from 1995 pilot, and 1999 mainstream)
GSIP	Geography Schools and Industry Project (1984-91)
GWG	(National Curriculum) Geography Working Group 1989-90
GYSL	Geography for the Young School Leaver Project (also called Avery Hill Project) (Schools Council)
HEFCE	Higher Education Funding Council (England) http://www.hefce.ac.uk
HIT	Humanities and Information Technology Project
HWG	(National Curriculum) History Working Group

continued

IGU-CGE	International Geographical Union, Commission for Geographical Education
INLT	International Network for Learning and Teaching Geography in Higher Education (from 1999) http://www.inlt.org
KS	Key stage (KS1-4 cover ages 5-16)
LEA	Local Education Authority
MSC	Manpower Services Commission
NAHA	National Association of Humanities Advisers
NC	National Curriculum (from 1988) http://www.nc.uk.net
NCC	National Curriculum Council (1988-1993)
NCVQ	National Council for Vocational Qualifications (1986-1997)
Ofsted	Office for Standards in Education (from 1992) http://www.ofsted.gov.uk
PoS	Programme of Study – the knowledge, skills and understandings which all pupils should be taught during a key stage
QAA	Quality Assurance Agency for Higher Education http://www.qaa.org.uk
QCA	Qualifications and Curriculum Authority – established 1997 from merger of SCAA and NCVQ http://www.qca.org.uk
RGS RGS-IBG	Royal Geographical Society – after 1995 merged with Institute of British Geographers http://www.rgs.org
SAT	Standard Assessment Task
SC	Schools Council (England and Wales, 1964-84)
SCAA	School Curriculum and Assessment Authority (England 1993-97)
SCDC	School Curriculum Development Committee (England and Wales, 1984-88)
SEAC	School Examinations and Assessment Council (England and Wales, 1988-93)
SEC	Secondary Examinations Council (England and Wales, 1984-88)
SEU	Standards and Effectiveness Unit (at DfEE from 1997, now DfES) http://www.standards.dfes.gov.uk
SoA	Statement of Attainment (statement describing attainment for a specific level of an attainment target)
TGAT	Task Group on Assessment and Testing (National Curriculum)
TLF	Teaching and Learning in the Foundation subjects (from 2000) One strand of the KS3 Strategy
UCAS	Universities and Colleges Admissions Service http://www.ucas.com
WO	Welsh Office

Year	RGS-IBG	GA
1980	7815	7203
1981	7917	6635
1982	8707	6163
1983	8527	6258
1984	8670	6463
1985	8433	6555
1986	8523	6520
1987	8655	7191
1988	9134	7044
1989	10,103	6873
1990	10,366	8499
1991	11,005	9672
1992	11,306	10,397
1993	11,428	10,844
1994	11,457	11,014
1995	12,665	11,443
1996	12,338	11,462
1997	12,456	11,547
1998	12,287	10,727
1999	12,723	9923
2000	13,039	9360
2001	13,488	10,003

2: **Membership of the RGS (with Institute of British Geographers after 1995) and of the Geographical Association, 1980-2001**

Source: RGS-IBG and GA.

3: KS3 national curriculum teacher assessment results for selected subjects, 1997-2000

Subject	Percentage of pupils at level 5 or above all pupils				boys				girls			
	1997	1998	1999	2000	1997	1998	1999	2000	1997	1998	1999	2000
Geography	58	59	61	63	54	55	56	63	63	64	66	68
English	61	62	64	64	51	54	56	56	70	70	72	72
History	56	58	60	63	56	53	54	63	62	64	66	69
Design and technology	56	60	63	65	56	53	55	65	64	68	71	73

Source: DfEE Standards website.

4a: GCSE Geography: some features of a changing system

National criteria Version and reason	Content requirements	Assessment requirements	Numbers of syllabuses	Characteristics of syllabuses
GCSE: The National Criteria: Geography 1985 (DES/WO, 1985) ■ to provide a common framework for all syllabuses in geography for the new GCSE examination.	Outlined aims under the headings of knowledge, skills and values, and set out guidelines for content, including: ■ first-hand study of a small area, preferably home area, as base for experiential learning ■ study of contrasting areas and/or themes within British Isles ■ consideration of UK's relationships with wider groupings, e.g. EEC ■ Study of geographical aspects of important social, environmental issues ■ Topics which focus on inter-relationships and interactions between people and environment.	All Mode 1 schemes must include a minimum of 20% school-based assessment interpreted by most syllabuses as 'a geographical enquiry'. Remaining component is terminal examination with roughly half the syllabuses having common papers and half differentiated papers. Grade descriptions provided for F and C grades.	Sixteen syllabuses (including one offered jointly by MEG and WJEC). First examination 1988.	Considerable variety in syllabus content. The majority of syllabuses were theme based. Two syllabuses, MEG A and Avery Hill (MEG/WJEC), had a strong issues focus; LEAG B had a more minimal focus on issues. Most syllabuses left teachers free to choose illustrative content. Only MEG B and LEAG D retained a regional flavour with the UK and West Africa as regional frameworks for examples. Coursework ranged from 20% to 50% of the assessment and included a variety of tasks based on fieldwork and on secondary data.
GCSE/KS4 Examinations Criteria 1993 (SEAC, 1993c) ■ to define the subject-specific essentials for GCSE courses based on the new KS4 NC programmes of study.	Minimal outline of content because the syllabuses must 'provide opportunities for candidates to meet the requirements of the programme of study as defined by the relevant geography order' (i.e. NC). NC Geography KS4 emphasised country studies, aspects of physical, human and environmental geography and international relations. Because of overlapping level-related content, it also required knowledge of localities and the home region.	Terminal examination at least 75% in non-modular schemes and at least 50% in modular schemes. Coursework must be not less than 20% and not more than 25% and must include 'an enquiry supported by fieldwork'. Three tiers of examination papers, each tier covering three or four NC levels.	Eleven full course syllabuses and several short course syllabuses were ready and sent to SEAC (May 1993) but their approval and implementation was first deferred (October 1993) then abandoned altogether (1994).	**Syllabuses never released for use in schools**, though some were amended in only a minor way to fit the new criteria (1995). Most were thematic syllabuses, though Avery Hill kept its 'issues-base' and the '14-18' syllabus focused on enquiry and decision-making. Home region requirement was dealt with in coursework.

continued

National criteria Version and reason	Content requirements	Assessment requirements	Numbers of syllabuses	Characteristics of syllabuses
GCSE Criteria for Geography 1995 (SCAA/ACAC, 1995b) ■ to provide a common framework for syllabuses in the new situation where geography is optional at KS4, and following on from revisions which have taken place to the NC KS1-2.	All syllabuses were required to include ■ balance of physical, human and environmental aspects ■ range of scales, environments and places ■ patterns and processes in geography ■ people-environment inter-relationships ■ geographical aspects of social, economic, environmental and political issues ■ significance and effects of attitudes and values ■ locational knowledge ■ range of geographical enquiry skills including IT.	Terminal examination must be at least 75% weighting in non-modular and 50% in modular schemes. Coursework must be not less than 20% and not more than 25%. Extended prose – special mention Grade descriptions provided for F, C and A. Two tiers of examination papers A*-D and C-G (with safety net for higher candidates).	Eleven full course syllabuses (including one offered jointly by MEG/WJEC), and five short course syllabuses. First examination/full course 1998.	The majority of syllabuses were thematic. Four syllabuses had a focus on issues, most notably the Avery Hill. ULEAC B emphasised people-environment themes and issues. Only one syllabus was based on a regional framework (NEAB B). Coursework mainly interpreted as one long or two short fieldwork investigations. Avery Hill syllabus also included a cross-unit task involving 'research' or problem solving.
GCSE Criteria for Geography 2000 (QCA, 2000g) ■ to address the changes made to geography KS1-3 in the NC Review and to general KS4 requirements (e.g. key; skills, sustainable development).	All specificators (syllabuses) are required to include the aspects noted above (1995 criteria) plus ■ acquisition and use of geographical vocabulary ■ specific mention of ICT, key skills, sustainable development ■ interdependence and global citizenship given a higher profile ■ decision making more explicit.	As above (1995 criteria). Internal and external assessment weightings are unchanged – 20/25% internal and 75-80% external. Two-tier system of examination papers continues – A*-D and C-G (and safety net for higher candidates).	Ten full course specifications, five short course specifications. (Also five Certificate of Achievement specifications for lower attainers.) First examination/full course 2003.	The specifications (syllabuses) are very similar to the previous set. Some changes were necessitated by rationalisation of awarding bodies (e.g. AQA A, B and C created from old NEAB and SEG). Five are thematic, another four are centred round issues. Only one (AQA B) has a regional framework. Coursework is mainly interpreted as one long or two short fieldwork investigations (as above).

4b: A-level Geography: some features of a changing system

National core or criteria Version and reason	Content requirements	Assessment requirements	Numbers of syllabuses	Characteristics of syllabuses
A-level Common Core for Geography 1983 (GCSE Examining Boards, 1988) ■ 'the wish for reassurance that there is broad comparability of knowledge and awareness amongst all candidates, irrespective of which board's syllabus they have studied' (p. 19).	Outlined what a student ought to have gained as a result of doing A-level geography 1. Important ideas in physical and human geography and at the interface between them 2. Understanding of processes of regional differentiation 3. Knowledge derived from study of a balanced selection of regions and environments 4. Understanding of and an ability to apply a variety of techniques 5. A range of skills and experiences 6. Understanding of geography's contribution to current issues 7. Heightened ability to respond to and make judgements about aesthetic and moral matters	No assessment criteria or requirements in the A-level common core. SEC and later SEAC approve syllabuses and assessment arrangements and undertake regular scrutinies of boards' examining procedures. Assessment objectives given in the A/AS core.	Twelve full A-level and, after 1987, ten AS syllabuses There was voluntary implementation of the common core. All the boards accepted the core, except Cambridge, on the grounds that it was 'amorphous as a framework and unhelpful as a statement' (p. 13) Oxford did not accept point 7.	Considerable variety of syllabuses and assessment arrangements. Some with a rigid separation of physical and human geography components, e.g. Oxford, AEB, JMB 'B'; most requiring an OS map question, some with a strong regional geography component, e.g. Oxford, Cambridge, London 210, JMB 'C'. One syllabus (Geography 16-19/London) had a distinctive issues and people-environment approach; one (Oxford and Cambridge) encompassed a systems approach and a stress on quantitative techniques; Oxford offered 'Economic geography' and Northern Ireland Board separate physical and human geography AS syllabuses.
A/AS Subject Core for Geography 1993 (SEAC, 1993d) ■ to provide a common basis for all A and AS syllabuses; to recognise changes resulting from the NC and new GCSE (KS4) Criteria.	Outlined a core for geography which would comprise about one-third of A-level syllabuses and two-thirds AS syllabuses. It required that all A/AS candidates must study: ■ a theme which emphasises interaction between people and environment at different spatial scales (including processes, issues, responses) ■ a chosen physical environment – characteristics, processes, interactions, etc. ■ a chosen human environment – characteristics, processes, interactions, etc. Plus for A-level candidates – personal investigative work including first-hand data.	*And* syllabus and assessment arrangements must conform to the 1994 SCAA Code of Practice including: ■ Syllabuses may be linear or modular ■ If modular, no module may occupy less than 15% assessment ■ Coursework maximum of 20%	Nine full A-level syllabuses, of which 3 could be modular or linear and all the rest were modular. Eight AS syllabuses. First A-level examination 1997.	Greater degree of standardisation of syllabus content. All syllabuses now offered various combinations of physical and human components plus some element focused on people-environment interactions. NEAB offered new approaches by looking at long- and short-term change in human and physical environments. The former 'Geography 16-19' kept an issues-based approach. No regional or place-based syllabuses, no specifically 'economic geography and no separate physical/human AS syllabuses.

continued

National core or criteria Version and reason	Content requirements	Assessment requirements	Numbers of syllabuses	Characteristics of syllabuses
A/AS Subject Criteria for Geography 1999 (QCA, 1999a) ■ to provide a framework for A/AS syllabuses which takes account of the new AS which comprises the first year of an A-level. Also recognises new priorities like key skills, and builds on changes at KS3 resulting from NC Review.	Required study of places, themes, and environments at different scales and in different contexts, in particular: ■ interactions between people and their environments at different scales (including processes, issues, responses) ■ physical processes (selected only for AS), their interactions, outcomes, changes over space/time ■ human processes (selected only for AS), their interactions, outcomes, changes over space/time ■ undertake a range of enquiry approaches and use a range of skills and techniques All these, in relation to 'chosen environments'. Also A-level candidates need to develop understanding of connections between different aspects of geography.	Assessment objectives and weightings given in the Criteria Also: there must normally be six units (A) and three units (AS); internal assessment must not exceed 30%; there must be a minimum of 20% synoptic assessment (requiring candidates to demonstrate understanding of connections between different aspects of the subject); the quality of written communication must be assessed. Other details in the QCA Code of Practice apply to all specifications and assessment arrangements.	All specifications (syllabuses) are unitised (modular) with assessment sessions in January and July, though unit tests can be taken in any session during the course. Eight full A-level specifications each with its AS specification representing the first year. First full cycle of examination for A-level 2002.	Specification (syllabus) content and approach are very similar to the previous set. Most A specifications look very similar with some units focusing on separate physical and human topics and some units which emphasis interactions. Two specifications have brought in fresh content, especially relating to change and environmental issues (EdExcel B, and OCR B). AQA B continues the features of the NEAB specification with its focus on change and processes. The specification of the former Geography 16-19 syllabus (EdExcel B) is no longer as distinctive compared with other specifications. No regional or place-based specifications. No distinctive AS specifications – all are basic introductions to the A-level specification to which they are linked.

5: The curriculum and assessment authorities for England

Organisation	Dates	Remit/Aims
Schools Council	1964 to 1982-84	'The object of the Schools Council shall be the promotion of education by carrying out research into and keeping under review the curricula, teaching methods and examinations in schools, including the organisation of schools as far as it affects the curricula.'
School Curriculum Development Committee	1983-88	'to promote education by supporting curriculum development relevant to the needs of school education in England and Wales.' Including supporting, reviewing, evaluating and disseminating curriculum development work, and undertaking any essential curriculum development activity.
Secondary Examinations Council	1983-88	'in regard to the activities of GCE and CSE examining boards: ■ to ensure that syllabuses and procedures for assessment at 16+ are in accordance with the national criteria which are to be proposed by boards and considered by the Secretaries of State ■ to approve new A-level syllabuses and revisions to existing syllabuses ■ to monitor the comparability of standards of both 16+ and 18+ examinations ■ to engage in research, if necessary, to support these activities.'
National Curriculum Council	1988-93	'to give independent professional advice on the school curriculum.' Including 'all aspects of the curriculum, not just the core and other foundation subjects. Its remit covers the curriculum for the under fives and for 16-19 year olds, as well as for pupils of compulsory school age.'
School Examinations and Assessment Council	1988-93	■ 'to keep all aspects of examinations and assessment under review ■ to advise the Secretary of State on, and if so requested by him, to carry out programmes of research and development for purposes connected with examinations and assessment ■ to advise the Secretary of State on the exercise of his powers under Section 5(I) of the Act (ERA).'
School Curriculum and Assessment Authority	1993-97	'to advise the Secretary of State on all aspects of the curriculum for maintained schools and of schools examinations and assessment.' 'The Authority keeps under review developments in all these areas and advises the Secretary of State on such matters as he or she may refer to the Authority or as the Authority may see fit. Specifically, and in addition, SCAA advises on the approval of external qualifications under ERA 1988 and as appropriate, programmes of research and development (and carries these out if requested).'
Qualifications and Curriculum Authority	1997-present	'The Education Act 1997 gave QCA a core remit to promote quality and coherence in education and training.' 'QCA's prime duty is to advise the Secretary of State for Education and Employment on all matters affecting the school curriculum, assessment and publicly funded qualifications offered in schools, colleges and workplaces ... For 2001-02, objectives include continuing to develop a broad and balanced curriculum for 3-19 year olds and creating a clear and coherent qualifications framework ... Through this work, QCA contributes to the development of public policy on education and training.'

Sources: Schools Council Report 1968-69; SCDC Annual Report 1984-85; SEC Annual Report 1983-84; Introducing the NCC 1988; An Introduction to SEAC 1989; SCAA Annual Report 1994-95; QCA: An Introduction, 1997.

References

ACAC (1996) *Geography: Exemplification of standards key stage 3*. Cardiff: ACAC.

Adey, P. and Shayer. M. (1994) *Really Raising Standards: Cognitive intervention and academic achievement*. London: Routledge.

Ainley, P. (2000) 'Missing the point about the learning and skills council, a comment on Coffield', *Journal of Educational Policy*, 15, 5, pp. 585-8.

Aldrich, R. (1990) 'The national curriculum: an historical perspective' in Lawton, D. and Chitty, C. (eds) *The National Curriculum*. London: University of London Institute of Education Bedford Way Series/Kogan Page.

Alexander, R. (1985) 'Teacher development and informal primary education' in Blyth, A. (ed) *Informal Primary Education Today*. Lewes: Falmer, pp. 153-66.

Ash, S. and Mobbs, D. (1987) 'The GYSL-TRIST Project', *Teaching Geography*, 12, 5, pp. 222-3.

Assessment Reform Group (1999) *Assessment for Learning: Beyond the Black Box*. Cambridge: University of Cambridge School of Education and the Assessment Reform Group.

Bailey, P. (1972) *Teaching Geography*. Newton Abbot: David & Charles.

Bailey, P. (1989) 'A place in the sun: the role of the Geographical Association in establishing geography in the national curriculum of England and Wales 1975-89', *Journal of Geography in Higher Education*, 13, 2, pp. 149-57.

Bailey, P. (1992) 'Geography and the national curriculum: a case hardly won', *The Geographical Journal*, 158, 1, pp. 65-74.

Bailey, P. and Binns, T. (eds) (1987) *A Case for Geography*. Sheffield: GA.

Bailey, P. and Fox, P. (eds) (1996) *Geography Teachers' Handbook*. Sheffield: GA.

Balchin, W.G.V. (1993) *The Geographical Association: The first hundred years 1893-1993*. Sheffield: GA.

Balchin, W.G.V. and Coleman, A.M. (1973) 'Graphicacy should be the fourth ace in the pack' in Bale, J., Graves, N. and Walford, R. (eds) *Perspectives in Geographical Education*. Edinburgh: Oliver & Boyd, pp. 78-86.

Bale, J. (1987) *Geography in the Primary School*. London: Routledge & Kegan Paul.

Bale, J. (1994) 'Geography teaching, post-modernism and the national curriculum' in Walford, R. and Machon, P. (eds) *Challenging Times: Implementing the national curriculum in geography*. Cambridge: Cambridge Publishing Services, pp. 95-7.

Bale, J. (ed) (2000) *Changing Geography series*. Sheffield: GA.

Bale, J., Graves, N. and Walford, R. (eds) (1973) *Perspectives in Geographical Education*. Edinburgh: Oliver & Boyd.

Ball, S.J. (1990) *Politics and Policy-Making in Education: Explorations in policy sociology*. London: Routledge.

Ball, S.J. (1993) 'Education policy, power relations and teachers' work', *British Journal of Educational Studies*, 41, 2, pp. 106-21.

Ball, S.J. (1994) *Education Reform: A critical and post-structuralist approach*. Milton Keynes: Open University Press.

Ball, S.J. (1999) 'Labour, learning and the economy: a policy sociology perspective', *Cambridge Journal of Education*, 29, 2, pp. 195-206.

Bantock, G.H. (1969) 'Discovery methods' in Cox, C.B. and Dyson, A.E. (eds) *The Crisis in Education, Black Paper 2*. London: Critical Quarterly Society.

Barber, M. (ed) (1996) *The National Curriculum: A study in policy*. Keele: Keele University Press.

Barber, M. and Sebba, J. (1999) 'Reflections on progress towards a world class education system' *Cambridge Journal of Education*, 29, 2, pp. 183-93.

Barnes, T. and Gregory, D. (eds) (1997) *Reading Human Geography: The poetics and politics of inquiry*. London: Hodder Headline.

Barrett Hacking, E. (1996) 'Novice teachers and their geographical persuasions', *International Journal of Research in Geographical and Environmental Education*, 5, 1, pp. 77-86.

Battersby, J. (1995) 'Rationale for the revised curriculum', *Teaching Geography*, 20, 2, pp. 57-8.

Becher, T. (1994) 'Significance of disciplinary differences', *Studies in Higher Education*, 19, 2, pp. 151-61.

Bednarz, S., Burkill, S., Lidstone, J. and Rawling, E. (2000) 'The International Network for Learning and Teaching Geography in Higher Education: developing links with school education', *Journal of Geography in Higher Education*, 24, 2, pp. 277-84.

Bell, L. (1999) 'Back to the future: the development of educational policy in England', *Journal of Educational Administration*, 37, 3, pp. 200-28.

Bennetts, T. (1985) 'Geography from 5-16: a view from the Inspectorate', *Geography*, 70, 4, pp. 299-314.

Bennetts, T. (1994) 'The Dearing review and its implications for geography', *Teaching Geography*, 19, 2, pp. 60-3.

British Educational Research Association (BERA) (2001) 'Special issue on the National Education Research Forum', *BERA Research Intelligence Newsletter*, no. 74. Southwell: BERA.

Biddle, D. (1999) 'Geography in schools: a report commissioned by the National Committee for Geography, Australian Academy of Science', *Australian Geographer*, 30, 1, pp. 75-92.

Black, P. and Wiliam, D. (1998) *Inside the Black Box: Raising standards through classroom assessment.* Cambridge: University of Cambridge School of Education and the Assessment Reform Group.

Blackie, J.H. (1967) *Inside the Primary School.* London: HMSO.

Blair, T. (1998) *The Government's Annual Report 1997-98.* London: The Stationery Office.

Blatch, Baroness (1993) 'Geography and the national curriculum', *Geography*, 78, 4, 359-66.

Blunkett, D. (1999) *National Curriculum Review: Letter to Sir William Stubbs (QCA),* 9 February.

Blyth, A. (1973) 'History, Geography and Social Science 8-13; a second generation project' in Taylor, P.H. and Walton, J. (eds) *The Curriculum: Research, innovation and change.* London: Ward Lock Educational, pp. 40-51.

Blyth, A. and Krause, J. (1995) *Primary Geography: A developmental approach.* London: Hodder & Stoughton.

Blyth, A., Cooper, K., Derricot, R., Elliott, G., Sumner, H. and Waplington, A. (1976) *Place Time and Society 8-13: Curriculum planning in history, geography and social science.* Bristol: Collins-ESL.

Boardman, D. (1985) 'Geography for the Young School Leaver' in Boardman, D. (ed) *New Directions in Geographical Education.* Lewes: Falmer, pp. 65-83.

Boardman, D. (ed) (1986) *Handbook for Geography Teachers.* Sheffield: GA.

Boden, P. (1976) *Developments in Geography Teaching.* London: Open Books.

Bowe, R. and Ball, S.J. with Gold, A. (1992) *Reforming Education and Changing Schools: Case studies in policy sociology.* London: Routledge.

Bowles, R. (2000) *Raising Achievement in Geography, Occasional Paper 1.* London: Register of Research in Primary Geography.

Bradford, M. (1995) 'The new A-level and AS geography syllabuses', *Teaching Geography*, 20, 3, pp. 145-8.

Bradford, M. (1996) 'Geography at the secondary-higher education interface; change through diversity' in Rawling, E. and Daugherty, R. (eds) *Geography into the Twenty-First Century.* Chichester: Wiley, pp. 277-88.

Bradford, M. (2001) 'The new A/AS framework', *Teaching Geography*, 26, 1, pp. 47-9.

Briggs, K. (1979) *Beginning the New Geography.* London: University of London Press.

Broadfoot, P. (1999) *Empowerment or Performativity? English assessment policy in the late 20th century.* Paper delivered at BERA Conference, Brighton, September.

Brooks, L. and Finch, R. (1939) *Geographies – Book 2: Seeing the world.* London: University of London Press.

Brown, S. and Smith, M. (2001) 'The secondary-tertiary interface' in Kent, W.A. (ed) *Reflective Practice in Geography Teaching.* London: Paul Chapman, pp. 262-77.

Bruner, J.S. (1960) *The Process of Education.* New York: Random House.

Burkill, S. (1980) 'Some comparisons of project approaches' in Rawling, E. (ed) *Geography into the 1980s.* Sheffield: GA, pp. 49-56.

Burtenshaw, D. (1991) 'Collateral damage in geography', Special Report, *Times Educational Supplement*, 29 March, p. 31.

Bushell, T. and Waugh, D. (1991) *Key Geography.* Cheltenham: Stanley Thornes.

Butt, G. (1997) *An Investigation into the Dynamics of the National Curriculum Geography Working Group 1989-90,* unpublished PhD thesis, University of Birmingham

Butt, G. and Lambert, D. (1993) 'Modules, cores and the new A/AS-levels', *Teaching Geography*, 18, 4, pp. 180-1.

Butt, G., Flinders, K., Hopkin, J., Lambert, D. and Telfer, S. (1998) 'Statutory teacher assessment at key stage 3 – beyond testing?', *Teaching Geography*, 23, 2, pp. 92-3.

Caistor, M. (1999) 'Geography's getting there!', *Primary Geographer*, 37, p. 25.

Callaghan, D. (1995) 'The believers: politics and personalities in the making of the 1988 Education Act', *History of Education*, 24, 4, pp. 369-85.

Capey, J. (1995) *General National Vocational Qualifications Assessment Review: Final report, chaired by Dr J. Capey*. London: National Council Vocational Qualifications.

Carhart, J., Orrell, K. and Wilson, P. (1986) 'A summary of the available draft or approved mode 1 GCSE Geography syllabuses', (insert) *Teaching Geography*, 12, 1.

Carr, W. and Hartnett, A. (1996) *Education and the Struggle for Democracy*. Milton Keynes: Open University Press.

Carter, R. (1993) 'The GA writes to Sir Ron', *Teaching Geography*, 18, 4, pp. 155-8.

Carter, R. (1994) 'Feet back on firmer ground', Geography Extra, *Times Educational Supplement*, 18 November, p. III

Carter, R. (ed) (1998) *Handbook of Primary Geography*. Sheffield: GA.

Catling, S. (1979) 'Reflections on the recent HMI report "Primary education in England"', *Teaching Geography*, 5, 2, pp. 73-7.

Catling, S. (1990) 'Subjecting geography to the national curriculum', *Curriculum Journal*, 1, 1, pp. 77-89.

Catling, S. (1991) 'Geography in primary practice in a period of transition' in Walford, R. (ed) *Viewpoints on Geography Teaching: The Charney Manor conference papers 1990*. York: Longman, pp. 95-102.

Catling, S. (1999) 'Geography in primary education in England', *International Research in Geographical and Environmental Education*, 8, 3, pp. 283-6.

Centre for Formative Assessment Studies (CFAS) (1999) *School Sampling Project: Monitoring the school curriculum 1998-99; secondary schools final report*. Manchester: CFAS.

Chalkley, B. and Craig, L. (2000) 'Introducing the first benchmark standards for higher education geography', *Journal of Geography in Higher Education*, 24, 3, pp. 395-8.

Chorley, R. and Haggett, P. (1967) *Models in Geography*. London: Methuen.

Cloke, P., Crang, P. and Goodwin, M. (1999) 'Introduction' to *Introducing Human Geography*. London: Arnold, pp. ix-xv.

Coldron, J. and Smith, R. (1999) 'Active location in teachers' constructions of their professional identities', *Journal of Curriculum Studies*, 31, 6, pp. 711-26.

Cole, J.P. and Beynon, N.J. (1968) *New Ways in Geography Books 1-4*. Oxford: Blackwell.

Collingwood, R.G. (1939) *An Autobiography*. Oxford: Oxford University Press.

Copnall, G. (2000) 'Cwricwlwm Cymru 2000', *Teaching Geography*, 25, 1, pp. 24-7.

Corney, G. (ed) (1992) *Teaching Economic Understanding through Geography*. Sheffield: GA.

Cox, C.B. and Boyson, R. (eds) (1977) *Black Paper 4*. London: The Critical Quarterly.

Cox, C.B. and Dyson, A.E. (eds) (1969a) *Fight For Education: A Black paper (1)*. London: The Critical Quarterly.

Cox, C.B. and Dyson, A.E. (eds) (1969b) *The Crisis in Education: Black paper 2*. London: The Critical Quarterly.

Cox, C.B. and Dyson, A.E. (eds) (1970) *Goodbye Mr Short: Black paper 3*. London: The Critical Quarterly.

Council for Environmental Education (CEE) (1998) *Education for Sustainable Development in the Schools Sector: A report to DfEE/QCA from the Panel for Education for Sustainable Development*. Reading: CEE.

Council of British Geography (1993) *Review of National Curriculum and Assessment Framework: Consultation response*, unpublished paper.

Counsell, C. (2000) 'Challenges facing the literacy co-ordinator', *Literacy Today*, 24, September, pp. 20-1.

Crang, M. (1998) *Cultural Geography*. London: Routledge.

Crick, B. (2000) *Citizenship for Students in Post-Compulsory Education and Training: A report*. London: QCA.

Crombie-White, R., Pring, R. and Brockington, D. (1995) *14-19 Education and Training: Implementing a unified system of learning*. London: Royal Society of Arts.

Curriculum Council for Wales (CCW) (1991) *Geography in the National Curriculum (Wales): Non-statutory guidance*. Cardiff: CCW.

CCW (1993a) *Monitoring Report on National Curriculum Geography in Wales 1993*. Cardiff: CCW.

CCW (1993b) *An Enquiry Approach to Learning Geography*. Cardiff: CCW.

CCW (1993c) *Approaches to Teaching and learning About Wales*. Cardiff: CCW.

Dainton, S. (1996) 'The national curriculum and the policy process' in Barber, M. (ed) *The National Curriculum: A study in policy.* Keele: Keele University Press, pp. 88-120.

Dale, R. (1989) *The State and Education Policy.* Milton Keynes: Open University Press.

Dalton, T.H. (1988) *The Challenge of Curriculum Innovation: A study of ideology and practice.* Lewes: Falmer.

Daugherty, R. (1981) 'Geography and the school curriculum debate' in Walford, R. (ed) *Signposts for Geography Teaching.* Harlow: Longman, pp. 119-28.

Daugherty, R. (1987) 'GCSE: the choice is yours', *Teaching Geography,* 12, 2, pp. 53-6.

Daugherty, R. (1989a) 'What will they do next?', *Teaching Geography,* 14, 4, pp. 146-8.

Daugherty, R. (ed) (1989b) *Geography in the National Curriculum.* Sheffield: GA.

Daugherty, R. (1994) 'Quality assurance, teacher assessments and public examinations' in Harlen, W. (ed) *Enhancing Quality in Assessment.* London: Paul Chapman for BERA, pp. 100-15.

Daugherty, R. (1995) *National Curriculum Assessment: A review of policy 1987-94.* Lewes: Falmer.

Daugherty, R. (1996) 'Defining and measuring progression in geographical education' in Rawling, E. and Daugherty, R. (eds) *Geography into the Twenty First Century.* Chichester: Wiley, pp. 195-215.

Daugherty, R. and Jones, S. (1999) 'Community, culture and identity: geography, the national curriculum and Wales', *The Curriculum Journal,* 10, 3, pp. 443-61.

Daugherty, R. and Lambert, D. (1994) 'Teacher assessment and geography in the national curriculum', *Geography,* 79, 4, pp. 339-49.

Daugherty, R. and Rawling, E. (1998) 'Quality and standards in geographical education', *Geography,* 83, 1, pp. 51-86.

Dearing, Sir Ron (1993) *The National Curriculum and its Assessment: Final report.* London: SCAA.

Dearing, Sir Ron (1996) *Review of Qualifications for 16-19 Year Olds: Full report.* London: SCAA.

Department for Education (DfE) (1992) *Choice and Diversity: A new framework for schools,* Cm 2021. London: HMSO.

DfE (1995) *Geography in the National Curriculum (England).* London: HMSO.

DfEE (1997) *Excellence in Schools,* Cm 3681. London: The Stationery Office.

DfEE (1998a) *The Learning Age: A renaissance for a new Britain.* London: The Stationery Office.

DfEE (1998b) *The National Literacy Strategy: Framework for teaching.* London: Standards and Effectiveness Unit of DfEE.

DfEE (1999a) *Key Skills Explained.* London: DfEE.

DfEE (1999b) *The National Numeracy Strategy and Framework for Teaching.* London: Standards and Effectiveness Unit of DfEE.

DfEE (2001) *Schools: Building on success,* Green Paper. London: DfEE.

DfEE and Department for Culture, Media and Sports (DCMS) (1999) *All Our Futures: Creativity, culture and education.* London: DfEE.

DfEE and Qualifications and Curriculum Authority (QCA) (1998 and updated 2000) *A Scheme of Work for Key Stages 1 and 2; Geography.* London: QCA.

DfEE/QCA (1999a) *Geography: The national curriculum for England, key stages 1-3.* London: DfEE/QCA.

DfEE/QCA (1999b) *The National Curriculum: Handbook for primary teachers (KS1&2).* London: DfEE/QCA.

DfEE/QCA (1999c) *The National Curriculum: Handbook for secondary teachers (KS3&4).* London: DfEE/QCA.

DfEE/QCA (2000a) *Consultation Paper on the Development of Vocational GCSEs.* London: QCA.

DfEE/QCA (2000b) *A Scheme of Work for Key Stage 3 Geography.* London: QCA.

DfEE and Teacher Training Agency (TTA) (1997 and 1998) *Teaching: High status, high standards,* Circulars 10/97 and 4/98. Hong Kong: DfEE.

DfEE, Welsh Office (WO) and Department for Education for Northern Ireland (DENI) (1997) *Qualifying for Success: A consultation paper on the future of post 16 qualifications.* London: DfEE.

Department of Education and Science (DES) (1959) *15-18: A report of the Central Advisory Council for Education (England)* (known as the Crowther Report). London: HMSO.

DES (1967) *Children and their Primary Schools, A report of the Central Advisory Council for Education (England)* (known as the Plowden Report). London: HMSO.

DES (1972) *New Thinking in School Geography*, Education Pamphlet 59. London HMSO.

DES (1977a) *Educating our Children: Four subjects for debate*. London: HMSO.

DES (1977b) *Education in Schools: A consultative document*, Cmnd 6869. London: HMSO.

DES (1977c) *Curriculum 11-16 Working Papers by HMI*. London: HMSO.

DES (1978) *The Teaching of Ideas in Geography: Some suggestions for the middle and secondary years of schooling, a discussion paper by HMI*. London: HMSO.

DES (1980a) *A Framework for the School Curriculum*. London: HMSO.

DES (1980b) *A View of the Curriculum, HMI Series Matters for Discussion 11*. London: HMSO.

DES (1981a) *Review of the Schools Council*. London: DES.

DES (1981b) *The School Curriculum*. London HMSO.

DES (1981c) *Geography in the School Curriculum 11-16, Working Paper*. London: DES.

DES (1985a) *Better Schools*. London: HMSO.

DES (1985b) *The Curriculum from 5-16, Curriculum Matters 2*. London: HMSO.

DES (1986) *Geography from 5-16: Curriculum Matters 7*. London: HMSO.

DES (1987) *The National Curriculum 5-16: A consultation document*. London: HMSO.

DES (1988a) *The Introduction of the General Certificate of Secondary Education in Schools 1986-88; Report by HM Inspectors*. London: DES.

DES (1988b) *Advancing A Levels* (Higginson Report). London: DES.

DES (1989a) *Aspects of Primary Education: The teaching and learning of history and geography*. London: HMSO.

DES (1989b) *A Report on Humanities Work in 20 Secondary Schools*. London: HMSO.

DES (1989c) *National Curriculum Geography Working Group: Terms of reference (Annex A) and supplementary guidance (Annex B)*. London: DES.

DES (1989d) *National Curriculum: From policy to practice*. London: HMSO.

DES (1991a) *Geography in the National Curriculum (England)*. London: HMSO.

DES (1991b) *Short Course, Geography at KS4*. London: DES.

DES and WO (1985) *GCSE: The national criteria, geography*. London: HMSO.

DES and WO (1987) *National Curriculum Task Group on Assessment and Testing: A report*. London: DES.

DES and WO (1989) *Interim Report of the National Curriculum Working Group*. London: DES.

DES and WO (1990) *Geography for Ages 5-16: Proposals of the secretaries of state for education and science and for Wales*. London: HMSO.

DES, Department of Employment (DoE) and WO (1991) *Education and Training for the Twenty First Century*. London: HMSO.

Department for Environment, Transport and the Regions (DETR) (2001) *Education for Sustainable Development – More relevant than ever. The third annual report of the Sustainable Development Education Panel*. London: DETR.

De Villiers, M. (ed) (1990) *Primary Geography Matters*; (1991) *Primary Geography Matters: Inequalities*; (1992) *Primary Geography Matters: Change in the primary curriculum*; (1993) *Primary Geography Matters: Children's worlds*; (1995) *Developments in Primary Geography: Theory and practice*. Sheffield: GA.

Dinkele, G., Cotterell, S. and Thorn, I. (1976) *Reformed Geography* (a series of five books). London: Harrap.

Dowgill, P. (1996) 'Reporting pupils' experience of the national curriculum geography' in Gerber, R. and Williams, M. (eds) *Qualitative Research in Geographical Education, Monograph No. 1*. London: Institute of Education, pp. 39-51.

Dowgill, P. (1999) 'Counting the cost of curriculum change', *Teaching Geography*, 24, 2, pp. 67-9.

Dowgill, P. and Lambert, D. (1992) 'Cultural literacy and school geography', *Geography*, 77, 1, pp. 143-51.

Ecclestone, K. (2000) 'Bewitched, bothered and bewildered: a policy analysis of the GNVQ assessment regime 1992-2000', *Journal of Education Policy*, 15, 5, pp. 539-58.

Elwyn Jones, G. (2000) 'The debate over the national curriculum for history in England and Wales 1989-90: the role of the press', *Curriculum Journal*, 11, 3, pp. 299-322.

Estyn (2000) *Aiming for Excellence in Geography: Standards and quality in primary schools*. Cardiff: Estyn (HMI for Education and Training in Wales).

Estyn (2001) *Good Practice in Geography: Standards and quality in secondary schools*. Cardiff: Estyn (HMI for Education and Training in Wales).

Evans, J. and Penney, D. (1995) 'The politics of pedagogy: making a national curriculum physical education', *Journal of Educational Policy*, 10, 1, pp. 27-44.

Evans, J. and Penney, D. (1999) *Politics, Policy and Practice in Physical Education*. London: E&FN Spon.

Everson, J.A. and Fitzgerald, B.P. (1969) *Settlement Patterns*. London: Longman.

Everson, J.A. and Fitzgerald, B.P. (1972) *Inside the City*. London: Longman.

Fitzgerald, B.P. (1969) 'The American High School Geography Project and its implications for teaching in Britain', *Geography*, 54, 1, pp. 56-63.

Foskett, N. and Marsden, B. (eds) (1998) *A Bibliography of Geographical Education 1970-1997*. Sheffield: GA.

Fry, P. and Schofield, A. (eds) (1993) *Teachers' Experiences of National Curriculum Geography in Year 7*. Sheffield: GA.

Fryer, R. (1997) *Learning for the Twenty First Century: First report of the Advisory Group for Continuing Education and Lifelong Learning*. London: NAGfCELL.

Fullan, M. (1991) *The New Meaning of Educational Change*. London: Cassell Educational.

Furlong, J., Barton, L., Miles, S., Whiting, C. and Whitty, G. (2000) *Teacher Education in Transition*. Milton Keynes: Open University Press.

Gagne, R.M. (1965) *The Conditions of Learning*. New York: Holt, Rinehart & Wilson.

Gallagher, R.M. with Parish, R., Williamson, J., King, A., Amor, P., Judd, M., Grenyer, R., Gallagher, P., Edwards, J. and Wood, J. (2000) *Geography 1 2 3 Series*. Oxford: Oxford University Press.

Galton, M. (2000) 'The national curriculum balance sheet for key stage 2: a researcher's view', *Curriculum Journal*, 11, 3, pp. 323-41.

Gardner, R. (1999) 'Is geography lost in space?', *Geographical Magazine*, August, pp. 104-5.

Gardner, R. and Craig, L. (2001) 'Editorial: Is geography history?', *Journal of Geography in Higher Education*, 25, 1, pp. 5-10.

Garnett, A. (1969) 'Teaching geography: some reflections', *Geography*, 54, 4, pp. 385-400.

GCE Examining Boards of England, Wales and Northern Ireland (1983) *Common Cores at Advanced Level*. GCE Boards.

Geographical Association (GA) (1990) *Response to the Final Report of the National Curriculum Geography Working Group* (internal paper). Sheffield: GA.

GA (1999a) 'Geography in the curriculum: a position statement from the GA', *Geography*, 84, 2, pp. 165-7.

GA (1999b) *Leading Geography: National standards for geography leaders in primary schools*. Sheffield: GA.

GA (1999c) *Leading Geography: National standards for geography leaders in secondary schools*. Sheffield: GA.

GA and National Council for Educational Technology (NCET) (1994, revised 1995) *Geography: A pupil's entitlement for IT (secondary)*. Sheffield/Coventry: GA/NCET.

GA/NCET (1995) *Geography: Primary Geography: A pupil's entitlement for IT*. Sheffield/Coventry: GA/NCET.

Geography Discipline Network (GDN) (1998) *A Series of Ten Teaching/Learning Guides for Geography in Higher Education*. Cheltenham: GDN.

GEES (the National Subject Centre for Geography, Earth and Environmental Sciences) (2001) 'Introducing the new National Subject Centre', *Planet*, 1. Plymouth: Learning and Teaching Support Network.

GeoVisions Project Team (1999) 'Co-operative research', *Teaching Geography*, 24, 2, pp. 70-1.

Giddens, A. (2000) *The Third Way and Its Critics*. Oxford: Polity Press in association with Blackwells.

Glesne, C. and Peshkin, A. (1992) *Becoming Qualitative Researchers*. New York: Longman.

Gold, J., Jenkins, A., Lee, R., Monk, J., Riley, J., Shepherd, I. and Unwin, D. (1991) *Teaching Geography in Higher Education*. Oxford: Blackwell.

Goldstein, H. and Woodhouse, G. (2000) 'School effectiveness research and educational policy', *Oxford Review of Education*, 26, 3, pp. 353-63.

Goodson, I.F. (1983) *School Subjects and Curriculum Change*. London: Croom Helm.

Goodson, I.F. (1987) 'Geography: aspects of subject history', *School Subjects and Curriculum Change* (a revised and extended edition). Lewes: Falmer, pp. 57-83.

Goodson, I.F. (1988a) 'Becoming a school subject' in Goodson, I.F. (ed) *The Making of Curriculum: Collected essays*. Lewes: Falmer, pp, 160-83.

Goodson, I.F. (1988b) 'Defining and defending the subject: geography versus environmental studies' in Goodson, I.F. (ed) *The Making of Curriculum: Collected essays*. Lewes: Falmer, pp. 89-107.

Goodson, I.F. (1998a) 'Introduction: studying subject knowledge' in Goodson, I.F. with Anstead, C.J. and Mangan, J.M. (eds) *Subject Knowledge: Readings for the study of school subjects*. Lewes: Falmer, pp. 1-12.

Goodson, I.F. (1998b) 'Nations at risk and national curriculum: ideology and identity' in Goodson, I.F. with Anstead, C.J. and Mangan, J.M. (eds) *Subject Knowledge: Readings for the study of school subjects*. Lewes: Falmer, pp. 150-64.

Goodwin, M. (1999) 'Citizenship and governance' in Cloke, P., Crang, P. and Goodwin, M. (eds) *Introducing Human Geography*. London: Hodder Headline, pp. 189-98.

Gordon, P., Aldrich, R. and Dean, D. (1991) *Education and Policy-Makiing in England in the Twentieth Century*. London: Woburn Press.

Goudie, A. (1993) 'Guest editorial: schools and universities: the great divide', *Geography*, 78, 4, pp. 338-9.

Graham, D. with Tytler, D. (1993) *A Lesson for Us All: The making of the national curriculum*. London: Routledge.

Graves, N.J. (1968) 'The High School Project of the Association of American Geographers', *Geography*, 53, 1, pp. 68-73.

Graves, N.J. (1971) *Geography in Secondary Education*. Sheffield: GA.

Graves, N.J. (ed) (1972) *New Movements in the Study and Teaching of Geography*. London: Temple Smith.

Graves, N.J. (1975) *Geography in Education*. London: Heinemann Educational.

Graves, N.J. (1979) *Curriculum Planning in Geography*. London: Heinemann Educational.

Graves, N.J. (1982) 'Geographical education', *Progress in Human Geography*, 6, 4, pp. 563-75.

Graves, N., Kent, A., Lambert, D., Naish, M. and Slater, F. (1990) 'Evaluating the Final Report', *Teaching Geography*, 15, 4, pp. 147-51.

Gravestock, P. and Healey, M. (eds) (2000) A series of eight guides to *Developing Key Skills in Geography in Higher Education*. Cheltenham: GDN.

Gregory, D. and Urry, J. (1985) 'Introduction' in Gregory, D. and Urry, J. (eds) *Social Relations and Spatial Structures*. Basingstoke: Macmillan, pp. 1-8.

Grimwade, K. (1997) 'Part 1 GNVQs – what implications do they have for geography?', *Teaching Geography*, 22, 3, pp. 140-2.

Grimwade, K. (ed) (2000a) *Geography and the New Agenda: Citizenship, PSHE and sustainable development in the secondary curriculum*. Sheffield: GA.

Grimwade, K. (ed) (2000b) *Geography and the New Agenda: Citizenship, PSHE and sustainable development in the primary curriculum*. Sheffield: GA.

Haggett, P. (1972) *Geography: A modern synthesis*. London: Harper & Row.

Haggett, P. (1996) 'Geography into the next century: personal reflections' in Rawling, E. and Daugherty, R. (eds) *Geography into the Twenty First Century*. Chichester: Wiley, pp. 11-18.

Hall, D. (1976) *Geography and the Geography Teacher*. London: George, Allen & Unwin.

Hall, D. (1991) 'Charney revisited: twenty five years of geographical education' in Walford, R. (ed) *Viewpoints on Geography Teaching: The Charney Manor conference papers*. Harlow: Longman, pp. 10-29.

Hall, D. (1996) 'Developments at A-level' in Rawling, E.M. and Daugherty, R.A. (eds) *Geography into the Twenty First Century*. Chichester: Wiley, pp. 145-72.

Harland, J., Kinder, K., Ashworth, M., Montgomery, A., Moor, H. and Wilkin, A. (1999) *Real Curriculum: At the end of key stage 2: Report one from the Northern Ireland cohort survey*. Slough: NFER.

Hart, C. (1982) *The Geographical Component of 17+ Pre-Employment Courses*. London: Geography 16-19 Project, Institute of Education.

Hart, C. (ed) with Chaffey, J., Crossley, S., Entwhistle, J., Foskett, N. and Foskett, R. (1985) *Worldwide Issues in Geography*. London: Collins Educational.

Harvey, D. (1973) *Social Justice and the City*. London: Edward Arnold.

Harvey, D. (1989) *The Condition of Post-modernity*. Oxford: Blackwell.

Hatcher, R. and Troyna, B. (1994) 'The policy cycle: a ball by ball account', *Journal of Educational Policy*, 9, 2, pp. 155-70.

Head, J. and Merttens, R. (2000) 'Series editors' preface' in Ross, A. *Curriculum Construction and Critique*. Lewes: Falmer, pp. ix-xi.

Healey, M. (2000a) 'Developing the scholarship of teaching in higher education: a discipline-based approach', *Higher Education Research and Development*, 19, 2, pp. 169-89.

Healey, M. (2000b) *Promoting Lifelong Professional Development in Geographical Education: Developing the scholarship of teaching in higher education in the 21st century*. Invited paper to plenary session of International Geographical Congress, August, Seoul, Korea.

Helburn, N. (1983) 'Reflections on the high school project' in Huckle, J. (ed) *Geographical Education: Reflection and action*. Oxford: Oxford University Press, pp. 20-8.

Helsby, G. and McCulloch, G. (eds) (1997a) *Teachers and the National Curriculum*. London: Cassell Educational.

Helsby, G. and McCulloch, G. (1997b) 'Introduction' in Helsby, G. and McCulloch, G. (eds) *Teachers and the National Curriculum*. London: Cassell Educational, pp. 1-18.

Hennessy, P. (2000) *The Prime Minister: The office and its holders since 1945*. London: Penguin.

Hickman, G., Reynolds, J. and Tolley, H. (1973) *A New Professionalism for a Changing Geography*. London: Schools Council.

Hillage, J., Pearson, R., Anderson, A. and Tamkin, P. (1998) *Excellence in Research in Schools*. London: DfEE and Institute of Employment Studies.

Hillgate Group (1987) *The Reform of British Education*. London: Hillgate Group.

Hirst, P.H. (1965) 'Liberal education and the nature of knowledge' in Achambault, R.D. (ed) *Philosophical Analysis and Education*. London: Routledge.

Hirst, P.H. (1974) *Knowledge and the Curriculum*. London: Routledge.

HMI (1998) *Assessment Report 1996/97*. London: The Stationery Office.

HMI Wales (1993) *A Survey of Geography in Key Stages 1, 2 and 3 in Wales 1992-93*. Cardiff: HMCI.

Hodgson, A. and Spours, K. (1999) *New Labour's Educational Agenda: Issues and policies for education and training from 14+*. London: Kogan Page.

Huckle, J. (ed) (1983) *Geographical Education: Reflection and action*. Oxford: Oxford University Press.

Huckle, J. (1997) 'Towards a critical school geography' in Tilbury, D. and Williams, M. (eds) *Teaching and Learning Geography*. London: Routledge, pp. 241-52.

Jackson, E. (2000) *Barnaby Bear series*. Sheffield: GA.

Jackson, P. (1996) 'Only connect: approaches to human geography' in Rawling, E.M. and Daugherty, R.A. (eds) *Geography into the Twenty First Century*. Chichester: Wiley, pp. 77-94.

Jenkins, S. (1990) 'Not just about maps', *Leader, The Times*, 7 June, p. 13.

Johnston, R.J. (ed) (1985) 'Introduction: exploring the future of geography', *The Future of Geography*. London: Methuen, pp. 3-26.

Johnston, R. (1991a) *Geography and Geographers: Anglo American geography since 1945* (fourth edition). London: Edward Arnold.

Johnston, R.J. (1991b) *A Question of Place: Exploring the practice of human geography.* Oxford: Blackwell.

Johnston, R.J. (1993) 'A changing world: a changing discipline' in Johnston, R.J. (ed) *The Challenge for Geography.* Oxford: Blackwell for Institute of British Geographers, pp. vi-ix.

Johnston, R.J., Taylor, P.J. and Watts, M.J. (1995) *Geographies of Global Change.* Oxford: Blackwell.

Joint Board for Pre-Vocational Education (1985) *The Certificate of Pre-Vocational Education (Part A CPVE framework and criteria for appraisal of schemes, Part B core competencies and vocational module specifications).* London: Joint Board.

Jones, G.W. (1998) *Geography and y Cwricwlwm Cymreig.* Paper presented at the conference of the Council of British Geography, Oxford, July.

Kavanagh, D. and Seldon, A. (1999) *The Powers Behind the Prime Minister.* London: Harper Collins.

Kelly, A.V. (1999) *The Curriculum: Theory and practice* (fourth edition). London: Paul Chapman.

Kent, A., Lambert, D. and Slater, F. (1991) 'A process of erosion, viewpoint', *The Independent,* 24 January, p. 19.

Kirkman, S. (1985) 'Sir Keith Joseph warns on geography', *Times Educational Supplement,* 21 June.

Knight, P. (1996) 'Subject associations: the cases of secondary phase geography and home economics 1976-94', *History of Education,* 25, 3, pp. 269-84.

Labour Party (1996) *Aiming Higher: Labour's proposals for the reform of the 14-19 curriculum.* London: The Labour Party.

Lambert, D. (1991) 'Too late for debate' Geography Extra, *Times Educational Supplement,* 29 March, p. 33.

Lambert, D. (1994) 'The national curriculum: what shall we do with it?', *Geography,* 79, 1, pp. 65-76.

Lambert, D. (1996) 'Assessing pupils' attainment and supporting learning in Kent, A., Lambert, D., Naish, M. and Slater, F. (eds) *Geography in Education: Viewpoints on teaching and learning.* Cambridge: Cambridge University Press, pp. 260-87.

Lambert, D. (2001) *Mind the Gap! An exploration into the role of subject expertise in supporting teaching excellence in geography.* Unpublished paper, Institute of Education.

Lambert, D. and Machon, P. (eds) (2001) *Citizenship through Secondary Geography Education.* London: Routledge/Falmer.

Lauder, H., Jamieson, I. and Wikely, F. (1998) 'Models of effective schools: limits and capabilities' in Slee, R., Weiner, G. and Tomlinson, S. (eds) *School Effectiveness for Whom? Challenges to the school effectiveness and school improvement movements.* Lewes: Falmer.

Lawrence, I. (1992) *Power and Politics at the DES* (Education Series Management). London: Cassell.

Lawton, D. (1986) 'The Department of Education and Science: policy-making at the centre' in Hartnett, A. and Naish, M. (eds) *Education and Society Today* Lewes: Falmer, pp. 19-36.

Lawton, D. (1992) *Education and Politics in the 1990s: Conflict or consensus.* Lewes: Falmer.

Lawton, D. (1994) *The Tory Mind on Education, 1979-94.* Lewes: Falmer.

Lawton, D. (1996) *Beyond the National Curriculum: Teacher professionalism and empowerment.* London: Hodder & Stoughton.

Layton, D. (1972) 'Science as general education', *Trends in Education.*

Leat, D. (ed) (1998) *Thinking Through Geography.* Cambridge: Chris Kington Publishing.

Livingstone, D. (1992) *The Geographical Tradition.* Oxford: Blackwell.

Lloyd, K. (1994) 'Place and practice: the current state of geography in the primary curriculum', *Primary Geographer,* 17, pp. 7-9.

Lowe, M.S. and Short, J. (1990) 'Progressive human geography', *Progress in Human Geography,* 14, 1, pp. 1-11.

Lowenthal, D. and Bowden, D. (1976) *Geographies of the Mind.* Oxford: Oxford University Press.

Macdonald, B. and Walker, R. (1976) *Changing the Curriculum.* London: Open Books.

Mackinder, H. (1887) 'On the scope and methods of geography', *Proceedings of the Royal Geographical Society,* 9, pp. 141-73.

Marsden, W.E. (1976) *Evaluating the Geography Curriculum.* Edinburgh: Oliver & Boyd.

Marsden, W.E. (1980) 'Introduction: geographical education in its historical context: research possibilities' in Marsden, W.E. (ed) *Historical Perspectives on Geographical Education* (research papers prepared for the IGU Congress, Tokyo). London: Institute of Education, pp. 1-7.

Marsden, W.E. (1989) 'All in a good cause – geography, history and the politicisation of the curriculum in nineteenth and twentieth century England', *Journal of Curriculum Studies*, 21, pp. 509-26.

Marsden, W.E. (1995) *Geography 11-16: Rekindling good practice*. London: David Fulton.

Marsden, W.E. (1997a) 'Taking the geography out of geographical education: some historical pointers', *Geography*, 82, 3, pp. 241-52.

Marsden, W.E. (1997b) 'Continuity after the national curriculum', *Teaching Geography*, 22, 2, pp. 68-70.

Marsden, W.E. and Hughes, J. (1994) *Primary School Geography*. London: David Fulton.

Marsh, C. (1997) *Perspectives: Key concepts for understanding curriculum*. Lewes: Falmer.

Martin, E., Benjamin, J., Prosser, M. and Trigwell, K. (1999) 'Scholarship of teaching: a study of the approaches of academic staff' in Rust, C. (ed) *Improving Student Learning: Improving student outcomes*. Oxford: Centre for Staff Learning and Development, Oxford Brookes University, pp. 326-31.

Martin, R. (2001) 'Editorial: of publishers and popularisers', *Transactions of the Institute of British Geographers* NS, 26, 1, pp. 3-6.

Marvell, A. (2000) 'Opportunities for a changing curriculum', *Teaching Geography*, 25, 4, pp. 170-4.

Massey, D. (1998) 'Spaces of politics' in Massey, D., Allen, J. and Sarre, P. (eds) *Human Geography Today*. London: Polity Press, pp. 279-94.

Massey, D. (1999a) 'Geography matters in a globalised world', *Geography*, 84, 3, pp. 261-5.

Massey, D. (1999b) 'Space-time science and the relationship between physical geography and human geography', *Transactions of the Institute of British Geographers* NS, 24, 3, pp. 261-76,

Massey, D. (1999c) 'The social place', *Primary Geographer*, 37, pp. 4-6.

Massey, D. (2000) 'Editorial: practising political relevance', *Transactions of the Institute of British Geographers* NS, 25, 2, pp. 131-3.

Massey, D., Allen, J. and Sarre, P. (1998) *Human Geography Today*. London: Polity Press.

Maund, D. and Wyatt, H. (1980) 'The role of the adviser in supporting curriculum development', *Teaching Geography*, 5, 4, pp. 176-8.

McEwan, I. (1987) *The Child in Time*. London: Pan Books/Jonathan Cape.

Mills, D. (ed) (1981, revised 1988) *Geography In Primary and Middle Schools*. Sheffield: GA.

McGuiness, C. (1999) *From Thinking Skills to Thinking Classrooms: A review and evaluation of approaches to developing pupils' thinking*. London: DfEE.

Morgan, J. (2000) 'To which space do I belong? Imagining citizenship in one curriculum subject', *Curriculum Journal*, 11, 1, pp. 55-68.

Morrish, M. (1981) 'Geography for business students', *Bulletin of Environmental Education*, 126, November.

Morrish, M. (2000) 'Teaching the new AS-level', Humanities Extra, *Times Educational Supplement*, November, p. 21.

Naish, M. (1980) 'Geography into the 1980s' in Rawling, E. (ed) *Geography into the 1980s*. Sheffield: GA, pp. 61-6.

Naish, M. (ed) (1992) *Primary Schools, Geography and the National Curriculum in England: Monitoring the implementation of geography in the primary curriculum* (Research Report produced by the British Sub-committee of the Commission for Geographical Education of the International Geographical Union). Sheffield: GA.

Naish, M. and Rawling, E. (1990) 'Geography 16-19: some implications for higher education', *Journal of Geography in Higher Education*, 14, 1, pp. 55-75.

Naish, M., Rawling, E. and Hart, C. (1987) *Geography 16-19: The contribution of a curriculum development project to 16-19 education*. London: Longman for School Curriculum Development Committee.

National Curriculum Council (NCC) (1990) *Consultation Report: Geography*. York: NCC.

NCC (1991a) *Geography: Non-statutory guidance*. York: NCC.

NCC (1991b) *INSET for National Curriculum Geography*, unpublished report of the NCC Geography INSET Working Party. York: NCC.

NCC (1992) *Implementing National Curriculum Geography*, unpublished report of the summary of responses to the NCC questionnaire survey of LEAs. York: NCC.

NCC (1993a) *An Introduction to Teaching Geography at KS 1&2*. York: NCC.

NCC (1993b) *Teaching Geography at KS1 &2: An INSET guide*. York: NCC.

NCC (1993c) *An Introduction to Teaching Geography at KS3*. York: NCC.

NCC (1993d) *Teaching geography at KS3: An INSET guide*. York: NCC.

Newby, P. (1980) 'The benefits and costs of the quantitative revolution', *Geography*, 65, 1, pp. 13-18.

Nichols, A. with Kinninment, D. (eds) (2001) *More Thinking Through Geography*. Cambridge: Chris Kington Publishing.

Norwood Report (1943) *Curriculum and Examinations in Secondary Schools*. London: HMSO.

Nuttall, D. (1989) 'National assessment: will reality match aspirations?' Paper delivered as part of conference *Testing Times* organised by Macmillan Education, 8 March.

Ofsted (1993-2001) *Annual Reports of Her Majesty's Chief Inspector of Schools*. London: HMSO.

Ofsted (1993a) *Geography at Key Stages 1, 2 and 3. The first year 1991-92*. London: HMSO.

Ofsted (1993b) *Geography at Key Stages 1, 2 and 3. Second year 1992-93*. London: HMSO.

Ofsted (1994) *General National Vocational Qualifications in Schools 1993/94: Quality and standards in GNVQs*. London: HMSO.

Ofsted (1995) *Geography: A review of inspection findings 1993/94*. London: HMSO.

Ofsted (1996a) *Subjects and Standards: Issues for school development arising from Ofsted inspection findings 1994/95; KS1 and 2*. London: HMSO.

Ofsted (1996b) *Subjects and Standards: Issues for school development arising from Ofsted inspection findings; KS3, 4 and Post 16*. London: HMSO.

Ofsted (1996c) *Assessment of General National Vocational Qualifications in Schools 1995/96*. London: HMSO.

Ofsted (1997) *Part One General National Vocational Qualification Pilot: The first two years 1995-97*. London: The Stationery Office.

Ofsted (1998a) *Secondary Education: A review of secondary schools in England 1993-97*. London: TSO.

Ofsted (1998b) *Standards in the Primary Curriculum 1996/97, Geography leaflet*. London: Ofsted.

Ofsted (1999a) *Primary Education 1994-1998: A review of primary schools in England*. London: TSO.

Ofsted (1999b) *Standards in the Secondary Curriculum 1997/98, Geography leaflet*. London: Ofsted.

O'Riordan, T. (1996) 'Environmentalism and geography: a union still to be consummated' in Rawling, E.M. and Daugherty, R.A. (eds) *Geography into the Twenty First Century*. Chichester: Wiley, pp. 113-28

Orrell, K. (1985) 'Geography 14-18' in Boardman, D. (ed) *New Directions in Geographical Education*. Lewes: Falmer, pp. 85-98.

Ozga, J. (1999) *Policy Research in Educational Settings: Contested terrain*. Milton Keynes: Open University Press.

Palôt, I. (2000) 'AS and A2 specifications', *Teaching Geography*, 25, 3, pp. 196-7.

Peck, J. (1999) 'Grey geography?', *Transactions of the Institute of British Geographers* NS, 24, 2, pp. 131-5.

Phillips, R. (1998) *History Teaching, Nationhood and the State: A study in educational politics*. London: Cassell.

Pickles, T. (1935) *Geographies for Senior Forms* (a series of 11 books). London: Dent.

Plaskow, M. (1985) *Life and Death of the Schools Council*. Lewes: Falmer.

Pollard, A., Broadfoot, P., Croll, P., Osborn, M. and Abbott, D. (1994) *Changing English Primary Schools? The impact of the Educaton Reform Act at key stage 1*. London: Cassell Education.

Pollard, J., Bryson, J. and Daniels, P. (2000) 'Shades of grey? Geographers and policy-making', *Transactions of the Institute of British Geographers* NS, 25, pp. 243-8.

Porritt, J. (1999) 'Introductory chapter', *Respect for the Earth: Sustainable development: Reith Lectures 1999*. London: Profile Books.

Powell, A. (ed) (1997) *Handbook of Post-16 Geography*. Sheffield: GA.

Power, S. and Whitty, G. (1999) 'New Labour's educational policy: first, second or third way?', *Journal of Educational Policy*, 14, 5, pp. 534-6.

Pring, R.A. (1972) 'Knowledge out of control', *Education for Teaching*, autumn.

Pring, R.A. (1995) *Closing the Gap: Liberal education and vocational preparation*. London: Hodder & Stoughton.

Pring, R.A. (2000a) *Philosophy of Educational Research*. London: Continuum.

Pring, R.A. (2000b) 'Editorial: Educational research', *British Journal of Educational Studies*, 48 1, pp. 1-3.

Quality Assurance Agency for Higher Education (QAA) (2000) *Benchmark Statement for Geography*. Gloucester: QAA.

Qualifications and Curriculum Authority (QCA) (1998a) *Geographical Enquiry at Key Stages 1-3*. London: QCA.

QCA (1998b) *Report of Findings from Phase III of Monitoring the National Curriculum: Geography*, unpublished Geography Team report. London: QCA.

QCA (1998c) 'Geography and history in the 14-19 curriculum: report of a conference', *Teaching Geography*, 23, 3, pp. 125-8.

QCA (1998d) *Developing the School Curriculum; a handbook for QCA staff involved in the review of the national curriculum* (internal document). London: QCA.

QCA (1998e) *National Curriculum Review: A progress report to the Secretary of State* (internal document). London: QCA.

QCA (1998f) *Maintaining a Broad and Balanced Curriculum*. London: QCA.

QCA (1998g) *Education for Citizenship and the Teaching of Democracy in Schools: Final report of the Advisory Group on Citizenship*. London: QCA.

QCA (1999a) GCE AS *and A-level Specifications: Subject criteria for Geography*. London: QCA.

QCA (1999b) *Learning through Work-Related Contexts: A guide to successful practice*. London QCA.

QCA (1999c) *Flexibility in the Secondary Curriculum*. London: QCA.

QCA (2000a) *Curriculum Guidance for the Foundation Stage*. London: QCA.

QCA (2000b) *Developing the Curriculum: A coherent 14-19 phase of education and training* (an informal consultation paper issued by the QCA 14-19 Team). London: QCA.

QCA (2000c) *Guidance on the Key Skills Units – Levels 1-3 – in Communication, Application of Number and Information Technology*. London: QCA.

QCA (2000d) *PSHE and Citizenship at Key Stages 1 and 2: Initial guidance for schools*. London: QCA.

QCA (2000e) *Citizenship at Key Stages 3 and 4: Initial guidance for schools*. London: QCA.

QCA (2000f) *Guidance on Disapplication of National Currriculum Subjects at KS4*. London: QCA.

QCA (2000g) *GCSE Criteria for Geography*. London: QCA.

QCA (2001) Review of Curriculum 2000; QCA's report on phase 1. Available on: www.qca.org.uk

QCA, Curriculum and Assessment Authority for Wales (ACCAC) and Northern Ireland Council for Curriculum and Examinations (CCEA) (1998) *GCSE and GCE A/AS Code of Practice*. London: QCA.

QCA, ACCAC and CCEA (2000) *Arrangements for the Statutory Regulation of External Qualifications in England and Wales*. London: QCA.

QCA and Department of Education and Employment (DfEE) (1998, revised 2000) *Geography; A Scheme of Work for KS1&2*. London: QCA/DfEE.

QCA/DfEE (1999a) *The Review of the National Curriculum in England: The consultation materials*. London: QCA.

QCA/DfEE (1999b) *The Review of the National Curriculum in England: The Secretary of State's proposals*. London: QCA/DfEE.

QCA/DfEE (2000) *Geography: A scheme of work for KS3*. London: QCA/DfEE.

QCA/DfEE (2001) *Citizenship: A scheme of work for KS3*. London: QCA.

Quicke, J. (2000) 'A new professionalism for a collaborative culture of organizational learning in contemporary society', *Journal of Educational Management and Administration*, 28, 3, pp. 299-315.

Ranger, G. (1991-94) *Enquiry Geography* series. London: Hodder & Stoughton.

Rawling, E. (ed) (1980) *Geography Into the 1980s*. Sheffield: GA.

Rawling, E. (1991a) 'Innovations in the geography curriculum 1970-90: a personal view' Walford, R. (ed) *Viewpoints on Geography Teaching: The Charney Manor Conference papers 1990*. York: Longman, pp. 33-8.

Rawling, E. (1991b) 'Spirit of enquiry falls off the map', *Times Educational Supplement*, 25 January, p. 18.

Rawling, E. (1991c) 'Making the most of the national curriculum', *Teaching Geography*, 16, 3, pp. 130-1

Rawling, E. (1992a) 'The making of a national geography curriculum', *Geography*, 77, 4, pp. 292-309.

Rawling, E. (1992b) *Programmes of Study: Try this approach*. Sheffield: GA.

Rawling, E. (1992c) *Supporting the Implementation of National Curriculum Geography: A role for the GA* (paper). Sheffield: GA.

Rawling, E. (1994) *GA Regions; Present and Future* (paper presented to GA Council), March.

Rawling, E. (1996) 'The impact of the national curriculum on school-based curriculum development in geography' in Kent, A., Lambert, D., Naish, M. and Slater, F. (eds) *Geography in Education: Viewpoints on teaching and learning*. Cambridge: Cambridge University Press, pp. 100-32.

Rawling, E. (1997a) 'Geography and vocationalism: opportunity or threat?', *Geography*, 82, 2, pp. 163-78.

Rawling, E. (1997b) 'Issues of continuity and progression in post-16 geography' in Powell, A. (ed) *Handbook of Post-16 Geography*. Sheffield. GA, pp. 11-30.

Rawling, E. (1999a) 'Geography in England 1988-98: costs and benefits of national curriculum change', *IRGEE*, 8, 3, pp. 273-8.

Rawling, E. (1999b) *Exploring Pedagogic Research and Teaching and Learning of Geography*, unpublished Seminar Report of the Higher Education Study Group of the RGS with IBG, May.

Rawling, E. (1999c) 'Time to re-invent curriculum development?', *Teaching Geography*, 24, 3, p. 108.

Rawling, E. (2000) *Understanding Teacher Supply in Geography*. The report of a conference organised by the Teacher Training Agency and RGS with IBG, 21 April. London: TTA/RGS-IBG.

Rawling, E. (2001a) 'National curriculum geography: new opportunities for curriculum development?' in Kent, A. (ed) *Reflective Practice in Geography Teaching*. London: Sage, pp. 99-112.

Rawling, E. (2001b) 'The politics and practicalities of curriculum change 1991-2000: issues arising from a study of school geography in England', *British Journal of Educational Studies*, 49, 2, pp. 137-58.

Rawling, E. (2001c, forthcoming) 'Education for sustainable development: a case study in curriculum policy', *Environmental Education Research*

Rawling, E.M. and Daugherty, R.A. (eds) (1996) *Geography into the Twenty First Century*. Chichester: Wiley.

Rice, R.E. (1992) 'Towards a broader conception of scholarship: the American context' in Whiston, T. and Geiger, R. (eds) *Research in Higher Education: the UK and the US*. Milton Keynes: Open University Press.

Roberts, M. (1990) 'Redrawing the map', Geography Extra, *Times Educational Supplement*, 13 April, p. 35.

Roberts, M. (1995) 'Interpretations of the Geography National Curriculum: a common curriculum for all?', *Journal of Curriculum Studies*, 27, 2, pp. 187-205.

Roberts, M. (1997) 'Reconstructing the Geography National Curriculum: professional constraints, challenges and choices' in Helsby, G. and McCulloch, G.M. (eds) *Teachers and the National Curriculum*. London: Cassell Educational, pp. 96-113.

Roberts, M. (2000) 'Teacher education: a research-based profession' in Fisher, C. and Binns, T. (eds) *Issues in Geography Teaching*. London: Routledge/Falmer, pp. 37-49

Robinson, R. (1992) 'Facing the future: not the national curriculum', *Teaching Geography*, 17, 1, pp. 31-2.

Robinson, R., Carter, R. and Sinclair, S. (1999) 'Wiser people, better world?', *Teaching Geography*, 24, 1, pp. 10-13.

Rose, G. (1993) *Geography and Feminism*. Cambrige: Polity.

Ross, A. (2000) *Curriculum Construction and Critique*. Lewes: Falmer.

RGS-IBG and GA (1998) *Geography: An essential contribution to education for life*. London: RGS-IBG.

Runnymede Trust (2000) *The Future of Multi-Ethnic Britain* (the Parekh Report). London: Profile Books.

Rynne, E. and Lambert, D. (1997) 'The continuing mismatch between students' undergraduate experiences and the teaching demands of the geography classroom', *Journal of Geography in Higher Education*, 21, 1, pp. 187-98.

Schofield, A. (1990) 'Where on Earth are we going?', Geography Extra, *Times Educational Supplement*, 13 April, p. 33.

School Curriculum and Assessment Authority publications (SCAA) (1993a) *Review Handbook for Subject and Key Stage Advisory Groups* (internal document). London: SCAA.

SCAA (1993b) *GCE A and AS Subject Core for Geography*. London: SCAA.

SCAA (1994a) *Geography in the National Curriculum: Draft proposals*. London: SCAA.

SCAA (1994b) *GCE A and AS Code of Practice*. London: SCAA

SCAA (1995a) *Corporate Plan 1995-1998*. London: SCAA.

SCAA (1995b) *Information Technology and the National Curriculum at Key Stage 1&2*. London: SCAA.

SCAA (1995c) *Key Stage 3: Information technology and the national curriculum; geography*. London: SCAA.

SCAA (1995d) *GCSE Regulations and Criteria (Geography)*. London: SCAA.

SCAA (1996a) *Consistency in Teacher Assessment: Exemplification of standards, geography KS3*. London: SCAA.

SCAA (1996b) *Consistency in Teacher Assessment: Optional tests and tasks, geography, KS3*. London: SCAA.

SCAA (1996c) *Teaching Environmental Matters through the National Curriculum*. London: SCAA.

SCAA (1996d) *Monitoring the School Curriculum 1995/96: Reporting to schools*. London: SCAA.

SCAA (1997a) *Expectations for Geography at Key Stages 1 and 2*. London: SCAA.

SCAA (1997b) *Curriculum Planning at Key Stage 2*. London: SCAA.

SCAA (1997c) *Geography and Use of Language (KS1/2)*. London: SCAA.

SCAA (1997d) *Geography and Use of Language (KS3)*. London: SCAA.

SCAA (1997e) *Monitoring the School Curriculum 1996/97: Reporting to schools*. London: SCAA.

SCAA (1997f) *Geography Position Statement* (internal Geography Team paper for National Curriculum Review Conference), July. London: SCAA.

SCAA (1997g) *Analysis of Educational Resources 1996/97: Key stage 3 geography textbooks*. London: SCAA.

SCAA and Curriculum Authority of Wales (ACAC) (1995a) *GCSE: Mandatory Code of Practice*. London: SCAA

SCAA and ACAC (1995b) 'GCSE Criteria for geography' in *GCSE Regulations and Criteria*. London: SCAA.

SCAA and ACAC (1997) *GCE A and AS Code of Practice*. London: SCAA.

School Examinations and Assessment Council (SEAC) (1991a) *Teacher Assessment at KS3* (pamphlet). London: SEAC.

SEAC (1991b) *KS3: Assessment in Practice*. London: SEAC.

SEAC (1992a) *Geography Standard Assessment Tasks: Key stage 1*. London: SEAC.

SEAC (1992b) *Teacher Assessment at Key Stage 3: Geography*. London: SEAC.

SEAC (1992c) *Principles for GCE A and AS Examinations*. London: SEAC

SEAC (1993a) *Children's work Assessed: Geography and History Key Stage 1*. London: SEAC.

SEAC (1993b) *Key Stage 3: Pupil's Work Assessed: Geography*. London: SEAC.

SEAC (1993c) *GCSE/KS4 Criteria for Geography*. London: SEAC.

SEAC (1993d) *GCE A and AS Examinations: Subject Core for Geography*. London: SEAC.

Schools Council (1974) *Dissemination and Inservice Training, The Report of the Schools Council Working Party on Dissemination 1972-73*, Pamphlet 14. London: Schools Council

Schools Council (1976) *The Schools Council 13-16 Project: A new look at history*. Edinburgh: Holmes MacDougal.

Scoffham, S. (ed) (1998) *Primary Sources: Research findings in primary geography*. Sheffield: GA.

Scruton, R. (1986) *World Studies: Education or indoctrination?*. Institute for European Defence and Strategic Studies.

Scruton, R., Ellis-Jones, A. and O'Keefe, D. (1985) *Education and Indoctrination*. Harrow: Educational Research Centre.

Semel, S. (1994) 'Writing school history as a former participant: problems in writing the history of an élite school' in Walford, G. (ed) *Researching the Powerful*. London: UCL Press, pp. 204-20.

Shaw, J. and Matthews, J. (1998) 'Communicating academic geography: the continuing challenge', *Area*, 30, 4, pp. 367-72.

Slater, F. (1982) *Learning Through Geography: An introduction to activity planning*. London: Heinemann.

Smith, D. (1977) *Human Geography: A welfare approach*. London: Edward Arnold.

Smith, P. (1997a) 'Standards achieved: a review of geography in primary schools in England 1995-96', *Primary Geographer*, 31, pp. 4-5.

Smith, P. (1997b) 'Standards achieved: a review of geography in secondary schools in England 1995-96', *Teaching Geography*, 22, 3, pp. 125-6.

Soja, E. (1989) *Post Modern Geographies*. London: Verso.

Soja, E. (1998) 'Thirdspace: expanding the scope of the geographic imagination' in Massey, D., Allen, J. and Sarre, P. (eds) *Human Geography Today*. London: Polity, pp. 260-78.

Stengel, B. (1997) 'Academic discipline and school subject: contestable curricular concepts', *Journal of Curriculum Studies*, 29, 5, pp. 585-602.

Stoddart, D. (1986) *On Geography and its History*. Oxford: Blackwell.

Stoddart, D. (1987) 'To claim the high ground: geography for the end of the century', *Transactions of the IBG* NS, 12, pp. 327-36.

Storm, M. (1987) 'How far is geography to do with knowing where places are?', *ILEA Geography Bulletin 26*. London: ILEA.

Sylva, K. (2000) 'Editorial', *Oxford Review of Education*, 26, 3, pp. 293-7.

Teacher Training Agency (TTA) (1999a) *Using Information and Communications Technology to Meet Teacher Training Objectives in Geography, Initial Teacher Training Secondary*. London: TTA.

TTA (1999b) *Using Information and Communications Technology to Meet Teacher Training Objectives in Geography, Initial Teacher Training Primary*. London: TTA.

Thomas, G. and Grimwade, K. (1997) 'Geography in the secondary school: a survey', *Teaching Geography*, 21, 1, pp. 37-9.

Thompson, L. (2000a) 'Target setting – not rocket science!', *Teaching Geography*, 25, 4, pp. 165-9.

Thompson, L. (2000b) 'Young people's Geovisions', *Teaching Geography*, 25, 2, pp. 99-102.

Tidswell, W.V. (1973) *Pattern and Process in Human Geography*. London: University Tutorial Press.

Tolley, H. and Reynolds, J. (1977) *Geography 14-18: A handbook for school-based curriculum development*. London: Macmillan for Schools Council.

Tomlinson, S. (1997) 'Education 14-19: divided and divisive' in Tomlinson, S. (ed) *Education 14-19: Critical perspectives*. London/Atlantic Highlands NJ: Athlone, pp. 1-17.

Tomlinson, S. (2001) *Education in a Post-welfare Society* (Introducing Social Policy series). Milton Keynes: Open University Press.

Tyler, R. (1949) *Basic Principles of Curriculum and Instruction*. Chicago: Chicago University Press.

UNESCO (1990) *Trends and Developments of Technical and Vocational Education*. Paris: UNESCO.

Unwin, D. (1980) 'Statistical inferences, viewpoints', *Teaching Geography*, 5, 3, p. 144.

Unwin, T. (1992) *The Place of Geography*. Harlow: Longman.

Walford, R. (1969) *Games in Geography*. London: Longman.

Walford, R. (1981) 'Language, ideologies and geography teaching' in Walford, R. (ed) *Signposts for Geography Teaching*. Harlow: Longman, pp. 215-22.

Walford, R. (1984) 'Geography and the future', *Geography*, 69, 3, pp. 193-208.

Walford, R. (1992) 'Creating a national curriculum: a view from the inside' in Hill, A.D. (ed) *International Perspectives on Geography Education*. Boulder CO/Skokie IL: IGU-CGE/Rand McNally, pp. 89-100.

Walford, R. (1999) *Analysis of Summer 1999 Examination Results*, unpublished paper prepared for COBRIG Conference, September.

Walford, R. (2000) 'Geography examined 1850-2000', *Geography*, 85, 4, pp. 303-10.

Walford, R. (2001) *Geography in British Schools: Making a world of difference 1850-2000*. London: Woburn.

Walford, R. and Williams, M. (1982) 'Recent involvement of GA in the curriculum debate', *Geography*, 67, 1, pp. 71-5.

Walker, D. (1998) 'Mayday!: Humanities get that sinking feeling!', *The Independent*, 12 March.

Wallace, M. (1993) 'Discourse of derision; the role of the mass media within the education policy process', *Journal of Educational Policy*, 8, 4, pp. 321-37.

Waugh, D. and Bushell, T. (1991) *Key Geography: Foundations*. Cheltenham: Stanley Thornes.

Weeden, P. and Wilson, P. (2001) 'GCSE geography, 2001: a geographical odyssey', *Teaching Geography*, 26, 2, pp. 94-6.

Welsh Office (WO) (1991) *Geography in the National Curriculum (Wales)*. Cardiff: HMSO.

WO (1995) *Geography in the National Curriculum, Wales*. Cardiff: HMSO.

Westaway, J. and Jones, B. (2000a) 'The revised curriculum in England', *Primary Geographer*, 40, (pull-out pages).

Westaway, J. and Jones, B. (2000b) 'The revised national curriculum for geography in England', *Teaching Geography*, 25, 1, pp. 28-30.

Westaway, J. and Jones, B. (2001) 'Changes to GCSE geography', *Teaching Geography*, 26, 1, pp. 4-6.

Westaway, J. and Rawling, E. (2001) 'The rises and falls of school geography', *Teaching Geography*, 26, 3, pp. 108-11.

Whitty, G., Power, S. and Halpin, D. (1998) *Devolution and Choice in Education: The school, the state and the market*. Milton Keynes: Open University Press.

Williams, R. (1962) *The Long Revolution*. Harmondsworth: Penguin.

Wise, M.J. (1977) 'Geography in the universities and in schools', *Geography*, 62, 4, pp. 249-58.

Wise, M.J. (1992) 'International geography: the IGU Commission on Education', *Geography and Education: National and International Perspectives*, pp. 233-46.

Wolf, A. (1993) 'Assessment issues and problems in a criterion-based system, *FEU Occasional Paper*. London: FEU.

Wolf, A. (1995) *Competence-based Assessment*. Milton Keynes: Open University Press.

Woods, P. and Wenham, P. (1995) 'Politics and pedagogy: a case study in appropriation', *Journal of Educational Policy*, 102, pp. 119-42.

Worsley, P. (1985) 'Physical geography and the natural environmental sciences' in Johnston, R.J. (ed) *The Future of Geography*. London: Methuen, pp. 27-42.

Young, M.F.D. (ed) (1971) *Knowledge and Control*. London: Collier Macmillan.

Young, M.F.D. (1998) *The Curriculum of the Future: From the new sociology of education to a critical theory of learning*. Lewes: Falmer.

Index